The Human Rights Act and the Criminal Justice and Regulatory Process

THE CENTRE FOR PUBLIC LAW AT THE
UNIVERSITY OF CAMBRIDGE

Director
PROFESSOR JACK BEATSON, QC

Assistant Directors
CHRISTOPHER FORSYTH
IVAN HARE

Supported by
CLIFFORD CHANCE

HART PUBLISHING – OXFORD
1999

Hart Publishing
Oxford and Portland, Oregon

Distributed in the North America (US and Canada) by
Hart Publishing
c/o International Specialized Book Services
5804 NE Hassalo Street
Portland, Oregon
97213-3644
USA

Distributed in Netherlands, Belgium and Luxembourg by
Intersentia, Churchillaan 108
B2900 Schoten
Antwerpen
Belgium

Distributed in Australia and New Zealand by
Federation Press
John Street
Leichhardt
NSW 2000

Hart Publishing is a specialist legal publisher based in Oxford, England.
To order further copies of this book or to request a list of other publications
please write to:

Hart Publishing, Salter's Boatyard, Folly Bridge Abingdon Road, Oxford, OX1 4LB
Telephone: +44 (0)1865 245533 Fax: +44 (0) 1865 794882
email: hartpub@hartpub.co.uk

British Library Cataloguing in Publication Data
Data Available

ISBN 1-84113-050-8 (paper)

Typeset in Times by John Saunders Design & Production, Reading, UK
Printed in Great Britain by by Watkiss Studios, Biggleswade, Beds.

THE HUMAN RIGHTS ACT
AND THE CRIMINAL JUSTICE
AND REGULATORY PROCESS

CONTENTS

INTRODUCTION

This volume largely consists of the papers presented at the Cambridge Centre for Public Law's winter conference on 9–10 January 1999. The Centre's first conference in 1998 examined the government's proposals for constitutional reform in a broad and interdisciplinary way. We decided that our second conference should focus on particular aspects of the impact of the Human Rights Act 1998.

We settled on criminal justice and regulation for a number of reasons. First, the Commonwealth experience (Canada and New Zealand) was that the introduction of a Bill of Rights had its most significant impact in the area of criminal justice. It is felt by many, including the former Attorney-General, Mr John Morris M.P., that the same will be true in the United Kingdom. Secondly, we thought that this was a topic which would be of interest not only to lawyers and judges, but also to policy-makers and administrators, and to which we in Cambridge could make a useful contribution.

We decided to examine regulatory proceedings alongside criminal justice because we considered that this would enable delegates to stand back from the detail of a particular context and get to grips with general principle. While the potential impact of the European Convention, in particular Article 6, on criminal justice is well known, there is less familiarity with its impact on regulatory proceedings. Those interested in regulation might learn from those interested in criminal justice and vice versa. There are, moreover, as the debate on the Financial Services and Markets Draft Bill shows, significant points of overlap between the two areas. Both involve investigation, hearings, appeals and other post-hearing action.

Once again, a very distinguished group of chairmen, speakers, panellists, and over 120 delegates, including many actively involved in the formulation, implementation and scrutiny of the new law, participated. The papers in this volume are in substantially the same form as the conference presentations: they represent 'work in progress'. We have also included several additional contributions. The first two, on interpretation, are the Lord Chancellor's 1999 Paul Sieghart Memorial lecture, also to be published in the *European Human Rights Law Review*, and Lord Lester of Herne Hill Q.C.'s article,

'The Art of the Possible', published in [1998] *European Human Rights Law Review* 665. The two others are new and concern regulation; Jack Beatson considers which Regulatory Bodies are subject to the Human Rights Act and Richard Nolan examines the impact of the Act on the powers conferred on office holders by the Insolvency Act. Finally, with the kind permission of the British Bankers Association, the London Investment Banking Association, the Futures and Options Association, Clifford Chance, Freshfields and Linklaters & Paines, we have included two Opinions given by Lord Lester of Herne Hill Q.C., Javan Herberg, and Monica Carrs-Frisk on the impact of the European Convention on the disciplinary framework in the draft Financial Services and Markets Bill.

The partners of Clifford Chance have again generously supported the Conference and this publication. Particular thanks are due to Michael Smyth and Richard Thomas for being so receptive to our idea, and to George Staple and Nicholas Jordan for taking time out of their busy professional lives, not only to attend the conference, but to write papers for it. We are also grateful for financial support from the Faculty of Law.

We are also grateful to many others. Our contributors met the deadlines we set, and our chairmen, Lord Bingham of Cornhill (who also gave the Keynote speech), Professor Sir David Williams Q.C., Mrs Justice Arden, Sir Frederick Crawford, and Lord Justice Laws kept a firm but gentle control over the conference proceedings themselves. Our panellists Lord Lester of Herne Hill Q.C., Michael Blair Q.C., H.H. Judge Paul Collins CBE and Ben Emmerson were the catalysts for a stimulating discussion bringing together a number of issues that had arisen in earlier sessions. Ben Emmerson also acted as a roving reporter in all the sessions, and fulfilled his brief splendidly.

Administrative support was provided by the University of Cambridge's Board of Continuing Education and our Centre Administrator, Philip Greenwood, who worked tirelessly to ensure everything ran smoothly. Our publisher Richard Hart has again been a good friend of the Centre.

Jack Beatson
Tony Smith

August 1999

CONFERENCE CHAIRMEN, SPEAKERS AND PANELLISTS

A.J. Ashworth Q.C., D.C.L., F.B.A.   *Vinerian Professor of English Law, University of Oxford*

The Hon Mrs Justice Arden   *Royal Courts of Justice*

The Rt Hon Lord Justice Auld   *Royal Courts of Justice*

Jack Beatson Q.C.   *Rouse Ball Professor of English Law, Director of the Centre for Public Law University of Cambridge*

The Rt. Hon. Lord Bingham of Cornhill   *Lord Chief Justice of England and Wales*

Michael Blair Q.C   *General Counsel, Financial Services Authority*

The Rt Hon Lord Justice Buxton   *Royal Courts of Justice*

H.H. Judge Paul Collins   *Director of Studies, Judicial Studies Board*

Madeleine Colvin   *JUSTICE*

Sir Frederick Crawford D.L.   *Chairman, Criminal Cases Review Commission*

The Hon. Mr Justice Eady   *Royal Courts of Justice*

Ben Emmerson   *Doughty Street Chambers*

Nicholas Jordan   *Clifford Chance*

David Kyle   *Criminal Cases Review Commission*

The Rt. Hon Lord Justice Laws   *Royal Courts of Justice*

The Hon. Lord Lester of Herne Hill Q.C.   *Blackstone Chambers*

A.T.H. Smith LL.D.   *Professor of Criminal and Public Law, University of Cambridge*

John Spencer   *Professor of Law, University of Cambridge*

George Staple Q.C.   *Clifford Chance*

David Thomas Q.C., LL.D.   *Reader in Criminal Justice, University of Cambridge*

Sir David Williams Q.C., D.L.   *Emeritus Vice-Chancellor & Emeritus Rouse Ball Professor of English Law, University of Cambridge*

THE CAMBRIDGE CENTRE FOR PUBLIC LAW

The aim of the Centre is to promote research in the area of public law and regulation, and to develop into a research centre of national and international reputation. Its interests include constitutional and administrative law and theory, institutions, civil liberties, human rights, judicial control and regulation and regulatory systems. Financial resources permitting, the Centre intends to do this by providing:

- A focal point for the exchange of ideas between academics, practitioners and others (including members of public and regulatory bodies, representatives of regulated industries and utilities, the Law Commission) through a conference, seminar and lecture programme.

- Support for scholars, practitioners and students through Visiting and Research Fellowships and Studentships.

- Dissemination of research output through publication.

An individual or corporate body may become a 'Friend of the Centre' and receive:

- The Centre's Annual Bulletin and selected publications
- The Centre's conference, seminar and lecture programme
- Priority booking and discount for the Centre's conference, seminar and lecture programme

Our website is at http://www.law.cam.ac.uk/ccpr/home.htm

For further information, please contact Jack Beatson (Director), Christopher Forsyth or Ivan Hare (Assistant Directors), or Philip Greenwood, Centre Administrator.

Centre for Public Law,
University of Cambridge,
Faculty of Law,
10, West Road,
Cambridge CB3 9DZ

Telephone ++ 44 (0)1223 330033/330080
Facsimile ++ 44 (0)1223 330055
Email public.law@law.cam.ac.uk

OTHER CENTRE PUBLICATIONS

Constitutional Reform in the United Kingdom: Practice and Principles, 1998, ISBN: 1-901362-84-0 (Hart Publishing Ltd, Oxford)

New Directions in European Public Law, edited by Jack Beatson and Takis Tridimas, 1998, ISBN: 1-901362-24-8 (Hart Publishing Ltd, Oxford)

1999/2000 CONFERENCE PROGRAMME

14 January 2000: The Enforcement of U.K. Anti-Discrimination Legislation:

One day conference to discuss the questions raised in the Discussion Paper to be issued by the Independent Review being conducted by the Centre for Public Law in association with the Judge Institute of Management Studies.

Attendance by invitation. Those interested should contact Mr Tufyal Choudhury at the Centre (tel/fax 01223 330060) or by email to *discrim@law.cam.ac.uk,*

19–20 February 2000: Freedom of Expression and Freedom of Information:

Weekend conference at Emmanuel College, Cambridge.

July 2000: Financial Regulation:

Two day conference in July 2000 organised jointly with the Cambridge Centre for Corporate and Commercial Law.

Further details and information about registration are available on the Centre's webpage (address above), or from Philip Greenwood at the Centre (tel/fax 01223 330080, email: *pg 211@cam.ac.uk*).

KEYNOTE SPEECH

LORD BINGHAM OF CORNHILL
LORD CHIEF JUSTICE

Our sincere thanks are due to Professors Beatson and Smith, and the Centre for Public Law for mounting this conference on the Human Rights Act and the Criminal Justice and Regulatory Process, which is certainly timely and will, I think, be valuable and influential.

A year ago, when the predecessor of this conference was held, the Human Rights Bill had embarked on its legislative career. That is now a matter of history. I permit myself two comments.

First, given the obstinacy with which incorporation was resisted over decades, it is striking how little serious opposition the Bill encountered. The barricades virtually collapsed at the first whiff of legislative grapeshot.

Secondly, the Bill emerged from the legislative process essentially unaltered. The provisions now contained in sections 12 and 13 do little more than emphasise what would have been obvious anyway. So, for better or worse, the Bill we started out with is in all essentials the Act we have ended up with.

Looking ahead to the future, I think one can fairly confidently make three predictions. The first is that once the Act comes into force we can expect a plethora of Convention points to be taken, relied on and pursued often by one side or the other to appeal. Experience elsewhere suggests that such a result is overwhelmingly likely. It is, I suppose, probable that the initial surge of work will subside to some extent after the first few years. But one cannot be too confident. I understand that the Supreme Court of Canada still devotes a considerable percentage of its time to cases raising human rights issues, and I believe that much the same is true of New Zealand.

It seems likely, secondly, that most of the points will arise in criminal proceedings. No doubt there will be civil cases concerned with privacy, freedom of association, freedom of expression, etc. But it seems likely that criminal suspects and defendants will prove the most eager claimants under the Convention. That again is confirmed by experience elsewhere.

Thirdly, it seems very probable that Article 6 will provide the most fruitful source of Convention jurisprudence in this country, as (I suspect, although I have carried out no census) it may well do in Strasbourg. Reliance will doubtless be placed on Article 5. But it seems probable that Article 6 will be the main staple.

To my knowledge, no public announcement has been made of the date on which it is proposed to bring the main body of the Act into force, and I am not privy to ministerial thinking. If I had to put money on a date, rather as if it were a general election, I should choose 1 October 2000. It is probably safe to say that the date will not be a great deal earlier. This projected two year delay has been the subject of some criticism by those who feel that it throws doubt on the government's sincerity in enacting the measure, and that it undesirably delays the date at which we must grapple with the thorny problems which the Convention is likely to raise. While I understand this view, I do not myself agree with it. I have no doubt about the government's sincerity: it introduced this measure as one of its first acts on coming in to office, and it seems to me to be much more than a gesture. Moreover, I see the delay as an indication of sincerity, because it seems to me to betray a clear intention that when the Act does come into force it shall do so effectively and successfully. If the Act were a mere gesture, it could be brought into force at once. This period of preparation seems to me to recognise that there are important things to be done if British incorporation of the Convention is to escape inclusion in the *Guinness Book of Great Legal Disasters*.

What are these things to be done?

The first task is educational, or what in judicial circles is known as judicial studies or training. Courts and tribunals are obliged, so as far as possible, to read and give effect to primary and subordinate legislation in a manner compatible with Convention rights (section 3) and to take account of what I shall loosely call Strasbourg jurisprudence (section 2). The problem of course is that most judges, magistrates and tribunal members are very largely ignorant of Convention rights and Strasbourg jurisprudence. This is not a criticism, since up to now ignorance has almost been a virtue. But there is a clear need to introduce magistrates and tribunal members to this new field of law and to give judges a much more comprehensive understanding of what is involved. This task is the more difficult to accomplish because the limited resources of the Judicial Studies Board are currently devoted to a programme, scarcely (if at all) less important, to prepare the judiciary for the all too imminent implementation of the Woolf reforms. There is also, of course, a need for the legal profession to educate itself. I have a lingering fear that the task of the courts in ruling on Convention issues may be made the more difficult by inequality of arms between prosecutors and defenders, with those appearing for defendants very much better versed in the niceties of Convention jurisprudence than those representing the Crown. This fear may, however, prove unfounded. I have no doubt that this educational task is one to which this conference will make a powerful contribution.

The second task facing us is prophylactic. It is very important that the time before implementation is used, and constructively used, to fill as many holes in the dyke as possible before the flood comes. Invaluable work has already been done, much of it by those present today, in identifying the obviously vulnerable points in our laws and procedures. More work, I know, is in train. Again, I feel sure that this is an area in which this conference will make a powerful contribution. There are distinguished and knowledgeable contributors who have written papers identifying points of law, evidence and procedure which are likely to cause trouble. I have no doubt more points will emerge in the course of discussion. It would be lamentable if we were to sit back and wait for obvious points to be taken in the course of contested litigation, when they could be much more quickly and inexpensively and fairly cured now. The record of this conference will prove an invaluable sourcebook over the next 18 months or so, and the sooner the record of the conference becomes available the better.

The third task is administrative: to try and ensure that when implementation day dawns we have administrative arrangements in place to try and ensure the efficient, expeditious and economical disposal of the issues raised. It would lay us open to serious criticism if the courts became bogged down in repeated arguments on the same points, sometimes with differing results. This is a matter very largely for judges and court officials to address.

I end with two notes of caution. First, while I do not intend to downplay the importance of the Convention or to disparage its significance, I do think it important that we keep our feet on the ground. Our procedures for arresting, charging, interrogating and identifying suspects and trying those accused of crime have been the subject of constant review over the last two or three decades, and have been the subject of comprehensive consideration by two Royal Commissions. We have not, doubtless, achieved a perfect answer. No answer ever will be perfect, because the balance between prosecutor and defender constantly alters, and continual adjustment is necessary. But I think we have every reason to believe that in most respects we comply with Convention standards. In many respects—for example in relation to bringing detained defendants to trial within a reasonable time—our self-imposed constraints are much more stringent than the Convention requires. We should not be too ready to find breaches of Articles 5 and 6, which are after all based on principles we have all been brought up to respect.

Lastly, I think it very important that the judges, particularly the most senior and conspicuous judges, should resist any temptation to cultivate reputations as liberals, or strict constructionists, or anything else. It has always been a great strength of our system that the judges decide cases as they come, without giving any thought at all to whether this or that decision will be favourably or unfavourably regarded by the *Guardian* or the *Daily Mail* or their equivalents in the legal profession. Critics of incorporation have predicted that it will lead to the politicisation of the judiciary. I, with many others, have resisted that suggestion. There has already developed, however, some tendency in the press to categorise some judges as 'liberal' and others as 'conservative'. Such descriptions are harmless so long as they are ignored, but would be dangerous if taken seriously. I think it is true of all the outstanding judges, in the past and in our own time, that none of them can be typecast. In every case it is possible to point to some judgments which may be regarded as liberal and forward-looking, and others which betray a more cautious and conservative approach. The judges must not give thought to their record, and should not be afraid of accusations of inconsistency or what others may see as such.

[ii]

AN OVERVIEW

THE RT. HON LORD JUSTICE LAWS*

I will first say something about the doctrine of margin of appreciation. It is the means by which the European Court of Human Rights at Strasbourg, as an international tribunal, recognises that national cultures vary and that the national authorities may be best placed to make the first judgment as to whether a particular measure taken within their jurisdiction offends against Convention rights. That is why the doctrine is not transferable to national courts; it is by definition a function of the jurisprudence of the Strasbourg Court as an international tribunal. There remains here in England some confusion about this. One hears it said that when the Human Rights Act 1998 comes fully into effect our courts will have to apply a margin of appreciation. It is not so; at least not as the term is understood in the Strasbourg jurisprudence. To assert otherwise is to make what Professor Gilbert Ryle would have called a category mistake.

This truth concerning the margin of appreciation is also one reason, I think, why section 2 of the Act of 1998 enjoins us to *take account of* rather than to *apply* the decisions of the Strasbourg court and the opinions of the Commission. The margin of appreciation is an important part of Strasbourg's case law; but for the reasons given we cannot apply it. It is no function of the domestic court's jurisdiction. It is different in nature from the *Wednesbury*[1] principle, which is of course a rule of national law imposed on themselves by the judges out of respect for the authority of democratically elected decision-makers.

This brings me to what will be the nature of our task. Our national judges will have to apply the substantive Convention rights in light of the Strasbourg jurisprudence. When a British court has arrived at a decision touching a Convention right and there follows a challenge in Strasbourg—I hope that successful ones will be rare—I would expect the Court of Human Rights to accord a margin of appreciation to the national court. Indeed the margin may be *greater* than has up to the present time been accorded by Strasbourg to our domestic governmental decision-makers, since by force of the 1998 Act our judges will for the first time be adjudicating directly on Convention rights; the Convention will be considered, not as a means of resolving ambiguity in statute or as a litmus of the common law, but as part of the substantive law of the United Kingdom.

And here lies the challenge. We must develop the common law and rules of statutory interpretation conformably with the Convention; but it is part of a *continuum* with everything that has gone before. It is not an alien add-on. Not because British lawyers were instrumental in the drafting of the Convention; that, though interesting, is history. It is because the principles of freedom and fairness which the Convention enshrines are the very principles respected by the common law. They are given new focus and emphasis, and we must grasp the opportunity to colour the international jurisprudence on human rights with the common law's subtle shades.

In our own jurisdiction, I expect (in the field of administrative law) to see *Wednesbury* mature into something closer to proportionality and pressing social need. And legitimate expectation will come more to

* These remarks were made in the concluding session of the Conference

[1] [1948] 1 KB 223.

embrace substantive expectations. In crime, section 78 of the Police and Criminal Evidence Act 1984 will look less like a general discretion (which anyway it is not), and more like a means of vindicating concrete requirements of fairness. Section 2 of the Criminal Appeal Act 1968 (a conviction must be quashed if it is unsafe, but not otherwise) will be developed so as to give more emphasis to the way in which a conviction has been arrived at, rather than being directed only to the narrower question whether the evidence must have proved the defendant's guilt to a reasonable jury. The substantive criminal and regulatory law, including sentencing, will be more expressly subject to the discipline of legal certainty ('prescribed by law' in the Convention text) and proportionality ('necessary in a democratic society'). Our civil law will develop so as to accord a right of privacy subject to public interest defences.

In the result our law will be modernised, but according to the methods of the common law. By this incremental approach we can fulfil the challenge of the Human Rights Act, while still respecting the will of the elected arm of government. The judges will not stick out their necks on poles of individual predilections, nor feel reluctantly driven to apply a foreign law. It is not 'foreign'; it is no more nor less than a revitalising of the common law. I would have said a phoenix; but the common law anyway shows no sign of terminal decay.

Our principles of statutory interpretation will change: section 3 of the Act of 1998, where it applies, will abolish the old lynch-pin of the search for Parliamentary intention. Our ideas of Parliamentary sovereignty will change: the pure Diceyan doctrine of implied repeal will go (in fact it went with *Factortame* [1990] 2 AC 85). Though Parliament may still make any law it chooses, if it is to enact a measure which is repugnant to Convention rights—what will come to be called an unconstitutional measure—it will have to do so by express words which put its intention to violate the Convention beyond doubt.

This is not Aladdin's new lamps for old. It is Robert Browning: 'Grow old along with me, the best is yet to be'. Our old constitution is given new blood by the Human Rights Act. It strengthens, does not dilute, the common law. And the common lawyers must administer it, according to their ancient methods.

PART I

The Constitutional Context

THE HUMAN RIGHTS ACT 1998: THE CONSTITUTIONAL CONTEXT

PROFESSOR A.T.H. SMITH*

HISTORICAL BACKGROUND

One of the most extraordinary features of the Human Rights Act 1998 is the speed with which it has been placed on the statute book. There had been interest in isolated quarters in enacting a Bill of Rights for Britain for the best part of a quarter of a century – a persistent background rumbling.[1] But I mean no disrespect when I describe that movement as desultory. Lord Scarman had sounded a trumpet blast in his Hamlyn Lectures,[2] but politicians and his fellow judges did not respond enthusiastically (publicly at least) to the call.[3]

The Conservative Party was consistently opposed to any such development, and the conversion of the Labour Party to the cause would have been describable as deathbed but for the fact that the patient arose and walked. A consultation paper was published on December 1996, by Jack Straw M.P. and P. Boateng M.P.,[4] setting out the Labour Party's plans to incorporate the European Convention,[5] and a White Paper was published very shortly after the government took office on 1 May.[6] The Bill to accomplish this objective, the Human Rights Bill 1998, was introduced into the House of Lords on October 23, 1997, and received its Royal Assent on November 9th 1998. Criminal lawyers who have for thirty years been waiting for the enactment of a criminal code,[7] witness the process with a mixture of awe and envy. But a somewhat undesirable side effect was that there was very little time to discuss and debate in any serious way any of the longer-term implications of what was proposed; very little change could be made to the package as contemplated in the White Paper, and very limited concessions – none of them structural – were made as the Bill made its way through Parliament.

The Act will not come in to force until the Secretary of State decides that the time is ripe,[8] although certain

---

* LL.D, Professor of Criminal and Public Law, University of Cambridge.

[1] See Professor M. Zander, *A Bill of Rights?* (1st ed., 1975). There had also been numerous attempts to legislate. See Lord Lester, Q.C., "The Mouse that Roared: The Human Rights Bill 1995" [1995] P.L. 198.

[2] *English Law - The New Dimension* (1974); R. Dworkin, *A Bill of Rights for Britain* (1990).

[3] It is fair to say that they did eventually respond, and were more or less unanimously in favour. See Lord Brown-Wilkinson, "The Infiltration of a Bill of Rights" [1992] P.L. 397; Rt. Hon. Sir Thomas Bingham, "The European Convention on Human Rights: Time to Incorporate" (1993) 109 L.Q.R. 390; Woolf, "Droit Public - English Style" [1995] P.L. 57; Sir S. Sedley "Human Rights: a Twenty-First Century Agenda" [1995] P.L. 386; Lord Lester Q.C., in "The Mouse that Roared: The Human Rights Bill 1995" [1995] P.L. 198, n.1 stated that his Bill had the support of most Law Lords, both serving and retired. As has been pointed out, this was "an entirely new and very significant development": M. Zander, *A Bill of Rights?* (4th ed., 1997).

[4] "Bringing Rights Home: Labour's plans to incorporate the European Convention on Human Rights into U.K. Law" [1997] E.H.R.L. Rev. 71.

[5] For comment, see J. Wadham, [1997] P.L. 75. And see [1997] E.H.R.L. Rev. generally: Lord Lester, "Towards a Constitutional Bill of Rights", *ibid.* 124; Sir N. Lyell, Q.C., M.P., "Whither Strasbourg? Why Britain Should Think Long and Hard Before Incorporating the European Convention on Human Rights", *ibid.* 132; J. Wadham, "Bringing Rights Half-Way Home", *ibid.* 141; K.D. Ewing and C.A. Gearty, "Rocky Foundations for Labour's New Rights", *ibid.* 146; D. Beyleveld, "The Concept of a Human Right and Incorporation of the European Convention on Human Rights" [1995] P.L. 577; T.H. Jones, "The Devaluation of Human Rights Under the European Convention" [1995] P.L. 430; More generally, see D. Feldman, *Civil Liberties and Human Rights in England and Wales* (Oxford: Clarendon Press) 1993, Ch. 16.

[6] *Rights Brought Home: The Human Rights Bill* (October 1997), Cm 3782.

[7] Since, that is, the Law Commission outlined its proposals in this connection in 1968. The title of the Rt. Hon. Lord Bingham's lecture, "A Criminal Code: Must we Wait Forever?" [1998] Crim. L.R. 694 captures the sense of exasperation that is experienced by advocates of such a code.

[8] Section 19, which requires Ministers to certify that any Bill introduced before Parliament complies with the Human Rights Act has already been implemented. Thus, the Rating (Valuation) Bill, the

provisions of the Act, having in effect a retrospective operation, have been held by the Divisional Court[9] to be factors that the Director of Prosecutions must take into account in deciding whether or not to give consent to a prosecution under an Act that is plainly at variance with Article 6 of the Convention. There are, however, clear signs that the government has somewhat belatedly realised just how significant an educational task awaits all participants in the legal process; judges (including county court judges and magistrates – the Act is intended to operate at every level in the legal hierarchy), civil servants (including in particular the Crown Prosecution Service), prosecuting and defence counsel, solicitors, and the police. The present signs are that the implementation date of the Act is to be set back even further, creating "a climate of indecision and uncertainty for all public authorities".[10]

As it is, the Act is but one of a series of more-or-less interconnected measures of constitutional reform: devolution to Scotland and Wales: reform of the House of Lords; freedom of information;[11] possible reform of the electoral system, and membership (ultimately) of the European Exchange Rate mechanism.

AN OVERVIEW[12]

The main purpose of the Act is to incorporate the European Convention on Human Rights, a treaty of the Council of Europe, to which the United Kingdom has been a signatory from the outset (in March 1951). We have become to some extent familiar with that Convention, and the decisions of the European Court, to which there has been, most unusually in the international law context, a right of individual petition since 1966.[13] Even in the criminal law context, we have been

found wanting by the European Court on an uncomfortable number of occasions. There have been what might be termed high profile reverses,[14] although not every decision has been adverse.[15] Even after the Human Rights Act becomes law, the Strasbourg procedure will not be discontinued. But it is clearly one of the aspirations of the promoters of the legislation that recourse to the European Court will needs be much less frequent.

The effect of the Act is to give the Convention the force of [ordinary][16] law in the United Kingdom. Thus, we are guaranteed the right to life (Article 2), freedom from torture or inhuman or degrading treatment, (Article 3), freedom from slavery or forced labour (Article 4); liberty and security of the person (Article 5); fair trial (Article 6); freedom from retrospective criminal laws (Article 7); respect for private and family life, home and correspondence (Article 8); freedom of thought, conscience and religion (Article 9); freedom of expression (Article 10); freedom of peaceful assembly and freedom of association, including the right to join a trade union (Article 11); the right to marry and found a family (article 12 and freedom from discrimination in the enjoyment of those rights and freedoms (Article 14).[17]

The articles differ somewhat in character. Some are absolute, and admit of no derogation or qualification; these include the prohibition of torture, slavery and the prohibition of retroactive criminal offences. The right to life admits of exceptions for lawful acts of war or from the use of force that is no more than is absolutely necessary in defence of a person against unlawful violence, effecting arrest or stopping escape of a detainee or for quelling a riot. Most of the Convention rights are however expressed to be subject to restrictions which ensure respect for other rights and freedoms. Thus,

---

Sexual Offences (Amendment) Bill and the Tax Credits Bill all bear the legend that "Mr Secretary . . . [Mr Chancellor of the Exchequer, in the case of the last mentioned] has made the following statement under section 19(1)(a) of the Human Rights Act 1998: In my view the provisions of the . . . Bill are compatible with the Convention rights".

[9] *R. v. D.P.P., ex parte Kebilene*, [1999] 3 W.L.R. 175.

[10] D. Pannick Q.C., *The Times* 18 May, 1999.

[11] The position here is rather more conventional, at least in terms of speed of the reform process. There is to be yet more consultation, about a measure whose gestation process stretches as far back as the early nineteen seventies.

[12] And see C. Ovey, "The European Convention on Human Rights and the Criminal Lawyer: An Introduction" [1998] Crim. L.R. 4.

[13] Technically, the United Kingdom government made a declaration under Article 25 of the Convention that the right of individual petition was to be recognised in respect of events occurring after January 14, 1966. See *Declarations recognising the competence of the European Commission of Human Rights to receive individual petitions and recognising as compulsory the jurisdiction of the European Court of Human Rights*, Cmnd. 2894. The background to this development is described by Lord Lester Q.C., "U.K. Acceptance of the Strasbourg Jurisdiction: What Really went on in Whitehall in 1965" [1998] P.L. 237.

[14] *Sunday Times* v. *U.K.* (1979) 2 E.H.R.R. 245; *Dudgeon* v. *U.K.* (1982) 4 E.H.R.R. 149 – homosexuality in Northern Ireland, breach of articles 8 and 13; *McCann* v. *U.K.* (1996) 21 E.H.R.R. 97 (death on the rock); *Welch* v. *U.K.* (1995) 20 E.H.R.R. 247 – retrospective confiscatory legislation in breach of Article 7: *Benham* v. *U.K.* (1996) 22 E.H.R.R. 293 (proceedings for poll tax payments criminal rather than civil in character); *Findlay* v. *U.K.* (1997) 24 E.H.R.R. 221 (Court Martial courts insufficiently impartial, as guaranteed by Article 6); *Saunders* v. *U.K.* (1996) 23 E.H.R.R. 313 (use of compulsorily extracted material in subsequent prosecution in violation of Article 6); *Bowman* v. *U.K.* [1998] 26 E.H.R.R. 1 – prohibition of certain advertising during elections in breach of Article 10.

[15] *Laskey, Jaggard and Brown* (1997) 24 E.H.R.R. 39 (consensual sado-masochism not in breach of Article 8); *Murray* v. *U.K.* (1996) 22 E.H.R.R. 29 (right to silence); *Wingrove* v. *U.K.* (1997) 24 E.H.R.R. 1 (censorship of blasphemous film permissible: not a prosecution); *S.W.* v. *U.K.; C.R.* v. *U.K.* (marital rape exemption abolition no breach of Article 7).

[16] Subject to what is said below, about Parliamentary Sovereignty.

[17] The United Kingdom is also a party to the First Protocol to the Convention, which guarantees the right to the peaceful enjoyment of possessions (Article 1), the right to education (Article 2 and the right to free elections (Article 3).

Articles 8 (privacy), 9 (thought conscience and religion) 10 (expression) and 11 (assembly) are broadly stated in para. 1 of the Article, then qualified, provided that any restriction is regulated by law, and is "necessary in a democratic society".

SOME CONSTITUTIONAL CONTEXT: THE STATUS OF THE HUMAN RIGHTS ACT

Three possible models

It is clear that a Bill of rights has, potentially, a destabilising effect upon the established interrelationship between Parliament, the Executive and the courts. Statements made by Ministers upon the Bill's introduction to Parliament, (and I refer here particularly to the remarks of the Lord Chancellor when he introduced the Bill to the House of Lords on 23 November 1997, which made it plain that it was intended to preserve the constitutional *status quo*,[18] at least so far as the position of the judiciary was concerned.

At least three alternative possibilities presented themselves for consideration.

1. We might have adopted the American model, giving the judiciary a power of judicial review of legislation; that would have involved a constitutional revolution. But that, in the language of the White Paper, "could not be reconciled with our own constitutional traditions" – although some would have preferred it.[19]
2. A second alternative was the Canadian model, giving a power of judicial review over legislation, but subject to legislative override – the so-called "notwithstanding" power, whereby the legislature could override an apparent conflict with the Charter.[20]
3. Yet a third possibility was to be found in the New Zealand model, giving the Bill the status of an

ordinary Act of Parliament.[21] That is, in the end, the option that was chosen, the model preferred, though with some significant adaptations. In the words of the White Paper, again:

"To make provision in the Bill for the courts to set aside Acts of Parliament would confer on the judiciary a general power over decisions of Parliament which under our present constitutional arrangements they do not possess, and would be likely on occasions to draw the judiciary in to serious conflict with Parliament. There is no evidence to suggest that they desire this power, nor that the public would wish them to have it."

The position thus arrived at was a non-negotiable part of the reform package, as was the content of the Bill itself. Even if, had we been able to start the process of enacting a Bill of Rights with a blank sheet, we would not have chosen the European Convention as a model, the Convention was the best available option. As a matter of practical politics, this approach seems to have much to commend it. The best is so often the enemy of the good, and it was long apparent that dissatisfaction with the existing constitutional arrangements for the protection of rights (measured in part by our performance at Strasbourg) was such that action was called for, and urgently.

The certification process

Borrowing from the New Zealand model, the Act provides that the responsible Minister will attach to any legislative proposal introduced before Parliament, a statement to the effect that the measure complies with the 1998 Act. But the White Paper contemplated that there may be exceptions, since

". . . there may be occasions where such a statement cannot be provided, for example because it is essential to legislate on a particular issue but the policy in question *requires a risk* to be taken in relation to the Convention or because the arguments in relation to the Convention issues raised are not clear-cut . . . Parliament would expect the Minister to explain his or her reasons during the normal course of the proceedings on the Bill".[22]

---

[18] But see his discussion of the changes that might be effected by the Act, in "The Development of Human Rights in Britain under an Incorporated Convention on Human Rights" [1998] P.L. 221. See also his Keynote address, in Cambridge Centre for Public Law, *Constitutional Reform in the United Kingdom: Practice and Principles* (1998), at p. 2.

[19] Such as the Provost of Queens College Oxford, Geoffrey Marshall; "Patriating Rights – With Reservations" in Cambridge Centre for Public Law, *Constitutional Reform in the United Kingdom: Practice and Principles* (1998), p. 73. See also I. Loveland, "Incorporating the ECHR into U.K. Law" (1999) 52 Parliamentary Affairs 113.

[20] For a discussion of the current Canadian position, See J. Black-Branch, "Entrenching Human Rights Legislation under Constitutional Law: The Canadian Charter of Rights and Freedoms" [1998] E.H.R.L.R. 312.

[21] The standard practitioners work is Adams, *Criminal Law and Practice in New Zealand*; see also G. Huscroft and P. Rishworth, *Rights and Freedoms: The New Zealand Bill of Rights 1990 and the Human Rights Act 1993* (Brooker's, Wellington, 1995). The judicial forward surge that followed the implementation of the Act in New Zealand has now been met with a retreat or "unprincipled backsliding" by judges who are said to be not well versed in "rights" jurisprudence; see most recently, in *Grayson* [1997] 1 N.Z.L.R. 399, and its critiques by A.S. Butler, "The End of Precedent and Principle in Bill of Rights Cases? A note on *R. v. Grayson* [1997] N.Z.L.Rev. 274, and S. Optican, "Rolling Back s.21 of the Bill of Rights" [1997] N.Z.L. Rev. 42. See also A. Butler, "The Bill of Rights Debate: Why the New Zealand Bill of Rights Act 1990 is a Bad Model for Britain" [1997] O.J.L.S. 323.

[22] Para. 3.3 of the White Paper.

This mechanism is intended to have an impact further back in the legislative process, and has been taken from a comparable New Zealand measure, where, however, it is the Attorney-General who certifies. It is intended that it should be a feature in the thinking of those who promote (and in the case of Parliamentary Counsel draft) legislation – already is well ingrained in such institutions as the Law Commission, when considering possible legislation on Binding over, for example, or the law of corruption. There would also be (possibly) a Parliamentary Committee (or Committees), which might conduct inquiries on a range of human rights issues relating to the Convention.

Incorporating the existing jurisprudence

Section 2 of the Act provides that a court or tribunal in determining a question which has arisen under the Act in connection with a Convention right must take into account any judgment, decision, declaration or advisory opinion of the European Court of Human Rights, and the opinions or decisions of various other identified agencies, so far as, in the opinion of the court or tribunal, it is relevant to the proceedings in which that question has arisen.

The effect of this section is to incorporate, at a stroke, the entire corpus of the jurisprudence of the European Court of Human Rights. This differentiates the developments here from those of Canada and New Zealand, and requires an instant familiarity with a body of law to which few English lawyers have hitherto aspired.[23]

The Act says that the court "must take in to account", and not that it must "apply". This is consistent with what was said in the White paper, which says that decisions of the Court "will not be binding".[24] This might be contrasted with the provisions of the European Communities Act 1972, section 3(1) which provides that:

"For the purposes of all legal proceedings any question as to the meaning or effect of any of the Treaties, or as to the validity, meaning or effect of any Community instrument, shall be treated as a question of law (and, if not referred to the European Court, be for the determination as such in accordance with the principles laid down by any relevant decision of the European Court".

---

[23] There are already in production several works on the Convention and its jurisprudence. One might make here of the latest part of Halsbury, eds Lord Lester of Herne Hill Q.C. and Professor D. Oliver, Volume 8(2), *Constitutional Law and Human Rights*, (1997) which contains a very useful overview of the Convention and the decisions of the European Court, and which is available as a stand-alone publication. Judgments of the European Court are quickly available on the internet.http://www.dhcour.coe.fr/.

[24] Para 2.4

The significance of the contrast may be no more than a reflection of the fact that the decisions of the European Court are not infrequently somewhat delphic in character; it is difficult, sometimes, to read them as giving rise to any clear *ratio decidendi* of the kind sought and applied by common lawyers. In *Funke* v. *France*,[25] for example, it was suggested by the court that the presumption of innocence might also include, by implication, a right not to incriminate oneself.

Principles of interpretation upon which the European Court has itself acted.

It may be useful at this point to draw attention to some principles upon which the European Court has itself acted.

1. A generous approach is taken when determining what comes within the scope of the protected fundamental rights. This is said to be consonant with the essential object and purpose of the E.C.H.R., which is "an instrument for the protection of individual human beings".[26] Adopting a narrow construction of the rights protected is to run the risk of denying Convention scrutiny in cases where a fundamental right may be affected, albeit indirectly.

This may well require from common lawyers a significant difference from their customary approach. Until relatively recently, it was not at all uncommon to find the higher courts in this country denying that a general issue of rights protection was involved at all in the resolution of the dispute before them. For example, Lord Diplock in *Harman* v. *The Home Office*, said:[27]

"My Lords, in a case which has attracted a good deal of publicity it may assist in clearing up misconceptions if I start by saying what the case is *not* about. It is *not* about freedom of speech, freedom of the press, openness of justice or documents coming into 'the public domain'; nor, with all respect to those of your Lordships who think the contrary, does it in my opinion call for consideration of any of those human rights and fundamental freedoms which in the European Convention for the Protection of Human Rights and Fundamental Freedoms (Rome, 4 November 1950; T.S. 71 (1953); Cmd 8969) are contained in separate articles each starting with a statement in absolute terms but followed immediately by very broadly stated exceptions."

That was, of course, some 15 years ago, and the general judicial receptivity to rights arguments has altered enormously since then.

---

[25] (1993) 16 E.H.R.R. 297, 1 C.M.L.R. 897.
[26] *Niemietz* v. *Germany* 16 E.H.R.R. 97, para 31.
[27] [1983] 1 A.C. 280 at 299E-F.

2. So far as the application of a test of proportionality is concerned, there appear to be four requirements to be fulfilled before interference can be justified:

(i) The interference must be lawful
(ii) it must serve a legitimate purpose
(iii) it must be necessary in a democratic society and
(iv) it is not discriminatory

3. It must be remembered that the Convention is regarded by the Court as a "living instrument". This means that the older a decision, the less value it may have as a guide to construction. What is seen to be proportionate in a democratic society will inevitably vary over time. Thus, the criminalisation of homosexuality was regarded as raising no admissible issue under the Convention during the 1960's and early 70's. Subsequently, it was ruled to be contrary to Article 8 when applied to acts between consenting adults in private in *Dudgeon* v. *United Kingdom*[28] and in *Sutherland* v. *United Kingdom*,[29] the Commission found that the continued unequal age of consent for male sexual behaviour (18) compared with heterosexual behaviour (16) violates Art. 8 read with Article 14.

Parliamentary Sovereignty[30]

It was noted earlier that the purpose of the Act is to give the Convention the force of "ordinary" law. But the Human Rights Act contains provisions that take it beyond what might be called "ordinary" law, because of the way in which it accommodates the doctrines of Parliamentary Sovereignty. The implied repeal of inconsistent past legislation requires a special mention. The doctrine of Parliamentary Sovereignty as formulated by Diecy was, in part, that later inconsistent legislation repeals an earlier inconsistent Act to the extent of the inconsistency. One consequence of this train of reasoning was that earlier debates on the wisdom of enacting a Bill of Rights rapidly became sidetracked. It was, according to the strict Diceyans, technically impossible to entrench a Bill of Rights. Any later and inconsistent Act would simply repeal it. Various stratagem, were suggested as to how this problem might be d, Perhaps the most famous was Professor Sir H.W.R. Wade's idea that the judges might be invited to swear a different oath pledging allegiance to a written Bill of Rights rather than to Parliamentary Sovereignty.[31]
Parliament successfully altered the standard doctrine

when it incorporated the Treaty of Rome through the European Communities Act 1972 (with consequences that became manifest in the *Factortame* litigation).[32] These developments make it clear that there are indeed situations in which the courts can treat even *later* enacted legislation as being inoperative if it conflicts with directly applicable European law.

It is explicit in the case of the Human Rights Act, however, that the reverse is to be the case. That is, the courts cannot declare legislation, not even *previously enacted* legislation invalid on the basis of incompatibility with the Human Rights Act; the Diceyan model has been placed in abeyance for the purposes of this legislation. Instead, and perhaps as a *quid pro quo*, the courts are given an entirely novel power, to make a declaration of incompatibility. Technically, perhaps, it would be open to the courts to invalidate earlier legislation in the event of any incompatibility – that would be consistent with the classic doctrine. But it seems most unlikely that they will seek to do so, in the face of the plain legislative injunctions.

Interpretation of legislation[33]

The Act gives to the courts considerable guidance as to how its own provisions are to be approached.

"3. – (1) So far as it is possible to do so, primary legislation and subordinate legislation must be read and given effect in a way which is compatible with the Convention rights.

(2) This section-

(a) applies to primary legislation and subordinate legislation *whenever enacted*;

(b) does not affect the validity, continuing operation or enforcement of any incompatible primary legislation; and

(c) does not affect the validity, continuing operation or enforcement of any incompatible subordinate legislation if (disregarding any possibility of revocation) primary legislation prevents removal of the incompatibility."

---

[28] (1981) 4 E.H.R.R. 149.
[29] (1997) 24 E.H.R.R. C.D. 22.
[30] See N. Bamforth, "Parliamentary Sovereignty and the Human Rights Act 1998" [1998] P.L. 572.
[31] *Constitutional Fundamentals* (1980) 47.

[32] *R.* v. *Secretary of State for Transport, ex parte Factortame (No 2)* [1991] A.C. 603. The precise significance of these developments for the doctrine of sovereignty is a matter of some dispute. See H.W.R. Wade, "Sovereignty: Revolution or Evolution" (1996) 112 L.Q.R. 568; T.R.S. Allan, "Parliamentary Sovereignty: Law Politics and Revolution" (1997) 113 L.Q.R. 443; J. Eekelaar, "The Death of Parliamentary Sovereignty - a Comment" (1997) 113 L.Q.R. 185.
[33] See D. Pannick, "Principles of interpretation of Convention rights under the Human Rights Act and the discretionary area of judgment" [1998] P.L. 545. See also P. Duffy Q.C., "The European Convention on Human Rights: Issues Relating to its Interpretation in the Light of the Human Rights Bill" in Cambridge Centre for Public Law, *Constitutional Reform in the United Kingdom: Practice and Principles* (1998).

This is said by the White Paper to go "far beyond the present rule which enables the courts to take the Convention into account in resolving any ambiguity in a legislative provision. The courts will be required to interpret legislation so as to uphold the Convention rights unless the legislation is so clearly incompatible with the Convention that it is impossible." The "rule of construction" is to apply to past was well as to future legislation. To the extent that it affects the meaning of a legislative provision, the court will not be bound by previous interpretations.

It should be emphasised that the demand for such an approach requires the courts to engage in a very different exercise from the one in which they conventionally suppose themselves to be engaging when approaching a statute. Currently, the courts reading statutes suppose themselves to be, in some form or another, in search of legislative intent. Under the Act, legislative intent becomes, in a sense secondary. Instead, the courts must look for some interpretation of the Act at hand that is consistent with the 1998 Act, as interpreted (perhaps) by the European Court.

The Declaration of incompatibility

The mechanism for ensuring that the law of the United Kingdom is brought into compliance with the provisions of the 1998 Act, should that be necessary – the declaration of incompatibility – is entirely novel. There is no counterpart in either the Canadian or New Zealand measures, and the precise operation of how the declaration will work in practice remains a matter of some speculation.

A declaration of incompatibility may be made by the court[34] if it is satisfied that there is an unavoidable conflict between the Convention rights and primary legislation (section 4(2). The same power is to apply in the case of subordinate legislation if it cannot be made compatible because of primary legislation. (sections 4(3) and (4).

Section 5 provides that, where a court is minded to make such a declaration, the Crown is entitled to be given notice in accordance with rules of court. A Minister or his nominee is then entitled to be joined as a party. In a criminal case, a person so joined may appeal

to the House of Lords against any declaration of incompatibility.

The declaration is not to affect the validity, continuing operation or enforcement of the offending provision, nor is it to be binding on the parties (section 4(6)). Instead, it may (if the Minister so chooses) lead to a "remedial order" amending the offending legislation.

Governmental response to the declaration

The Act provides for a fast-track procedure for changing legislation in response either to a declaration of incompatibility by our own higher courts or to a finding of a violation of the Convention in Strasbourg. The appropriate Government Minister will be able to amend the legislation by Order so as to make it compatible with the Convention. The Order will be subject to the approval by both Houses of Parliament before taking effect. However, where the need to amend the legislation is particularly urgent, the Order will take effect immediately, but will expire after a short period if not approved by Parliament. The order may operate retrospectively, though it cannot operate in such a way as to impose criminal liability retrospectively.

The upshot is something of a Pyrhic victory. The applicant has established that he or she ought to have won the case, because his rights have been infringed, but he loses since the declaration does not actually affect the outcome of the proceedings in question. Victory is secured only if the Minister choses to make the operation of the amending legislation retrospective,; justice is done, not according to law but by Ministerial fiat. And that, as Sir William Wade has pointed out, is hardly consistent with the declaration in the European Convention and the First schedule of the Human Rights Act itself, that the rights of citizens are to be determined by independent and impartial tribunals.[35]

Some tentative predictions

Professor M. Taggart, in summarising the New Zealand experience thus far, said:[36]

"The abiding impression of the first seven years of [Bill of Rights] jurisprudence is the utter domination of criminal cases. From the literally thousands of cases in which the Bill of Rights has been invoked on behalf of an accused, a large number have been reported and a disproportionately large

---

[34] Section 4(5) provides that "in this section 'court' means:
  (a) the House of Lords;
  (b) the Judicial Committee of the Privy Council;
  (c) the Courts-Martial Appeal Court;
  (d) in Scotland, the High Court of Justiciary sitting otherwise than as a trial court or the Court of Session;
  (e) in England and Wales or Northern Ireland, the High Court or the Court of Appeal.

[35] Cambridge Centre for Public Law, *Constitutional Reform in the United Kingdom: Practice and Principles* (1998), at p.67.
[36] "Tugging on Superman's Cape: lessons from experience with the New Zealand Bill of Rights Act 1990" in Cambridge Centre for Public Law, *Constitutional Reform in the United Kingdom: Practice and Principles* (1998).

number have gone up to the Court of Appeal. One indicator of the amount of case law is that the treatment of the Bill of Rights in the leading criminal law lose-leaf text runs to over 250 pages. All of this is consistent with Canadian experience".

The adoption of the New Zealand Constitutional model was a sign that the government did not want to upset the constitutional status quo any further than might be necessary. In this respect, there is a very major difference between the position here and in Canada, since there is to be no power of judicial review. Instead, there is to be a "declaration of incompatibility". When the courts make such a pronouncement (and there are widely varying predictions as to the likely frequency with which they might come to do so), they return the initiative to take remedial action back to the Executive. So at least the intention is to proceed cautiously.

But there is inevitably a degree of unpredictability as to how the enactment will alter the current public perceptions of adjudication required of the judiciary. The New Zealand measure was widely perceived in advance of its implementation to be a toothless document. But as Taggart points out, "it did not take the judiciary long to shake the media, the legal profession, politicians and the public out of this apathy".[37] In particular, in *Simpson v. Att.-Gen [Baigent's case]* [38] in which the Court of Appeal invented a damages remedy

against the state for breach of the Charter, the court appears to have stepped beyond the sphere of competence originally contemplated by Parliament.

What approach the judges will take remains to be seen, and it is perhaps foolish even to try to predict. Newspapers have fastened upon this aspect of the Act and have fostered the expectation that there will be a far higher judicial profile when the Act becomes law.[39] That the judiciary are involved in policy "up to their necks"[40] has been disconcertingly illustrated by the developments in the case involving Senator Pinochet. One prominent counsel,[41] has urged that the courts should adapt the doctrine of "margin of appreciation"[42] in such a way as to display deference to the opinions of the legislature and the executive where this appears appropriate, and to develop principles indicating where deference is or is not appropriate. What will be required of the judiciary, as the jurisprudence evolves, is some articulation in the light of the Act, of the respective spheres of Parliament, the executive and the judiciary.

---

[37] *Constitutional Reform* (1988): p. 86. "In the shell game of constitutional reform, ...it is often difficult to keep your eye on the pea. And once the reform is securely in place, history often is quickly forgotten, pushed down by the imperative to make the best (as the judges see it) of what we have in a forward looking manner".

[38] [1994] 3 N.Z.L.R. 667. For criticism, see J. Smillie, "'Fundamental' rights, parliamentary supremacy and the New Zealand Court of Appeal" (1995) 111 L.Q.R. 209, and the reply by A. Hunt, (1995) 111 L.Q.R. 565.

[39] In a letter to *The Times*, Dr P. Allott has expressed the view that the Human Rights Act ("Minima Carta", he calls it) "is a pale shadow of one of the worse features of the American Constitution, the politicising of the judiciary and the 'judicialising' of politics".

[40] The expression used by Sir H.W.R. Wade in *Constitutional Fundamentals* (1980) at. p. 62.

[41] D. Pannick [1998] P.L. 545.

[42] The doctrine whereby an international tribunal such as the European Court of Human Rights displays reluctance to substitute its own judgment for that of the national court, out of deference to the latter's greater expertise in making assessments of national factors and conditions. Its precise sphere is a matter of some controversy. See e.g. D. Pannick, "Principles of Interpretation of Convention Rights uner the Human Rights Act and the Discretionary Area of Judgment" [1998] P.L. 545; R. Singh, M. Hunt and Marie Demetriou, "Is there a Role for the 'Margin of Appreciation' in National Law after the Human Rights Act?" [1999] E.H.R.L.R. 15.

2

ACTIVISM AND RESTRAINT: HUMAN RIGHTS AND THE INTERPRETIVE PROCESS

THE RT. HON. LORD IRVINE OF LAIRG
LORD CHANCELLOR*

1. INTRODUCTION

My subject tonight is 'Activism and Restraint: Human Rights and the Interpretative Process'.

When scholars begin to write the legal history of the twentieth century, they will need to allocate a considerable space to their chapters on public law. Judicial activism in the development of a mature system of public law is likely to come to count as the century's single greatest judicial achievement.

Lord Diplock expressed his view that he regarded the progress towards a developed system of administrative law as 'one of the greatest achievements of the English courts' in his judicial lifetime.[1] But it has been on the anvil of interpretation of statutory materials by judges that much of this progress has been made. In developing their powers of judicial review, and in beginning to articulate a doctrine of common law constitutional rights, the judges have been careful to explain that their creativity has been an interpretative one. The activism which has driven the dramatic expansion of public law has thus been tempered by the restraint which our constitution requires.

The tendency in the United Kingdom towards growing judicial supervision of the executive finds its broader, international counterpart in the increasing importance which is attached—at both national and transnational level—to the protection of human rights.

As the United Nations High Commissioner for Human Rights remarked last December, on the occasion of the fiftieth anniversary of the Universal Declaration of Human Rights, we have seen in the last 50 years that 'a culture of human rights is growing throughout the world'. Although a wide range of factors determines the extent to which this culture can take effect in any particular legal system, the trend—in recent years—towards the legalisation of human rights has been central. The eminent jurist, Hersch Lauterpacht, was in the vanguard of those who recognised the importance of embracing fundamental rights not merely as aspirational rhetoric, but as enforceable legal principle.[2]

It is the task of translating the text of the European Convention on Human Rights into principles of domestic law upon which British courts will soon embark: and, just as the interpretative process has been crucial, during the twentieth century, to the development of administrative law, so it will also take centre stage when our courts begin to exercise a more substantive public law jurisdiction as the new millennium dawns.[3]

* This is a very lightly revised version of the 1999 Paul Sieghart Memorial Lecture delivered at Kings College London under the auspices of the British Institute of Human Rights. The lecture will also be published in the *European Human Rights Law Review.*

[1] *Inland Revenue Commissioners* v. *National Federation for Small Businesses and Self-Employed Ltd.* [1982] AC 617, 641.

[2] See, e.g., *An International Bill of the Rights of Man* (New York: Columbia University Press, 1945).

[3] It is the courts' interpretative duty, under the Human Rights Act 1998, s. 3(1), to construe national law in a manner which is consistent with the Convention rights which lies at the heart of the legislative scheme. Indeed, it is this interpretative approach to fundamental rights which facilitates the co-existence of strong rights protection and respect for parliamentary sovereignty. See further Cm 3782, *Rights Brought Home: The Human Rights Bill* (London: HMSO, 1997), 9–11, and my 1998 National Heritage Lecture to the Historical Society of the United States Supreme Court, 'Constitutional Change in the United Kingdom: British Solutions to Universal Problems' (publication forthcoming).

However, while the centrality of interpretation will remain constant, the nature of the interpretative challenge faced by the courts will evolve. They will be confronted, for the first time, with an instrument that enumerates—in the expansive terms which are the universal language of constitutional texts—the fundamental rights of people.

It is, therefore, timely to examine the nature of the interpretative process in the human rights arena. I shall turn, shortly, to the experiences of other jurisdictions, since there is much which a comparative perspective can offer. I will also address the prospects for human rights adjudication in the United Kingdom. Let me begin, however, by focusing on the particular challenges which fundamental rights interpretation poses and the factors which shape the judiciary's response.

2. TEXTUAL PRESCRIPTION AND JUDICIAL RESPONSE: THE ALCHEMY OF HUMAN RIGHTS INTERPRETATION

2.1 The special challenge of human rights adjudication

Interpretation is, at root, an exercise in textual analysis. It is, therefore, the words of a bill of rights with which judges must primarily be concerned as they seek to adjudicate in cases which engage fundamental norms. Although many eminent judges held that the judicial function entailed nothing other than this literal approach to construction,[4] this declaratory theory long ago gave way to more open recognition that law-making—within certain limits—is an inevitable and legitimate element of the judge's role.[5] Acceptance of this truism reveals the real nature of the interpretative process. In particular, it indicates that, when construing a statutory provision, the judge may well have to choose between competing meanings by reference, for instance, to the underlying rationale of the legislative scheme. Lord Simonds famously rebuked the late Lord Denning for advocating such an approach, commenting that it would

be 'a naked usurpation of the legislative function under the thin disguise of interpretation'.[6] In this, as in so many other matters, Lord Denning was rather ahead of his time; yet, as was sometimes—although not inevitably—the case, Lord Denning's heterodoxy came, in time, to be accepted as the new orthodoxy.[7]

These truths concerning the nature of the interpretative process apply with particular force to human rights instruments. As the Chief Justice of Hong Kong observed, in a case about which I shall have a good deal more to say later, 'A constitution'—or, for that matter, a bill of rights—'states general principles and expresses purposes without condescending to particularity and definition of terms. Gaps and ambiguities are bound to arise . . .'[8] As he approaches the interpretation of a constitutional text, the task of the judge is therefore a delicate one. Two particular imperatives weigh upon him, and pull in different directions.

First, it is important that the courts are not so timid in their interpretation of a rights instrument that it loses its utility as an effective guarantee of the citizen's fundamental entitlements. The dictum which one New Zealand commentator[9] has dubbed 'the celebrated Cardozo-via-Wilberforce aphorism' is often cited, but remains as pertinent as ever. According to this formulation, rights texts must be given 'a generous interpretation avoiding what has been called the "austerity of tabulated legalism", suitable to give individuals the full measure of [their] fundamental rights and freedoms'.[10]

---

[4] Lord Simonds was a forceful exponent of the declaratory theory of the judge's role. See, e.g., his remarks in *Scruttons* v. *Midland Silicones Ltd.* [1962] AC 446, 467–9. Lord Devlin expressed similar views in 'Judges and Lawmakers' (1976) 39 *MLR* 1.

[5] See, e.g., Lord Reid, 'The Judge as Law Maker' (1972) 12 *Journal of the Society of Public Teachers of Law* 22. For a relatively early articulation of the legislative function of the courts, see B. Cardozo, *The Nature of the Judicial Process* (New Haven, Conn.: Yale University Press, 1921), 98–141; for more recent perspectives, see A. Lester, 'English Judges as Lawmakers' [1993] *PL* 269; Lord Bingham of Cornhill, 'The Judge as Lawmaker: An English Perspective' in P. Rishworth (ed.), *The Struggle for Simplicity in Law* (Wellington: Butterworths, 1997).

[6] *Magor and St. Mellons Rural District Council* v. *Newport Corporation* [1952] AC 189, 191.

[7] A good example of this in the public law field is the approach which Lord Denning took to the scope of judicial review. In *Laker Airways Ltd.* v. *Department of Trade* [1977] QB 643, 705, he said that, 'Seeing that the prerogative is a discretionary power to be exercised for the public good, it follows that its exercise can be examined by the courts just as any other discretionary power which is vested in the executive'. The House of Lords accepted this conclusion some years later in *Council of Civil Service Unions* v. *Minister for the Civil Service* [1985] AC 374. In *The Discipline of Law* (London: Butterworths, 1979), 61, Lord Denning wrote that, 'The great problem before the courts in the twentieth century has been: In an age of increasing power, how is the law to cope with the abuse or misuse of it?' It was this healthy attitude to the supervision of governmental power which underpinned Lord Denning's valuable contributions to the development of English public law; and it was his equally keen awareness of the scope for abuse of power in relationships between citizen and citizen which was the impetus for many of his decisions in the private law sphere.

[8] *Ng Ka Ling* v. *Director of Immigration* [1999] 1 HKLRD 315, 339–40, *per* Li CJ giving the unanimous judgment of the Court of Final Appeal.

[9] P. Rishworth, 'Lord Cooke and the Bill of Rights' in P. Rishworth (ed.), *The Struggle for Simplicity in Law* (Wellington: Butterworths, 1997), 321.

[10] *Minister of Home Affairs* v. *Collins MacDonald Fisher* [1980] AC 319, 328, *per* Lord Wilberforce.

However, it is equally crucial that human rights are not stretched by courts so far that they become distorted caricatures. As Lord Woolf remarked in a Privy Council decision[11] on the Hong Kong Bill of Rights Ordinance, 'it is necessary to ensure that disputes as to the effect of the Bill are not allowed to get out of hand. The issues involving the . . . Bill of Rights should be approached with realism and good sense, and kept in proportion. If this is not done the Bill will become a source of injustice rather than justice and it will be debased in the eyes of the public.'[12] This is wise counsel, and it will apply to our own Human Rights Act just as it does to Hong Kong's Bill of Rights.

2.2 The role of the judiciary and the courts' interpretation of human rights texts

The challenge for the courts is to work out where the correct balance lies between these competing imperatives of activism and restraint. A rich and complex alchemy of factors impacts upon this judicial balancing exercise. But a crucial factor is the prevailing conception in society of the role and function of the courts within the broader legal and constitutional order.

The more keenly it is felt that the judges are guardians of fundamental rights who serve a central role in ensuring accountable government, the more likely they are to take an interventionist approach, broadly reading the rights themselves while narrowly construing any provisions which appear to inhibit their application. In contrast, a judiciary which less readily perceives that it is part of a constitutional machinery which secures individuals' rights against legislative encroachment and executive abuse is likely to take a very different approach to the interpretation of a human rights instrument.

I need hardly point out to so distinguished an audience that there can be no clearer illustration of this than the historic judgment of the United States Supreme Court in *Marbury* v. *Madison*.[13] The vacuum created by the US Constitution's silence on the courts' powers over unconstitutional legislation had to be filled by judicial decision. The Supreme Court's conclusion, that the judicial branch could set aside such legislation, was inspired by a particular conception of the purpose and role of the courts and the nature of their relationship with the other institutions of government.

However, to acknowledge the particular importance and sensitivity of the judicial decision-making process in the field of human rights interpretation does not mean that the judges have *carte blanche* to do as they please.[14] This follows for a number of reasons.

First, the text itself provides, to some extent, a limit on the judges' freedom. Although the expansive language of human rights instruments means that they cannot constitute precise directions which judges simply enforce, they do at least point towards the acceptable parameters within which constitutional adjudication may occur.[15] The text thus reminds that judge that, in the words of Cardozo, 'even when he is free, [he] is not wholly free . . . He is not a knight-errant, roaming at will in pursuit of his own ideal of beauty or of goodness'.[16]

Secondly, the conclusions which previous courts have reached also constitute—through the doctrine of precedent—a significant limit on the scope of the judges' interpretative freedom. But in this regard as in so many others, human rights are something of a special case. Professor Jack Beatson, in his inaugural lecture at Cambridge, pointed out that 'in its application on any date the language of [an ordinary] Act [of Parliament], though necessarily embedded in its own time, is nevertheless to be construed in accordance with the need to treat it as current law'.[17] This same principle applies—but with much greater force—to human rights instruments. To quote Cardozo again: 'Statutes are designed to meet the fugitive exigencies of the hour . . . A constitution'—or a bill of rights—'states or ought to state not rules for the passing hour, but principles for an expanding future'.[18] It is for this reason that the European Convention on Human Rights is regarded as 'a living instrument which . . . must be interpreted in the light of present day conditions'.[19] Consequently, while past decisions on the meaning of human rights texts furnish judges with invaluable guidance, they certainly do not fix any immovable limit

[11] The Privy Council ceased hearing appeals from Hong Kong upon the transfer of sovereignty to the People's Republic of China on 1 July 1997. The Hong Kong Special Administrative Region's Court of Final Appeal is now the highest appellate tribunal in the jurisdiction.

[12] *Attorney-General of Hong Kong* v. *Lee Kwong-kut* [1993] AC 951, 975.

[13] (1803) 1 Cranch 137.

[14] For further discussion, from the perspective of English law, of the limits which the constitution imposes on judicial decision-making in the public law field, see section 4 below, and my lectures 'Judges and Decision-Makers: The Theory and Practice of *Wednesbury* Review' [1996] *PL* 59 and 'Principle and Pragmatism: The Development of English Public Law under the Separation of Powers' (Hong Kong, September 1998).

[15] By stating such parameters, the text of human rights legislation also serves a democratic function by furnishing the judges with a catalogue of rights which has received the imprimatur of an elected legislature: see further my 'Response to Sir John Laws' [1996] *PL* 636.

[16] Cardozo, n. 5 above, at 141.

[17] 'Has the Common Law a Future?' [1997] *CLJ* 291, 302.

[18] Cardozo, n. 5 above, at 83.

[19] *Tyrer* v. *United Kingdom* (1978) Series A, vol. 26, para. 31

on the courts' interpretative freedom,[20] as the US Supreme Court's *volte-face* in *Brown* v. *Board of Education* on the constitutionality of racial segregation illustrates.[21]

Finally, the jurisprudence of constitutional courts in other jurisdictions is a useful source of guidance to any judge seeking to give meaning to a human rights instrument. The South African Constitutional Court has embraced this comparative ethos with particular zeal.[22]

Thus we reach the position that, while there are many factors which, quite properly, shape and guide the interpretation of human rights instruments, their linguistic texture and their evolutive nature necessarily leave the judges with a significant margin of interpretative autonomy. As I have already suggested, it is the prevailing conception of the constitutional role of the judiciary which shapes its behaviour within this area of decision-making freedom.

Before I develop this theme further, I enter an important caveat. The content of this perception of the courts' role should emphatically not be determined by the attitudes of individual judges. While there will always exist subtle differences of emphasis and opinion between members of the Bench, the overarching conception of the judiciary's role, which determines the premise on which it approaches constitutional texts, necessarily consists in a complex amalgam of strands within a wider consensus in society about the nature and purpose of the judicial function.

This phenomenon can be observed in the development of English public law over the course of the twentieth century. As I noted at the outset, the growth of judicial review is one of the pre-eminent legal innovations of recent decades. And, although the courts fashioned our modern system of administrative law, it would be misleading to suggest that these developments occurred at their unilateral instance. The expansion of judicial review must be understood within a broader

constitutional setting. The explosion of regulatory power led to the courts coming to be regarded as a central part of a broader constitutional mechanism securing responsible government. In this manner, the growth of review, and the perception of the judicial function upon which it is founded, constituted a mature response to the changing needs of good governance.[23]

The role of the judiciary in this context is also shaped by the perception of judicial independence. I regard independence, along with judicial impartiality and open justice, as a closely related trinity.

Judicial independence is a fundamental article of Britain's unwritten constitution. It is a critical aspect of the doctrine of separation of powers. In their own sphere the judges are independent, free of executive influence or control. There is no higher duty of the office I occupy than to ensure from within Government that judicial independence is both respected and maintained absolutely. And, as you know, under our arrangements, the fulfillment of that duty is strengthened and supported by my separate, but related, roles as Cabinet Minister and Head of the Judiciary. So, judges are independent of Government, with an absolute power over the decisions within their own courts, which can only be overturned by the equally absolute decisions of senior judges in higher courts. In return, the trust we place in our judiciary is that they will carry out their duties impartially. Judicial impartiality, which I would define as the absolute recognition and application by judges of an obligation of fidelity to law, is the *quid pro quo* from the judiciary for the guarantee from the state of their judicial independence in their distinct sphere within the separation of powers.

But just as judicial impartiality is the other side of the coin of judicial independence, so open justice, as witnessed by attentive media, is a strong spur to judicial impartiality in practice. And each element in this trinity is especially highlighted in a period in which the importance of public law adjudication in the United Kingdom is heightened. I will return to the position in the UK later. First, however, let me draw upon the experiences of other jurisdictions to illustrate my thesis in comparative perspective.

[20] British courts, when they begin to adjudicate on the ECHR, will, of course, benefit from the existence of a ready-made body of case law in the form of the jurisprudence of the European Commission and Court of Human Rights. Although s. 2(1) of the Human Rights Act 1998 requires British courts to have regard to these decisions, they will not constitute 'precedent' in the technical sense.

[21] Compare *Plessy* v. *Ferguson* (1896) 153 US 537 and *Brown* v. *Board of Education of Topeka* (1953) 347 US 483.

[22] The Master of the Rolls has noted that English courts, too, are becoming increasingly outward-looking, suggesting in his 1991 F.A. Mann Lecture that it would not be long before 'England . . . ceased to be a legal island, bounded to the north by the Tweed, and joined, or more accurately rejoined, the mainstream of European legal tradition, at least as an associate member'. See Sir Thomas Bingham, '"There is a World Elsewhere": The Changing Perspectives of English Law' (1992) 41 *ICLQ* 513, 514.

[23] See further Sir Stephen Sedley, 'Governments, Constitutions, and Judges' in G. Richardson and H. Genn (eds.), *Administrative Law and Government Action* (Oxford: Clarendon Press, 1994) and 'The Sound of Silence: Constitutional Law Without a Constitution' (1994) 110 *LQR* 270. For a broader perspective, see M. Cappelletti, *The Judicial Process in Comparative Perspective* (Oxford: Clarendon Press, 1989), ch. 1.

3. PERSPECTIVES ON ACTIVISM AND RESTRAINT IN THE INTERPRETATION OF HUMAN RIGHTS

3.1 The *Immigrant Children* cases: interpretation in Hong Kong's new constitutional order

3.1.1 Introduction

Hong Kong is my first port of call. Its courts are still coming to terms with a new set of constitutional arrangements. It is only eight years since the International Covenant on Civil and Political Rights was incorporated into Hong Kong law,[24] and it is less than two years since the Basic Law, which now forms the written constitution of the Hong Kong Special Administrative Region, entered into force upon the transfer of sovereignty from the United Kingdom to the People's Republic of China.[25]

The most challenging questions of construction which have arisen under Hong Kong's new constitutional texts relate to the rights of permanent residence and abode which Article 24 of the Basic Law confers upon certain categories of persons. The issues raised by these *Immigrant Children* cases[26] can be divided into two broad categories. Before I turn to the substantive questions about the scope of the entitlements granted by the Basic Law, let me examine two broader issues which arose, concerning the interrelationship of Hong Kong's institutions of government.[27]

3.1.2 The institutional issues

First, the scope of the Court of Final Appeal's competence to interpret Hong Kong's constitution had to be decided. The Basic Law requires the Court to refer to the National People's Congress the interpretation of matters which relate to the responsibilities of the central government or which impact upon its relationship with Hong Kong.[28] The way in which this issue was approached by the Court was crucial, since a broad construction would have transferred a substantial degree of interpretative competence from the Hong Kong judiciary to the mainland authorities.[29] After due consideration, the Court held that the duty to refer questions of interpretation related only to a very narrow range of issues and that it was a matter for the Court to determine whether, in any particular case, such an issue was properly engaged.[30] While this construction did not place unbearable strain on the text of the Basic Law, it did not necessarily constitute the most natural construction of the relevant words.

Three principal factors underpinned the Court of Final Appeal's approach, each of which affected its underlying conception of the constitutional role and function of the judicial branch. First, the Court held that the construction of constitutional texts calls for a particular interpretative method. A 'literal, technical, rigid or narrow approach' had to be rejected; instead, it was said that Hong Kong's courts should 'give a generous interpretation to the . . . constitutional guarantees' enshrined in the Basic Law, 'in order to give to Hong Kong residents the full measure of [their] fundamental rights and freedoms'.[31] Secondly, Li CJ—giving the judgment

---

[24] This was effected by the Hong Kong Bill of Rights Ordinance. For an interesting discussion of the Hong Kong courts' early Bill of Rights jurisprudence, see J.M.M. Chan, 'Hong Kong's Bill of Rights: Its Reception of and Contribution to International and Comparative Jurisprudence' (1998) 47 *ICLQ* 306.

[25] Following the transfer of sovereignty, the ICCPR remains part of Hong Kong's domestic law by operation of Art. 39 of the Basic Law.

[26] There are two separate *Immigrant Children* decisions. The first case, *Ng Ka Ling* v. *Director of Immigration (sub nom: Cheung Lai Wah (An Infant)* v. *Director of Immigration)* [1997] 3 HKC 64 (Court of First Instance); [1998] 1 HKC 617 (Court of Appeal); [1999] 1 HKLRD 315 (Court of Final Appeal), dealt with a particularly broad range of issues, and it was in this case that the Court of Final Appeal took the opportunity to explain, in some detail, its approach to constitutional adjudication (on which see below). The other *Immigrant Children* decisions are cited as *Chan Kam Nga* v. *Director of Immigration* [1998] 1 HKLRD 142 (Court of First Instance); [1998] 1 HKRD 752 (Court of Appeal); [1999] 1 HKLRD 304 (Court of Final Appeal).

[27] A further institutional issue also arose, regarding the constitutionality of Hong Kong's Provisional Legislative Council. This question had been the subject of considerable dispute in earlier cases before the lower courts. In *Hong Kong Special Administrative Region* v. *Ma Wai Kwan David* [1997] 2 HKC 315, the Court of Appeal held that the provisional legislature had been lawfully constituted in accordance with the requirements of the Basic Law. The issue was raised again in *Cheung Lai Wah (An Infant)* v. *Director of Immigration (No. 2)* [1998] 2 HKC 382, but the Court of Appeal held itself bound by its

earlier decision. The question was authoritatively determined by the Court of Final Appeal in *Na Ka Ling* v. *Director of Immigration* [1999] 1 HKLRD 315, 355–7, which held that the Provisional Legislative Council was lawfully constituted.

[28] Basic Law, Art. 158(3). This had not been in issue when the case was before the lower courts, since Art. 158(3) applies only to courts which make 'final judgments which are not appealable'.

[29] Such a construction was urged by counsel for the Director of Immigration who suggested that, even when the predominant question related to a provision of the Basic Law not falling within one of the special categories delineated by Art. 158(3), reference should still be made to the National People's Congress if another provision of the Basic Law, which did relate to one of the matters mentioned in Art. 158(3), was arguably relevant to the interpretation of the predominant provision. See *Ng Ka Ling* v. *Director of Immigration* [1999] 1 HKLRD 315, 343–4.

[30] *Ibid.*, at 344–5. Thus the reference duty arises only when the Court concludes that the 'predominant' provision of the Basic Law requiring interpretation relates to one of the matters set out in Art. 158(3). The fact that other provisions of the Basic Law which do relate to Art. 158(3) issues are arguably relevant to the construction of the predominant provision is insufficient to trigger the duty to refer.

[31] *Ibid.*, at 340, *per* Li CJ.

of the Court—held that constitutional adjudication called for a 'purposive approach' which recognised that one of the fundamental objectives of the Basic Law was 'to implement the unique principle of "one country, two systems"'.[32] This policy, said the Court, was advanced by the Basic Law's conferral of 'a high degree of autonomy' upon Hong Kong and its courts.[33] Thirdly, and most explicitly, the Court of Final Appeal emphasised that it is the 'constitutional role' of Hong Kong's courts to act 'as a check on the executive and legislative branches of government to ensure that they act in accordance with the Basic Law'.[34]

It is not my purpose, this evening, to analyse the correctness or otherwise of the decision at which the Court actually arrived. The determination of the constitutional dynamics of a particular legal order is properly for its own institutions to establish. My point is simply this: that, in light of the manner in which the Court perceived its function, it is wholly unsurprising that it favoured a construction of the Basic Law which emphasised the role of the judiciary as the primary interpreter of the constitution. Naturally, in considering this, attention was paid to the text of the constitution; but it is undeniable that the premises on which the Court approached the terms of the Basic Law exerted a strong influence on the conclusion which it reached.

The same ethos pervaded the Court's treatment of the second institutional issue, which concerned the competence of the judiciary to review the validity of legislation on the ground of its incompatibility with the Basic Law or the ICCPR. Although the Court's comments on this point were *obiter*, they are nevertheless important given both the authoritative source from which they issued and the light which they shed on the Court's broader approach to constitutional adjudication.

While the Court said that it 'undoubtedly' had jurisdiction to set aside enactments of Hong Kong's own Legislative Council,[35] the more controversial question was whether a similar jurisdiction could be exercised over legislation passed by China's National People's Congress. In an earlier case before a lower court, Chan CJHC had suggested that the relationship between the courts of the Hong Kong Special Administrative Region and the National People's Congress was analogous to that which had previously existed between the colonial courts and the

Westminster Parliament.[36] On this view, there was no jurisdiction in the courts to review the legislative acts of the sovereign. The Court of Final Appeal disagreed fundamentally, stating that the Court's jurisdiction to review legislation for consistency with the Basic Law extends to legislation passed by the National People's Congress, though this jurisdiction was subject to the provisions of the Basic Law itself, including the provision that the power of interpretation of the Basic Law, vesting in the Standing Committee of the National People's Congress, was paramount.

These different approaches to the sovereignty question disclose a broader shift in ethos which, to date, has been evident during the short history of Hong Kong's new constitutional order. The earlier decisions of the lower courts disclosed what may be termed a 'sovereigntist' approach to constitutional adjudication, which places less emphasis on the role of the court as a guardian of fundamental rights and as part of a constitutional machinery which supervises the other branches of government. This approach can be detected not only in the early decisions on the Basic Law, but also in some of the colonial courts' judgments, prior to the transfer of sovereignty, on the Bill of Rights Ordinance. In contrast, the *Immigrant Children* decision marks a shift away from a 'sovereigntist' view of the adjudicative function, towards a constitutionalist conception which underscores the courts' role as a constitutional check on the legislature and the executive. The Court's decision that it has jurisdiction to invalidate legislation passed by the National People's Congress thus stands as an important symbol of this change of ethos; in particular, it will serve as a useful marker for the lower courts as they continue to adjust to the demands of Hong Kong's new constitutional order.

However, before leaving the institutional implications of the Immigrant Children decision, I wish to offer one

---

[32] *Ibid.*, at 339, *per* Li CJ.

[33] *Ibid.*, at 337, *per* Li CJ.

[34] *Ibid.*

[35] *Ng Ka Ling* v. *Director of Immigration* [1999] 1 HKLRD 315, 337.

[36] *Hong Kong Special Administrative Region* v. *Ma Wai Kwan David* [1997] 2 HKC 315, 334–5. This suggestion was based upon Art. 19(2) of the Basic Law which directs that, 'The courts of the Hong Kong Special Administrative Region shall have jurisdiction over all cases in the Region, except that the restrictions on their jurisdiction imposed by the legal system and the principles previously in force in Hong Kong shall be maintained'. Chan CJHC opined that, following the transfer of sovereignty, the National People's Congress replaced the Westminster Parliament as Hong Kong's sovereign legislature, so that the courts' incapacity to question enactments of the latter transferred, by operation of Art. 19(2), to the former. It should be pointed out that Chan CJHC later expressed doubts as to the correctness of these comments. In *Cheung Lai Wah (An Infant)* v. *Director of Immigration (No. 2)* [1998] 2 HKC 382, 395, he said that, 'It may be that in appropriate cases . . . the HKSAR courts do have jurisdiction to examine the laws and acts of the NPC which affect the HKSAR for the purpose of, say, determining whether such laws or acts are contrary to or inconsistent with the Basic Law . . .'

further thought. While the Court of Final Appeal's assertion of jurisdiction over mainland legislation is of symbolic importance for the future direction of constitutional jurisprudence in Hong Kong, the rejection of the notion of a sovereign legislature whose enactments cannot be questioned is not an ineluctable element of a shift from a 'sovereigntist' to a constitutionalist approach. It is quite possible for courts to adopt a more constitutionalist ethos in the public law sphere without questioning the ultimate supremacy of the legislature. The jurisprudence of the courts in New Zealand and the United Kingdom, to which I shall turn shortly, are cases in point.

3.1.3 The substantive issues

First, let me make some brief remarks about the substantive issues raised by the *Immigrant Children* decision. The Basic Law provides that Chinese nationals, at least one of whose parents is a permanent resident of Hong Kong, should themselves be regarded as permanent residents: importantly, acquisition of this status triggers a right of abode.[37] Shortly after the transfer of sovereignty, the Provisional Legislative Council, mindful of the possibility of a huge influx of people possessing—or claiming to possess—the status of permanent residency, enacted legislation to regulate and impose order upon the immigration process.[38] The effect of this legislation was twofold. First, it defined, in greater detail than the Basic Law, the conditions which had to be satisfied in order to establish permanent residency by descent; the applicants contended that this definition was unduly narrow and, hence, unconstitutional. Secondly, the legislation directed that those seeking to exercise a right of abode should, before going to Hong Kong, prove their status as permanent residents and obtain permission to travel from the mainland authorities; breach of these regulations entailed the commission of a criminal offence, and this provision took effect retroactively.

The lower courts upheld all of these legislative initiatives, apart from one aspect of the definition of permanent residency.[39] In stark contrast, the Court of Final

Appeal held that all but one of them was invalid for breach of either the Basic Law or the ICCPR.[40] The text of those constitutional instruments did not alter as the litigation progressed up the appellate hierarchy. Rather, the Court of Final Appeal reached conclusions which differed from those of the lower courts because it adopted a particularly constitutionalist conception of its function which impacted fundamentally on its interpretative approach.[40a] So, the dissimilar treatment of these substantive aspects of the *Immigrant Children* cases further illustrates the relationship between a court's perception of its constitutional role and the ultimate decisions which it reaches on the scope of fundamental rights. Let me outline a further example of this phenomenon.

3.2 South Africa and the United Kingdom: access to the courts' supervisory jurisdiction

The conception of the judicial function which prevails in a society is revealed with particular clarity by the courts' treatment of legislative attempts to attenuate their jurisdiction. The more acutely it is felt that courts are guardians of individual liberties, the more likely they are to construe ouster provisions in a way which preserves the judiciary's capacity to adjudicate in disputes between the citizen and the state.

English courts attach great importance to the citizen's right of access to justice; and judges have now come to speak of this as a constitutional right.[41] The *locus*

[37] Basic Law, Art. 24(2) and (3).

[38] See Immigration (Amendment) (No. 2) Ordinance (No. 122 of 1997); Immigration (Amendment) (No. 3) Ordinance (No. 124 of 1997).

[39] See *Ng Ka Ling* v. *Director of Immigration (sub nom: Cheung Lai Wah (An Infant)* v. *Director of Immigration)* [1997] 3 HKC 64 (Court of First Instance) and [1998] 1 H.K.C. 617 (Court of Appeal); *Chan Kam Nga* v. *Director of Immigration* [1998] 1 HKLRD 142 (Court of First Instance) and [1998] 1 HKLRD 752 (Court of Appeal). The part of the legislative scheme referred to in the text which the lower courts, in *Ng Ka Ling*, impugned as unconstitutional related to a provision which recognised an illegitimate child as the descendent only of its mother (unless the child was legitimated by subsequent marriage of both parents, in which case the child would

then be recognised as the descendent of its mother and its father). It should also be noted that, in *Chan Kam Nga*, the Court of First Instance held unconstitutional a legislative provision which refused to recognise a child as having been 'born of' a permanent resident if the parent became a permanent resident only after the birth. However, the Court of Appeal upheld the constitutionality of this provision.

[40] The only aspect of the legislative scheme upheld by the Court of Final Appeal, in *Ng Ka Ling*, n. 39 above, was a requirement that persons claiming to be permanent residents had to substantiate their claims to the satisfaction of Hong Kong authorities based on the mainland before travelling from the mainland to Hong Kong. The further requirement, that permission to travel had to be obtained from mainland authorities, was impugned as unconstitutional.

[40a] Since this lecture was delivered, the Standing Committee of the National Peoples Congress has exercised its power under the basic law, Article 158(1), by reinterpreting certain of the provisions of the basic law which were at stake in the *Immigrant Children* cases. For present purposes, it is sufficient to observe that these developments do not detract from the fact that the Courts' decisions in these cases clearly illustrate my argument that the judicial response to a constitutional text turns on, inter alia, the judiciary's perception of its constitutional functions.

[41] See, e.g., *R.* v. *Secretary of State for the Home Department, ex parte Leech (No. 2)* [1994] QB 198; *R.* v. *Lord Chancellor, ex parte Witham* [1998] QB 575.

classicus of this genre is still the seminal *Anisminic*[42] decision in which the House of Lords went to considerable lengths to preserve the availability of judicial review in the face of a statutory provision which, on a literal construction, appeared to preclude it. My theme this evening is usefully illuminated by comparing *Anisminic* with the 1988 judgment of the South African Appellate Division in the *UDF* case.[43] The two decisions concerned very similar ouster clauses, yet the respective courts reached sharply contrasting conclusions.

It is well known that the Foreign Compensation Act 1950 provided that the determinations of the Commission established under that Act could 'not be called in question in any court of law'.[44] The Law Lords, in *Anisminic*, held that this only immunised valid determinations of the Commission: that is, determinations within jurisdiction. 'What would be the purpose,' asked Lord Wilberforce, 'of defining by statute the limit of a tribunal's powers if, by means of a clause inserted in the instrument of definition, those limits could safely be passed?'[45] By interpreting the ouster provision in this way, it was possible for the House of Lords to set aside a decision made under a jurisdictional error of law.

This decision has provoked considerable debate and disagreement ever since it was handed down. Many commentators have suggested that the House of Lords ignored Parliament's intention and treated the right of access to court as a constitutional fundamental which not even Parliament could abrogate.[46] It is not my intention, this evening, to address this aspect of *Anisminic* in any detail.[47] It is sufficient for me to say that I do not share this view; but to add that, although the courts are right to presume that Parliament does not intend to attenuate access to justice, there must exist some formulation which is strong enough to overcome that presumption.[48] This proposition follows straightforwardly from Parliament's sovereign status. For present purposes, my interest in *Anisminic* lies simply in the fact that the House of Lords went to such lengths in order to hold that jurisdiction was preserved in the face of a preclusive clause.

The *UDF* case[49] reveals a very different approach. Section 3 of the South African Public Safety Act 1953 conferred broad emergency powers on the State President. Relying on these powers, regulations were made which imposed severe restrictions on the freedom of the press. The United Democratic Front challenged these provisions on the ground that they were unacceptably vague. However, section 5B of the Act provided that 'no court shall be competent to enquire into or give judgment on the validity of any proclamation' made under section 3. Had the Appellate Division desired to effect judicial review in spite of this preclusive provision, the necessary conceptual tools lay ready to hand. The *ultra vires* doctrine had long been regarded as the juridical basis of review in South Africa.[50] It was therefore open to the court to hold that the vague regulations had been made beyond jurisdiction with the consequence that—by analogy with *Anisminic*—the ouster clause did not protect vague regulations from review. However, the Appellate Division rejected this analysis, choosing not to accept the concept of jurisdiction as the organising principle of administrative law. By holding that vagueness was not a jurisdictional matter, the court precluded itself from applying *Anisminic* logic.

Thus, the preclusive provision in the Public Safety Act succeeded before the Appellate Division where the equivalent provision of the Foreign Compensation Act had spectacularly failed before the House of Lords. As with the divergent conclusions of the various courts in the Hong Kong *Immigrant Children* decisions, the reason for this difference cannot be attributed to textual considerations, since the two ouster provisions were almost identical. It is the different premises upon which the two courts approached their interpretative task—and, in particular, their divergent perceptions of their constitutional functions—which explains the radically different conclusions at which they arrived. This much is apparent from the respective historical contexts in which the decisions were reached.

Professor Wade has written that, during the middle part of the twentieth century, 'a deep gloom settled on [English] administrative law . . . The courts showed

---

[42] *Anisminic Ltd.* v. *Foreign Compensation Commission* [1969] 2 AC 147.

[43] *Staatspresident* v. *United Democratic Front,* 1988 (4) SA 830.

[44] S. 4(4).

[45] [1969] 2 AC 147, 208.

[46] H.W.R. Wade, 'Constitutional and Administrative Aspects of the *Anisminic* Case' (1969) 85 LQR 198; H.W.R. Wade and C.F. Forsyth, *Administrative Law* (7th edn., Oxford: Clarendon Press, 1994), 734–9.

[47] My views on the subject of sovereignty can be found in 'Judges and Decision-Makers: The Theory and Practice of *Wednesbury* Review' [1996] *PL* 59.

[48] As the Divisional Court recognised in *R.* v. *Lord Chancellor, ex parte Witham* [1998] QB 575.

[49] The judgments in this case are in Afrikaans. For discussion in English, see N. Haysom and C. Plasket, 'The War Against Law: Judicial Activism and the Appellate Division' (1988) 4 *South African Journal on Human Rights* 303; E. Mureinik, 'Administrative Law' [1988] *Annual Survey of South African Law* 34; J. Grogan, 'The Appellate Division and the Emergency: Another Step Backward' (1989) 106 *SALJ* 14; M.L. Matthews, 'Vandalizing the Ultra Vires Doctrine' (1989) 5 *South African Journal on Human Rights* 481; C.F. Forsyth, 'Of Fig Leaves and Fairy Tales: The Ultra Vires Doctrine, the Sovereignty of Parliament and Judicial Review' [1996] CLJ 122.

[50] See L. Baxter, *Administrative Law* (Cape Town: Juta and Co., 1984), 303: 'The ultra vires doctrine was adopted at the Cape almost as soon as the Supreme Court was established'.

signs of losing confidence in their constitutional function . . . and they showed little stomach for continuing their centuries-old work of imposing law upon government.'[51] There can be no better illustration of this than the House of Lords' decision in *Liversidge* v. *Anderson*.[52] The majority's conclusion—strongly opposed by Lord Atkin[53]—that a subjective language clause could preclude any proper judicial scrutiny of the decision-making process stands in stark contrast to the modern judiciary's attitude in this field. As subsequent decisions have demonstrated,[54] it would have been relatively easy to interpret the subjective provision in a manner which preserved a meaningful role for judicial review. Ascribing such an interpretation to the clause in *Liversidge* would certainly have involved considerably less difficulty than the House of Lords' creative construction of the much stronger ouster clause in *Anisminic*.[55]

The substantial differences in approach which these cases disclose can be explained only by reference to the sea change which had taken place, in the intervening 25 years, in the prevailing conception of the courts' public law role. To quote Sir William Wade again, 'In the 1960s the judicial mood completely changed. It began to be understood how much ground had been lost and what damage had been done to the only defences against abuse of power which still remained.'[56] The courts realised—more clearly than ever before, in light of the rate at which the state was expanding—that their public law jurisdiction was a crucial cornerstone in the constitutional machinery for securing responsible government. The decision in *Anisminic* formed an integral element of the courts' reinvention of their constitutional function; and the House of Lords' unwillingness interpretatively to denude itself of the power to adjudicate on disputes between the citizen and the state clearly illustrates the conception of the judicial function which underpinned the renaissance of English administrative law.

The *UDF* case formed part of a very different—and particularly dark—chapter in the history of South African public law. The state of emergency was ongoing, and the courts were beginning to adopt an unduly deferential attitude to the executive and legislative branches. By the time of the *UDF* case a culture was developing within some parts of the judiciary which tended to overlook the courts' duty to impose standards of legality on government. There was at least the risk of South Africa's courts becoming 'more executive minded than the executive'.[57] A South African critic used stronger language still, arguing that the court had displayed 'an excess of enthusiasm for the preservation of the powers of the State President, a reckless neglect of the consequences for the legal system and, indeed, a suicidal disregard for the functions of the judiciary'.[58] The attributability of the *UDF* judgment to a change in the conception of the courts' role is made all the more apparent by the fact that, as I have already explained, the appeal court chose to reject an orthodox jurisdictional analysis, which would have reduced the impact of the ouster clause,[59] in favour of a wholly novel approach which had the opposite effect.

The *Immigrant Children* case demonstrates that the way in which a court perceives its constitutional function can impact fundamentally on how it interprets the text of a human rights instrument. Taken together, the *Anisminic* and *UDF* decisions illustrate that this conception of the judicial function exerts similar influence on the construction of ordinary legislation which touches individuals' rights. Each of these points will assume a heightened relevance in this country as our courts begin both to attribute meaning to the European Convention and to construe municipal statutes against that background. Before I deal with these domestic prospects in more detail, let me refer, briefly, to the experiences of two other jurisdictions.

3.3 Canada and New Zealand: constitutional innovation and judicial reaction

It is widely acknowledged that the Canadian Bill of Rights 1960 largely failed in its attempt to engender in Canada a culture of fundamental rights; even the draftsman admitted that it 'received a very poor recep-

---

[51] H.W.R. Wade and C.F. Forsyth, *Administrative Law* (7th edn., Oxford: Clarendon Press, 1994), 17–19.

[52] [1942] AC 206.

[53] For discussion of—and a fascinating insight into—the disagreement between Lord Atkin and the majority, see R.F.V. Heuston, 'Liversidge v. Anderson in Retrospect' (1970) 86 *LQR* 33.

[54] E.g. *Secretary of State for Education and Science* v. *Tameside Metropolitan Borough Council* [1977] AC 1014. See further H.W.R. Wade and C.F. Forsyth, *Administrative Law* (Oxford: Clarendon Press, 1994), 442–59.

[55] The fact that *Liversidge* v. *Anderson* was a wartime decision naturally had some impact on the House of Lords' approach; but this cannot constitute a full explanation. This decision formed part of a much broader retreat from effective judicial supervision of government which extended well beyond the period 1939–45.

[56] H.W.R. Wade and C.F. Forsyth, *Administrative Law* (Oxford: Clarendon Press, 1994), 19.

[57] Lord Atkin levelled this criticism at the majority in *Liversidge* v. *Anderson* [1942] AC 206, 244.

[58] M.L. Matthews, 'Vandalizing the Ultra Vires Doctrine' (1989) 5 *South African Journal on Human Rights* 481.

[59] For an example of such orthodox reasoning, see the earlier decision in *Minister of Law and Order* v. *Hurley* 1986 (3) SA 586.

tion from the legal profession'.[60] This was in spite of the fact that a strong approach to the protection of human rights was envisaged, according to which the Bill of Rights would prevail over incompatible legislation.[61] In fact, this situation was held to have arisen in only one case[62] in spite of the fact that, according to Canadian academic opinion, the courts could have reached this conclusion on many more occasions.[63] As Professor Zander remarks, Canada's experience in the 1960s shows that the 'mere enactment' of a Bill of Rights 'changes nothing'.[64]

New Zealand's Bill of Rights Act 1990 provides an interesting counterpoint.[65] This modest[66] measure operates only by interpretation and confers no powers on the courts to invalidate or declare the incompatibility of legislation which infringes human rights.[67] Many

commentators predicted, on this basis, that the legislation would have little effect.[68] History, however, has proved them wrong.

The key to the success of the New Zealand fundamental rights legislation was the manner it which it was approached by the courts.[69] Under the Presidency of Sir Robin Cooke, whose views on the importance of protecting human rights are well known,[70] New Zealand's courts took it upon themselves to act—in the words of Hardie Boys J—as 'the ultimate guardians of personal liberty'.[71] It was this view of the judicial function which ensured that the Act's potential as a guarantee of civil liberties was realised. The best illustration of this is to be found in *Baigent's Case*.[72] In spite of the facts that the Bill of Rights lacked a remedies clause and that there were certain oblique indications that this omission was deliberate,[73] the Court nevertheless created, in this case, a new public law remedy for breach of the Bill of Rights. It is quite clear that it was the Court's view of its constitutional duty which led it to take this activist step: it refused to countenance a Bill of Rights that constituted 'no more than legislative window dressing',[74] holding instead that judges must have power to take remedial action when they discover human rights abuses.

---

[60] E.A. Driedger, 'The Meaning and Effect of the Canadian Bill of Rights: A Draftsman's Viewpoint' (1977) 9 *Ottawa Law Review* 303. See also J. Black-Branch, 'Entrenching Human Rights Legislation under Constitutional Law: The Canadian Charter of Rights and Freedoms' [1998] *European Human Rights Law Review* 312, 315–9. As is well known, Canada's experience with its Charter of Rights and Freedoms 1982 has been markedly different. Although—as would be expected—there exists a diversity of opinion in Canada concerning the extent to which the Charter has succeeded in protecting individuals' rights, there can be no doubt that it has been received with immeasurably greater enthusiasm than the earlier Bill of Rights. Although space does not permit detailed consideration of this matter, the divergent attitudes of the judiciary to the Bill of Rights and the more recent Charter certainly provide at least a partial explanation for the failure of the former and the success of the latter. The literature on the Charter is enormous; however, a useful overview of its impact to date can be found in R. Penner, 'The Canadian Experience with the Charter of Rights: Are there Lessons for the United Kingdom?' [1996] PL 104.

[61] Canadian Bill of Rights, s. 2. See further Driedger, n. 60 above, at 307–10. The Bill was not fully entrenched, since it was possible for legislation, by express provision, to take effect notwithstanding conflict with the Bill of Rights; a similar approach is to be found in s. 33(1) of the Canadian Charter of Rights and Freedoms 1982.

[62] *R.* v. *Drybones* [1970] SCR 282.

[63] See especially H. Arthurs in 'Minutes of Evidence taken before the Select Committee on a Bill of Rights' (House of Lords: 1977).

[64] M. Zander, *A Bill of Rights?* (4th edn., London: Sweet and Maxwell, 1997), 127.

[65] For an overview, see M. Taggart, 'Tugging on Superman's Cape: Lessons from Experience with the New Zealand Bill of Rights Act 1990' in J. Beatson, C.F. Forsyth and I.C. Hare (eds.), *Constitutional Reform in the United Kingdom: Practice and Principles* (Oxford: Hart Publishing, 1998).

[66] It had originally been intended that New Zealand should have a fully entrenched rights instrument, but this proposal did not win sufficient public support. The 1990 Act rose from the ashes of the failed attempt at entrenchment. See further P. Rishworth, 'The Birth and Rebirth of the Bill of Rights' in G. Huscroft and P. Rishworth (eds.), *Rights and Freedoms* (Wellington: Brooker's, 1995), ch. 1.

[67] See New Zealand Bill of Rights Act 1990, ss. 4 and 6. The New Zealand measure is, in terms of its text, weaker than the United Kingdom's Human Rights Act 1998 in two respects. First, the interpretative duty under s. 6 of the New Zealand Act appears to be slightly less robust than the formulation found in s. 3 of the UK legis-

lation. Secondly, the British Act's declaration of incompatibility and fast-track amendment machinery (see ss. 4 and 10, respectively) have no analogues in the New Zealand legislation.

[68] However, *cf.* P. Rishworth, 'The Potential of the New Zealand Bill of Rights' [1990] *NZLJ* 68.

[69] For detailed discussion, see A. Adams, 'Competing Conceptions of the Constitution: The New Zealand Bill of Rights Act 1990 and the Cooke Court of Appeal' [1996] *New Zealand Law Review* 368. Adams identifies three distinct 'discourses' within the Court of Appeal's Bill of Rights jurisprudence during the period 1990–5. She locates Lord Cooke of Thorndon firmly within the first such discourse which emphasises the constitutional status of the Bill of Rights. Although Adams argues that the judges within the other two discourses approached the Bill of Rights with less enthusiasm, it was the generous, constitutional approach to the legislation which determined the outcome of many of the leading cases.

[70] Lord Cooke of Thorndon has, both judicially and extra-curially, consistently asserted that certain norms are so fundamental that they lie beyond the competence of even a sovereign Parliament. See *L* v. *M* [1979] 2 NZLR 519, 529; *Brader* v. *Ministry of Transport* [1981] 1 NZLR 73, 78; *New Zealand Drivers' Association* v. *New Zealand Road Carriers* [1982] NZLR 374, 390; *Fraser* v. *State Services Commission* [1984] 1 NZLR 116, 121; *Taylor* v. *New Zealand Poultry Board* [1984] 1 NZLR 394, 398; 'Fundamentals' [1988] *NZLJ* 158. For discussion, see P. Rishworth, 'Lord Cooke and the Bill of Rights' and M. Kirby, 'Lord Cooke and Fundamental Rights' in P. Rishworth (ed.), *The Struggle for Simplicity in the Law* (Wellington: Butterworths, 1997).

[71] *R.* v. *Te Kira* [1993] 3 NZLR 257, 275.

[72] *Simpson* v. *Attorney-General (Baigent's Case)* [1994] 3 NZLR 667.

[73] Specifically, the White Paper had included a remedies clause, but the legislation did not. This may be thought to indicate an intention to exclude remedies from the Bill of Rights.

[74] [1994] 3 NZLR 667, 691, *per* Casey J.

As one commentator has observed, the New Zealand courts' response to the Bill of Rights demonstrates that 'entrenchment no longer seems as important . . . as it once did';[75] rather, what mattered was that the enactment of the Bill of Rights 'coincided with a spring-tide of judicial enthusiasm for the enforcement of fundamental rights and control of government power'.[76]

4. ACTIVISM, RESTRAINT AND THE PROSPECTS FOR HUMAN RIGHTS ADJUDICATION IN THE UNITED KINGDOM

4.1 The Human Rights legislation: a constitutional balancing act

Let me conclude this address by turning to the prospects for human rights adjudication in the United Kingdom.

The Human Rights Act is founded upon a division of functions between the different branches of government, which reflects the British conception of the separation of powers principle on which our constitution is based. Under the Act our courts have to interpret statutes 'so far as possible' to be compatible with Convention rights; if this is impossible they have been given a unique power to declare legislation to be incompatible, but then it is for the executive to initiate, and Parliament to enact, remedial legislation, with a fast track process available for that purpose.[77] This balance which inheres in the text of the Act can be secured in practical terms only by a measured judicial response to the challenge of seeking, so far as is possible, to interpret national law consistently with the Convention.

If the courts were to adopt a very narrow view of this duty of consistent construction, their ability interpretatively to guarantee Convention rights would be severely curtailed. Instead of reading municipal law in a way which gave effect to individuals' rights, the courts would tend to discover irreconcilable conflicts between UK law and the Convention which would then require legislative correction. In contrast, a judiciary which took an extremely radical view of its interpretative duty would be likely to stretch legislative language—beyond breaking point, if necessary—in order to effect judicial vindication of Convention rights. Such an approach would yield virtually no declarations of incompatibility: the judges would, in effect, be taking it upon themselves

to rewrite legislation in order to render it consistent with the Convention, and so excluding Parliament and the executive from the human rights enterprise.

Both of these approaches would be wrong. The constitutional theory on which the Human Rights Act rests is one of balance. It requires courts to recognise that they have a fundamental contribution to make in this area, while appreciating that the other elements of the constitution also have important roles to play in securing the effective protection of the Convention rights in domestic law. Thus the Act, while significantly changing the nature of the interpretative process, does not confer on the courts a licence to construe legislation in a way which is so radical and strained that it arrogates to the judges a power completely to rewrite existing law: that is a task for Parliament and the executive. The interpretative duty which the courts will soon begin to discharge in the human rights arena is therefore a strong one; but it is nevertheless subject to limits which the Act imposes, and which find still deeper resonance in the doctrine of the separation of powers on which the constitution is founded.[78]

It is my view that the manner in which English courts have developed public law to date discloses a well-balanced conception of the judicial function which will provide a sound foundation for the judiciary as it begins to work out the precise content of its interpretative duty under the Human Rights Act. Let me illustrate by highlighting three specific contexts in which the courts have successfully balanced the competing imperatives of activism and restraint in their recent public law jurisprudence.

4.2 The existing judicial review jurisdiction

I began, this evening, by commenting on the remarkable growth of judicial review over recent decades. Although this is a striking example of judicial activism, the judges have nevertheless striven to find constitutional balance as they have pushed public law

---

[75] P. Rishworth, 'Affirming the Fundamental Values of the Nation: How the Bill of Rights and the Human Rights Act affect New Zealand Law' in P. Rishworth and G. Huscroft (eds.), *Rights and Freedoms* (Wellington: Brooker's, 1995), 71.

[76] *Ibid.*, at 76.

[77] See, principally, ss. 3, 4 and 10.

[78] A different, but related, challenge will arise once the Scottish Parliament begins to legislate. According to the Scotland Act 1998, s. 28(6), the courts must seek to avoid reaching the conclusion that Scottish legislation is invalid (on the ground of its being *ultra vires*) by construing it narrowly. Although this interpretative duty is different in nature from that which the Human Rights Act creates, the importance of balance will remain constant: the courts will have a fundamental contribution to make in seeking to ensure that the Scottish Parliament's legislation is effective (in the sense of being *intra vires*) while preserving the integrity of the distribution of legislative competence between Westminster and Edinburgh which the Scotland Act embodies. Thus, by utilising interpretative methodology to secure the protection of fundamental rights and the efficacy of Scottish legislation, both the Human Rights Act and the Scotland Act recognise that the interpretative process will be of central importance to the success of the constitutional reform programme.

forward, tempering their interventionism with appropriate restraint.

For instance, the courts have, in general, been careful to preserve the distinction between appeal and review, appreciating that it would be an affront to Parliament's sovereignty—according to which the legislature can choose on whom to confer discretion—for the judges to arrogate to themselves primary decision-making power by enquiring into the merits of executive action. These issues recently crystallised in the context of legitimate expectation.[79] In the *Hamble Fisheries* case,[80] Sedley J had expressed the view that whether an agency could depart from a substantive expectation was 'ultimately a matter for the court'.[81] It is clear to me that—at the present stage of the development of English administrative law—this did constitute an unduly interventionist approach. Orthodoxy has now been restored by the Court of Appeal which held, in *Hargreaves*,[82] that it is not for a court to determine that an agency may not depart from the substance of its policy. Only if frustration of the expectation would be *Wednesbury* unreasonable may a court intervene on substantive grounds.[83] This reflects a proper balance between judges and decision-makers, and demonstrates the capacity of the courts to temper activism with restraint.[84] Although the Human Rights Act will shift that balance, it is crucially important that this will occur pursuant to legislative intervention, rather than at the unilateral instance of the judicial branch. I shall return to this subject shortly.

The importance of maintaining balance also pervades the law of judicial review at the level of constitutional theory. Although some academics,[85] and

certain judges in their extra-curial capacity,[86] have questioned the contemporary relevance of the *ultra vires* doctrine, British courts[87] consistently adhere to it as the juridical basis of review.[88] In this way, the judiciary has been able to confer considerable protection on citizens, as they interact with the state, in a manner that respects the ultimate sovereignty of the legislature.[89] Moreover, by postulating a relationship between legislative intention and judicial review, the *ultra vires* principle demonstrates that the prevention of maladministration is a co-operative endeavour which involves both Parliament and the courts.

4.3 The doctrine of common law constitutional rights

In recent cases—such as *Leech*[90] and *Witham*[91]—the courts have conferred particularly strong protection on the individual's right of access to justice, by characterising it as a 'constitutional right'. Two aspects of this discourse exemplify the judiciary's careful balancing of the activist expansion of public law against the restraint which constitutional propriety demands.

At a structural level, the courts have been careful to reconcile their decisions with orthodox constitutional

---

[79] On the subject of legitimate expectation, see generally C.F. Forsyth, 'The Provenance and Protection of Legitimate Expectations' [1988] *CLJ* 238.

[80] *R. v. Ministry of Agriculture, Fisheries and Food, ex parte Hamble (Offshore) Fisheries Ltd.* [1995] 2 All ER 714.

[81] *Ibid.*, at 735.

[82] *R. v. Secretary of State for the Home Department, ex parte Hargreaves* [1997] 1 WLR 906.

[83] See *ibid.*, at 921, *per* Hirst LJ, 'On matters of substance . . . *Wednesbury* provides the correct test'. Similarly, at 924, Pill LJ explained that a court would prevent departure from the substance of a policy 'only if . . . the decision to apply the new policy in the particular case was unreasonable in the *Wednesbury* sense'.

[84] See further my comments in 'Judges and Decision-Makers: The Theory and Practice of *Wednesbury* Review' [1996] *PL* 59, 71–2. For a different view, see P.P. Craig, 'Substantive Legitimate Expectations in Domestic and Community Law' [1996] CLJ 289.

[85] See, e.g., D. Oliver, 'Is the Ultra Vires Rule the Basis of Judicial Review?' [1987] *PL* 543; P.P. Craig, 'Ultra Vires and the Foundations of Judicial Review' [1998] *CLJ* 63; D. Dyzenhaus, 'Reuniting the Brain: The Democratic Basis of Judicial Review' (1998) 9 *Public Law Review* 98.

[86] See, e.g., Lord Woolf of Barnes, '*Droit Public*—English Style' [1995] PL 57; Sir John Laws, 'Law and Democracy' [1995] *PL* 72 and 'Illegality: The Problem of Jurisdiction' in M. Supperstone and J. Goudie (eds.), *Judicial Review* (2nd edn., London: Butterworths, 1997); Sir Stephen Sedley, 'The Common Law and the Constitution' in Lord Nolan and Sir Stephen Sedley (eds.), *The Making and Remaking of the British Constitution* (London: Blackstone Press, 1997), 16–18.

[87] Unlike some of their Commonwealth counterparts. For instance, the High Court of Australia now regards certain principles of judicial review as autonomous common law rules rather than as interpretative constructs. See, principally, *Kioa* v. *Minister for Immigration and Ethnic Affairs* (1985) 159 CLR 550 and, for discussion, P. Bayne, 'The Common Law Basis of Judicial Review' (1993) 67 *ALJ* 781. South African courts also went down this path in the 1980s (see the *UDF* decision, discussed above), although judicial review in South African law now rests on new constitutional foundations, on which see A.J.H. Henderson, 'The Curative Powers of the Constitution: Constitutionality and the new Ultra Vires Doctrine in the Justification and Explanation of the Judicial Review of Administrative Action' (1998) 115 *SALJ* 346.

[88] For recent and authoritative confirmation of the centrality of *ultra vires*, see *Boddington* v. *British Transport Police* [1998] 2 WLR 639.

[89] On the constitutional importance of the *ultra vires* doctrine, see C.F. Forsyth, 'Of Fig Leaves and Fairy Tales: The Ultra Vires Doctrine, the Sovereignty of Parliament and Judicial Review' [1996] *CLJ* 122; M.C. Elliott, 'The Ultra Vires Doctrine in a Constitutional Setting: Still the Central Principle of Administrative Law' [1999] *CLJ* 129; M.C. Elliott, 'The Demise of Parliamentary Sovereignty? The Implications for Justifying Judicial Review' (1999) 115 *LQR* 119.

[90] *R. v. Secretary of State for the Home Department, ex parte Leech (No. 2)* [1994] QB 198.

[91] *R. v. Lord Chancellor, ex parte Witham* [1998] QB 575.

theory,[92] acknowledging that, in a state based on an acceptance of Parliamentary supremacy, constitutional rights can subsist only as interpretative constructs, which take effect by way of presumption and which yield in the face of clear contrary enactment.[93] This is of a piece with both the courts' adherence to the *ultra vires* doctrine and the scheme of the Human Rights Act.

On the plane of substance, the judiciary have shown similar sensitivity. Take, for instance, the *Lightfoot* case.[94] The applicant, who wished to present a petition for bankruptcy, was unable to afford the court fees which she was first required to pay. Claiming that this was an infringement of her constitutional right of access to justice, she sought judicial review of the delegated legislation which determined the level of the fees.[95] After careful consideration, Laws J concluded that the applicant was seeking recourse to an essentially administrative regime rather than a core judicial function and, for this reason, held that the right of access to justice was not properly engaged. Thus, while this constitutional right is of great significance, it is important to recognise its limits. As Laws J observed, 'A sound principle may be undermined, even destroyed, if it is pressed into service in areas to which it does not necessarily belong'.[96] Although this case was concerned with the scope of an unwritten common law right, the courts will have to conduct precisely the same type of balancing exercise as they begin to interpret the norms which the Convention enumerates.

4.4 Human rights and the European Convention in English courts

Let me offer one final example of the judiciary's willingness to balance activism and restraint in the public law field. English courts have not been impervious to the growing international trend towards the legalisation of human rights. The judicial review jurisdiction and the doctrine of common law rights both contribute to the protection of fundamental rights in the UK. Moreover, the courts have ascribed some

relevance to the European Convention,[97] using it to resolve ambiguities in legislation[98] and to develop the common law where it is incomplete or uncertain.[99] However, the judiciary have consistently refused to embrace the Convention as a direct limit on the decision-making powers of the executive.[100] Notwithstanding that they have been described as 'straining at the leash' to do so,[101] the courts have recognised that to take such a step unilaterally would substantially affront the separation of powers, at a stroke reducing agency autonomy and usurping Parliament's constitutional responsibility for the domestication of international treaties.[102] Once again, activism in public law yields to the restraint of constitutional propriety.[103]

5. CONCLUSION

Over the course of the twentieth century, the changing nature of governance within the United Kingdom has substantially altered the prevailing conception of the judicial function. As Lord Mustill said of the courts' public law jurisdiction:

'To avoid a vacuum in which the citizen would be left without protection against a misuse of executive powers the courts have had no option but to occupy the dead ground [left by Parliament]

---

[92] See M.C. Elliott, 'Reconciling Constitutional Rights and Constitutional Orthodoxy' [1997] *CLJ* 474.

[93] This reasoning is especially clear in Laws J's judgment in *Witham*, n. 91 above.

[94] *R. v. Lord Chancellor, ex parte Lightfoot* [1998] 4 All ER 764. For comment, see M.C. Elliott, '*Lightfoot*: Tracing the Perimeter of Constitutional Rights' [1998] *Judicial Review* 217.

[95] Specifically, she claimed that the relevant provisions of the Insolvency Fees Order 1986 (SI 1986/2030) were *ultra vires* their putative legal basis (*viz.* Insolvency Act 1986, s. 415(3)).

[96] [1998] 4 All ER 764, 773.

[97] For a useful summary of the present relevance of the ECHR in English law, see Lord Bingham of Cornhill, HL Deb., 3 July 1996, cols. 1465–7.

[98] See *R. v. Secretary of State for the Home Department, ex parte Brind* [1991] 1 AC 696.

[99] See *Attorney-General* v. *British Broadcasting Corporation* [1981] AC 303, 352, *per* Lord Fraser.

[100] See especially *Brind*, n. 98 above; *R. v. Ministry of Defence, ex parte Smith* [1996] QB 517. For an interesting empirical study, see F. Klug and K. Starmer, 'Incorporation through the Back Door?' [1997] *PL* 223, especially 228–32.

[101] M.J. Beloff and H. Mountfield, 'Unconventional Behaviour: Judicial Uses of the European Convention in England and Wales' [1996] *European Human Rights Law Review* 467, 495.

[102] See further my 'Constitutional Change in the United Kingdom: British Solutions to Universal Problems' (publication forthcoming), and n. 3 above.

[103] The Court of Appeal's decision in *R. v. Secretary of State for the Home Department, ex parte Ahmed and Patel* [1998] INLR 570 does not detract from my thesis. In this case, it was held—by applying reasoning similar to that of the High Court of Australia in *Minister of State for Immigration and Ethnic Affairs* v. *Teoh* (1995) 183 CLR 273—that British accession to a treaty, such as the ECHR, can found a legitimate expectation that the executive, in exercising its prerogative powers, will respect the provisions of the treaty. However, given that, as I have already mentioned, substantive expectations can be protected only through the doctrine of *Wednesbury* unreasonableness, the *Ahmed and Patel* judgment does not place administrators under a directly enforceable duty to act consistently with the Convention rights. It will be the Human Rights Act which does that.

in a manner, and in areas of public life, which could not have been foreseen 30 years ago.'[104]

On this view, we have witnessed a shift from what I have termed a 'sovereigntist' to a constitutional perception of the role of the judiciary, which emphasises the courts' role as an integral component in a constitutional machinery that seeks to secure accountable government.

The impact of this change of perception on the interpretative process has been profound. More extensive and more exacting limits have been read into executive powers. Provisions which appear to inhibit judicial supervision of government are construed narrowly and robustly. And a new, interpretative doctrine of common law constitutional rights has been articulated.

Crucially, however, the judiciary's activist endeavour in the field of public law has been tempered with appropriate restraint. The courts have consistently accepted the limits of their role within the British state. They have appreciated that their function of providing effective protection for citizens against maladministration must be discharged in a manner which takes account of other values which society embraces, such as the democratic imperative of parliamentary sovereignty and the need to respect the executive's area of decision-making autonomy. In this manner it has been possible for English courts to fashion a modern regime of administrative law, without challenging the established axioms of the legal order. It is their realistic perception of the judicial role that explains the successful track record of our courts in the difficult task of balancing the competing demands of intervention and restraint.

The Human Rights Act will prove a catalyst that will further fuel the ongoing development of the constitutional function of British courts. It will concentrate attention, more than ever before, on the judiciary's role as the guardian of individuals' rights; this, in turn, will further strengthen the constitutionalist basis on which the courts approach the interpretative process. New and demanding questions will arise for the courts as they begin to interpret a written catalogue of human rights. They will have to resolve hard cases concerning the precise scope of citizens' rights under the Convention and the rigour with which rights infractions must be justified.

However, the typology of change in English public law is one of evolution, not revolution. While the new human rights legislation will raise fresh interpretative challenges, the courts' overarching goal—of securing respect for individuals' rights in a manner which is sensitive to the broader framework of the separation of powers—will remain constant. The existing corpus of administrative law—and the forces which have shaped it—form a firm foundation on which to build the superstructure of a new, rights-based public law for Britain in the twenty-first century.

A former Chief Justice of the US Supreme Court famously remarked that a 'constitution is what the judges say it is'.[105] More recently, Sir Stephen Sedley observed that 'the reverse is true as well: if the judges are not prepared to speak for it, a constitution is nothing'.[106] That is very true. In this manner, the challenge which courts must confront as they seek to interpret fundamental rights texts is ultimately that of saying neither too little nor too much. As I have explained this evening, it is—in large part—the conception of the courts' function which determines the judicial response to this conundrum. In their development of public law to date, English courts have demonstrated a healthy understanding both of their role and of its limits. The task which they will shortly face, as they begin to apply a set of written constitutional rights, is a difficult one; yet it is, without any doubt, one that is well worth undertaking, and to which—I am confident—our judges will rise with characteristic pragmatism and sound judgment.[107]

---

[104] R. v. Secretary of State for the Home Department, ex parte Fire Brigades Union [1995] 2 AC 513, 567.

[105] Former Chief Justice Hughes, speaking when he was Governor of New York.

[106] Sir Stephen Sedley, 'The Sound of Silence: Constitutional Law Without a Constitution' (1994) 110 LQR 270, 277.

[107] I am indebted to Mark Elliott, Research Student at Queens' College, Cambridge, for his high quality assistance in the preparation of this Lecture.

3

THE ART OF THE POSSIBLE: INTERPRETING STATUTES UNDER THE HUMAN RIGHTS ACT

LORD LESTER OF HERNE HILL QC*

This is a historic moment in the life of the European Convention on Human Rights and in the life of the British Constitution. With the implementation of Protocol 11, some 800 million inhabitants in 40 European countries now have direct access to a new and permanent European Court of Human Rights; a court which we hope will be able to meet the formidable challenges that lie ahead. Meanwhile, Parliament has enacted a series of measures that will profoundly alter the ways in which we are governed from London, Edinburgh, Belfast and Cardiff; the ways in which our Convention rights are protected and enforced; and the relationship between the three branches of government. The papers given at this conference discuss the implications of only one of these constitutional measures—the *Human Rights Act 1998*—but inevitably do so in the context of the wider changes taking place within the Council of Europe and the European Union as well as in the governments of Scotland, Northern Ireland, Wales, England and the United Kingdom as a whole.

Thirty years ago, because it had not been made part of the law of the land, our courts did not treat the European Convention as relevant when interpreting and applying domestic law. The first judicial reference to the Convention that I have been able to discover was in 1972, by Lord Kilbrandon, in his dissenting speech in *Broome* v. *Cassell*.[1] According to Lord Kilbrandon, ever since ratification of the Convention by the United Kingdom, in 1951, there had been a constitutional right

to free expression, derived from Article 10 of the Convention. In 1974, Lord Reid, in giving judgment for the House of Lords, in *Waddington* v. *Miah*,[2] referred to the presumption that Parliament, when enacting penal legislation, would not intend to breach Article 7 of the Convention by creating retrospective criminal liability. In 1975, in *Blathwayt* v. *Baron Cawley*,[3] Lord Wilberforce observed that the Convention was a legitimate source in enabling the courts to decide questions of public policy. Between 1976 and 1981, the English Court of Appeal vacillated as to the relevance of the Convention to the exercise of statutory powers to control immigration, eventually deciding that it was legally irrelevant to the exercise of those powers by Ministers or immigration officers.[4]

In 1982, Lord Diplock, giving judgment for the House of Lords in *Garland*,[5] recalled the well-established principle that the words of a statute passed after an international treaty has been ratified and dealing with the subject matter of the international obligation of the United Kingdom:

'are to be construed, if they are reasonably capable of bearing such a meaning, as intended to carry out the obligation, and not to be inconsistent with it.'

In 1982, in *Raymond* v. *Honey*,[6] Lord Wilberforce referred to Article 6 of the Convention and the case law

---

* Lord Lester of Herne Hill QC is a barrister, practising at Blackstone Chambers and a Liberal Democrat member of the House of Lords. This paper is a revised version of his lecture to the Statute Law Society's Eighteenth Annual Conference held in Edinburgh on 10 October 1998 and published in [1998] *EHRLR* 665.

[1] *Broome* v. *Cassell* [1972] AC 1027 at 1133 (HL).

[2] *Waddington* v. *Miah* [1974] 1 WLR 692 at 694 (HL).

[3] *Blathwayt* v. *Baron Cawley* [1976] AC 397 at 426 (HL).

[4] Anthony Lester, 'Fundamental Rights: The United Kingdom Isolated?' [1984] *PL* 46 at 66–8.

[5] *Garland* v. *British Rail Engineering* [1983] 2 AC 751 at 771B (HL).

[6] *Raymond* v. *Honey* [1983] 1 AC 1 (HL).

of the European Court of Human Rights, in construing the Home Secretary's very broad statutory powers to censor prisoners' correspondence. The House of Lords struck down Home Office rules which unnecessarily restricted a prisoner's right of access to the courts.

Also in 1982, in their powerful joint dissenting speech in *Home Office* v. *Harman*,[7] Lord Scarman and Lord Simon of Glaisdale relied upon the guarantee of free expression in Article 10 of the Convention, in explaining why, in their view, the communication to a journalist of confidential information that had been read out in open court did not constitute a common law contempt of court.

In 1987, in the *Spycatcher* case,[8] although a majority of the House of Lords granted interlocutory injunctions restraining publication of extracts from Peter Wright's book after it had been published in the United States, and were later found by the European Court thereby to have breached Article 10 of the Convention, they were agreed that Article 10 provided the relevant standard in determining whether the grant of an injunction was necessary.

In 1991, in *Brind*,[9] the House of Lords decided that the Convention could not be relied upon to review the exercise of broad delegated statutory powers, in the particular case, the power to censor broadcasts. To do so, they reasoned, would be to incorporate the Convention into domestic law through the back door when Parliament had failed to open the front door to the Convention. The Law Lords rejected the argument for which I was responsible that, just as the courts would imply common law requirements of fairness and rationality into apparently unfettered statutory powers, so they should imply the requirement, derived from the Convention and the common law, that such powers should not be exercised excessively or without a sense of proportion. Lord Bridge of Harwich said this:

"When confronted with a simple choice between two possible interpretations of some specific statutory provision, the presumption whereby the courts prefer that which avoids a conflict between our domestic legislation and our international treaty obligations is a mere canon of construction which involves no importation of international law into the domestic field. But where Parliament has conferred on the executive an administrative discretion without indicating that it must be exercised within the Convention limits, to presume that it must be exercised within Convention limits would be to go far beyond the resolution of an ambiguity ... and I cannot escape the conclusion that this would be a judicial usurpation of the legislative function."

[7] *Home Office* v. *Harman* [1983] 1 AC 280 (HL).

[8] *Attorney-General* v. *Guardian Newspapers and Times Newspapers* [1987] 1 WLR 1248 (HL).

[9] *R* v. *Secretary of State for the Home Department, ex p. Brind* [1991] 1 AC 696 (HL).

As the unsuccessful advocate in *Brind*, I am comforted by Francis Bennion's criticism of the decision[10] and by the fact that that all-too-persuasive Treasury Devil, John Laws, in his scholarly capacity, apparently believes that the Law Lords were wrong to have been persuaded by his arguments.[11] Happily that will be of only academic interest, in the light of the Human Rights Act, to which I now turn.[12]

According to Dicey's theory of the British Constitution, all Acts of Parliament are equal in the eyes of the law, whether they are the Act of Union with Scotland or the Dentists Act, with no special legal weight to be given to a constitutional measure as fundamental or organic law. Even Dicey could not live with that austere mechanical doctrine when it came to his challenge to the constitutionality of Asquith's Irish Home Rule Bill.

These days our courts will surely regard the Human Rights Act as no ordinary law. It is a fundamental constitutional measure of greater contemporary significance to the protection of civil and political rights than any previous measure except for the European Communities Act in areas where Community law governs. The Act will give effect to a fundamental international instrument by which all three branches of government of the United Kingdom are bound. It occupies a central position in the Government's programme of constitutional reform, enabling people in this country to enforce their Convention rights against public authorities before our courts. In the Lord Chancellor's words, it will have 'a profound and beneficial effect on our system of law and government and will develop over the years a strong culture of human rights'.[13] That is why the Act may not be brought fully into force until 2000, and why some £6 million is being spent by the Judicial Studies Board in training judges, magistrates and tribunal members about the subject-matter of the Act.

[10] Francis Bennion, *Statutory Interpretation: A Code* (3rd ed. London: Butterworths, 1997) at 634.

[11] Sir John Laws, 'Is the High Court the Guardian of Fundamental Constitutional Rights?' [1993] *PL* 59.

[12] In *R* v. *Secretary of State for the Home Department, ex parte Ahmed* [1998] INLR 570, the Court of Appeal presided over by Lord Woolf MR upheld the principle declared by the High Court of Australia in *Minister of State for Immigration and Ethnic Affairs* v. *Teoh* (1995) 183 CLR 273 that ratification of an international human rights convention creates a legitimate expectation, absent statutory or executive indications to the contrary, that administrative decision-makers will act in accordance with the convention when exercising prerogative powers. See, further, Lord Lester of Herne Hill QC, 'Government Compliance with International Human Rights Law: A New Year's Legitimate Expectation' [1996] *PL* 187.

[13] Third Reading, House of Lords, 5 February 1998, HL Deb., vol. 585, col. 839.

The Act provides for all legislation to be interpreted as far as possible in a way that is compatible with Convention rights. To quote the Lord Chancellor again: 'The Convention rights are the magnetic north and the needle of judicial interpretation will swing towards them'.[14]

One obvious and important change of direction is away from the *Brind* decision which is effectively overruled. By virtue of section 6, it is unlawful for a public authority (including a court or tribunal) to act in a way which is incompatible with a Convention right. The exercise of discretion under broad delegated powers, such as the Home Secretary's power to censor broadcasts in *Brind*, must be interpreted in accordance with the requirements of the Convention. More generally, every public power whose exercise interferes with a Convention right will have to be invoked only where necessary and in accordance with the principle of proportionality. This will have far-reaching implications for the judicial review of administrative action.

The drafting of the Act is elegant and concise. It is a subtle measure, designed to pass into legislation by respecting the ceremonial forms required by the English dogma of the sovereignty of Parliament.[15] That is why the courts will not have the same power and duty as they would have had under the first of my two Private Member's Bills, and as they already have under the European Communities Act, to set aside inconsistent provisions in Acts of Parliament. Instead, where it is impossible to reconcile a legislative provision with Convention rights, the senior courts[16] may make a declaration that the provision is incompatible with the Convention. In that event, the Government will be able, if it wishes, to make remedial orders removing the incompatibility, using a special procedure that reconciles the need for a speedy remedy with the need for effective parliamentary scrutiny. By making a declaration of incompatibility, the judiciary will give an invitation to the executive and the legislature to consider, as a matter of urgency, whether to repair the legislation. It is an invitation, which they will be unlikely to refuse.

The political compromise represented by an interpretative Bill of Rights of this kind was envisaged by Hersch Lauterpacht in his brilliantly original and prophetic study of the need for an 'International Bill of Rights' published in 1945.[17] Lauterpacht suggested that in situations where no interpretation will be able to deprive of its obvious meaning an Act of Parliament

clearly designed to change or to abrogate an obligation of the Bill of Rights, the courts, while giving effect to the statute, should be given the right—and must be under the duty—to declare that the statute is not in conformity with the Bill of Rights.[18]

Section 3 of the Act imposes a duty on courts and tribunals to strive to avoid a mismatch between domestic legislation and the Convention. It uses these strong words: 'So far as it is possible to do so, primary legislation and subordinate legislation must be read and given effect in a way which is compatible with Convention rights'. It applies to primary and subordinate legislation whenever enacted.[19] It does not affect the validity, continued operation or enforcement of any incompatible primary legislation[20]; nor of any incompatible subordinate legislation if (disregarding any possibility of revocation) primary legislation prevents removal of the incompatibility.[21] In Northern Ireland, where so much of the governing legislation is subordinate, and where primary legislation is likely only rarely to prevent removal of any incompatibility, the courts may have more occasions to set aside incompatible subordinate legislation than in Great Britain.

Unlike the Constitution of South Africa,[22] section 3 does not say that the courts must prefer a 'reasonable interpretation of the legislation that is consistent with international law over any alternative interpretation that is inconsistent with international law'. Indeed, the Government opposed an Opposition amendment that would have required the courts to adopt a reasonable rather than a possible interpretation, because the likely result of the amendment would have been that that 'the courts would not go so far down the road of interpreting legislation'.[23]

The fact that section 3 requires a possible interpretation rather than a reasonable interpretation or a reasonably possible interpretation does not mean that the courts will adopt an arbitrary or perverse interpretation. What it does mean is that special principles of interpretation will need to be used in interpreting legislation under the Act, 'without necessary acceptance of all the presumptions that are relevant to legislation of private law'.[24]

---

[14] *Ibid.*, at col. 840.

[16] See further, Nicholas Bamforth, 'Parliamentary sovereignty and the Human Rights Act 1998' [1998] *PL* 572.

[16] S. 4(5).

[17] Hersch Lauterpacht, *An International Bill of the Rights of Man* (New York: Columbia University Press, 1945).

[18] *Ibid.* at 192.

[19] S. 3(2)(a).

[20] S. 3(2)(b).

[21] S. 3(2)(c).

[22] Art. 233 of the Constitution of the Republic of South Africa, 1996, Act 108 of 1996.

[23] Committee Stage, HC, 3 June 1998, HC Debs, vol. 313, col. 421.

[24] *Minister of Home Affairs* v. *Fisher* [1980] AC 319 at 329C–E (PC), *per* Lord Wilberforce (in relation to the interpretation of the chapter of the Constitution of Bermuda protecting human rights).

Section 3 requires courts where necessary to prefer a *possible* interpretation of legislation that is consistent with Convention rights to any alternative interpretation that is inconsistent with Convention rights. Where necessary the courts will therefore prefer a possible but strained interpretation to an interpretation that more closely reflects the structure and text of the impugned legislative provision. There is nothing novel about that. But I hope the courts will be able to do better in explaining their reasons than did the House of Lords in one case where, citing from a Victorian judgment about the proper construction of an informal commercial transaction, Lord Russell of Killowen said, of a phrase in the Equal Pay Act 1970, 'this beats me' adding that he would 'jettison the words in dispute as making no contribution to the manifest intention of Parliament'.[25]

Courts and tribunals will no doubt imply words into a statute where there is an ambiguity or an omission[26] to give effect to a Convention right and the implied words are necessary to remedy the defect. They will give a restrictive interpretation to subordinate legislation or delegated powers that threaten Convention rights so as to ensure that those rights are not unnecessarily restricted. Enactments made before the coming into force of the Human Rights Act will be interpreted in accordance with the principle that, in the absence of clear words to the contrary, Parliament is to be presumed to have intended them to be compatible with the United Kingdom's obligations under the Convention. Where necessary the courts will imply words into an enactment to save it from being declared to be incompatible with Convention rights.[27]

Because of its great constitutional and international importance, the courts will not treat provisions of the Act as impliedly amended or repealed by subsequent legislation. As with European Community law, they will surely require nothing less than an express intention in subsequent legislation to amend or repeal provisions of the Act.[28] They will be assisted in this robust approach

[25] *O'Brien* v. *Sim-Chem Ltd* [1980] 1 WLR 1011 at 1017 (HL).
[26] On the remedying of omissions, see Mary Childs, 'Constitutional Review and Underinclusive Legislation' [1998] *PL* 647.
[27] Cf. *Attorney-General of The Gambia* v. *Jobe* [1984] 1 AC 689 at 702B–E (PC).
[28] See e.g. *Macarthys Ltd* v. *Smith* [1980] 3 WLR 929 at 948 (CA), *per* Lord Denning MR. Cf. Lauterpacht, *supra* n.17: 'as the Bill of Rights will . . . be a fundamental international instrument to which Great Britain is a party, nothing short of an express enactment deliberately designed to abrogate the Bill of Rights or part thereof will be interpreted to that effect by English courts. Failing any such express and undoubted intention to violate the international obligation of Great Britain, the courts, following an accepted canon of interpretation, will construe the statute so as to negative the intention to depart from a binding treaty which has been adopted, in significant circumstances of solemnity, as part of the law of the land.'

by the parliamentary procedure prescribed by section 19 involving statements of compatibility by ministers in charge of Bills. Where the minister has made a statement to the effect that in his view the Bill's provisions are compatible with the Convention rights, the courts will readily conclude that nothing in the Bill was intended to override such rights.

The courts will not usurp the legislative powers of Parliament by adopting a construction which it could not be supposed that Parliament had intended by enacting the Human Rights Act and by previously or subsequently enacting the impugned statutory provision. Where only a fanciful or perverse construction is possible to make the statute compatible with Convention rights, or where the problem created by the apparent mismatch between the statute and Convention rights requires extensive redrafting and a choice among different legislative options, the courts will make a declaration of incompatibility.[29] By doing so, they will be marking the boundary between the powers of the judiciary, the legislature and the executive in deciding how the constitutional principles contained in the Act are to be applied.[30]

Where a statutory provision cannot be saved by judicial interpretation from a declaration of its incompatibility, the system will in one sense have failed. Ever since the United Kingdom ratified the Convention in 1951, our statute book has been meant to match the requirements of the Convention; yet the courts will have been compelled to rule that there is a breach of a Convention right, required by legislation, for which they are unable to provide a remedy. The choice that will then face the Government will be between making a remedial order, for which precious parliamentary time will have to be found, and leaving the claimant to seek redress from the European Court of Human Rights, armed with a favourable judgment from the domestic court and with a high probability of success.

The inventive and imaginative process of statutory interpretation that is called for involves no judicial usurpation of the legislative function. On the contrary, it is Parliament itself that has used its legislative function to command the courts to interpret past and future statutes wherever possible so as to be compatible with Convention rights. That is the plain intention of Parliament to which the courts will give full faith and

[29] Taking into account Lord Clyde's advice with respect to the interpretation of a statute where the validity of the legislation has to be tested against the provisions of European law: see *Clarke (AP)* v. *Kato, Smith and General Accident Fire & Life Assurance Corporation PLC*, [1998] 1 WLR 1647 at 1665, per Lord Clyde.
[30] See *Matadeen* v. *Pointu and Others* [1998] 3 WLR 18 at 27A (PC), *per* Lord Hoffmann.

credit by seeking wherever possible to interpret statutes compatibly with the international treaty obligations by which the United Kingdom is bound. As the White Paper observed, the interpretative obligation:

'goes far beyond the present rule which enables the courts to take the Convention into account in resolving any ambiguity in a legislative provision. The courts will be required to interpret legislation so as to uphold the Convention rights unless the legislation itself is so clearly incompatible with the Convention that it is impossible to do so'.[31]

During the Committee Stage the Lord Chancellor said:

'We want the courts to strive to find an interpretation of legislation which is consistent with Convention rights so far as the language of the legislation allows, and only in the last resort to conclude that the legislation is simply incompatible with them'. [32]

At Third Reading, the Lord Chancellor said:

'in 99% of the cases that will arise, there will be no need for judicial declarations of incompatibility'. [33]

Similarly, in the Commons, the Home Secretary, Jack Straw, said:

'We expect that, in almost all cases, the courts will be able to interpret legislation compatibly with the Convention'. [34]

And

'we want the courts to strive to find an interpretation of legislation that is consistent with Convention rights, so far as the plain words of the legislation allow, and only in the last resort to conclude that the legislation is simply incompatible with them'.[35]

I respectfully disagree with Dr Geoffrey Marshall's criticism of the drafting of section 3, and his contention that 'the more faithfully the courts follow the injunction to read legislation as being compatible with the Convention the less effect the Convention will have'.[36] It all depends upon whether the courts will give a liberal interpretation to Convention rights and a restrictive interpretation to legislation that is in conflict with those rights. The case law of Commonwealth constitutional courts, including the Privy Council, indicate a willingness to do as the Government and Parliament plainly intend; namely, to be sympathetic, imaginative and inventive in interpreting the Human Rights Act and the law of the Convention. This means that the courts will need, where possible, to read provisions into ambiguous or incomplete legislation[37] and to give a restrictive interpretation to provisions that are clear but sweep too broadly. The judicial interpretation of legislation under the Human Rights Act, like the politics that gave shape to the Act, will involve the art of the possible.

Convention rights often conflict with one another or with other vital public interests: the right to life versus personal autonomy, human dignity and equality of treatment; free speech versus personal privacy or fair trial; religious freedom versus the rights of others; or private property versus environmental protection. The rights and their limits have to be interpreted purposively and dynamically, and in accordance with legal principles that reflect the fair balance inherent in the Convention as a whole.

When the courts obey the command in the Human Rights Act where possible to make statutes (or, for that matter, the common law) compatible with Convention rights, they will have to deal with controversial and difficult ethical, social and legal issues that English judges 20 years ago would have regarded as not justiciable, or as political issues that would be better dealt with by Parliament. But if the courts are to be true to the object and purpose of the Human Rights Act they will not be able to avoid making their own judicial decisions on such issues. They must either interpret domestic law so as to conform to the Convention or, if this is impossible, declare under Section 4 that the impugned statutory provision is incompatible with Convention rights.

In the latter event, the courts will in theory have a discretion whether to make a declaration of incompatibility. But in practice (as Lauterpacht anticipated) they will surely regard themselves as under a duty to make a declaration. This is the only remedy they will be able to give for the breach of the victim's Convention rights. A judicial declaration will send a clear signal to the executive and legislative branches so as to enable them to remedy the position under the special procedure prescribed by section 10 and Schedule 2. Without such a declaration, the Government will be unable to take remedial action under section 10. If no remedial action

---

[31] *Rights Brought Home: The Human Rights Bill*, Cm 3782, 1997 at para. 2.7.

[32] Committee Stage, HL, 18 November 1997, HL Debs, vol. 583, col. 535.

[33] Third Reading, HL, 5 February 1998, HL Debs, vol. 583, col. 840.

[34] Second Reading, HC, 16 February 1998, HC Debs, vol. 306, col. 780.

[35] Committee Stage, HC, 3 June 1998, HC Debs, vol. 313, cols. 421–2.

[36] Geoffrey Marshall, 'Interpreting interpretation in the Human Rights Bill' [1998] *PL* 167 at 170.

[37] Compare the reading into Alberta's Individual's Rights Protection Act of sexual orientation by the Supreme Court of Canada, in *Vriend* v. *Alberta* (1998) 156 DLR 4th 385, with the Privy Council's refusal to read into the Civil Service Act of Antigua and Barbuda a restriction upon the freedom of expression of civil servants, in *de Freitas* v. *Permanent Secretary of Ministry of Agriculture and Others* [1998] 3 WLR 675, *per* Lord Clyde. See also Mary Childs, 'Constitutional Review and Underinclusive Legislation' [1998] *PL* 647.

is taken and recourse to the European Court becomes necessary, a declaration will make it clear that the only reason the victim has been deprived of an effective domestic remedy is because of an incompatible legislative provision that the Government and Parliament have failed to amend or abrogate.

In spite of the absence of a power to set aside plainly inconsistent legislation, the role of British courts will be closely analogous to the role of constitutional courts in other common law countries in deciding whether legislation passes muster against the standards of constitutional Bills of Rights. Even though our courts are specifically required by section 2 to take account of Strasbourg jurisprudence, comparative constitutional case law from elsewhere in the Commonwealth, including decisions of the Privy Council, interpreting similar language and concepts to those contained in the Convention, will also be strongly persuasive. This increasingly rich body of Commonwealth constitutional case law will be especially persuasive in common law contexts, or in areas where the European Court has failed to lay down coherent legal principles, for example, when giving a very wide margin of appreciation to the national authorities.[38]

The Privy Council recently explained the judicial approach in interpreting a constitutional measure, such as the Human Rights Act, comparing it with the approach in construing a commercial contract.[39] Lord Hoffmann said this:

'The context and purpose of a commercial contract is very different from that of a constitution. The background of a constitution is an attempt, at a particular moment in history, to lay down an enduring scheme of government in accordance with certain moral and political values. Interpretation must take these purposes into account. Furthermore, the concepts used in a constitution are often very different from those used in commercial documents. They may expressly state moral and political principles to which judges are required to give effect in accordance with their own conscientiously held views of what such principles entail. It is however a mistake to suppose that these considerations release judges from the task of interpreting the statutory language and enable them to give free rein to whatever they consider should have been the moral and political views of the framers of the constitution. What the interpretation of commercial documents and constitutions have in common is that in each case the court is concerned with the meaning of the language which has been used. As Kentridge AJ said in giving the judgment of the

South African Constitutional Court in *State* v. *Zuma* 1994 (4) BCLR 401 at 412. "If the language used by the lawgiver is ignored in favour of a general resort to 'values' the result is not interpretation but divination".'[40]

The task is made more difficult under the Human Rights Act, because the lawgiver is not only Parliament but also the framers of the Convention as subsequently interpreted by the European Court and Commission of Human Rights. That is the price to be paid for using the Convention as a substitute for a full constitutional Bill of Rights.

In applying the moral and political principles contained in the Convention, the British judge, like the European Court, must make value judgements. There is nothing new in that. Even in the absence of a statute guaranteeing human rights, our courts have always had to make difficult value judgements, when interpreting legislation or developing the common law. They do so as independent judges acting judicially, not as knights errant roaming at will in pursuit of their own ideal of beauty or of goodness.[41]

Madame Justice Bertha Wilson has pointed out, in the context of interpreting legislation under the Canadian Charter of Rights and Freedoms, that when the courts review legislation under the Charter they are primarily concerned with the effect of the legislation, rather than with ascertaining the intention of the legislation.[42] The same is true when reviewing legislation under the Human Rights Act. The first question the courts must ask is: does the legislation interfere with a Convention right? At that stage, the purpose or intent of the legislation will play a secondary role, for it will be seldom, if ever, that Parliament will have intended to legislate in breach of the Convention. It is at the second stage, when the Government seeks to justify the interference with a Convention right, under one of the exception clauses, that legislative purpose or intent becomes relevant. It is at that stage the principle of proportionality will be applied.

The Privy Council has recently adopted a three-fold analysis of the relevant criteria for dertermining whether a limitation of a human right is arbitrary or excessive. In *de Freitas*, the Privy Council held that a court must ask itself:

'whether: (i) the legislative objective is sufficiently important to justify limiting a fundamental right; (ii) the measures designed to meet the legislative objective are rationally

[38] See generally, Nicholas Lavender, 'The Problem of the Margin of Appreciation' [1997] *EHRLR* 380 and David Pannick, 'Principles of interpretation of Convention Rights under the Human Rights Act and the Discretionary Area of Judgment' [1998] *PL* 545.

[39] *Matadeen* v. *Pointu and others* [1998] 3 WLR 18 (PC) (in the context of the protection given to human rights by the Constitution of the Republic of Mauritius).

[40] *Ibid.*, at 25G–H.

[41] To paraphrase the celebrated statement by Benjamin N. Cardozo, *The Nature of the Judicial Process* (New Haven, Conn.: Yale University Press, 1921) at 102.

[42] Madam Justice Bertha Wilson, 'The Making of a Constitution: Approaches to Judicial Interpretation' [1988] *PL* 370 at 371–2.

connected to it; and (iii) the means used to impair the right or freedom are no more than is necessary to accomplish the objective.'[43]

These criteria will be relevant in interpreting legislative restrictions of Convention rights under the Act. Our courts have already had the task of deciding in areas where Community law governs, whether a statutory rule is necessary and proportionate to its aims. This has involved the judicial review of Acts of Parliament against European standards, requiring the courts to evaluate the measure's impact in the light of its aims, having regard to evidence about its policy and the social and economic context in which it operates. That is what is also required in interpreting legislation in the light of Convention rights. Suppose, for example, that a given measure were alleged to discriminate unfairly in a field covered by the Convention. Advocates will have to deploy arguments and submit evidence about the history of the measure, the Government's reasons for maintaining it in force, the social and economic impact of the measure, the legislative pattern in other European countries, and the moral and political principles upon which the relevant Convention rights are based.[44]

As the impact of the Human Rights Act comes to be understood, British judges will increasingly be called upon to act as constitutional judges when interpreting legislation and developing the common law, and to fashion new remedies for the citizens of Europe within their jurisdiction. They will have to move from their relatively sheltered position as lions under the throne of the sovereign Queen in Parliament to become a co-ordinate branch, separate and independent, but working in partnership with the other two branches of government.

The present generation of senior judges is well equipped to meet the new challenges. They no longer make 'a fortress out of the dictionary',[45] refusing to look at Royal Commission reports, White Papers, or reports of parliamentary debates to enable them to interpret legislation wisely. Like Justice Holmes, they recognise that a word 'is not a crystal, transparent and unchanged, it is the skin of a living thought'.[46] The present Government and Parliament are paying the judiciary a large compliment in entrusting them with the power and the duty to protect basic civil and political rights as part of the law of the changing British Constitution. I hope and believe that the judges will repay the compliment by being imaginative and sympathetic when interpreting statutes under the Human Rights Act.

---

[43] See *de Freitas* v. *Permanent Secretary of Ministry of Agriculture, Fisheries, Lands and Housing* [1998] 3 WLR 675 (PC), *per* Lord Clyde, adopting the analysis formulated by the Supreme Court of Zimbabwe, *per* Gubbay CJ, drawing upon the jurisprudence of South Africa and Canada.

[44] Cf. *R* v. *Employment Secretary, ex p. Equal Opportunities Commission* [1995] 1 AC 1 (HL).

[45] '[I]t is one of the surest indexes of a mature and developed jurisprudence not to make a fortress out of the dictionary; but to remember that statutes always have some purpose or object to accomplish, whose sympathetic and imaginative discovery is the surest guide to their meaning': *Cabell* v. *Markham*, 148 F 2d 737 at 739 (2nd Cir. 1945), *per* Learned Hand J, aff'd. 326 US 404 (1945).

[46] *Towne* v. *Eisner* 245 US 418 at 425 (1919).

4

THE JUDICIAL STUDIES BOARD AND THE ECHR

H.H. JUDGE PAUL COLLINS C.B.E.*

The successful growth of judicial education programmes in recent years now means that it is unthinkable that any major legal innovation could be unaccompanied by a JSB course for the judges whose work might be affected. Judges expect and rightly demand training in new law. It is the obligation of the JSB under its constitution (a Memorandum of Understanding with the Lord Chancellor's Department) to identify training needs and attempt to fulfil them. Who can guess what impact accession to the European Communities might have had in 1972 if the JSB had been in existence?

Under the leadership of its Chairman, Lord Justice Henry, the JSB signalled its intentions towards the ECHR by a flag raising seminar in the Lord Chief Justice's court on 29 September 1997. Lord Scarman, Lord Lester, Lord Woolf, Lord Justice Henry, the late Judge Ryssdael, Judge Martens, Advocate-General Jacobs QC, Laws J, and the late Peter Duffy QC contributed to a day chaired by Lord Bingham. Very many members of the senior judiciary attended; lively exchanges indicated keen interest in the opportunities presented to judges and some awareness of potential problems. Immediately afterwards the JSB set up an ECHR working group which the writer had the privilege of chairing until December 1998, being succeeded by Sedley LJ. The Lord Chancellor and the Home Secretary earmarked substantial funds for the whole national effort of judicial, magisterial and tribunals training at the time of the White Paper heralding the Human Rights Bill and the role of the JSB is central.

The remit of the JSB requires it to train the full and part time judiciary, some 3,500 in all; to co-ordinate the training for the lay magistracy, some 30,000 souls, to be

delivered by Magistrates Courts Committees; and to offer advice and help to the myriad of tribunals of different kinds and sizes. The working group addresses the needs of all these constituencies, although it has delegated the detailed planning for magistrates and tribunals to two dedicated working groups. From the outset judges, academics, practitioners, human rights groups and officials from the LCD contributed to the working group's informal and enthusiastic meetings. It would only be right to single out Peter Duffy QC as a storehouse of knowledge and understanding of the subject and a source of wise practical advice as to the planning of the JSB's programme.

The increasing demands on judges' time meant that the working group had to reject the possibility of residential training for judges in the substantive law of the ECHR. A different route had to be mapped out. The JSB Criminal Committee, then led by Judge LJ, began from January 1998 to include a talk on the impact of the ECHR on criminal litigation in its Crown Court Continuation seminars. The family and civil seminars have followed suit to an increasing degree. Although implementation is not expected until later in 2000, human rights points are being taken with increasing frequency, particularly in the Crown Court, and appellate judgments often take the provisions of the Convention into account. The JSB does not believe that the early introduction of human rights materials into its ordinary courses is precipitate. In early 2000 every full- and part-time judge will attend a one day seminar dedicated to the Act and the Convention. Of course, there will be no attempt to summarise the mass of jurisprudence. What the seminars will aim at is providing judges with a conceptual toolkit to enable them to operate with confidence in the new environment of human rights. This means not only proactively giving effect to the guaranteed rights but also being astute to

* Director of Studies at the JSB

detect points without merit which might threaten to clog up the justice system. The seminars will balance presentations on fundamental notions and the judicial approach against syndicate sessions where judges will discuss practical exercises in small groups, slanted towards the interests of particular disciplines. The JSB is not a law school and does not aim to teach judges human rights law, but to place them firmly within the human rights context and enable them to handle human rights arguments. It is expected that judges at all levels, full- and part-time, will attend seminars together, a practice successfully adopted in the training for the civil justice reforms.

The seminars will not stand alone. They will fall inside the programme which has already begun and will be accompanied by written materials which are still under discussion. The JSB is represented by Sedley LJ on the LCD Project Board for human rights implementation and the sources of information for judges are crucial. The Court Service has recently announced funding to provide every full time judge with high specification laptop computers, replacing those which have done sterling duty under the now defunct JUDITH project. These will give access by modem link to the Court Service intranet which is being developed and which will be the first point of reference for human rights materials. For a glimpse of what judges can do for themselves, a visit to Judge Sean Overend's ECHR website at www.beagle.org is recommended. The intranet will be able to display existing jurisprudence and materials and also be able to give speedy prominence to homegrown material, which will undoubtedly explode in quantity after implementation.

Human rights development by judges will be an integral part of JSB judicial training after implementation. It remains to be seen whether further dedicated seminars are thought desirable or whether treating human rights as an inseparable element in the ordinary day-to-day work of judges is better calculated to maintain judicial awareness.

It is recognised that the Court of Appeal and High Court judges will need more assistance than other judges initially; the burden on them may be very great. There will be a series of evening seminars at the Royal Courts of Justice where a Lord Justice and a practitioner or academic will examine different aspects of human rights law with their colleagues.

Training the lay magistracy is an enormous task. The JSB has no remit to train their clerks, who will give the vital legal advice. The relevant working group has commissioned an experienced team of magistrates' trainers to produce a training pack to support a one-day awareness seminar and the JSB will hold 'training the trainers' days to brief training officers in the use of the materials in the context of the seminar programme which the JSB will construct. Ultimately, it is the statutory responsibility of Magistrates Courts Committees to train justices, though the JSB must advise the Lord Chancellor as to the effectiveness of that training. As so many points are likely to be brought up in the magistrates' courts, the importance of this training cannot be overemphasised. The few words devoted to it here should not be taken as any guide to the effort being put into making it as effective as possible.

The JSB has now held two seminars for tribunal heads and training officers. Its role is purely advisory; it has no jurisdiction, even over those tribunals for which the Lord Chancellor is responsible. And there are many others, sponsored by other government departments. At the beginning of March 1999 there was considerable concern as to the rate at which tribunals were preparing themselves for implementation. Some were well advanced with ambitious and competent programmes; some were alarmingly unaware of the scope of the task ahead; some had not accepted the invitation to the seminars and the state of their preparation has to be imagined. The JSB has drawn the situation to the attention of those who may be able to do something about it and will offer help and advice to tribunals within its ability. But the JSB has neither the staff nor the resources to create human rights training programmes for the many tribunals with widely differing jurisdictions. A comparatively small number of places will be available at judicial seminars for some tribunal chairmen. Tribunals will present a fertile ground for human rights arguments in large numbers and it must be hoped that all of them will put the necessary training arrangements in hand.

A national training programme so large and without precedent is daunting but exciting. Initial and continuing education in human rights for all those who sit in judgment has been well recognised by ministers as a prerequisite for successful implementation. For the JSB, the opportunity to emphasise its position at the centre of judicial life, so soon after its massive training programme for the civil justice reforms is one to be seized with alacrity.

PART II

Criminal Justice
and the Act

5

THE EUROPEAN CONVENTION AND CRIMINAL LAW

ANDREW ASHWORTH*

In practical terms the greatest impact of the European Convention on Human Rights, when the Human Rights Act 1998 is eventually implemented, will fall on the criminal process. Criminal procedure will probably bear the brunt, but not far behind will come the law of evidence, the criminal law and sentencing. And even if we may have to wait almost two more years before the Act is brought into force, it is apparent that appellate courts are already paying attention to the Convention and to the Strasbourg jurisprudence when it is thought relevant.[1]

So far as the criminal law is concerned, there seems to be an assumption that the Convention's effects will fall mainly on some of the offences created by the Criminal Justice and Public Order Act 1994, and that it is defence lawyers who can expect the greatest assistance from the Strasbourg case law. In this paper I will try to sustain a different argument—that the Convention will have implications both for offences and for defences, both for defendants and for (potential) victims, both for defence lawyers and for prosecutors. I begin (1) with a brief *Rundschau* of the possible effects of the Convention on criminal law; give brief consideration to (2) the concept of a 'criminal charge'; devote detailed attention to (3) possible changes in the law on justifiable force; mention some of the issues surrounding (4) breach of the peace; and then conclude.

Before that, however, I should draw attention to the essentially practical question of how different people in the criminal justice system are likely to approach the

challenge of the Human Rights Act. While many would wish to maintain that questions about the application of the ECHR to English criminal law can usually be resolved by careful legal analysis, others would argue that differences of attitude and disposition towards the ECHR are likely to be the key. Of course, solicitors and counsel may well view the ECHR as an Aladdin's cave, to be raided for dazzling new arguments; and I have argued that prosecutors should make a thorough search of the cave too, as indeed the CPS are doing. But also significant in practice will be the approach to the ECHR taken by the government and its advisers, and by the magistracy, justices' clerks and the judiciary. I would suggest that the possible approaches—of which there is already evidence, both in statements from the Home Office and in some judicial statements—can be ranged along a continuum from the minimalist to the maximalist. The extreme positions might be characterised as follows.

The minimalist wishes the ECHR to remain in the background, and to interfere with ordinary business as little as possible. He or she will not necessarily be an opponent of the Human Rights Act, but may be someone who recognises the need for it and yet maintains that it should have a residual role. Minimalists will tend to emphasise the pockets of discretion in the new scheme, for example, that section 2 of the Human Rights Act merely requires courts to 'take account of' the Strasbourg jurisprudence, not to follow it; they will tend to cite decisions like *Schenk* v. *Switzerland*,[2] with which they will associate the proposition that the admission of evidence will not render a trial unfair no matter what rights of the defendant have been infringed along the way, and *Laskey* v. *UK*,[3] with which they will associate the proposition that states are free to criminalise sado-

* QC, DCL, FBA, Vinerian Professor of English Law, University of Oxford.
[1] For two recent examples, see *Thomas et al.* [1998] Crim.LR 887 (on ss. 23–26 of the Criminal Justice Act 1988, absent witnesses, and Art. 6.3(d)) and *Manchester Crown Court ex parte Appleby, The Times*, 19 November 1998 (time limits for prosecution and Arts. 5.3 and 6.1), and *Kebilene* [1999] 3 WLR 175..

[2] (1991) 13 EHRR 242.
[3] (1997) 24 EHRR 39.

masochistic activities for the protection of health and morals, even when consenting adults in private are involved; and minimalists will seem impelled towards arguments that the ECHR is really an embodiment of the common law, especially the right to a fair trial in Article 6, so that no new outcomes can really be expected.

Maximalists, on the other hand, are likely to be enthusiasts for the Convention, perhaps people who have applauded most of the respects in which Strasbourg judgments adverse to the UK have led to reforms in criminal justice, or perhaps simply people who want to see the introduction of a constitutional document that will help to prevent some legislative excesses. Maximalists will tend to emphasise sections 3 and 6 of the Human Rights Act, requiring courts to construe legislation in conformity with the ECHR so far as possible, and requiring public authorities to act in conformity with the Convention; they will tend to cite decisions such as *Saunders* v. *UK*[4], on the privilege against self-incrimination, and *A* v. *UK*[5] on the force that may be used in parental chastisement; and they may predict that the Criminal Justice and Public Order Act offences will be laid waste, and that legislative provisions on disclosure and adverse inferences from silence will need to be substantially remodelled.

Elements of these tendencies can be found in all the papers for this conference. Perhaps no-one ever believed that we would be engaged in the neutral, value-free vivisection of the Convention and its jurisprudence. And, not least because we are also embarking on a new phase in Strasbourg (Protocol 11, the abolition of the Commission and the introduction of the new, expanded Court), the Convention may well prove to be not just a living instrument but very much a negotiable instrument. The question I am raising concerns the standpoint from which the various parties will seek to negotiate it.

1. CRIMINAL LAWS AND CONVENTION RIGHTS

What are the major points of impact of the Convention on criminal law? To give a general impression of this, the Articles may be considered in turn:

Article 2 *(right to life):* self-defence and justifiable force in the prevention of crime, etc; abortion;

Article 3 *(right not to be subjected to torture or inhuman or degrading treatment):* the defence of parental chastisement;

Article 5 *(right to liberty and security of person):* the defence of insanity;

Article 6.2 *(presumption of innocence):* burden of proof; offences of strict liability;

Article 8 *(right to respect for private life):* homosexual offences (both generally and in respect of private premises, and the age of consent as compared with heterosexual offences); child abduction; failing to leave, or re-entering, land after the issuance of a notice to gypsies or other travellers (sections 77–80 of the Criminal Justice and Public Order Act 1994);

Article 9 *(freedom of religion):* blasphemy (also Article 10);

Article 10 *(freedom of expression):* obscenity; racial hatred offences; contempt of court; criminal libel; incitement to disaffection;

Article 11 *(freedom of assembly):* breach of the peace (also Articles 5 and 10); various offences under the Public Order Act 1986 and Criminal Justice and Public Order Act 1994 concerned with processions and demonstrations.

No doubt there are other offences and defences that might be added to this list, but already there is much to consider. Many of those possible conflicts between the Convention and English criminal law will require careful analysis and detailed attention to the Strasbourg jurisprudence.[6] Moreover, the Convention is also relevant to the way in which the criminal courts operate: Article 7, prohibiting retrospective criminal liability, has been interpreted as setting standards of certainty and quality of law, and as restricting the creative powers of the courts to 'reasonably foreseeable' applications (extensions) of existing offences.[7]

What is also noticeable, from the above list, is the possible impact of the Convention on the ambit of general defences to criminal liability. The defence of parental chastisement will need to be re-shaped and restricted following the judgment of the European Court in *A.* v. *UK*.[8] The ambit of the defence of insanity, with its extraordinary coverage of states including epilepsy, hyperglycæmia, and sleepwalking,[9] will need to be reconsidered.[10] And the Strasbourg jurisprudence now gives some support to the introduction of a defence of

---

[6] For fuller analysis, in conjunction with the relevant Strasbourg jurisprudence, see B. Emmerson and A. Ashworth, *Human Rights and Criminal Proceedings* (Sweet & Maxwell, 1999, forthcoming), ch. 3.

[7] *C.R. and S.W.* v. *UK* (1995) 21 EHRR 363.

[8] (1999) 27 EHRR 611.

[9] See A. Ashworth, *Principles of Criminal Law* (2nd edn., 1995), 204–6.

[10] *Winterwerp* v. *Netherlands*, 2 EHRR 387 (1979); see further P.J. Sutherland and C. Gearty, 'Insanity and the European Court of Human Rights', [1992] Crim.LR 418, and E. Baker, 'Human Rights, M'Naghten and the 1991 Act' [1994] Crim.LR 84.

---

[4] (1996) 23 EHRR 313.   [5] [1998] Crim.LR 892.

entrapment.[11] Whereas it will be for the accused's legal representatives to question the compatibility of offence definitions with the Convention, it will fall to the prosecution to draw attention to respects in which the interests of victims or potential victims ought to receive protection from the court (e.g. the right to life, the right not to be subjected to inhuman or degrading treatment, etc.).

In part 3 below I intend to focus on the relationship between the Article 2 jurisprudence and the English rules on justifiable force, after a brief discussion (in part 2) of the concept of a criminal charge. The hope is that detailed examination of at least one major point of impact of the Convention on English criminal law, rather than a general but superficial survey, will help to illuminate the prospects and the difficulties attending implementation. I have chosen a contestable example, so as to probe the boundaries of the Convention and its jurisprudence.

2. THE CONCEPT OF A CRIMINAL CHARGE

It has long been established that the concept of a 'criminal charge' or 'offence' has an 'autonomous meaning' under the Convention, that is, that a state's own characterisation of the proceedings is not conclusive.[12] The principles on which the issue should be decided were laid down by the Court in *Engel* v. *Netherlands* (1976),[13] and the leading decision is now that of *Benham* v. *UK* (1996),[14] a case in which the applicant had been committed to prison for non-payment of the community charge. Among the breaches of the Convention he alleged were a failure to grant appropriate legal assistance, as required by Article 6.3(c), and in order to bring his case within this provision he needed to establish that he had been 'charged with a criminal offence'. In English law it was plain that he had not: the proceedings for recovery of an unpaid community charge were civil in nature. However, the Court went on, following the *Engel* case, to consider the substance of the matter, paying attention to the nature of the proceedings (notably, that they were 'brought by a public authority' and that they had 'punitive elements', in that committal to prison was only possible after a finding of 'wilful refusal to pay or culpable neglect'), and also to the severity of the penalty (here, a 'relatively

severe' maximum penalty of three months' imprisonment, and an actual penalty of 30 days' imprisonment).[15] The Court therefore decided that the applicant had been 'charged with a criminal offence', and found against the UK government on this point. The *Benham* case therefore establishes that the label put upon proceedings, either at common law or by statute, is not conclusive for the purposes of the ECHR.

When the Human Rights Act is in force, courts will be required to apply the above tests to the substance of the case if it is contended, despite its characterisation in English law, that it involves an 'offence' or 'criminal charge'. The government recently conceded in Strasbourg that 'breach of the peace' is a 'criminal charge' under the Convention, despite the existence of a Divisional Court ruling that states otherwise.[16] These would be rather unusual decisions for English courts to have to make, but the question may arise in relation to the civil proceedings, under section 1 of the Crime and Disorder Act 1998, which give rise to the making of an anti-social behaviour order; and also in relation to means enquiries for fine default.[17]

3. JUSTIFIABLE FORCE AND THE RIGHT TO LIFE

Article 2 declares everyone's right to life, but allows exceptions when deprivation of life 'results from the use of force which is no more than absolutely necessary (a) in defence of any person from unlawful violence; (b) in order to effect a lawful arrest or to prevent the escape of a person lawfully detained; (c) in action lawfully taken for the purpose of quelling a riot or insurrection'. The scope and application of the exceptions were considered in the Gibraltar shooting case, *McCann and others* v. *UK* (1996),[18] where the European Court differed from the Commission's finding and held (by ten votes to nine) that the UK had violated Article 2 in the shooting by SAS soldiers of three IRA terrorist suspects.

The Government's argument had been that the three suspects were believed to have a radio-controlled detonator which would activate a car bomb, and that it was necessary to kill them to prevent the imminent detonation. In the event, neither a radio-controlled device nor a car bomb was found. The majority judgment began

---

[11] *Teixeira de Castro* v. *Portugal* (1999) 28 EHRR 101.

[12] For discussion, see D.J. Harris, M. O'Boyle and C. Warbrick, *The Law of the European Convention on Human Rights* (1995), 166–73

[13] A.22 (1976).

[14] (1996) 22 EHRR 293.

[15] (1996) 22 EHRR at 323–24. See also *Ravnsborg* v. *Sweden* (1994) 18 EHRR 38.

[16] The decision is *R.* v. *County Quarter Sessions Appeals Committee, ex parte Metropolitan Police Commissioner* [1948]. 1 KB 260. The concession was made to the Court in *Steel* v. *UK* [1998] Crim.L.R. 893, discussed in part 4 below

[17] *R.* v. *Corby JJ, ex parte Mort, The Times*, 13 March 1998.

[18] (1996) 21 EHRR 97.

by stating that the purpose of Article 2 is to secure practical and effective protection of each individual's life; it emphasised that this right is only to be taken away where 'absolutely necessary', a 'stricter and more compelling test' than that applicable to the phrase 'necessary in a democratic society' under paragraph 2 of Articles 8 to 11; it stated that its inquiries concern not only the actions of the law enforcement officers but also the planning of any law enforcement operation, to ascertain whether it was organised so as to 'minimise, to the greatest extent possible, recourse to lethal force'; and it explained that the actions of the officers should be judged on the facts that they honestly believed, for good reasons, to exist. In this case the Court found that the soldiers themselves had not violated Article 2 because, on the information given to them, they did have good reason for the beliefs that led them to fire the shots. However, the majority of the Court held that the immediate reaction of the soldiers, in shooting the three suspects dead, lacked 'the degree of caution in the use of firearms to be expected from law enforcement personnel in a democratic society, even when dealing with dangerous terrorist suspects'. The Court went on to hold that the UK government had violated Article 2, through its failure to ensure that the operation was planned so as to minimise the risk of death: the killings had not been shown to be 'absolutely necessary' for the 'defence of any person from unlawful violence'.

In the subsequent case of *Andronicou and Constantinou* v. *Cyprus* (1998)[19] the Court differed from the Commission's finding of a violation of Article 2 and held (by five votes to four) that there had been no breach. The case arose from a siege, in which Andronicou was holding Ms Constantinou hostage. Andronicou was known to be unstable, and to have a gun, and when Ms Constantinou was heard to scream the special police unit went in. They used tear-gas and then, when Andronicou fired at them as they entered his house, they replied with several rounds of automatic fire. Andronicou was killed instantly; Ms Constantinou was wounded and died shortly afterwards. The majority of the Court accepted that it must consider the 'planning and control' of the operation, and must determine whether the force used was 'strictly proportionate' to the purpose, on the facts that the officers honestly believed, for good reasons, to exist. In view of the deployment of machine guns in a confined space the Court regretted that so much fire power had been used, but narrowly concluded that the use of lethal force could not be said to have exceeded what was absolutely necessary for the purpose of defending the lives of Ms Constantinou and of the officers themselves.

The application of Article 2 to the facts created great difficulty in these cases: not only did the Commission and the Court take different views, but the Court's decisions were both by the narrowest of majorities and contain some powerful dissenting judgments. Moreover, the Court has stated that in interpreting Article 2 it is neither determining the compatibility of a State's laws with the Convention nor determining the criminal liability of any party.[20] However, it would surely be undesirable for domestic criminal law to be patently inconsistent with the Article 2 jurisprudence when the Human Rights Act comes into force, and arguments can only be raised in the European Court if they were first raised in the national courts. The jurisprudence starts from the proposition that the right to life of everyone (including suspected or actual offenders) should be protected so far as possible: this emphasis on the right to life is not usually to be found as the starting point in English criminal cases, where the focus is upon whether the court has been left in reasonable doubt over the justifiability of the killing. This is one of the general shifts in reasoning which the Human Rights Act ought to bring about: the duty laid on public authorities by section 6 to act in conformity with the Convention suggests that they should demonstrate their awareness of the individual rights engaged in each situation, whether this be the police acting so as to prevent a breach of the peace (are the rights of freedom of expression and of freedom of assembly being respected?) or a court dealing with a defence to homicide based on justifiable force (was the victim's right to life adequately respected?).

There are at least four detailed issues that warrant further consideration.[21] First, the European jurisprudence is most closely concerned with cases in which there was a killing by law enforcement officers or other State agents. The English approach is not to differentiate between private individuals and State agents in the standards of reasonableness laid down. There has been criticism of this,[22] and it seems that the Article 2 jurisprudence requires law enforcement officers to plan their operations so as to minimise the risk to life, and to act only on reasonable grounds. The requirement of proper planning suggests that the ambit of criminal liability might be spread wider than the law enforcement officers who actually caused the death, and raises the possibility that commanding officers might in some circumstances be prosecuted for aiding and abetting the

---

[19] (1998) 25 EHRR 491.

[20] (1996) 21 EHRR 97 at paras. 155 and 173.
[21] See also J. Rogers, 'Justifying the Use of Firearms by Policemen and Soldiers: A Response to the Home Office Review of the Law on the Use of Lethal Force' (1998) 18 *LS* 486, which came to hand after this paper had been written.
[22] A. Ashworth, n. 9 above, 132–43.

killing. In that context, it is relevant to add that Article 2 applies to unintentional killings,[23] and that where, for example, there is evidence of gross negligence on the part of senior officers which led to deaths, a prosecution for manslaughter might have a realistic prospect of resulting in conviction.[24] This line of argument was strengthened by the decision in *Osman* v. *UK* (1998),[25] where the Court recognised that States have a positive obligation to take reasonable preventive measures to protect an individual whose life is known to them to be at risk from the criminal acts of another. More generally, one implication of section 6 of the Human Rights Act 1998, requiring public authorities to act in accordance with the Convention, is that senior law enforcement officers should train their personnel and plan their operations so as to preserve life to the maximum degree.

The second point is the European Court's insistence, in the two decisions above, that the beliefs on which officers act should be based on 'good reason', a more demanding standard than the 'honest belief' held sufficient in *Gladstone Williams* (1984)[26] and *Beckford* v. *R.* (1988).[27] This will require English courts to reconsider their attachment to the subjective test of mistake, at least where the defence is based on justifiable force. This would be a tremendous blow to those who have long campaigned for the courts to adopt a subjective test of mistake throughout the criminal law,[28] although it would give support to those others who have argued that the subjective test ought to be modified in certain types of case where it is fair to impose some kind of duty of care.[29] Did the defendant in *Gladstone Williams* have 'good reason'? Would an intoxicated defendant ever have 'good reason'? On the other hand the application of Article 2 in *Andronicou* suggests that, even in respect of trained law enforcement officers, some indulgence should be granted to 'heat of the moment' reactions, along the lines of *Palmer* v. *R.* (1971).[30] The decisions in *McCann* and *Andronicou* are so different in their approach and orientation that one could argue that, in practice, the later one detracts considerably from the earlier.

[23] See the Commission's decision in *Stewart* v. *UK* (1984) 39 DR 162.

[24] Cf. the facts of the well-known tort case of *Alcock* v. *Chief Constable of South Yorkshire* [1992] 1 AC 155, arising out of the Hillsborough football stadium disaster.

[25] Judgment of 28 October 1998; to be reported in [1999] Crim.LR (February).

[26] (1984) 78 Cr.App.R 276.

[27] [1988] AC 130.

[28] J.C. Smith and B. Hogan, *Criminal Law* (8th edn., 1996, by J.C. Smith), comment at 91 that 'it may now perhaps be safely assumed that the courts will give full effect to' the ruling in *Morgan* v. *DPP* [1976] AC 182.

[29] E.g. C. Wells, 'Swatting the Subjectivist Bug' [1982] Crim.LR 209; Ashworth, n.9 above, 232.

[30] [1971] AC 814.

Thirdly, the term 'absolutely necessary' seems stronger than the term 'necessary' in English law, for example in section 3 of the Criminal Law Act 1967. It may be advisable for English courts to advert to this aspect of cases in which a justificatory defence to homicide is raised. In effect, this goes hand in hand with recognition that each person has a right to life which should only be taken away in the extreme circumstances set out in Article 2.2. No doubt English judges will argue that this much is implicit in the approach they have always taken. Even if that is so, it would be advisable for it to be explicit in the future. The tendency of Parliament and the judiciary to subsume all considerations within the concept of 'reasonableness' will need to be curbed, and the separate issues confronted.

A fourth cluster of points relate to the precise wording of the exceptions to Article 2. Although the killing must be 'absolutely necessary' for the achievement of one of the three stated purposes, there is no requirement of proportionality on the face of Article 2: that defect in the drafting has, however, been remedied by the case law, and in *Andronicou* the Court stated that the force must be 'strictly proportionate'.[31] The first exception to Article 2 refers to the 'defence of any person from unlawful violence'. The reference is to 'violence' rather than to 'killing', suggesting that it may indeed be in conformity with the Convention to deprive a person of the right to life when that person is inflicting, or about to inflict, serious but non-life-threatening injury on another. The wording also leaves open the question of how imminent the 'unlawful violence' must be. This was an issue before the Commission in *Kelly* v. *UK* (1993),[32] where soldiers in Northern Ireland had opened fire on a stolen car containing three youths which was speeding away from a checkpoint, and one of the occupants was killed. In the civil action that followed, the Northern Ireland courts accepted that the soldiers suspected the youths of being terrorists and thought that they would continue terrorist (therefore life-threatening) activities if allowed to drive away. How far into the future might such terrorist activities take place, and does this affect the 'prevention of crime' justification? These important questions were not resolved by the Commission, which pointed out that the prevention of crime is not mentioned as an exception to Article 2 and could therefore not be relied upon. But the same issue of 'imminence' arises in relation to the 'unlawful violence' exception in Article 2.2(a). In

[31] See the Commission's decision in *Stewart* v. *UK* (1984) 39 DR 162, and the Court's statement in *Andronicou and Constantinou* (1998) 25 EHRR 491, at para. 171.

[32] (1993) 74 DR 139, on which see the valuable discussion by Sir John Smith, 'The Right to Life and the Right to Kill in Law Enforcement' (1994) *NLJ* 354.

McCann the point was not tested because it was assumed that the detonation of the alleged bomb was indeed imminent.

In rejecting the application in *Kelly*, the Commission held that the soldiers' use of deadly force was justified according to Article 2.2(b), as 'absolutely necessary . . . in order to effect a lawful arrest'. Sir John Smith has demonstrated that there was no power of arrest in the circumstances of that case, and that the Commission misunderstood the position.[33] Moreover the case raises a fundamental question about the drafting of Article 2: how can a killing be necessary to effect an arrest, since by definition there can be no arrest if the person has been killed? There are also further questions about the scope of the exceptions: Article 2.2(c) creates an exception for cases of killing in the course of lawful action to quell a riot or insurrection (which must be 'strictly proportionate', as for the other exceptions),[34] but the absence from Article 2.2 of any general 'prevention of crime' exception means that killing to protect property is always a breach of the Convention. Only if the term 'unlawful violence' in the Convention were to be given an artificially wide meaning could imminent cases of burglary or arson be brought within Article 2, although there might be an argument that robbery (which is defined so as to require an element of force) and most rapes would satisfy the requirement.[35]

To these points about the structure of Article 2 should be added the observation that neither Article 3, on 'inhuman or degrading treatment', nor Article 5, on security of the person, includes an express exception for the justifiable use of force. There is some authority to support the view that the law applicable when an injury is caused in self-defence or in effecting an arrest is similar to that applicable in cases where death is caused,[36] and such an exception ought to be implied in order to cure the defective drafting of the Convention in this respect. It is common sense that the rights conferred by Articles 3 and 5 should be subject to exceptions in favour of justifiable force, in the same way and for the same reasons as the right to life in Article 2.

All the above remarks have been directed to killings by law enforcement officers. But the State has a more general duty to ensure that the law protects the lives of citizens from unjustifiable deprivation by other individuals.[37] Although a private citizen would be unlikely to violate Article 2 rights by failing to plan an 'operation' with sufficient care and respect for life,[38] a private citizen might use force against another without 'good reason' and that might lead to an acquittal under current English law whilst violating the Article 2 right of the victim. This suggests that the rules of English law on mistaken belief in the need for justifiable force require alteration generally, and not just in their application to law enforcement officers.

In conclusion, it will be evident that a fair amount of the argument above is speculative. The leading decisions from Strasbourg are not unambiguous, and the drafting of the relevant Articles of the Convention leaves much to be desired. However, I hope to have made out at least a *prima facie* case for reconsideration of the English law on justifiable force when the Human Rights Act is implemented. When most commentators' eyes are turned towards the offences in the Criminal Justice and Public Order Act 1994, we should not neglect the other aspects in which criminal law will be challenged (including common law defences), nor should we overlook the responsibilities on prosecutors to draw attention to these points. In respect of justifiable force, the relevant rules exist chiefly at common law, with the somewhat elliptical section 3 of the Criminal Law Act 1967 playing little more than a background role. In 1993 the Law Commission put forward a draft Criminal Law Bill, clauses 27 to 30 of which would effectuate a welcome revision and restatement of English law on justifiable force.[39] Only a few changes would be needed to accommodate the Convention points made above. But the provisions on justifiable force did not appear in this government's Consultation Document on reforming the 1861 Act,[40] and it is not clear what the next move will be, or when it will occur.

---

[33] *Ibid.*, at 355.

[34] *Stewart* v. *UK* (1984) 39 DR 162.

[35] For comparison, see the extended notion of a 'violent offence' for the purpose of s. 2(2)(b) of the Criminal Justice Act 1991, as defined in s. 31 of that Act, discussed in *Archbold 1998* para. 5–131.

[36] This is certainly implicit in the decision of the Commission in *Hurtado* v. *Switzerland* (1994) 5 HRCD 2, to the effect that an application under Art. 3 in a case where considerable force had been used by Swiss police to arrest the applicant did not disclose a violation.

[37] *Osman* v. *UK* (above, n.19); and by analogy with the Court's decision on Art. 3 and parental chastisement in *A* v. *UK* [1998] Crim.LR 892.

[38] There may be rare cases where this is relevant: see, e.g. *Field* [1972] Crim.LR 435, discussed by A. Ashworth, 'Self-Defence and the Right to Life' [1976] *Camb.LJ* 282, at 292–6.

[39] Law Com. No. 218, *Legislating the Criminal Code: Offences against the Person and General Principles* (Cm 2370, London, HMSO)

[40] Home Office, *Violence: Reforming the Offences against the Person Act 1861* (February 1998).

4. BREACH OF THE PEACE

In *Steel* v. *UK* (1998)[41] the five applicants claimed that their arrests and detention for breach of the peace violated their rights of freedom of expression. All of them were involved in protests, and in the cases of the first two applicants the protests took the form of physically obstructing the activities of others. The Court, citing *Chorherr* v. *Austria*,[42] held that nonetheless their conduct constituted an expression of opinion. However, the Court went on to hold that their arrest, detention and subsequent conviction and imprisonment were 'not disproportionate' and were 'necessary in a democratic society' to avert the danger of disorder and violence.[43] In relation to the other three applicants, who were distributing leaflets and holding a placard, the Court not only held that they were exercising their freedom of expression but also held unanimously that their arrest was a disproportionate response which violated Articles 10 and 11. Theirs had been an 'entirely peaceful' protest which was not likely to provoke others to violence, and so the police had insufficient grounds for fearing a breach of the peace. In another complex case decided by the Court on the same day, *McLeod* v. *UK*,[44] it was found that the police violated the applicant's right to respect for her home, under Article 8, by entering 'in order to prevent a breach of the peace' when they had failed to check the court warrant under which the former husband claimed authority and when the house was occupied only by an elderly woman.

One implication of these two decisions is that both the police and the courts ought to become far more conscious of, and deferential towards, the declared rights of individuals before they purport to exert their authority under the time-honoured 'breach of the peace' powers. When the Human Rights Act comes into force, it will be necessary to recognise that every citizen has rights under Article 8 to respect for their home and private life, under Article 10 to freedom of expression, and under Article 11 to freedom of assembly. It is true that each of those Articles contains a second paragraph that provides for an exception if the interference with the right is 'necessary in a democratic society . . . for the prevention of disorder and crime', and so forth. But the decisions in *Steel* and *McLeod* illustrate the importance that ought to be given under the Convention to the notion of proportionality between any limitation on a right and the justification offered for it, and to the importance of keeping interference with rights to a minimum.

5. CONCLUSIONS

This selective discussion has offered an overview of points at which the Convention may have an impact on English criminal law, a brief analysis of the concept of a 'criminal charge', a consideration of the problems attending the 'breach of the peace' power, and a fairly detailed analysis of the law on justifiable force. I have not given detailed consideration to the position of 'regulatory offences' under the Convention, because that question is closely connected with the burden of proof and may therefore be discussed in another session. But the decision in *Salabiaku* v. *France*[45] does not give unqualified approval to offences of strict liability, referring vaguely to 'reasonable limits' (a qualification not tested in any subsequent decision), and there may be grounds for arguing against strict liability offences that may result in imprisonment.[46]

The purpose of my detailed analysis of one particular issue was to look closely at some European Court and Commission decisions, which will have to be taken into account by English courts under section 2 of the Human Rights Act, and to tease out some of their implications for the existing rules of English law. I started this paper by referring to the increasing frequency with which appellate courts are already citing the Convention and decisions of the European Court. The next 12 months will be a period of some uncertainty, as lawyers will doubtless begin to address Convention-based arguments to courts that have demonstrated an interest in receiving them. The retraining of the legal profession is beginning, but it seems that the judiciary will have to wait for their formal training until closer to the time of implementation. The pace of change in the universities is difficult to assess, but it is fair to say that the contents of most textbooks and casebooks used in the teaching of Criminal Law and of Evidence do not yet reflect the importance of the Convention. Law schools will need to reflect urgently on the approach to be taken to the Convention: what is to be avoided, in my view, is the temptation to hive off the Convention as a separate subject or topic, rather than regarding it as part and parcel of all existing courses (e.g. Criminal Law, Family Law, Administrative Law, etc.) to which it is relevant.

---

[41] [1998] Crim.LR 893.

[42] (1995) 17 EHRR 358, cited at para. 92 of *Steel*.

[43] The first applicant was held on arrest for 44 hours and then imprisoned for 28 days when she refused to be bound over to keep the peace. Four judges dissented from the finding that this was 'not disproportionate' and held that her Art. 10 right had been violated, two of them going so far as to describe the length of custody as 'manifestly extreme'.

[44] (1999) 27 EHRR 493 (*February*).

[45] (1991) 13 EHRR 379.

[46] See the encouraging aside of Brooke LJ in *B* v. *DPP* [1998] 4 All ER 265, at 276. For further discussion, see B. Emmerson and A. Ashworth, *Human Rights and Criminal Proceedings* (forthcoming), ch. 3.

But there is a powerful argument for some basic instruction on the substance of the ECHR at an early stage in legal education, so that references to the Convention can be placed in their context by students.

What is evident from, at least, parts 1 and 3 of this paper is that there are several respects in which English criminal law may have to be changed so as to bring it into conformity with the Convention. The Law Commission, to its credit, began some years ago to refer to the implications of the Convention for the topics on which it published Consultation Papers and Reports.[47] But in other respects there has been little interest among official committees in conformity with the Convention—the nadir being the extraordinary failure of the Royal Commission on Criminal Justice (1993) to refer at any stage to the ECHR, let alone to adopt it as a

source of principles. No doubt the Home Office is already undertaking a review of these matters, as of similar conflicts in the fields of criminal procedure, evidence and sentencing. On some matters there is room for argument, as we have seen, and it may therefore be right to wait and see what the appellate courts make of the possible conflict. But on other points the need to change the law is plain, and in the next couple years we will have to face a whole host of logistical problems (should there be legislation before implementation of the Human Rights Act? Should it be for the Law Commission or the Home Office to work on it? Should the aim be to produce a statute with a jumble of Convention-proofing amendments, or should we take a little longer and aim to combine the new amendments with more substantive reforms that have been waiting for some time? What should the courts do if there is no legislative amendment on, for example, the defence of parental chastisement or self-defence? And so on). No doubt there are those who know the answers to these and other pertinent questions; they certainly need to be discussed.

---

[47] See, e.g., Law Com. No. 222, *Criminal Law: Binding Over* (Cm 2439, London: HMSO, 1994), a particularly courageous report because it suggested a curtailment of the powers of the courts and therefore attracted the usual response; and also Law Commission Consultation Paper No. 139, *Consent in the Criminal Law* (1995).

6

THE CONVENTION AND THE ENGLISH LAW OF CRIMINAL EVIDENCE

THE RT. HON. LORD JUSTICE BUXTON

AN ENGLISHMAN ABROAD

Most English lawyers spend their summer holidays in France. After a few weeks, life on the *terrasse* beginning to pall, they find their way to the nearest substantial town, and are drawn irresistibly to the *Palais de Justice*. Being English lawyers, neurotically trained in the ways of English judges, they arrive promptly for the beginning of the trial: only to find that it is more like the end of the criminal trials that they are used to, since the proceedings commence with the presiding judge, part of the tribunal of fact, not only reading out the accused's criminal record, but cross-examining him upon it. More culture shocks await. Evidence is called by the prosecution, as part of the trial itself, as to the psychological profile of the accused. The trial is conducted on the basis of a written dossier, available to the tribunal of fact before the trial starts, and liberally referred to during oral testimony. There are no formal directions of law, so the basis on which the court is proceeding is not made explicit. Prosecuting counsel, far from being an independent private practitioner, is a member of the same professional corps as the judge. Above all, that necessary feature of any properly conducted trial of a serious charge, The English jury is nowhere to be seen. The English lawyer returns to his château reinforced in his belief that other countries have nothing to teach him about criminal procedure and the rights of the accused.

That was, until 1998. On his return home this year, the English lawyer finds the Human Rights Act 1998 (the 1998 Act), based on an international convention (the ECHR) that draws on other peoples' laws, and which he has a nasty feeling is about to turn the English criminal trial upside down. That feeling will be reinforced, if he is the unusual sort of English criminal

lawyer who reads the law periodicals, by the fact that for the last twelve months it has been impossible to stumble over an article on evidence or procedure that does not suggest, albeit often in somewhat vague terms, that everything will be different once we are under the 1998 Act. And the practitioners' bible, in the course of announcing that the ECHR may invade almost every aspect of the criminal trial, tells him that he must now 'embark upon a fairly steep [*sic*] learning curve'.[1]

The present writer fully sympathises with the feelings of unease to which this new learning has given rise. In an attempt to elucidate where we are in fact going this paper will first offer some background observations about the ECHR in general, and then review some examples of the possible operation of the 1998 Act in the English criminal trial.

THE ECHR AND ENGLISH JURISPRUDENCE

England has the great distinction of having been one of the first signatories of the ECHR, in 1950, and one of the first countries to create a right of individual petition to Strasbourg. It is usually assumed that English lawyers made a substantial contribution to the drafting of the ECHR,[2] and introduced into it such elementary common law notions as the right to a public trial and to equality of arms between defence and prosecution, both of which had seemed to be under serious threat in pre-war Europe. It may, however, be a mistake to assume that

---

[1] *Archbold News*, issue 3 for 1998 (hereafter, *Archbold News*), at 8.

[2] We think that there has been no systematic study of the English contribution to the *travaux préparatoires*. The materials for such a study are presumably available in Foreign Office archives, and could have considerable practical as well as academic value. We commend that enquiry as an appropriate enterprise for the Centre for Public Law.

the English contribution thought much more deeply than that into the potential problems of a criminal trial. Compared with today, English criminal practice in the 1950s was in an age of innocence. That was the era of 'Dixon of Dock Green', the era in which the leading judicial observer of the criminal trial could write:

The vast majority of criminals who come into the dock at Assizes or Sessions are pitiable creatures, a nuisance rather than a danger to the state. The English police are able to fulfill their difficult role because it is not necessary for them to develop a strong animus or sense of hostility against the criminal, as might well be the case if they had constantly to match themselves against violent and bitter enemies of society.[3]

The ECHR was thus not formulated against today's background of huge and sophisticated international frauds; drug importation and dealing on a massive scale; allegations of child abuse of the most extensive and horrible kind, to which the witnesses are the terrified and alienated children themselves; and serious cases of police corruption; all of which fall to the lot of present day policemen, judges and juries.

One must of course be careful in emphasising that point too strongly, or even perhaps at all. It is precisely when the system is under the sort of pressure that we have just indicated that first principles protecting the rights of those who are the objects of criminal proceedings need to be most kept in mind. The ECHR however, at least as interpreted by the European Court of Human Rights (the Strasbourg Court), is as we shall demonstrate in the next section not an absolute but an organic code, and one that is applied with at least some regard to the exigencies of the case and of the particular member state. It is in that spirit that we have to reflect on the fact that general statements that seemed a sufficient codification of principle in 1950 may need some considerable interpretation in the context of the criminal litigation of the 1990s.

WHOSE MARGIN OF APPRECIATION? AND ALLIED QUESTIONS

We have referred to the ECHR being, in the hands of the Strasbourg Court, an organic and flexible set of principles, that are applied by giving weight to the traditions and indeed the needs of the member states. The principal device whereby that is achieved is through the doctrine of the 'margin of appreciation', first substantively developed by the Court in a British case,

Handyside v. *UK*,[4] which concerned whether a conviction for possessing an obscene article could be justified under Article 10(2) of the ECHR as a limitation upon freedom of expression that was necessary for the 'protection of morals'. The Court said:

'By reason of their direct and continuous contact with the vital forces of their countries, state authorities are in principle in a better position than the international judge to give an opinion on the exact content of those requirements [of morals] as well as on the "necessity" of a "restriction" or "penalty" intended to meet them . . .'[5]

The doctrine is closely linked to the principle of proportionality, whereby, as the Court stated in *Soering* v. *UK*[6]:

'inherent in the whole of the Convention is a search for a fair balance between the demands of the general interest of the community and the protection of the individual's fundamental human rights.'

However, one man's, one country's, self-determination is another man's breach of principle, and there are developing arguments that the doctrine of margin of appreciation on the part of the objects of a human rights code, that is to say the member states who are governed by the ECHR, is incompatible with the reasons why such a code exists in the first place. That view has been recently given strong expression by Judge de Meyer of the Strasbourg Court, in his dissenting judgment in *Z* v. *Finland*[7]:

'[The Court] has already delayed too long in abandoning this hackneyed phrase and recanting the relativism it implies . . . where human rights are concerned, there is no room for a margin of appreciation which would enable the States to determine what is acceptable and what is not.'

For the moment, however, the doctrine, characterised as it was by Judge de Meyer, is firmly established in the Strasbourg jurisprudence. How does that affect the use and interpretation of the ECHR as part of English domestic law?

The 'Convention rights' introduced into English law are 'the rights and fundamental freedoms set out in [inter alia] Articles 2 to 12 of the Convention'.[8] That is to say, what the English court has to apply is the text. But in determining questions arising in relation to such Convention rights the English court must 'take into

---

[3] P. Devlin, *The Criminal Prosecution in England* (1960), 112.

[4] 1 EHRR 737 (1976).

[5] *Ibid.*, paras [48]–[49].

[6] (1989) 11 EHRR 439.

[7] [1997] EHRLR 442.

[8] 1998 Act, s.1(1)(a).

account', *inter alia*, the Strasbourg jurisprudence.[9] That is a comparatively weak form of guidance. It is to be contrasted with section 3 of the European Communities Act 1972:

'For the purpose of all legal proceedings any question as to the meaning of any of the Treaties . . . shall be treated as a question of law and if not referred to the European Court be for determination as such in accordance with the principles laid down by and any relevant decision of the European Court.'

By that formula the English judge is bound by the jurisprudence of the Luxembourg court, once he has managed to work out what it is. The position in relation to Strasbourg is rather more flexible.

How then should the English judge approach his task? On one level the jurisprudence of the Strasbourg Court, which is what the English judge has to take into account, goes no further than to say that in some cases *that court* will in effect excuse a breach of the literal terms of the ECHR in deference to the interests of the member state. That is because the task of the Strasbourg Court is to adjudicate upon individual petitions brought by citizens against a member state, and not to control the functioning of the state's internal legal order: therefore if the state in fact breaches the ECHR, it matters not for the Strasbourg Court whether that was done with the ECHR rules in mind or not. But in so providing the Strasbourg jurisprudence necessarily establishes that the stated norms of the ECHR are not absolute but relative, and leave room within their verbal statement for state discretion. The present writer is not clear how that aspect of the ECHR has been handled by those member states where, by the doctrine of the self-execution of treaties, the ECHR has long been part of the *domestic* law: in France, for instance, since the ratification of the ECHR in 1974.[10] The prospects for England are equally obscure. It would seem open in principle to an English court to fall back on the margin of appreciation in any type of circumstance where the Strasbourg Court has not ruled to the contrary, but it will do so really without any guidance as to how to proceed or as to the limits within which it can act.

[9] 1998 Act, s. 2(1).

[10] This is an important and urgent subject for further study, and is the second of the research projects that I would urge upon the Centre for Public Law. In what follows I make some very partial and no doubt misleading reference to experience in France, which is the only signatory of the ECHR with whose law, or language, I am even remotely familiar. I have been assisted by a paper prepared by M. Régis de Gouttes, Advocate General at the Cour de Cassation. But I hope that by the time I have to address these problems as a judge rather than as a commentator there will be available in England, and in English, detailed omparative materials on the domestic application of the ECHR in a range of other member states.

Although the doctrine of the margin of appreciation is not expressly cited by the Strasbourg Court in respect of complaints about criminal proceedings under Article 6, very similar expressions of policy have been directed at the Strasbourg Court's role in respect of the rules of criminal procedure of the member states. Thus in assessing the application of Article 6.3(d), which gives to every person the right 'to examine or have examined witnesses against him and to obtain the attendance and examination of witnesses on his behalf under the same conditions as witnesses against him' the Court has said that:

'the taking of evidence is governed primarily by the rules of domestic law and it is in principle for the national courts to assess the evidence before them. The [Strasbourg] Court's task . . . is to ascertain whether the proceedings in their entirety, including the way in which evidence was taken, were fair.'[11]

The principle is therefore the overall fairness of the proceedings: a consideration that led to the granting of relief by the Strasbourg Court in *Saidi* itself. But, in the domestic application of the ECHR, who decides that latter issue, and subject to what rules? Faced with what appears to be the breach of a Strasbourg-approved norm can the English court fall back on its own estimation that the trial is, or on appeal was, fair; or does the court have to speculate as to what Strasbourg may make of it? Given the weight accorded to national procedures in the Strasbourg jurisprudence, and the acknowledged relativism of much of the ECHR, it seem that an English court should properly decide the issue of fairness for itself. It may of course be a courageous Crown Court judge, and even more a courageous bench of lay magistrates, that goes down that route. We can say nothing more helpful on this iusse than that the comments that follow have to be read against the background of that substantial area of uncertainty.

THE PROPER ROLE OF HUMAN RIGHTS

One of the paradoxes of the present jurisprudence of the ECHR is that at the same time as the Strasbourg Court has stressed the autonomy of member states, it has found it impossible to resist the temptation seriously to limit that autonomy in specific areas that might not seem to have much to do with 'human rights' as they were probably thought of in 1950. We mention this aspect of the problem to remind ourselves that the English judge, occupied in 'taking into account' the

[11] *Saidi* v. *France* (1993) 17 EHRR 251 at para. [43]. See also *Schenk* v. *Switzerland* (1991) 13 EHRR 242.

Strasbourg jurisprudence, and be he never so confident that his appreciation is the same as Strasbourg's, must be aware that it is nonetheless difficult to forecast the legal problems to which the Strasbourg Court will see the ECHR as providing a solution.[12]

We give one example of what may be an uncomfortable development. All systems from time to time encounter the phenomenon of the appellant in flight: having given instructions for an appeal the prisoner escapes from custody, and therefore is not available to be present at the hearing of that appeal. Jurisprudence of the French Cour de Cassation, dating back to the last century, holds uniformly that in such circumstances the appeal cannot proceed: broadly because the appellant, by seeking relief from a court at the same time as he refuses to comply with the requirements of another court, purports to dictate the terms on which the State shall do justice. That position has been condemned by the Strasbourg Court as entailing a breach of Article 6.1 of the ECHR.[13] The Cour de Cassation has refused to accept that ruling, in a series of cases starting with *Aff. Guerin* in 1994.[14] Within the French system, therefore, the fugitive must lose: his only recourse is in Strasbourg.

The same problem has been addressed by the English courts in somewhat different terms, most recently in *Gooch*.[15] In a judgment manifestly less elegant or principled than the French authorities the Court of Appeal (Criminal Division) (CACD) held, in an Anglo-Saxon spirit of pragmatism, that whilst there was no absolute rule that a case would not be heard in the appellant's (culpable) absence, special circumstances were required before that could be done. The very strong element of judicial discretion inherent in that ruling would seem to be as inconsistent as is the absolute French rule with the jurisprudence of the Strasbourg Court as stated in *Poitrimol*.[16]

From this history we conclude that the domestic laws of France and England, though different from each other, may in dealing with this problem both be in breach of the Strasbourg jurisprudence. We find that a disturbing conclusion. The problem is a practical, or if not that a jurisprudential, issue, in relation to which the rules adopted by mature democracies, with legal systems admired and copied throughout the world, may legitimately differ both from each other and from some generally expressed norm. It is quite disproportionate to consider such a question as being on anything like the same level as the fundamental freedoms that the ECHR rightly protects. That such an issue has become a matter of ECHR jurisprudence is a strong warning to the English judge to look over his shoulder when addressing almost any matter in the criminal law of evidence.

With those on the whole disobliging background reflections we turn to, or at least approach somewhat nearer to, the actual subject-matter of this paper.

IS IT SAFE?

We start at the wrong end, with consideration of how the Court of Appeal (Criminal Division) should approach appeals giving rise to ECHR questions. The CACD's powers are a creature of statute: section 2(1) of the Criminal Appeal Act 1968 as substituted by the Criminal Appeal Act 1995, which provides that the CACD:

(a) shall allow an appeal against conviction if they think that the conviction is unsafe;
(b) shall dismiss such an appeal in any other case.

The effect is therefore to make the 'safety' of the conviction the only criterion for determining an appeal: even though the trial that led to that conviction may have been unsatisfactory in some other way.[17] That state of affairs is moderately controversial, not least in making it possible for a conviction to be upheld by the CACD on the basis of evidence that should not have been considered by the trial court[18]; but it seems clearly to be what Parliament wants.[19] The approach is different from that of the Strasbourg Court, which appears to regard breaches of the ECHR as having an absolute nature, leading to relief without close scrutiny

---

[12] The discussion is confined to the criminal law, and to its procedural aspects, but we cannot forebear from mentioning in passing the remarkable decision in *Osman* v. *United Kingdom*, *The Times*, 5 November 1998. There the Strasbourg Court appears to have held that the rules of the *substantive* English law of negligence (on the basis of which law, properly applied, the plaintiff's claim was struck out) could constitute a failure to afford the plaintiff a fair trial under art. 6.1 of the ECHR. It may or may not be premature to see in this the germ of a doctrine analagous to that of substantive due process that has haunted American constitutional law: and given such power to American judges.

[13] *Poitrimol* v. *France* (1993) 18 EHRR 130. The Strasbourg Court has recently cited *Pointrimol* with approval, in the face of the rebellion in France referred to below, in *Guerin* v. *France*, 29 July 1998.

[14] 19 January 1994, Bull. 27.

[15] [1998] 2 Cr. App. R 130.

[16] We may perhaps add that all concerned in *Gooch* proceeded in total oblivion of any possibility that the ECHR had anything to do with the matter. If the CACD in *Gooch* did comply with the Strasbourg jurisprudence it talked prose without knowing it.

[17] *Chalkley and Jeffries* [1998] 2 Cr App R 79.

[18] This point is forcefully made by Sir John Smith in a note at [1998] Crim. LR 809.

[19] There were available to the draftsman, but rejected, other formulae, including that adopted in Scotland of 'miscarriage of justice': see para. 1 of Sched. 2 to the Criminal Justice (Scotland) Act 1980, and the discussion at (1993) 109 *LQR* 68–71.

THE CONVENTION AND THE ENGLISH LAW OF CRIMINAL EVIDENCE

of the effect of the breaches on the result of the proceedings.[20]

How then should the CACD proceed when faced with, for example, a case where illegally obtained evidence has been admitted in breach or arguable breach of the ECHR jurisprudence (on which substantive issue see below), but where it is satisfied that the resulting conviction is entirely safe? By section 3 of the 1998 Act:

'So far as it is possible to do so, primary legislation [in casu, section 2 of the Criminal Appeal Act] must be read and given effect in a way which is compatible with Convention rights.'

But is it possible to read section 2 in a way that is compatible with Convention rights, in the sense that appeals are allowed because of breaches of the ECHR even though the resulting conviction is safe? It may simply be said that in the new world anything is possible. But does that extend to giving section 2 a meaning that is different from that identified in *Chalkely and Jeffries*? And if the issue is, as it is, the *meaning* of section 2, it is difficult to see that the section can have a different meaning in ECHR cases from that which it bears in non-ECHR cases.

To achieve coherence with the Strasbourg jurisprudence, therefore, section 2(1)(b) of the 1968 Act would have to have added at its end something like:

'unless the Court considers that in the trial leading to the conviction there was a breach of a Convention right as defined in section 1(1) of the Human Rights Act 1998.'

That, however, would not be the reading of section 2 that section 3(1) of the 1998 Act calls for, but its rewriting.

Nor can it be said that the CACD, as a 'public authority' as defined by section 6(3) of the 1998 Act, is constrained by section 6(1) of the 1998 Act to act in a way which is compatible with a Convention right. Any supposed failing in that respect of a court is, by section 9(1)(a) of the 1998 Act, only challengeable by way of appeal: but such appeal has to be determined according to the existing, *domestic*, rules of jurisdiction. The notion that the 1998 Act creates new procedures, or new causes of action, in the domestic law is as great a heresy when expressed in the criminal field as it is in the civil jurisdiction.[21]

And so does that impasse, if it is such, place the CACD under an obligation to make a declaration of incompatibility in respect of section 2, under section 4 of the 1998 Act, when faced with a trial in which a Convention right has been infringed but the resulting conviction has been safe? Adversary argument would be welcome. But the answer would seem to be in the negative, for broadly the same order of reasoning as was addressed in the previous paragraph. Section 2 is not *incompatible* with Convention rights, any more than it is incompatible with rights granted by the common law or by other statutes. It merely provides that where the conviction is in overall terms safe breach of such rights will not suffice to lead to its being quashed.

The position would therefore seem to be that the CACD has to consider complaints about a trial based on breaches of the ECHR, but only has jurisdiction to act on those complaints if it thinks that the outcome of the trial was unsafe, whether because of those complaints or otherwise: and however much it may consider that the complaints, when renewed in Strasbourg, will result in the granting of relief against the United Kingdom.

Leaving these uncomfortable reflections with the expectation that no-one will think of taking a point this arcane, we pass rapidly to issues of substance, that will burden trial courts, at all levels, as well as the CACD. We address only the most obvious issues: while noting that in the coming months and years almost every aspect of criminal evidence and procedure will be argued to be at least potentially vulnerable to the ECHR.

HEARSAY, ORALITY AND CONFRONTATION

'Article 6(3)(d) amounts to an express prohibition on the admission of hearsay evidence adduced by the prosecution'.[22] However, while Article 6.3(d) is undoubtedly of importance for English criminal trials, some caution must be exercised before analysing it in

---

[20] See e.g. *Saunders* v. *UK* (1996) 23 EHRR 313 at para [86]: 'The Court . . . cannot speculate as to the question whether the outcome of the trial would have been any different had [there not been a breach of the rule against self-incrimination] and . . . underlines that the finding of a breach of the Convention is not to be taken to carry any implication as regards that question'.

[21] A parallel issue has arisen in the French jurisprudence, which I do not have the linguistic sophistication to elucidate: I commend the question to the Centre for Public Law's comparative study. It will be

recalled that in *Saidi*, n. 11 above, the Strasbourg Court gave relief on grounds of the overall lack of fairness, in ECHR terms, of the French procedures in question. When the matter returned to France, the Cour de Cassation held that the criticisms recorded by the Strasbourg Court did not have direct effect in France, and were not receivable when the case was judged in cassation: *Aff. Saidi*, Cour de Cassation, 4 May 1994. Such an attitude would not, we think, be open to an English court, in view of the specific terms of s. 3 of the 1998 Act. The conflict does, however, further underline the potential tension between general Strasbourg rules and the specific domestic procedures that are called on to apply those rules.

[22] *Archbold News*, n.1 above, 6. *Archbold News* correctly goes on to stress that the Strasbourg Court will examine the disputed evidence in the context of the case as a whole, to determine the overall fairness of the proceedings.

English 'hearsay' terms. Putting the matter crudely for the sake of exposition, two different cases have to be examined. (I) A gives evidence at the trial, in the course of which he repeats, or in substance repeats, something said by B. (II) A does not give evidence at the trial, but his testimony, which in itself is not hearsay, is presented in written form. Both cases are regarded by English lawyers as infringing the rule against hearsay.

Article 6.3(d) however does not concern itself with the nature of the *evidence*, but rather provides that the defendant has the right:

'to examine or have examined witnesses against him and to obtain the attendance and examination of witnesses on his behalf under the same conditions as witnesses against him.'

That provision addresses case II, since it has been read as demanding 'confrontation' of the accused by those testifying against him.[23] Whether it addresses case I as well, where there is indeed a testifying witness, is somewhat obscure. The issue is difficult to explore not least because the compulsive orality of the English trial is not part of the other major traditions that have contributed to the ECHR: certainly, it is difficult to think of civil law courts having patience with, or even understanding, the kind of agonised theoretical debate that occupied so much valuable judge-time in the English courts in *Kearley*.[24] The principle of confrontation thus really does not touch the common law notion of hearsay as a rule of *evidence*, which applies to both sides, and at least in theory has something to do with the reliability of the testimony. Rather, it is a rule of *procedure* or propriety, giving procedural or, as some seem more recently to have argued, moral rights to the defendant.[25]

The jurisprudence of Article 6.3(d) does however have obvious implications for the use of pre-trial statements in cases where the maker of the statement is unable or unwilling to appear at the trial.[26] The use of such pre-trial statements is regulated in English domestic law by the fairly detailed provisions of sections 23 to 26 of the Criminal Justice Act 1988 (CJA 1988), the provisions of which may not entirely correlate with the requirements of the Strasbourg jurisprudence.

This issue has already been considered by the CACD

in *Gokal*[27] where the use of section 23 statements was challenged on grounds, *inter alia*, of breach of the ECHR. Although the ECHR was not then part of English law, the court took the ECHR argument very seriously, as indeed had the trial judge. The defendant in *Gokal* had had no opportunity to question the maker of the statements, but he was able, by the operation of paragraph 1 of Schedule 2 to the CJA 1988, to adduce evidence casting doubt on the credibility of the maker: evidence which, by reason of his absence from the trial, the maker would not be able to controvert. The CACD viewed that possibility, together with the obligation on the trial judge to give an appropriate warning to the jury as to the general quality of uncross-examined evidence and any particular matter casting doubt on the maker's reliability,[28] as satisfying the requirement that the proceedings should overall be fair to the defendant.[29]

The court also drew some assistance from the observation of the Strasbourg Court in *Barbera*[30] that Article 6.3(d) entailed that:

'all the evidence must in principle be produced in the presence of the accused at a public hearing with a view to adversarial argument.'

The CACD concluded that that requirement would be fulfilled in the case before it, since the statements would be the subject of criticism and of adversary argument; but that in itself may not be enough, since the 'evidence' referred to in the Strasbourg jurisprudence would seem to be the substance of the testimony, rather than the form in which it is couched.[31]

We think that it will not be seriously questioned that, applying the overall ECHR test of general fairness, the decision of the CACD in *Gokal* was correct.[32] That is likely to be the outcome of most challenges to the use of

---

23 See e.g. *Unterpertinger* v. *Austria* (1991) 13 EHRR 175.

24 [1992] 2 AC 228.

25 For more on this distinction, see Professor Friedman [1998] Crim LR 697. The assumptions made in and underlying the text above do not entirely march with Professor Friedman's analysis. I apologise for the fact that the structure of this paper does not permit the theory to be examined more fully.

26 That was the position in *Unterpertinger*, and also in *Delta* v. *France* (1994) 16 EHRR 574.

27 [1997] 2 Cr App R 266. The case involved an international fraud of great complexity, the sum in issue being alleged to be $1.2 billion, which involved the calling of witnesses from 11 different countries, including New Zealand, Hong Kong, the USA and five countries in Africa, together with some three weeks of accountancy evidence. The jury trial lasted for 129 days. This is criminal litigation of an order that was not contemplated by those who drafted the ECHR in 1950; and the nature of which one hopes is understood by those who now make decisions in Strasbourg.

28 *Beck* (1982) 74 Cr. App. R 221.

29 See [1997] 2 Cr. App. R at 280D.

30 (1989) 11 EHRR 360 at para. [78].

31 See *Delta* v. *France* (1994) 16 EHRR 574 at para. [34].

32 We may additionally mention that the admission of the statements was further challenged in *Gokal* at first instance as an infraction of the ECHR right against self-incrimination, in that the accused might, in order to controvert the statements, have to enter the witness-box, a course that otherwise he might not have taken. That argument was rejected as obviously unfounded. Whether to give evidence remained a matter of the defendant's choice; but in any event nothing in the Strasbourg jurisprudence gives the defendant a *right* not to

CJA 1988 evidence, bearing in mind in particular the stringent requirements of the CJA 1988 as to its admissibility.[33] Some problems however remain.

First, the criterion of fairness imposed by the ECHR is the fairness of the whole *trial*, not the fairness of the adduction of the particular *evidence*. In many cases that will be a distinction without a difference; but as *Archbold News* points out, citing *Trivedi* v. *United Kingdom*,[34] importance is attached in deciding the former issue to the availability of other evidence supporting the contested testimony. Defendants may therefore be able to argue that the fact that the evidence is particularly helpful to the prosecution case is a good ECHR reason for *not* admitting it. As *Archbold News* says, that would represent a significant shift in English practice. Not only is such a balancing operation not now required of the court, but there is even some suggestion that the importance of a piece of testimony is more rather than less reason for admitting it under the CJA 1988 provisions.[35]

Secondly, importance is attached in the Strasbourg jurisprudence to the fact that the maker of the statement may have been confronted at *some* stage of the proceedings, even if not at final trial.[36] *Archbold News* indicates that that requirement might be satisfied if the statement had been given at an old-style committal. Any suggestion that procedure of that discredited type might have to be reintroduced in order to avoid ECHR difficulties in the case of witnesses absent at the trial scarcely bears contemplation.

As we have pointed out, the 'confrontation' principle does not turn on the *reliability* of the evidence whose admission is contested; nor on the possibility, provided by the CJA 1988, of challenging the evidence by methods other than confrontation; nor does the Strasbourg approach in terms of the overall fairness of the proceedings put reliability into the equation, since the undesirability of non-contested evidence is seen in procedural rather than evidentiary terms. The principle is maintained in the Strasbourg jurisprudence in a spirit of *fiat justitia ruat coelum*:

'The Court is fully aware of the undeniable difficulties of the fight against drug-trafficking-in particular with regard to obtaining and producing evidence-and of the ravages caused to society by the drug problem, but such considerations cannot justify restricting to this extent the rights of the defence.'[37]

This all represents a marked difference from the English approach. It is the point at which the tension between English practice and Strasbourg jurisprudence seems to be at its height.

Finally on Article 6.3(d), difficulties may be looming if ECHR lawyers look too literally across the Atlantic to the wording of the confrontation clause of the Sixth Amendment:

'[i]n all criminal trials the accused shall enjoy the right....to be confronted with the witnesses against him.'

This provision[38] has been seen in the USA as potentially causing difficulties in trials involving child witnesses, where evidence has been given by video link or the accused has been screened from the witnesses. Both of these methods are now regarded by English lawyers as valuable means of achieving a fair (to the public interest) trial in cases involving child victims of a type not contemplated when the ECHR, or the Sixth Amendment, were originally formulated. The compromise reached in the USA appears to be that reasons, of a fairly extreme sort, specific to the witness, must be adduced before the court affords protection.[39] That does not represent a great step away from present English practice, where admission of video evidence is strictly controlled and screening only

---

testify, however much issues may arise as to the conclusions that can be drawn from the fact that he has not testified: on which latter point see below.

[33] We have already mentioned the provisions of Sched. 2. It should also be noted that where the prosecution seek the admission of CJA 1988 evidence (that is, in the Art. 6.3(d) case) they must satisfy the factual requirements of the Act to the standard of beyond reasonable doubt. That obligation almost certainly goes beyond what the ECHR requires, and would be found unusual in most jurisdictions signatory to the ECHR: see the next following section of this paper.

[34] [1997] EHRLR 520; for this and the point that follows see *Archbold News*, n.1 above, at 6.

[35] *Batt* [1995] Crim. LR 240.

[36] See e.g. *Asch* v. *Austria* (1993) 15 EHRR 597 at para. [27].

[37] *Saidi* v. *France* (1995) 17 EHRR 251 at para. [44].

[38] Which for the reasons already stated in respect of Art. 6.3(d) is not, or at least is not only, a hearsay provision. The conceptual distinction between the hearsay rule and the confrontation rule was identified by the US Supreme Court in *California* v. *Green*, 399 US 149 (1930); Professor Friedman suggests that the matter has been somewhat obscured since that date. The analytical point however remains of the first importance.

[39] E.g. per the Supreme Court in *Maryland* v. *Craig*, 110 SC 3157: would the witness be traumatised. In that case the giving of the evidence of a 6-year-old alleged victim of sexual abuse by a one-way television link was upheld by the Supreme Court, but only by 5 votes to 4. Some indication of the flavour of the debate may be gained from the judgment of Justice Scalia, writing for the minority (110 SC at 3171 and 3174): the decision of the majority 'failed conspicuously to sustain a categorical guarantee of the Constitution . . . unwillingness to testify in the presence of the defendant . . . cannot be a valid excuse under the Confrontation Clause, whose very object is to place the witness under the sometimes hostile glare of the defendant'. The jurisprudence of the ECHR fortunately permits of a more rounded approach, that respects the rights of the witness as well as of the accused.

allowed in exceptional cases.[40] It would be very regrettable if ECHR requirements were allowed to disturb that practice.[41]

THE STANDARD OF PROOF

Every English lawyer has as part of his life-blood that anything that has to be proved by a prosecutor has to be proved beyond reasonable doubt. That does not seem to be the view of the Strasbourg jurisprudence: commentators of authority point out that there is no requirement under the Strasbourg jurisprudence of a particular standard of proof, but only more generally a need for 'conviction' of the national court.[42] At the lowest, therefore, care must therefore be taken before it is automatically assumed that any requirement of culpability based on a lower standard than the present will infringe the ECHR.[43]

ILLEGALLY OR DUBIOUSLY OBTAINED EVIDENCE

The House of Lords has recently reiterated that the illegal origins of evidence does not, in English domestic

law, affect its *admissibility*.[44] These issues are, rather, addressed under the discretionary provisions of section 78 of PACE. In the Strasbourg jurisprudence many of the cases have concerned evidence obtained by phone tapping and other surveillance techniques, which principally come into consideration under Article 8. Section 78 is, however, cast in such vague terms, and its concept of fairness of the *proceedings* has been interpreted so loosely, that a judge might well think that he had to read and give effect to it so as to recognise Article 8 rights. Whether other breaches of the law, not obviously founding breach of an ECHR right,[45] give rise to ECHR issues as to a fair *trial* is much more doubtful. We at the moment see no reason why the 1998 Act should alter the courts' present practice in these respects.

ENTRAPMENT

This topic is an unusual feature of English law, because it turns on the propriety of the way in which the evidence has been obtained rather than on its reliability. That is because of the doctrine's origins in the USA, where the doctrine is confessedly used as a means of disciplining police and other public officers.[46] That approach, although not clearly articulated as such in English law, has played a substantial role in decision-making under section 78 of PACE.

In the recent case of *Texeira* v. *Portugal*[47] the Strasbourg Court held that a person with no previous drugs record who was persuaded by police officers to buy drugs on their behalf had not had a fair trial, because:

'the two officers did not confine themselves to investigating his criminal activity, but instead incited the commission of the offence, which would not have been committed without their intervention.'

We see this as broadly the same as the tests in *Smurthwaite and Gill*[48] and *Williams and O'Hare* v. *DPP*[49]; certainly, *Texeira* would not seem to call for a

---

[40] See generally *Archbold* (1998 edition), paras. 8–60 to 8–67.

[41] A perhaps important distinction between Art. 6.3(d) and the Sixth Amendment is that while the former is an 'equality of arms' provision, giving the defendant only the same rights as the prosecution, the Sixth Amendment gives no right to confrontation to the prosecution: *US* v. *Di Maria*, 727 F 2d 265. This aspect of Art. 6.3(d) may not yet have been properly explored. It would certainly seem arguable that the English rules, being rules of *evidence*, and therefore binding both sides, do not infringe a rule that only demands equality. We would also remark, with diffidence, that the Sixth Amendent, and Art. 6.3(d) interpreted in terms of 'confrontation', are limited to giving the accused to right to be confronted by, that is to see and hear, the witness; it is difficult to see that a literal reading of either provision gives the defendant a further right to be seen by the witness.

[42] Van Dijk and Van Hoof, *Theory and Practice of the European Convention on Human Rights* (3rd edn., 1998), 460. What the national court must not do is treat the defendant as if he were guilty before it has convicted him on the evidence: *Schenk* v. *Switzerland* (1988) 242 at para, [51]. That is far different from saying that the national court, in performing that task, must apply rules as to the standard of proof that we suspect are to be found in the law of only one of the signatories to the Convention.

[43] For example, it has been suggested that the recent Home Office proposals to extend civil forefeiture proceedings to the proceeds or instruments of all crime (Working Group on Confiscation, Third Report, 42) would be vulnerable in Strasbourg because they would 'enable the state to confiscate money and assets without having to prove any criminality . . . the test would be a balance of probabilities, not beyond reasonable doubt': *Sunday Times*, 15 November 1998, in an article quoting the opinions of two senior academics. That assumes, we would respectfully suggest wrongly, that the ECHR demands the common law standard of proof of criminality.

[44] *Khan (Sultan)* [1997] AC 558. We understand that the case itself is under consideration in Strasbourg.

[45] E.g. failure by the police when searching a drugs suspect in the street to observe the requirements of para. 2.4(i) of PACE Code A. We doubt whether that lapse would, in itself, generate any ECHR right or liability. In that, as in every issue not yet passed on by Strasbourg, we may well be wrong.

[46] As demonstrated by *US* v. *Perl*, 584 F(2d) 1316 (1978): entrapment by an agent of a *foreign* government not a defence.

[47] [1998] Crim LR 751, with valuable commentary by Professor Ashworth.

[48] (1994) 98 Cr. App. R 437.   [49] (1994) 98 Cr. App. R 208.

wider exclusion of evidence than is at present practised in England. This outcome is achieved in the Strasbourg Court by concluding that under Article 6 the defendant had been deprived of a fair 'trial' from the beginning: with, therefore, no occasion for the adoption of the usual balancing exercise. The English courts cannot complain of that, having themselves accepted that 'proceedings' under section 78 of PACE include, or at least requires the consideration of, the gathering of evidence pre-trial.[50]

INFERENCES FROM SILENCE

In *Murray* v. *United Kingdom*[51] a challenge to the Northern Ireland powers to draw inferences from silence failed. As *Archbold News* points out,[52] that is not conclusive as to the fate of sections 34 to 37 of the Criminal Justice and Public Order Act 1994. Perhaps surprisingly, in view of previously assumed allocation to the national court of decisions on the nature of evidence or sources of proof that are admissible, the Strasbourg Court in *Murray* submitted the case to assessment by the test of general fairness of the trial, pointing to the safeguards in the legislation and the fact that independent evidence of guilt was strong. Fortunately, however, the latter point has to some extent been anticipated by section 38(3) of the 1994 Act, which prevents a conviction being obtained solely on the basis of an inference from silence. English judges may do well to put some further stress on that requirement in their directions to juries.

BURDENS AND PRESUMPTIONS

As a document with substantial English input, it is hardly surprising that Article 6.2 of the ECHR provides that:

'Everyone charged with a criminal offence shall be presumed innocent until proved guilty by law.'

There seems to be a belief amongst English criminal lawyers that article 6.2 may therefore call seriously into question any provision that places any part of the burden of proof or disproof on the defence.[53] That in our judgement is misconceived. The issue was addressed by the Strasbourg Court in *Salabiaku* v. *France*:

'Presumptions of fact or of law operate in every legal system. Clearly the Convention does not prohibit such presumptions in principle. It does however require the Contracting States to remain within certain limits in this respect as regards the criminal law . . . Article 6(2) does not therefore regard presumptions of fact or of law provided for in the criminal law with indifference. It requires States to confine them within reasonable limits which take into account the importance of what is at stake and maintain the rights of the defence.'[54]

The English rule is that any burden of proof placed on the defence has to be discharged only to the level of balance of probabilities, and not to that imposed on the prosecution of beyond reasonable doubt. That can hardly be said to infringe the (ECHR) rights of the defence. And it would be difficult to argue that the present examples of reverse burdens in English criminal law are outside any 'reasonable limits' envisaged by the Strasbourg jurisprudence.

It is much to be hoped that these considerations will be borne closely in mind by those seeking to attack reverse burdens on ECHR grounds. It is also important that legislators recognise the comparative freedom that the Strasbourg jurisprudence gives them in this respect. The requirement that the prosecution *dis*prove any matter relied on by the defence, and to the normal criminal standard, far from advantaging defendants, has led to reluctance to recognise even the possibility of particular defences, precisely because of the difficulty under English criminal procedure of disproving to the required standard of certainty anything asserted by the defence. That is, for example, undoubtedly one of the reasons for the refusal to take what would otherwise be the proper step of recognising the defence of duress in cases of murder. Because of those difficulties the Law Commission proposed, in its report on general defences in the criminal law, that in order to make the defence of duress more rational, and more acceptable, the burden of establishing its elements should be placed on the defendant.[55] The Law Commission concluded that that proposal would not infringe Article 6.2 of the ECHR. I respectfully agree.[56]

---

[50] *Matto* v. *Wolverhampton Crown Court* [1987] RTR 337.

[51] (1996) 22 EHRR 29.

[52] Above n. 1, at 6.

[53] *Archbold News*, above n.1, 7: 'Defence lawyers will be able to argue that a reverse onus clause breaches the presumption of innocence in Article 6(2)'.

[54] (1991) 13 EHRR 379 at para [28].

[55] Law Com No 218 (1993), paras. 33.1–33.16.

[56] The Cour de Cassation has on several occasions upheld provisions imposing presumptions of fact in the face of challenges on ECHR grounds: e.g. *arret* of 20 January 1989, Bull. No 33. We are not aware that any of this jurisprudence has been challenged in Strasbourg.

AND TO WHAT EXTENT WOULD THE ECHR ALLOW US TO DO THINGS DIFFERENTLY?

This paper started with an old-fashioned English lawyer contemplating the changes in his life that may be brought about by the ECHR. It finishes by carrying that process through to its logical conclusion, by reflecting on how English procedure could be altered further without infringing any requirement of the ECHR.

The ECHR imposes no requirement of jury trial, for any sort of offence, and therefore permits any currently proposed reduction in the availability of jury trial. Indeed, in *Murray* v. *United Kingdom*[57] the English delegate to the Strasbourg Commission pointed out that jury trial was more, not less, vulnerable to attack on grounds of general fairness than would be trial by judge alone, since a discretionary decision by a judge is scrutable and appellable whilst a verdict by jury is not.[58] The ECHR does not prevent the tribunal of fact being in full possession of the accused's criminal record,[59] provided that a proper trial of the present accusation still takes place. Under the ECHR a court can rely on the previous statement of a witness in preference to his oral testimony.[60] The ECHR would seem to permit the introduction of similar fact evidence and evidence of propensity to an extent far greater than is permissible in English domestic law. The ECHR creates no right to unlimited cross-examination of witnesses, provided that the same restrictions are imposed on the prosecution. The ECHR may well not require prosecution allegations to be proved beyond reasonable doubt. It is very unlikely that the ECHR would stand in the way of a regime in which the prosecution as well as the defence could appeal against the result of a criminal trial.

It would seem, therefore, that there could be a radical reduction in what are seen in English eyes as rules necessary for the protection of the accused without there being any breach of the ECHR. Compared with the fundamental requirements mentioned in the last paragraph, which form a very significant part of the basis of English criminal trial, the issues that the ECHR does worry about, such as admission of the statements of absent witnesses, entrapment and inferences from silence, may seem, for all the importance that they have when considered in the case of a particular defendant, to be in overall terms rather small beer.

CONCLUSION

The future presents a puzzling picture. The only part of present English criminal procedure or evidence that seems to be under serious threat is the regime under sections 23 to 26 of the CJA 1998, which most English lawyers would regard as a balanced and fair solution to the problem of eliciting the testimony of dead, sick, foreign or terrorised witnesses. On the other side of the coin, it would seem that much now thought to be of crucial importance could be removed from our procedure without any infringement of the Strasbourg regime. How an English judge should apply the Strasbourg jurisprudence, and to what extent he can use his own standards of fair procedure, remains in some obscurity. The best conclusion is that all concerned in the criminal process must keep their nerve, and their faith in the wisdom of the common law[61]: and hope that practitioners, and legal aid authorities, carefully study the whole of the Strasbourg jurisprudence before assuming that anything that incommodes the defence must be a breach of the ECHR.

AFTERWORD

The above text was completed on 2 December 1998. I venture to add two observations only arising out of the discussion at the January 1999 Conference.

1. There appeared to be a view amongst those attending the Conference that the effect of the 1998 Act would be to liberate English judges from some of the shackles that at present bind them (for instance, the obligation to seek the intention of Parliament in construing legislation; and to interfere with administrative decisions only if they were unreasonable in the *Wednesbury* sense); and that in pursuit of that freedom judges should revert to human rights texts from throughout the world, such as the recent legislation in Hong Kong, Australia, Canada and South Africa.

I do not comment in the wider context of the general application of the 1998 Act, but in relation to the present subject of criminal evidence and procedure I would counsel caution. The 1998 Act is very specifically drafted to retain the binding status of previous legislation until it is reversed by legislative, not by judicial, action (section 10); and to require the judges to have regard to the Strasbourg jurisprudence and nothing else. The latter is, for better or worse, a specific text, directly interpreted by an authoritative court that has

---

[57] N. 52 above.

[58] *Per* Mr N. Bratza (as he then was), 22 EHRR at 53–4.

[59] See Law Commission Report, *Previous Misconduct* (LCCP 141), at para. 1.11 n. 25. That was decided by the Strasbourg Commission as long ago as 1965, and we believe that the point has never thereafter been questioned.

[60] *Doorson* v. *Netherlands* (1996) 22 EHRR 330 at para. [78].

[61] See e.g. *per* Lord Browne-Wilkinson in *Re Arrows (No 4)* [1995] 2 AC 75 at 95F–H: in respect of fundamental rights such as the privilege against self-incrimination supra-national conventions reflect the common law.

shown little inclination to seek inspiration from outside the traditions of the signatory nations. When trying to envisage what the Strasbourg Court would conclude in an undecided case (which is inevitably the task forced on the English judge) it is very far from clear that the judge is entitled to assume that that Court would have recourse to jurisprudence in Canada or South Africa. That is so even where the texts of other countries' human rights documents are in the same verbal terms as the Convention: for instance in the case of the Hong Kong provisions. It is *a fortiori* an occasion for caution when other countries have chosen to legislate in terms different from those of the Convention.

2. During discussion of the problems posed for Convention issues by section 2(1) of the Criminal Appeal Act 1968, much was made of the observation of Lord Steyn in *Mohammed* v. *The State* [1999] 2 AC 111 in the course of considering the effect of a breach of section 5(2) of the Constitution of Trinidad and Tobago (which is not in the same terms as any part of Convention) that 'a breach of a defendant's constitu-

tional right to a fair trial must inevitably result in the conviction being quashed'. That observation was *obiter* in the case in which it was made, since the Privy Council did not think that the breach there in issue of a specific right to counsel was necessarily a breach leading to quashing; and of course doubly *obiter* so far as the Convention is concerned. The argument does however underline the need for caution in seeking to apply the supposed Convention rules as to 'fair trial'. The overriding obligation under the Convention to consider the fairness of the proceedings as a whole before condemning them as a breach of Article 6 makes it in fact very unlikely that a conviction that was achieved in breach of Article 6 would not be equally held to be in English domestic terms unsafe. Somewhat similarly, caution must be exercised before practices at an interlocutory or pre-trial stage that are alleged to be in breach of Article 6 are seen as requiring the abandonment of the whole proceedings: see the observations of the Divisional Court in *R.* v. *Stratford JJ ex p. Imbert The Times*, 25 February 1999.

7

EUROPEAN CONVENTION AND THE RULES OF CRIMAL PROCEDURE AND EVIDENCE IN ENGLAND

J.R. SPENCER*

Lord Justice Buxton starts his excellent paper with a section call 'an Englishman abroad' in which he gives his reaction to watching a French criminal trial. Although he is too polite to our neighbours to make the point expressly, I get the impression that he finds French trials a pretty rum affair. This view will certainly be shared by many British readers, some of whom will reason, 'If that apology for criminal trial is acceptable to our fellow Europeans, we needn't worry too much about our rules of criminal procedure and evidence being contrary to the European Convention on Human Rights'.

Over the last eight years, I have spent time both studying modern continental criminal procedure and teaching continental lawyers about ours. From that background I propose, first, to put a gloss on the hypothetical Englishman abroad's reaction to French trials and, secondly, to convey what I believe to be the reactions of many continental criminal lawyers towards criminal procedure in England. From this, I will make suggestions about the parts of our trial procedure which, from a continental perspective, might well be thought to fall foul of the European Convention. I shall then make particular mention of one of the ways in which the European Convention has already had an impact on trial procedure on the other side of the Channel. And I shall end with some general and rather pessimistic remarks about the drafting of the Human Rights Act and some possibly undesirable side-effects that it may have on criminal procedure in England in the next few years.

THE ENGLISHMAN ABROAD—AND THE ASPECTS OF CONTINENTAL CRIMINAL PROCEDURE THAT ARE LESS OBVIOUS

The first thing that often strikes English observers about French criminal trials—and criminal trials in other Continental countries—is that they seem to be very fast. We expect a trial to last a morning in an English magistrates' court, and perhaps two days in the Crown Court, but in France 'trials' seem to take perhaps 20 minutes. What the Englishman abroad often fails to grasp, however, is that in France—as in most other Continental countries—no such thing exists as pleading guilty. One of the most basic rules of a Continental criminal trial is that the court itself is has an official responsibility to attempt to find the truth: which means that it is not allowed to treat the defendant's admission as conclusive, but must look behind this at the other evidence. Thus when the Englishman abroad is stunned by the speed of continental trials he is not actually comparing like with like. Three-quarters, or perhaps seven-eighths of the cases he is watching would in England not be 'trials' at all, but non-trials resulting from a plea of guilty. Thus the French proceedings that shock him because they take only 20 minutes would, perhaps, in England take only ten. In England, dealing with even a particularly horrible murder can take as little as 30 minutes where the defendant obligingly pleads guilty[1]— a speed which would, in such a case, be viewed as quite indecent haste in most parts of continental Europe.

The second thing that the Englishman abroad notices about French and most other continental criminal trials is that the court starts off by hearing about the defendant's criminal record where—there as so often here—he has one. In so far as most French 'trials' are what would be in England guilty pleas, in which the only issue is the sentence, this is not particularly surprising. Where the defendant asserts his innocence, however, hearing his

---

* Professor of Law, University of Cambridge..
[1] See the case of *Armstrong*, *The Times*, 28 July 1995.

criminal record rehearsed does rightly come as something of a shock. Most continental lawyers, however, and most continental opinion seem to be unimpressed with the common law rule that prohibits the court from looking at the defendant's criminal record in order to help it decide whether he is guilty, which is felt to be illogical and sentimental. Even the Italians, who ditched their previous French-based code of criminal procedure in favour of an allegedly 'Anglo-Saxon' one in 1988, could not bring themselves to import this aspect of the common law of evidence as part of the package. (By contrast, there is wide disquiet on the Continent about the court in a contested case hearing the defendant's 'psychological profile'—and not all continental systems allow this.)

The third thing that strikes the Englishman abroad is that continental criminal trials usually take place without a jury. But the Englishman who is shocked by this often fails to understand two things.

The first is how rare, statistically, jury trials have now become in England. In Blackstone's day, jury trial was the almost invariable method by which criminal cases were decided. Today, it accounts for between 1 and 2 per cent of cases only. The huge majority of cases are handled by the magistrates' courts, and even in the 10 per cent or so that go to the Crown Court, most are dealt with by judge alone following a plea of guilty.[2]

The second is that continental Europeans do not all share the Anglo-Saxon's rosy view of jury trial. At the time of the Great Revolution, juries were introduced into France, on a short-lived wave of anglomania, whence they spread to the rest of Europe as the French overran it, bringing French criminal procedure with them. But the experience proved generally disappointing. Frenchmen, uneasily conscious that thousands executed in the Terror were sent on their way to the guillotine by juries, became sceptical about juries as a safeguard against State oppression and the conviction of the innocent. Whilst a few European countries have retained juries in the English form, most—like France itself—have replaced the traditional jury with some kind of composite panel in which both judges and lay persons sit together. (In France such courts, called *Cours d'assises*, try a very small number of the most serious cases.) In Holland—in some ways the most liberal democracy in Europe—juries do not exist at all. Seen by the Dutch as an unwelcome foreign imposition, juries were suppressed when the French were driven out of the Netherlands at the fall of Napoleon, and there is no desire to re-import them. Small wonder that when the European Convention on Human Rights was

drawn up, no one thought it essential to include a guarantee of jury trial!

A fourth thing that the Englishman abroad notices about a trial in France is the *dossier*—a big file, or pile of files, containing (in a serious case) a record of all the researches carried out ahead of trial by the *juge d'instruction*. To this document the president of the court makes frequent reference. An important element in this dossier will usually be the record of the various occasions on which the defendant was questioned by the *juge d'instruction*. The Englishman abroad is inclined to see this dossier, and the process by which it is compiled, as more than a little oppressive. It goes against the common lawyer's grain to think of the suspect-turned-defendant being repeatedly interrogated during the pre-trial phase when, in England, the police would have formally charged him and he would be thenceforth immune from further official questioning. It also seems to be making the prosecution's job too easy for them to put all this pre-collected material into the presiding judge's hands, for him to read and digest ahead of trial. For a large body of legal opinion on the Continent, however, the *dossier* and its compilation by an official person other than the police is thought to be an important safeguard for the innocent, as well as an deserved graveyard for the guilty. Being brought before a *juge d'instruction* (or the equivalent) is important for the innocent defendant, because it gives him an official opportunity to dispute or retract any confession he has made, or is said to have made, to the police. It also gives him the chance to suggest lines of enquiry to the *juge d'instruction* which would lead to the exposure of his innocence—lines which the *juge d'instruction* is expected to follow if they look serious, because it is the duty of a *juge d'instruction* to investigate *à charge et à décharge*. Furthermore the defence have—and always have had—full access to the whole *dossier* ahead of trial; which means (in principle at least) that they have, and have always had, access not only to the evidence on which the prosecution propose to base their case, but also what in England we call 'unused material'[3]. In fact, so strongly is a properly compiled *dossier* felt to be a safeguard for the innocent that a one usual complaint about French criminal procedure today is the fact that more and more cases are bypassing the *juge d'instruction* via forms of accelerated procedure where, in order to

---

[2] Even among educated lay people this is not generally understood. When I recently asked a number of my University colleagues to guess what proportion of criminal cases go to jury trial in England, the answers ranged from 20 per cent to 50!

[3] In practice, defence access to what we would call 'unused material' is sometimes limited by the failure of the authorities to include certain pieces of background information in the *dossier*. On this see Stewart Field, 'The Legal Framework of Covert and Proactive Policing in France'; Ed Cape and Taru Spronken, 'Proactive Policing: Limiting the Role of the Defence Lawyer' and J.R.Spencer, 'Proactive Policing the Principles of Immediacy and Orality', all in Stewart Field and Caroline Pelser (eds.), *Invading the Private: State Accountability and New Investigative Methods in Europe* (Aldershot: Dartmouth, 1998).

save time and money, the *dossier*—such as it is—is compiled by the police.

Nobody should imagine, of course, that continental lawyers believe their criminal procedure to be perfect. Complaints are often made. And it is unwise to generalise about them, because criminal procedure on the Continent varies from place to place, and the complaints vary with it. (And in deciding how much weight to put on them, it is important to remember that in the continental systems, the Bar never prosecutes and public prosecutors—who in some countries are jointly trained and administered with the judges—never defend. In consequence, informed legal opinion about criminal procedure tends to be sharply polarised in a way that it is not in the United Kingdom.[4])

In France, two of the most serious complaints that are heard concern not the trial stage, but what goes on before the trial. The first concerns the *garde à vue*—in English terms, the power of the police to detain for questioning. It is widely felt that at this stage in the proceedings the suspect has too few safeguards and the police too extensive powers.[5] The second concerns delay, particularly in serious and complex cases. The traditional exhaustive investigation by a *juge d'instruction* has a corresponding disadvantage, which is that it takes time. Where things go wrong with it, as sometimes happens, it can take a very long time indeed: cases can sometimes take four or five years to come to trial—or even longer. This problem is accentuated by the fact that in France it is the *juge d'instruction* who also decides whether the suspect is released on bail or not, and French practice has traditionally been to keep in custody many people who in England would be released on bail.

Some criticisms are also heard relating to the *audience de jugement* (i.e. trial). In the continental systems that remain most faithful to the French model[6]

the defendant and the witnesses are examined by the presiding judge; judges, on the whole, are happy with this arrangement, but many barristers (to use the English term to describe the continental near-equivalent) think it would be fairer if this job were done, as in England, by the prosecution and defence. In France and the systems that most closely follow it, the *procès verbaux*[7] of the pre-trial questioning of witnesses count in principle as evidence, even if the original maker of the statement does not appear at trial to testify orally and to subject himself to questioning. This too has given rise to criticism—of which more later in this paper.

THE FOREIGNER ABROAD—ENGLISH CRIMINAL PROCEDURE WHEN SEEN THROUGH EUROPEAN EYES

The not-so-well-informed foreigner abroad goes to the Old Bailey where he watches part of a jury trial, and initially assumes that this is how all criminal offences are handled. If he (or she) has English friends, he sometimes asks them how this country can afford to provide this Rolls-Royce trial for every common criminal and crime, and learns to his surprise that we do not; that most cases are handled by the magistrates' courts, and that even in the Crown Court most defendants opt out of jury trial by pleading guilty. Increasingly puzzled, the foreigner asks why this is so: what is it about English criminals, as compared with French or Dutch or German ones, that makes them so keen to admit their guilt? And when he learns that this happens in part because we reward guilty pleas by offering a reduction in the sentence of around 30 per cent, his astonishment knows no bounds. Continental judges and prosecutors usually think the idea is outrageous, because it means guilty people getting more lenient sentences than their crimes deserve. Defence lawyers point out that routinely giving lighter sentences to the majority of defendants who plead guilty is the same as routinely giving heavier sentences to the minority who exercise their right to make the State prove them guilty as alleged, and ask how we think this is compatible with the 'fair trial' requirement in Article 6(1) of the European Convention, and—more particularly—with Article 6(2): 'everyone charged with a criminal offence shall be presumed innocent until proved guilty according to law'. Well-informed continental lawyers also ask how this squares with the rule of English evidence under which extra-judicial confessions are excluded if they were produced by threats or promises. And they also ask how, under such a system,

[4] In his book *Presumed Guilty—the British Legal System Exposed* (Mandarin, 1993) Michael Mansfield criticises English criminal procedure bitterly and says we could solve its problems if we borrowed heavily from France. His source of information on the French system was, as he explains, a *juge d'instruction*. If he had spoken to an *avocat* instead, I believe he would have written a very different book.

[5] The French police can hold a suspect for 24 hours, extensible to 48 on the authorisation of the public prosecutor. Before 1993 the suspect had no right to see a lawyer. In 1993 he acquired the right to see one, but only after 20 hours had elapsed! At the time of writing, the government has introduced legislation to widen the suspect's rights.

[6] As derived from Napoleon's *Code d'instruction criminelle* of 1808. This represented a compromise between pre-Revolutionary French criminal procedure and the procedure installed by the Revolutionaries, which contained elements borrowed from the common law. The *Code d'instruction criminelle* was imposed on most of western Europe during the French occupation; but the involuntary recipients chose to keep it, usually with their own modifications, after 1814.

[7] I.e. official written records.

we avoid innocent persons being pressured to admit crimes they did not commit by the threat of heavier punishment if they continue to assert their innocence.[8] I have used forceful language to describe the Continental reaction to our 'sentence discount', but I do not think that I am exaggerating. Although in England the desirability of this practice seems to be the one single issue on which judges, barristers and Home Office officials habitually agree, I really do believe that this is one aspect of English criminal procedure that might one day be found in conflict with the Convention.

Let us suppose that the foreigner abroad has recovered from this shock, and that the conversation with his English friend comes back to jury trials. 'I waited around the corridors of the Old Bailey for a couple of days while the jury were considering their verdict' says the foreigner, 'and I was surprised to find that after all that time, the only thing they said was "guilty". How much longer will parties have to wait before they get the jury's written reasons?' The foreigner then suffers another shock when he learns that in England juries never give their reasons—and that far from seeing anything wrong with this, we actually fine and imprison people for trying to find out what those reasons were.[9] To the Continental lawyer, the requirement that a court should give reasons for its decision is regarded as an essential safeguard against arbitrary criminal justice. Some countries, like the Netherlands, for example, even go to the extent of writing it into their national constitutions.[10] What is meant by a 'reasoned decision' varies of course from one European country to another. In some, like Italy, the court must actually explain why it believed one lot of evidence rather than another.[11] In others, like France, a *motivation* can be more rudimentary. In France, furthermore, juries in the *cour d'assises* are excused from the duty to produce reasons. But in France, unlike in England, this is a matter for disquiet, not congratulation.[12] In broad terms, the more important the case, the more important it seems to continental lawyers that the

court should be required to give its reasons. To them, it would seem particularly perverse that English magistrates, who decide the less serious cases, can be required to produce reasons for their acquittals or convictions, whilst English juries, which decide the more serious ones, are not merely excused from giving reasons, but are actually forbidden to do so. Here too, I believe, there is a risk that one day English criminal procedure may found not to deliver the 'fair trial' that is guaranteed by Article 6(1) of the Convention—a right that certainly includes in principle the right to a reasoned decision.[13]

Another thing that often strikes the foreign visitor unfavourably about English criminal procedure is the weak position of the victim. Not only does the English victim lack the right, enjoyed by victims in many Continental countries, to become an official party to the proceedings (*partie civile*). The alleged victim, particularly in a sex case, is likely to be put through an unpleasant ordeal in the witness-box. Our general insistence on oral evidence, and our practice of examining even vulnerable witnesses adversarially, mean that the ordeal the English victim undergoes in court is often both longer and nastier than what happens to her or his counterpart in continental Europe: and the habits of our tabloid press often make sure that the degrading details are relayed to a national audience, even if nowadays the victim will be described as someone 'who cannot be named for legal reasons'. At first sight, this might seem to have nothing much to do with the Convention. Articles 5 and 6, which are the ones principally relevant to criminal procedure, are exclusively concerned with the rights of suspects and defendants. However, article 8 of the Convention protects the right to 'privacy and family life'. In *X* v. *The Netherlands*[14] the European Court of Human Rights upheld a complaint by a mentally handicapped woman that Dutch criminal procedure wrongly made it impossible to prosecute the son-in-law of the directress of the residential home in which she lived for taking sexual advantage of her. This failure, said the ECHR, meant that Dutch law failed properly to protect her right to privacy. It may well be that the current English rules of evidence, which make many mentally handicapped persons incompetent as witnesses, potentially bring this country into a similar difficulty.[15] It

---

[8] Cf. Andrew Ashworth, *The Criminal Process—an Evaluative Study* (Oxford: OUP, 1994), 275–84.

[9] Contempt of Court Act 1981 s.8.

[10] Grondwet, art. 121: 'Except where law otherwise provides, courts shall sit in public and their decisions shall contain the grounds on which they are based . . .' See Geert Corstens, *Het nederlands strafprocesrecht* (2nd ed., 1995) 583–6.

[11] Code of Criminal Procedure, Art. 546.

[12] 'These are the arguments for and against the jury. It would be impossible, nowadays, to have this institution suppressed, because it has entered into our spirit and is often seen in France as the most obvious expression of democracy. But perhaps a step forward is necessary in order to make sure that the Cour d'assises give reasons for their decisions, and to remove the oracular quality from their verdicts, which are sometimes flatly contrary to the simplest truth . . .' R. Merle and A. Vitu, Traité de droit criminel—procédure pénale (4th edn., 1989), 603.

[13] Van Dijk and Van Hoof, *Theory and Practice of the European Convention on Human Rights*, (3rd edn., 1998), 324. Three respected British commentators say that 'In the case of a jury trial, given that such trials are not contrary to article 6, the requirement to give reasons must be limited so as to take account of the way that jury trials operate': D.J.Harris, M.O'Boyle and C.Warbrick, *Law of the European Convention on Human Rights* (1995), .215). *Sed quaere*.

[14] (1985) Series A No 91.

[15] The Youth Justice and Criminal Evidence Act 1999, which received the Royal Assent just as this paper finally went to press, will make such persons competent.

is also not beyond the bounds of possibility that our current rules, which make it virtually impossible to clear the court when adult witnesses give evidence in sex cases and easy for the newspapers to publicise their testimony when they do, could some day also be held in breach of Article 8. Of course, there is serious a complication here, because whereas Article 8 of the Convention protects the right of privacy, Article 10 also protects the right of free speech. As far as the English courts are concerned, section 12 of the Human Rights Act—enacted with a genuflection towards the media—instructs our national courts to give free speech a high priority where this conflicts with other convention rights. But it is possible that the Strasbourg court might be less in awe of the media than is the UK Parliament[16].

ARTICLE 6 (3)(D) OF THE CONVENTION— ORALITY AND CONFRONTATION

I shall now turn to one of the possible conflicts between English criminal procedure and the Convention which Buxton LJ discusses in detail in his paper: the principle of orality and confrontation as enunciated by Article 6(3)(d). This enumerates, among the other minimum rights guaranteed to defendants in criminal cases, the right:

'to examine or have examined witnesses against him and to obtain the attendance and examination of witnesses on his behalf under the same conditions as witnesses against him.'

As Buxton LJ explains, this provision has already attracted the attention of a number of writers on the English law of evidence, and has already been considered by our Court of Appeal. He seems to share the view of certain other commentators that this provision could in future spell big trouble for us.

In this respect I am less worried than he is. I am less happy than he is with the current state of English law, and more inclined to think than an intelligent application of Article 6(3)(d) would actually improve it.

In order to evaluate the likely impact of Article 6(3)(d), I think it is sensible to look at the various decisions of the ECHR in the context of what had been previously been going on in the various national legal systems from which the cases came.

All the key cases came from jurisdictions where criminal procedure was based on the traditional French model, one aspect of which is that (to put it into English

terms) there is no hearsay rule and the *procès-verbaux* of any previous official interrogation of the witnesses are treated as admissible evidence. In the past, this used to mean that the prosecution could invite the court to convict a defendant—even in what we would recognise as a 'fought case'—on the basis of the written statement of a witness who did not give evidence at trial. In the days when all serious cases were handled by a *juge d'instruction* this did not greatly matter, because (at least in France) the *juge d'instruction* usually arranges *une confrontation* between the defence and any accusing witness whose evidence the defence disputes. However, the declining use of *juges d'instruction* meant an increasing number of cases in which the court was invited to convict on the basis of what were, in effect, police witness-statements: *procès-verbaux* of police interviews with witnesses, who did not attend trial, and whom the defence had had no earlier chance to question. To make matters even worse for the defence, the rule that *procès-verbaux* count as evidence was also made the basis for introducing anonymous testimony. In the Netherlands, particularly, prosecutors began to invite the courts to convict on the basis of written statements taken ahead of trial from persons whom the defence were not only unable to confront or question, but whose identity itself remained concealed: informers, and sometimes under-cover police officers.

It is against this background that the European Court of Human Rights has decided a string of important cases under article 6(3)(d).[17] On my reading, the rule to be deduced from them is that Article 6(3)(d) requires the defence, in principle, to be allowed a chance to confront and question all persons on whose evidence the prosecution relies and whose evidence the defence contests; that this requirement is satisfied whether the opportunity was given in the course of a pre-trial *instruction*, or at the trial itself; that despite this general requirement, evidence from untested and even anonymous sources may be admissible in extraordinary circumstances—both where it is genuinely impossible for the evidence to be tested by the defence (e.g. because the witness is dead), and where allowing such a confrontation would put the witness in real danger (e.g. because the defendant's friends, having discovered his identity, would kill him); but that where such untested evidence is admitted, the conviction must not be based on this alone. My view is that, in the systems where they came from, these decisions have effected a much-needed reform. Their result is that in in countries like France, Holland and

---

[16] As originally conceived, the Youth and Criminal Evidence Bill would have given the court the power to evict not only the public but also the press when certain types of witness are giving evidence; but this did not survive to become part of what is now the Youth Justice and Criminal Evidence Act 1999.

[17] *Unterpertinger* v. *Austria* (1991) 13 EHRR 175; *Kostovski* v. *The Netherlands* (1990) 12 EHRR 434; *Delta* v. *France* (1993) 16 EHRR 574; *Saidi* v. *France* (1994) 17 EHRR 251; *Doorson* v. *The Netherlands* (1996) 22 EHRR 330; *Van Mechelen* v. *The Netherlands* (1998) 25 EHRR 647.

Austria, it is no longer possible for the courts to convict a defendant on the basis of written *dossiers* made up of statements taken from witnesses whom the defence have not been able to confront or question. '*Verhoor getuigen AH-overval doet rechtbank zelf*', proclaimed a headline in a Dutch newspaper that I saw in 1993.[18] This means (I think!) 'The trial court in the AH robbery case intends to hear the witnesses itself'; a course of action so obvious that it would not be worth mentioning in England, but which in 1993 seemed sufficiently unusual in the Netherlands for a serious newspaper to make a story of it.

If such was the base-line against which the case law on Article 6(3)(d) developed, we might initially suppose that English law has little to worry about in this respect. Some years ago, this might indeed have been the case. But it is questionable, in my view, whether this is so today. English law, like every other system that values the principle of orality and immediacy, has had to make some allowance for the problem of the presumptively honest witness who is genuinely unable to testify at trial. But regrettably, I think the way we have changed the law over the last ten years to do this is an undesirable one, and goes against the values that Article 6(3)(d) has forced some of our Continental neighbours to adopt.

For centuries, the trial of any serious offence was invariably preceded by what we now call an 'old-style committal', in which a magistrate heard the prosecution witnesses orally on oath, the defence had a chance to put their questions, and the resulting deposition was taken down in writing. In most cases this was, of course, a tremendous waste of time. But it did have one real advantage in that it preserved the evidence of key witnesses in a reliable and pre-tested form—which could then be used at trial if the witness died or disappeared.[19] This procedure was supplemented by various piecemeal provisions under which magistrates could, subject to similar safeguards, take depositions from certain witnesses who were thought unlikely to be able to testify at trial. In recent years there has been an official drive to suppress committal proceedings, and with them the provisions about special depositions.[20] At the same time, Parliament has created various new exceptions to the hearsay evidence rule, which make admissible in evidence the statements that absent witnesses gave to the police. The 'documentary hearsay'

provisions of the Criminal Justice Act 1988 permit this in limited circumstances. In 1996, these were followed by some new provisions in the Criminal Procedure and Investigations Act, the astonishing—and possibly unintended—effect of which seems to be to render witness-statements taken by the police admissible at trials on indictment virtually whenever the presiding judge thinks that this would be a good idea.[21] Then, two years later, this was followed by the Criminal Justice (Terrorism and Conspiracy) Act 1998, one provision of which now renders admissible as showing that a defendant belongs to a terrorist organisation the opinion of a police officer that he does so. As the police officer's opinion will often be founded on what an anonymous informer told him, this provision opens the door—in effect—to testimony from anonymous witnesses.

As I am less happy with the statutory hearsay provisions than Buxton LJ is, I do not share his unease at the thought that we might have to reintroduce some of the old procedures for taking formal depositions to avoid trouble with the Convention. It seems obvious to me that there is no way in which a police witness-statement can be as good and reliable a piece of evidence as a statement taken by a judge or magistrate, in the course of which the witness is put on oath and asked questions by the defence. I therefore think—as I have explained elsewhere[22]—that we ought to set up a machinery that enables us to preserve the evidence of certain witnesses in this form in those cases where it is possible to do so. This was recognised in Italy when in 1988 they introduced a new 'Anglo-Saxon' criminal procedure, which in principle relies on oral evidence at trial rather than on written *procès-verbaux*. In order to alleviate the most obvious problems of disappearing witnesses and evidence, the Italian system incorporates something called an *incidente probatorio*, under which the evidence of a witness who looks as if he may be unavailable at trial can be formally heard and recorded in advance of trial before a judge. This idea was also put forward in England by the Pigot Committee in 1989, which recommended a similar arrangement for taking the evidence of children,[23] although the Home Office of the day would not accept it. If compliance with Article 6(3)(d) of Convention pushes us in this direction, I for one shall not be sorry.

---

[18] *NRC Handelsblad*, 8 September 1993.

[19] Glanville Williams, 'Power to Expedite Criminal Trials' [1959] *Crim. LR* 82.

[20] Like s. 105 of the Magistrates' Courts Act 1980, a provision dating from the 19th century which permitted depositions to be taken from persons dangerously ill, now repealed by Sch. 1 of the Criminal Procedure and Investigations Act 1996.

[21] See *Emmins on Criminal Procedure* (7th edn., 1997) 277–8.

[22] 'Orality and the Evidence of Absent Witnesses' [1994] *Crim. LR* 628.

[23] Report of the Advisory Group on Video Evidence (Home Office, December 1989).

A FINAL POINT: HOW WILL THE HUMAN RIGHTS ACT AFFECT ENGLISH CRIMINAL PROCEDURE?

The first part of this paper has been concerned with the possible impact of the Convention on current English criminal procedure. This final section is about a connected but different point—namely, the possible impact in this area of the Human Rights Act itself, rather than the Convention that it was designed to make 'directly effective'.

Will the Act achieve its purpose, in so far as this was to enable the English courts to resolve conflicts between the Convention and English criminal procedure themselves, and without the cases being decided against us—to our international embarrassment—in Strasbourg? I have an uneasy feeling that the answer here is 'no'.

In my opinion, the major threat to human rights in criminal procedure these days is not so much case law but statute: and in particular, laws rushed through Parliament in times of moral panic by governments who know they have a problem, do not know what to do about it, but feel an urgent need to be seen to be doing something.

However, as we all know, the Human Rights Act neither stops Parliament enacting laws that interfere with Convention rights, nor frees the courts from their obligation to obey them if it does. If, to take an extreme and (I hope!) fanciful example, a future law-and-order Parliament decided to re-enact Henry VIII's Statute for the Boiling of Poisoners,[24] British judges would have to sentence poisoners to be boiled. The most they could do about it would be to issue a 'declaration of incompatibility'—and encourage all concerned to take the case to Strasbourg. To take a less fanciful example, the Criminal Justice (Terrorism and Conspiracy) Act 1998, which contains the previously-mentioned provisions

about policemen's opinion evidence, was hurried through Parliament in two days in the wake of the Omagh bombing, at the very time Parliament was also engaged in passing the Human Rights Act. If our courts find the provisions of this Act to be incompatible with the Convention, they will have to apply them nonetheless. Thus despite the Human Rights Act, English criminal procedure will not necessarily escape occasional embarrassing examination in Strasbourg.

On the other hand, the Human Rights Act certainly does require the courts to depart from case law if this can be shown to be contrary to Convention Rights. This means that, although the English courts will not be able to overturn statutes, every decision of an English court that has settled—however sensibly—a disputed point of criminal procedure or evidence stands to be reopened by defence counsel in an attempt to persuade the courts to reconsider the matter in the light of the Convention, and in particular the amorphous requirement in Article 6(1) of a 'fair trial'.

Some years ago, English case law gave defendants a new right, which is to ask the court to stop the prosecution because it amounts to an 'abuse of process'. Abuse of process is a concept which—like 'fair trial'—is distinctly vague, and over a few years it has given rise to a large body of reported cases. If this new doctrine of abuse of process has sometimes enabled justice to be done, it is equally true that 'abuse of process' is sometimes argued—with waste of time—in cases devoid of merit, and that it is therefore something that has helped to make English criminal procedure even slower and more expensive than it was before. If we are pessimistic, it is possible to foresee the Human Rights Act working out in a similar way. In dealing with unmeritorious arguments based on the Convention, I expect that our judges will heed Buxton LJ's advice to keep their nerve and preserve their faith in the underlying common sense and fairness of the common law. But even unmeritorious arguments that ultimately fail can take up valuable time and public resources.

---

[24] (1530) 22 Hen. VIII ch.9.

8

INVESTIGATION AND SURVEILLANCE

THE RT. HON. LORD JUSTICE AULD

A NEW WAY OF THINKING

Michael Beloff has described as 'impressive' the readiness and resourcefulness of the United Kingdom judiciary in making use of the European Convention before incorporation.[1] Whilst that may be true of the higher judiciary, in particular the House of Lords, lesser judicial mortals may take some time to get the hang of it. As one of the latter, I am enthusiastic about the advent, but nervous about the mechanics of application, of human rights to our domestic law.

Inspired by the compelling advocacy of those who have fought so hard and long for the statutory incorporation of the European Convention, not least by Lord Lester, I am determined to take human rights seriously and to give them practical effect where our domestic law is lacking. However, you will detect in my use of the word 'determined' some anxiety about the task. That is because—like many other United Kingdom judges—I am unfamiliar with and uneasy about the use of such grand concepts as fundamental rights, whatever their provenance, as working tools in the daily determination of cases. Judicial training is necessary and urgent; a sympathetic and constructive judicial attitude to the new legal order is vital[2]; and in cases like mine some preliminary psychiatric treatment would also come in handy to broaden the focus of what pass for my judicial thought processes.

GUIDANCE RATHER THAN REGULATION—THE MARGIN OF APPRECIATION

This paper is mainly concerned with the impact of the Convention right of respect for privacy on the conduct and final outcome of a criminal trial in the United Kingdom. Section 6 of the Human Rights Act 1998 requires courts to regard as unlawful breaches by public authorities of Convention rights unless such conduct was required by or in pursuance of or compatible with primary legislation. Section 2(1) of the Act provides that a court or tribunal, in determining a question in connection with a Convention right, 'must take into account' relevant decisions or opinions of the ECHR etc. As to a remedy for an unlawful breach of a Convention right, section 7(1) enables a victim (a) to bring proceedings against the authority or (b) to 'rely on the Convention right in any legal proceedings'. As to the latter, the Act does not provide that a breach is necessarily a defence to a criminal proceeding;[3] section 8(1) provides courts and tribunals with a broad discretion as to how it should mark such a breach, viz., 'it may grant such relief or remedy, or make such order, within its powers as it considers just and appropriate'.

As Buxton LJ has observed,[4] the provision in section 2(1) that courts and tribunals 'must take account of' ECHR jurisprudence is 'a comparatively weak form of guidance'. That is so both as to the fact of breach and as to the way in which it should be marked in each individual case, not always distinct questions.

[1] John Maurice Kelly Memorial Lecture in Dublin in October 1997.

[2] See Lord Cooke, 'The New Zealand Experience' [1997] *EHRLR* 490, at 495.

[3] Consistently with the approach of the ECHR; see e.g. *Saunders* v. *UK* (1996) 24 EHRR 313.

[4] Ch. 6 above.

THE RIGHT TO RESPECT FOR PRIVACY

As to the right of privacy provided by Article 8—or as it describes it, the 'right to respect for private and family life', the Article provides:

1. 'Everyone has the right to respect for his private and family life, his home and his correspondence.
2. There shall be no interference by a public authority with the exercise of this right except such as is *in accordance with the law* and is *necessary* in a democratic society in the interests of national security, public safety or the economic well-being of the country, *for the prevention of disorder or crime*, for the protection of health or morals, or for the protection of the rights and freedoms of others' [my emphases].

See also Article 1 of the First Protocol, entitling every person 'to the peaceful enjoyment of his possessions'.

Acknowledging a 'right of privacy', or the more positive notion[5] of a right of 'respect' for it, is one thing; drawing the legal boundaries of that right in particular circumstances is another; determining the effect on a criminal trial and on its final outcome of a breach of those boundaries is yet another. My first impression in this context is that the right, in its definition and application and in the effect of its breach, has soft edges.

But for our statutory incorporation of this right, the courts may well have developed it as part of the common law.[6] The Supreme Court of the United States has long recognised such a right, albeit by reference to the US Constitution.[7] However, although the notion will soon be here as part of our statutory law, there will still much work for the courts in determining the forms and extent of its application.

As good a starting point as any is that of Brandeis J in 1928,[8] who spoke of 'the right to be let alone'. But it is only a starting point. Intrusive investigation and surveillance may take other and less technical forms than those provided for by Part III of the Police Act 1997 and the other statutes[9] referred to by Madeleine Colvin in the excellent Report of Justice, 'Under Surveillance— Covert Policing and Human Rights' and in her equally valuable paper for this Conference. There are degrees of privacy and any number of ways in which there can be greater or less intrusion on it. Is it, as a number of academic commentators have suggested, 'a condition of limited accessibility'?[10] How private, for example, is a confidential garden conversation deliberately listened to by a non trespassing policeman on the other side of the hedge or in a restaurant or bar, or the content of confidential papers left carelessly around, or the breach of a volunteered confidence? How private is the conduct of an offender in his home viewed through an open window from afar through binoculars? Even if private for this purpose, does the intrusion count as unlawful simply because it is intrusion and is not expressly permitted or regulated by domestic law?

Whilst United Kingdom courts will soon have to exercise their functions consistently and in conformity with the Convention, the test by which such compliance will fall to be judged is one of considerable generality, leaving a margin of appreciation to meet our system, its procedures and the individual facts of each case. See, as an example of the ECHR's acknowledgement of this scope for national determination, its decision in *Handyside* v. *UK*[11] in which, speaking of restrictions on the right to freedom of expression, it stated:

'By reason of their direct and continuous contact with the vital forces of their countries, state authorities are in principle in a better position than the international judge to give an opinion on the exact content of these requirements as well as on the "necessity" of a "restriction" or "penalty" intended to meet them.'

There is nothing new or peculiar to European Human Rights about this; it is a familiar and inevitable feature of the application of law of a 'federal' nature to a collection of legal systems of different origins and legal traditions. Holmes J stated the blunt necessity for it as long ago as 1905[12] in relation to the United States Constitution:

'The Constitution is made for people of fundamentally

---

[5] See Gomien, Harris and Zwaak, the main contributors to a recent work published under the ægis of the European Directorate of Human Rights, *Law and practice of the European Convention on Human Rights and European Social Charter* (1996), 228–31.

[6] In *R.* v. *Khan (Sultan)* [1997] AC 558 (HL), Lords Browne-Wilkinson, Slynn and Nicholls reserved for future decision the question whether there was a general right of privacy in English law.

[7] The US Constitution does not expressly mention a right of privacy, but the Supreme Court has held in a line of decisions that it provided for it, drawing on the concept of personal liberty and restrictions upon state action in the Fourteenth Amendment and/or the reservation of right to the people in the Ninth Amendment; see *per* Blackmun J, giving the opinion of the majority in the abortion case of *Roe* v. *Wade*, 410 US 113 (1973).

[8] In a dissenting judgment, in which the majority upheld the government's right to place wiretaps on telephones without judicial warrants, repeating almost word for word an article he had written about 40 years before in the *Harvard Law Review* (1980) entitled 'The Right to Privacy'.

[9] Interception of Communications Act 1985; Security Service Acts of 1989 and 1996; and Intelligence Services Act 1994.

[10] See Elizabeth Paton-Simpson, 'Private Circles and Public Squares: Invasion of Privacy by the Publication of "Private" Facts' (1998) 61 *MLR* 318, 319 and the references there given.

[11] 1 EHRR 737 (1979–80),, at 753–4, para. 48.

[12] In *Lochner* v. *New York*, 198 US 45, 76 (1905).

differing views, and the accident of our finding certain opinions natural and familiar or novel and even shocking ought not to conclude our judgment upon the question whether statutes embodying them conflict with the Constitution of the United States.'

The ECHR has indicated that the margin of appreciation is narrower than that of *Wednesbury* rationality.[13] However, the sheer breadth of the Convention's descriptions of some of its rights, in particular in this context, to 'respect for private and family life' and to 'a fair hearing', leaves a considerable margin for decision even on that narrower test.

Concentrating for the moment on the right to respect for privacy, there are the heavily qualified provisions in Article 8.2 permitting interference with it for the purposes there specified. To justify such interference for any of those purposes, the act must be 'in accordance with the law', it must be 'necessary', that is, there must be a pressing social need for it, and it must be 'proportionate'. There must also be some adequate system of regulation to enable the courts to satisfy themselves as a matter of fact that there has been no abuse.

As to the lawfulness of the act, this must mean lawfulness according to the domestic law of each member state. Madeleine Colvin, in introducing the 1998 Justice Report, commented on the increasing use by enforcement authorities of ever more sophisticated technologies in their investigation of crime, and concluded that:

'the present legislative and procedural framework governing . . . [modern surveillance] activities is out of date, inconsistent and unable to provide the safeguards required to ensure fairness, accountability and compliance with the Human Rights Act 1998.'

The criticisms made in the Report, and again by Madeleine in her paper for this Conference, of the inadequacies of the present and proposed[14] statutory regulation of the various forms of technological surveillance are well made. There is a need for some comprehensive statutory system regulating the use of surveillance devices and methods by the police and other enforcement authorities, and one which has regard to the Convention right of respect to privacy and ECHR jurisprudence giving effect to it. However, given the constant development of new technology in the field and of the increasingly innovative and vigorous forms of police investigation, it cannot be expected that such a code, even with regular up-dating, will provide for all forms of intrusive technological investigation.

Moreover, as I have indicated, much intrusive investigation of crime will continue in its old-fashioned, non-technological way; there is clearly a limit to the comprehensiveness of statutory regulation in this field.

The Justice Report appears to equate lawfulness—or as it is put in Article 8.2, 'in accordance with the law'—with an express statutory grant of power to do the act in question. Thus, at pages 8 and 10 it appears to regard as illegal an activity which has not been made the subject of statutory regulation and enforcement; at page 11 it speaks of the ECHR's requirement for this purpose[15] of 'a clear basis in law: either in an Act of Parliament or common law rule'. As to the latter, it apparently has in mind a common law rule positively authorising the activity in question, as distinct from not prohibiting it, because the next sentence states, in clear reference to some of the existing procedures:

'A Home Office Circular or set of guidelines is incapable of satisfying this requirement. Such laws must be readily accessible and adequately precise so that citizens will be aware of the circumstances in which they apply.'

As Lord Nolan reminded us in *Khan (Sultan)*,[16] 'under English law, there is in general nothing unlawful about a breach of privacy'. The advent of the Convention right to respect for privacy in Article 8.1, coupled with its relaxation by Article 8.2 if lawful and necessary for one of the specified purposes, did not at first sight seem to me to require as a qualification for relaxation that the activity in question has been expressly authorised and regulated by domestic law. However, there are indications in the jurisprudence of the ECHR that the obligation in Article 8.1 to secure 'respect' for the right to privacy may in certain circumstances require member states, in their application of the safeguards for relaxation in Article 8.2, positively to provide for such safeguards, particularly in the case of the conduct of public authorities.[17]

This is no doubt an example of what the Lord Chancellor had in mind in his recent statement[18] that the Convention represents a switch from the traditional common law approach to the protection of civil liberties, described by Dicey in 1885[19] as a 'negative' right, to a positive guarantee of such a right.[20] It is also a good

---

[13] The decision must be based on an 'acceptable assessment of the relevant facts'; and see per Simon Brown LJ in *Ex p. Smith*, describing it as 'only . . . a limited "margin of appreciation"': [1996] QB 517, 541.

[14] I.e. Part III of the Police Act 1997.

[15] In *Malone* v. *UK* (1985) 7 EHRR 14 and *Huvig* v. *France* (1990) 12 EHRR 528.

[16] N. 6 above, at 175.

[17] See e.g. *Johnston & Ors* (1986) Series A no. 112, 25, para. 55; *Airey* v. *Ireland* (1979) Series A no. 32, 17, paras. 32–3; and *Halford* v. *UK* (1997) 24 EHRR 523, at 544, para. 49.

[18] 'Rights Brought Home' *1998/99 The Inner Temple Yearbook* 8.

[19] 'Introduction' to the *Study of Law of the Constitution*.

[20] Cf. Gomien, Harris and Zwaak, who, n. 5 above at 157, express the view that 'Article 6 is arguably the only Article . . . that creates an exclusively affirmative obligation for the High Contracting Parties, rather than an obligation that, at least in part, requires a state to refrain from interfering in the exercise of a right by an individual'.

example of the need for newcomers to the jurisprudence of human rights to beware of adopting old jurisprudential tools for new tasks. Nevertheless, the approaches of the ECHR and the Commission are not entirely consistent on this matter[21]; and, as a matter of practicality a state cannot reasonably be expected to legislate for—so as positively to render lawful and regulate—all forms of possible intrusive conduct by public authorities in the investigation of crime.

I say nothing about the requirement of 'necessity' in Article 8.2 as part of the justification for relaxation of the right to respect for privacy provided in Article 8.1. The concepts of pressing social need and proportionality are already well recognised in our law; and that slippery concept, 'margin of appreciation', is all important. I can add nothing of value in a paper such as this to Madeleine Colvin's succinct treatment of the matter in the Justice Report and in her paper for this Conference.

THE RIGHT TO A FAIR HEARING

The Convention right to respect for privacy is further softened, in the context of investigation and surveillance of criminal activity, by its inter-action with the right to a fair hearing contained in Article 6. Article 6, which is headed 'Right to a fair trial', provides in Article 6(1) that '[i]n the determination of . . . any criminal charge against him, everyone is entitled to a fair and public hearing'. It continues by indicating some, but not all, particular respects in which that is to be achieved.

In future, United Kingdom courts will have to determine the admissibility of evidence of surveillance and other forms of investigation in criminal cases in accordance with the provisions of the Convention. In doing so, they will be required to 'take into account', *inter alia*, the jurisprudence of the ECHR. The trouble is that Article 6, in its provision of the right to a fair hearing, states precepts of a general nature, all too familiar in the common law and in section 78 of the Police and Criminal Evidence Act 1984. Moreover, the ECHR has described its task under Article 6 as the determination whether 'the proceedings in their entirety, including the way in which the evidence was taken, were fair'[22].

Article 6, on its own terms, and the stance of the ECHR give little practical guidance as to the effect and application of this broad test on a case by case basis. The ECHR, when it has considered the matter, has acknowledged the widely differing approaches of member states to the investigation and manner of trial of crime, and has resorted to the overall fairness of the proceedings, leaving to each member state the detailed manner of its achievement of that end. Where it is considered that there is no relaxation under Article 8.2, that is, that the surveillance or other investigative methods are a breach of the right to respect to privacy under Article 8.1, the criminal court at first instance must go on to consider the effect, if any, that the breach should have on the criminal trial. That is where the right to a fair hearing under Article 6 and the ECHR's principle of 'equality of arms' come into play. In particular, the court should consider whether the undoubted breach should be reflected by exclusion of the evidence because it would be unfair to admit it.

Part III of the Police Act 1997 does not appear to affect or create an exception to that general rule. As Peter Carter, QC has recently observed[23] (subject to the establishment in English law of a right of privacy), the complex and flexible provisions of that Act and the likely uncertainty in many cases whether there has been a material breach of them 'all clearly suggest that, in the absence of strong policy arguments to the contrary, evidence obtained as a result of a breach ought not be treated per se inadmissible'. Thus, his view is that there is nothing in the 1997 Act to unseat the rule in *Sang*, and as applied to section 78 in *Khan (Sultan)*, that, absent unfairness in the proceedings in admitting illegally obtained evidence other than post-offence admissions or confessions, a trial judge has no discretion to exclude relevant and admissible evidence on the ground that it was illegally obtained.[24]

However, as Peter Carter acknowledged,[25] and Lord Nolan stated in *Khan (Sultan)*,[26] a breach of Article 8 would, as a matter of common sense, be a relevant consideration to the exercise of the common law or section 78 'discretion'[27] to exclude unfair evidence. Nevertheless, as I have said, it is uncertain how much

---

[21] Cf. the Commission's rulings in *Hutcheon* v. *UK*, 27 November 1996; *Smith* v. *UK* [1997] EHRLR 277; and Commission ruling in *Contrera* v. *Spain*, 11 April 1997; see also Gomien, Harris and Zwaak, n. 5 above, 229–31.

[22] *Saidi* v. *France* (1994) 17 EHRR 251, at 269, para. 43.

[23] In his article, 'Evidence Obtained by Listening Device' (1997) 113 *LQR* 468, at 476.

[24] Cf. the more exclusionary approach of the New Zealand and Canadian courts, which owes more to the particular terms of their respective domestic human rights legislation than to any overriding principle of fairness of the sort to be found in Art. 6. See *Simpson* v. *A-G* [1994] 3 NZLR 667, at 703; and s. 24(2) of the Canadian Charter of Rights; *R* v. *Burlingham* [1995] SCR 206; and *R.* v. *Feeney* [1997] 2 SCR 13.

[25] N. 23 above,

[26] At 174–5.

[27] I have put the word 'discretion' in quotation marks because the task of determining admissibility for this purpose does not strictly involve an exercise of discretion. It is to determine whether the evidence 'would have such an adverse effect on the fairness of the proceedings that the court ought not to admit it'.

the Article or the ECHR's treatment of it adds to that task. In *Schenk* v. *Switzerland*[28] the ECHR held that the fact that evidence had been unlawfully obtained did not *per se* make it inadmissible; the test was whether it made the trial as a whole unfair, and that was primarily a matter for the national court.

The ECHR, other than to consider whether the overall proceedings were unfair, is reluctant to interfere in domestic rules of admissibility of evidence, which vary considerably according to the different systems of the member states. As Gomien, Harris and Zwaak have commented,[29] its focus on the general right to a 'fair hearing' has resulted in 'a rather amorphous body of case-law'. Its position is generally to leave it to the judgment of the national courts. The House of Lords noted in Khan (Sultan) the similarity of the Strasbourg Court's approach and English law on the matter, Lord Nicholls in particular, observing:[30]

'the decision of the European Court of Human Rights in *Schenk* v. *Switzerland* . . . confirms that the use at a criminal trial of material obtained in breach of the rights of privacy enshrined in Article 8 does not of itself mean that the trial is unfair. Thus the European Court of Human Rights case law on this issue leads to the same conclusion as English law.'

Lord Nolan also pointed to the primacy of the domestic courts in this respect, noting the ECHR's[31]:

'acceptance of the proposition that the admissibility of evidence is primarily a matter for regulation under national law, and its rejection of the proposition that unlawfully obtained evidence is necessarily inadmissible.'

In the light of that comity, I do not know how much assistance on the broad notion of fairness the United Kingdom courts can hope to obtain from the very general terms of Article 6 that it does not already derive from the same notion in common law or section 78 of the 1984 Act, still less from the somewhat diffident jurisprudence of the ECHR[32] in its consideration of it in relation to member states' differing systems.[33] As Lord Taylor CJ said in *R.* v. *Christou*[34]:

'the criteria of unfairness are the same whether the trial judge

is exercising his discretion at common law or under the statute [i.e. Section 78]. . . . What is unfair cannot sensibly be subject to different standards depending on the source of the discretion to exclude it.'

I am, therefore, puzzled as to what the authors of the Justice Report have in mind in the following passage at page 61 of it:

'Leaving it to individual states and their national courts to decide upon the procedural detail means that there is a certain amount of discretion on whether a given course is compatible with Article 6. This will become more important following implementation of the Human Rights Act 1998, with questions of disclosure and admissibility of evidence being tested more directly against the requirements of Article 6. Arguments based on the Convention will be able to be raised at trial and upon appeal. The courts themselves, in the terms of the Act, will be obliged to give effect to convention rights. In short, they will be obliged for the first time to consider the compliance of procedural rules with the overall fairness requirements of Article 6 and to fill in those gaps where the Strasbourg Court has not ventured, in recognition of the varying state systems.'

If the Canadian experience of the working of its 1982 Charter of Rights and Freedoms, as seen through the eyes of one academic commentator, Terence G. Ison,[35] is anything to go by, those may be over-ambitious expectations for the contribution of Convention rights to this part of our criminal law:

'It is usually in criminal law that significant achievements are claimed for the Charter. It is sometimes said that many innocent people have been acquitted as result of it. The reality is that we do not know how many innocent people have been acquitted as a result of the Charter, or even whether anyone has. Most of the acquittals are on process grounds, so there was never a finding of guilt or innocence. Moreover, in all of these cases, the accused could have been acquitted just as well without the Charter. For example, many have been acquitted because of unreasonable delay in bringing the prosecution. If the court wanted to acquit them on that ground, it could have done so just as well under the Magna Carta. If the court did not want to acquit them on that ground, the Charter would not have required it to do so. In some other cases, the court chose to reject evidence that was illegally obtained. It could have made the same choice following traditional case law development.

With regard to the admissibility of confessions, the Charter has changed the doctrinal rationales, but it is doubtful whether it has made any difference to the results. Under the Charter, the admissibility of confessions is determined by an evolving body of case law, just as it was before the Charter. With or

---

[28] (1991) 13 EHRR 242, at 265–6, para. 46.

[29] N. 5 above, 259.

[30] N. 6 above, at 583.

[31] *Ibid.*, at 581.

[32] The jurisprudence of the ECHR suggests that the UK's incorporation of the Convention in the 1998 Act will not effect any change. See *Murray* v. *UK* (1996) 22 EHRR 29, and also *Saunders* v. *UK* in which the Court, having found a breach of Art. 6, declined to speculate about the outcome of the criminal proceedings if there had been no such breach.

[33] So vividly illustrated by John Spencer in his characteristically engaging paper, Ch 7 above.

[34] [1992] QB 979 at 988.

[35] 'A Constitutional Bill of Rights—The Canadian Experience' (1997) 60 *MLR* 499, at 507; see also David Beatty 'The Canadian Charter of Rights: Lessons and Laments' (1997) 60 *LQR* 481; cf. Professor Anne Bayefsky, 'The Canadian Experience' [1997] *EHRLR* 496.

without the Charter, the law relating to the admissibility of confessions becomes what the judges think it should be.'

The authors of the Justice Report, under the heading 'Admissibility of evidence', accuse the courts of a lack of vigilance in not excluding evidence obtained in breach of the present Home Office guidelines on informants or intrusive surveillance.[36] In the ensuing treatment of the matter they go on to criticise as a 'narrow interpretation' of the Convention the Khan (Sultan) decision that a breach of privacy regarded by the Court of Appeal and the House of Lords as minor in comparison to the seriousness of the offence charged did not require exclusion of the evidence. Their reasoning is that a breach of a Convention right—a 'fundamental' right—demands more attention by the courts than any domestic rule of law governing the fairness of the proceedings.

However, it seems to me—as it did to Lord Taylor—that the concept of fairness is the same whether it comes packaged as a Convention or other 'fundamental' right or simply as a well established requirement of a national law. As a matter of admissibility of evidence, its effect on criminal proceedings is the same, namely, whether the admission of the evidence would be unfair or unjust.

To introduce into the exercise of determining admissibility a requirement for the court to mark its disapproval of the breach or 'to set the limits of fairness in the system as a whole', as recommended by Justice,[37] is to confuse it with the court's quite separate role in staying or otherwise controlling proceedings for abuse of process.[38] English courts may and do exercise the latter power even where they are of the view that there has been no unfairness in the instant proceedings. In doing so, they may balance the public interest of prosecuting those charged with serious criminal offences against that of marking their disapproval of public authorities' conduct which brings the administration of justice into disrepute[39]—an exercise not appropriate to the determination of the fairness of admitting evidence at common law or under section 78.

It may be that a court, in conducting that balance and in the exercise of its discretion, should give special weight to the fundamental nature of a right seriously breached. However, to confine any express declaration of such power to breaches of Convention rights and to seek to achieve it in part by the amendment of PACE, as

Justice recommends,[40] is to suggest a narrowing of the protection which the courts can already provide in their abuse of process jurisdiction. It would also unnecessarily and confusingly combine it with the courts' quite distinct role in determining the admissibility of evidence against the criterion of fairness in each individual case. I make the same point about the narrower but more exclusionary solution suggested by Peter Carter,[41] that in the event of a right of privacy being established in English law, the second Sang rule prohibiting the exclusion of evidence purely on the ground that it has been improperly obtained,[42] should be statutorily 'slightly relaxed' to permit a non-discretionary exclusionary rule 'narrow in scope, . . . tailored to meet a specific and compelling policy' and 'couched in unambiguous terms'. With respect, such an approach still confuses evaluation of the fairness of the admission of evidence with the exercise of a discretion to exclude it purely as a mark of disapproval of the way in which it was obtained[43].

In my view, the proper jurisdiction for the courts in ensuring proper regard for 'fundamental' rights, whether secured by the Convention or otherwise, is the first of the two mentioned by Justice in its Recommendation 14,[44] namely the power to control the proceedings in the exercise of their discretion as an abuse of process.

Although the exercise of that power has always arisen in response to what amounted to a plea in bar, it seems to

---

[36] At 70.

[37] See the Justice Report, Recommendation 14, 76.

[38] See *R. v. Chalkley and Jeffries* [1998] QB 848 (CA), at 874D–876C.

[39] See *R. v. Latif and Shahzad* [1996] 1 WLR 104 (HL), *per* Lord Steyn at 112G–113B.

[40] Recommendation 14,'Because of the covert and secret nature of proactive policing methods, the courts need to be more willing to uphold standards of propriety in police conduct. The abuse of process doctrine and the exclusionary principle of section 78 should be used to set the limits of fairness in the system as a whole. PACE should be amended to state specifically that the courts *may* exclude evidence that has been obtained in breach of a fundamental right guaranteed by the Human Rights Act 1998 if its admission would prejudice the integrity of the criminal justice system.' See also Katharine Grevling 'Fairness and the Exclusion of Evidence' (1997) 113 *LQR* 667, at 684–5. Cf. the stronger suggestion at 75 of the Justice Report, which goes further than the ECHR was prepared to go in *Schenk* and Lord Nolan in *Khan (Sultan)*, n. 6 above, at 581: 'The status of European Convention rights is much higher, and more fundamental, than the PACE Codes of Evidence, so that a breach of the Convention should *normally* lead to an exclusion of the evidence' [my emphasis].

[41] (1997), 113 *LQR* 468, at 479–80.

[42] 'Save with regard to admissions and confessions and generally with regard to evidence obtained from the accused after commission of the offence, he has no discretion to refuse to admit relevant admissible evidence on the ground that it was obtained by improper or unfair means. The court is not concerned with how it was obtained', *per* Lord Diplock at [1980] AC 437D–E.

[43] Something that neither the common law nor s. 78 intends, despite its inclusion of the words 'including the circumstances in which the evidence was obtained', and the jurisprudence of the ECHR does not require; see *Khan (Sultan)*, *per* Lord Nolan at 577–8 and 582; *Chalkley and Jeffries*, n. 38 above, at 874D–875G; *Schenk*, at 265–6, para. 46; see also Carter, n. 41 above, 478.

[44] See also the Justice Report, 60–1.

me strongly arguable that it is not just a power to stay the proceedings. It is a general and inherent power to protect as necessary the court's process from abuse, and includes the safeguarding of an accused person from oppression or prejudice.[45] In my view, the courts should be able to tailor the protection to the abuse. Where appropriate they should be able to make such order, say by excluding improperly obtained evidence, as would mark and remove the abuse but permit the continuance of the proceedings. Rather than turning to Parliament to garnish in that way the now well established Common law jurisdiction of abuse of process, I would leave it to the courts.

ON APPEAL

The difficulty of the abuse of process route to underlining, if and where appropriate, the special importance of fundamental rights, such as the right to respect for privacy, is the possible failure to give effect to such rights in criminal cases at the appellate stage. In the light of the new section 2(1) of the Criminal Appeal Act 1968,[46] restricting the Court of Appeal's power to quash a conviction only when it considers it to be unsafe, it is doubtful whether it can do so on the strength of an abuse of process which it considers does not result in unsafety.[47]

The Court of Appeal might take the view that a conviction in a trial which should never have taken place should be regarded as unsafe for that reason or

[45] *Connelly* v. *DPP* [1964] AC 1254 (HL), *per* Lord Devlin at 1354, *per* Lord Pearce at 1361 and 1364, and, particularly, *per* Lord Morris at 1301.

[46] As substituted by the Criminal Appeal Act 1995.

[47] See *Archbold*, (1999 edn.), para. 7–46a.

that, despite the statutory basis of the Court of Appeal's jurisdiction, there is some inherent or ancillary jurisdiction permitting it to intervene. However, my instinct is that neither would be a jurisprudentially respectable solution; and I believe that failure to make provision for this form of challenge to a conviction in the new Section 2(1) was an oversight. Some amendment of the sub-section is required to give the Court clear power to quash a conviction where, regardless of its unsafety, it considers there has been an abuse so outrageous as to make it an affront to justice to allow the conviction to stand. Such a power should not be confined to abuses constituting violations of human rights.

FINAL THOUGHT

Those who have spent some time actively advancing and preparing for the advent of human rights to our law will no doubt recognise in what I have written the classic signs of a narrowly based common law judge in need of shock treatment to enable him to cope with these strange foreign notions called 'fundamental rights'. However, for the reasons I have given, it does seem to me that there are practical limits to what may be expected to result from the Convention in the field of investigation and surveillance, at least in the short term. I hope that a sympathetic and constructive shift in judicial attitude and time, will prove me wrong. I also give my firm support to Justice's recommendation for a comprehensive rationalisation of the legislative and procedural framework for the control of surveillance and other intrusive forms of investigation, and for the establishment of a corresponding system of legal controls, all with the relevant Convention rights clearly in mind.

9

SURVEILLANCE AND THE HUMAN RIGHTS ACT

MADELEINE COLVIN*

INTRODUCTION

Surveillance covers any activity that involves the covert watching of a location or persons or the covert listening to communications between people over a period of time. It therefore covers a spectrum of activities from physical observation through to the use of advanced technology. Increasingly, the police, Customs and Excise and other law enforcement agencies,[1] both in the UK and elsewhere, are turning to these surveillance methods as part of the shift towards proactive, intelligence-led policing. This employs covert investigative methods to target known or suspected criminals rather than waiting to investigate a crime after it has happened. In this context, the use of sophisticated aural and visual surveillance—alone or together with the activities of informers and undercover police officers—provides both intelligence on potential crimes and the evidence to prosecute those that are committed.

However, this growing reliance by law enforcement agencies on new technology with its greater potential for intrusion can represent serious interference with privacy rights as guaranteed by Article 8 of the European Convention on Human Rights. The interference may occur in two ways: the actual process of watching and listening or the subsequent holding of recorded data. In terms of the surveillance process, new technology now offers powerful devices such as aerial cameras with high magnification power, night vision technology and the stroboscopic camera that can take hundreds of pictures in a matter of seconds. Alongside this is other equipment routinely used to survey public places: the automatic vehicle recognition system

(AVRS) which identifies number plates and the increasingly prevalent closed circuit television (CCTV) systems.

These methods invariably result in a permanent visual or auditory record that potentially gives rise to a second kind of interference on information privacy rights as guaranteed under Article 8. Described as 'the life blood of the modern police service',[2] criminal intelligence data can now be stored, analysed and disseminated in radically different ways both nationally and internationally. Much of the data, though, may be highly speculative and will inevitably include information about individuals and events that are not criminal.[3]

This paper examines existing law and procedure covering the use of technical surveillance devices with the requirements of Article 8. It also raises the need for regulatory controls over other forms of surveillance such as operations using informers and undercover police. However, the paper's focus on privacy rights is not intended to lessen the fact that such methods may also impact on fair trial rights under Article 6 of the European Convention. For example, in many cases, the defence is either not aware of the covert operation or the material obtained is withheld under the rules on disclosure of evidence. This is especially so in relation to undercover operations. In other cases, the courts have to decide whether to admit evidence that may have been unfairly, or unlawfully, obtained. As mentioned below, the principles of fairness entrenched in Article 6 may well be relevant in these circumstances.[4]

---

* Legal Policy Director at JUSTICE.

[1] Although this paper focuses on police investigations, the issues are also relevant to other agencies such as the Security Service (MI5).

[2] *Policing with Intelligence; Criminal Intelligence*, HMIC Thematic inspection report on good practice, 1997/98.

[3] For a full discussion of privacy information rights in relation to criminal intelligence data, see Chap. 4 of the report, *Under Surveillance—Covert Policing and Human Rights Standards*, (London: JUSTICE, 1998).

[4] See *ibid.*, Chap. 3 (Fair Trial Issues).

FUNDAMENTAL RIGHTS

It is well-established that in a democratic society, intrusions by state organs into a person's private life should not take place except where there is a pressing social need to do so, and the intrusion is provided by law. This is a principle of law incorporated in several international human rights instruments, including Article 8 of the European Convention:

'Article 8: Right to respect for private and family life
1.Everyone has the right to respect for his private and family life, his home and his correspondance.
2.There shall be no interference by a public authority with the exercise of this right except such as is in accordance with the law and is necessary in a democratic society in the interests of national society, public safety or the economic well-being of the country, for the prevention of disorder or crime, for the protection of health or morals, or for the protection of the rights and freedoms of others.'

Despite differences in the various methods used, Article 8 as developed by the European Court of Human Rights places strict standards on the regulation and supervision of surveillance techniques based on these principles.[5] In each case, the following questions need to be asked:

• *Does the interference have a basis in law?*
This is the principle of legality that requires that any interference with Article 8 is ' in accordance with the law': either an Act of Parliament or common law rule. This law must be 'accessible and precise' so that citizens are able to foresee the circumstances in which the authorities are empowered to interfere. It must therefore define the nature of the offences that may give rise to the interference, identify the types of activities that can be undertaken and its duration.[6] Unpublished guidelines from either a Department of State or the policing agency itself do not satisfy the test as they are not legally binding.[7] In practice, such laws are often accompanied by a more-detailed statutory code of practice or non-statutory guidelines.
• *Is the restriction justified in terms of a legitimate aim set out in Article 8(2)?*
Such interference with privacy is to be tolerated in a democratic society only in so far as it is undertaken in order to fulfill one of the legitimate purposes of Article 8(2). That is, it is undertaken for reasons either of national security, public safety or the economic well-being of the country or it is for the prevention of

disorder or crime, the protection of health or morals or the protection of the rights and freedoms of others. This list is intended to be exhaustive.
• *Is the interference 'necessary in a democratic society'?*
It has to be shown that the interference is both necessary to fulfil a pressing social need and is proportionate in its response to that need. The test of necessity is a strict test: whilst it is not synonymous with 'indispensable', it means more than 'reasonable' or 'desirable'.[8] To be proportionate, it must be shown that only such measures as are strictly necessary to achieve the required objective are taken. This means that particularly intrusive methods should be used only in the investigation of serious offences and when less intrusive methods are not available or are unlikely to succeed. In applying the test, account must also be taken of the collateral effect on others who may be affected, such as family members and business associates.[9]

In addition, Article 8 requires that the exercise of intrusive powers must be subject to a system of checks and balances. Since, for example, covert surveillance 'can undermine or even destroy democracy on the ground of defending it', there must be procedures to ensure accountability in the exercise of the power and to protect against abuse.[10] Although states enjoy a certain 'margin of appreciation'on the exact nature of the checks and balances, the European Court has identified the need for prior scrutiny of the use of the power in individual cases and for independent oversight to monitor and report on the activities as a whole.

As well as privacy implications, covert policing methods may give rise to arguments under Articles 6 and 13 of the European Convention. For example, there are two important facets of Article 6 which are especially relevant to covert surveillance policing. First, it is well established that the right to a fair trial does not simply come into play once trial proceedings start: it also involves consideration of fairness at the investigative stage, to the extent that that affects the trial or the evidence it considers. Secondly, the European Court has developed the principle of equality of arms: that both sides in the proceedings should have equal access to documents and evidence.[11] This raises questions on the doctrine of public interest immunity in criminal cases

---

[5] *Klass* v. *Germany* 2 EHRR 214 (1978); *Malone* v. *UK* (1984) 7 EHRR 14; *Huvig* v. *France* (1990) 12 EHRR 528.
[6] *Huvig* v. *France* [1990] 12 EHRR 528.
[7] *Malone* v. *UK* 7 EHRR 14 (1984).

[8] *Handyside* v. *UK* 1 EHRR 737 (1976); *Dudgeon* v. *UK* (1982) 4 EHRR 149.
[9] See the recent ECtHR decision in *Lambert* v. *France*, 24 August 1998.
[10] *Klass* v. *Germany* 2 EHRR 214 (1978).
[11] *Jespers* v. *Belgium* (1981) 27 DR 61.

and the new disclosure regime under the Criminal Procedure and Investigations Act 1996.[12]

In addition, Article 13 requires that domestic law must provide an effective remedy before an independent body (usually a court or tribunal) for those whose rights may have been breached.[13] The nature of the remedy may be determined by the sensitivity of the information.[14]

Regulating the use of covert investigation methods on the basis of these rights and principles has two important advantages. From the individual citizen's point of view, it means that actions taken against them are the subject of safeguarding controls. For the police and other investigative agencies, regulation provides a legitimate basis and framework from which to operate. If procedures are followed correctly and the substance of regulations adhered to, it greatly lessens the likelihood of a successful challenge to the methods used or to a court ruling that the evidence is deemed inadmissible.

SURVEILLANCE BY TECHNICAL DEVICES

A recent report on surveillance methods published by JUSTICE[15] concludes that the present *ad hoc*, piecemeal approach to the regulation of surveillance devices is unsatisfactory. In particular, it has led to significant inconsistencies in current laws and procedures as between the different areas, the different agencies which may be involved and the activities which are regulated. This conclusion is based on looking at several principal Acts governing the power to eavesdrop on private communications: the Interception of Communications Act 1985 (IOCA), Part III of the Police Act 1997[16] and, in relation solely to the security services, the Security Service Acts of 1989 and 1996 and the Intelligence Services Act 1994.

Interception of Communications Act 1985

The Interception of Communications Act 1985 (IOCA) was introduced following the *Malone* case[17] to satisfy the principle that interceptions should be 'in accordance with the law' if they are to comply with Article 8. However, it has proven to be of limited scope only,

failing to keep pace with technological developments. Its remit for example, extends only to the interception of mail and telecommunications on *public* telecommunication systems, not private networks.[17a] This alone has created a number of anomalies:

- In 1994 the House of Lords in the case of *Effik*[18] ruled that the public telecommunications system ends in the BT/cable socket in the wall. This means that when the radio signal from the hand set to the base unit is intercepted, as with cordless telephones, such systems fall outside the ambit of the1985 Act. It appears that section 5 of the WirelessTelegraphy Act 1949 is now being relied upon as the legal basis for such interceptions, as it is for radio pagers.[19] Although this section requires prior authorisation from a designated official within the Home Office, Scottish Office or Northern Ireland Office, it lacks any of the other safeguarding procedures of IOCA and therefore may well not comply with the full requirements of Article 8. In any event, as Customs officials are deemed to be Crown servants, they are exempt even from this system of authorisation.

- Also in 1994, the Court of Appeal held that 'the interception of a communication takes place when, and at the place where, the electrical impulse of the signal which is passing along the telephone line is intercepted in fact'.[20] This determines, therefore, that where public and private networks are both used as part of a call, it is the physical point of interception that matters if it is to be covered by IOCA. As telecommunications on mobile phones do not, by definition, pass through an elaborate cable network and it is impossible to pinpoint the exact place of interception, this interpretation casts doubt on whether such phones fall within IOCA; current Home Office advice is that they do.[21]

- This same point, though, is creating difficulties in terms of electronic (e-mail) communications. Although it is generally accepted that for interceptions of e-mail to be lawful, the IOCA regime must be followed, this is only so long as the mail is travelling over the public telephone networks and the leased lines connecting Internet Service Providers (ISPs). During transmission, however, e-mail messages spend some time at one or other ISPs before being transferred on: these areas are deemed to lie in the private

---

[12] For a full discussion of this, see Chap. 3 of *Under Surveillance*, n. 3 above..

[13] App. No. 18601/91 See *Esbester* v. *UK* 2 April 1993.

[14] *Klass* v. *Germany* 2 EHRR 214 (1978) 67; but see also *Chahal* v. *UK* (1996) 23 EHRR 413.

[15] *Under Surveillance—Covert Policing and Human Rights Standards*, n. 3 above.

[16] This came into force on 22 February 1999.

[17] (1985) 7 EHRR 14.

[17a] Since writing this paper the Home Office has published a consulation paper: 'Interception of Communications in the United Kingdom', June 1999.

[18] (1994) 99 Cr.App.R. 312.

[19] See also *R.* v. *Taylor-Sabori*, CA 25 September 1998 concerning the admissibility of pager messages sent from Holland to the UK through the BT Radio Paging System.

[20] *Ahmed and Others*, CA, 29 1994, March unreported (per Evans LJ)

[21] Police Bill 1996, *Hansard* ,11 March 1997, col.158.

network (unless they also happen to be public telecom-munications operators) and therefore interceptions at this point are outside the controls of IOCA[22] (see below, for further discussion of e-mail interceptions).

- In the case of *Halford* v. *UK*[23] the European Court held Article 8 was violated by the interception of a private telephone system as such networks fall outside the IOCA provisions. Alison Halford, who was a senior police officer, alleged that her Chief Constable had ordered the interception of her internal office telephone during the course of discrimination proceedings taken against the police force.

The exemption for 'participant monitoring' under section 1(2) of IOCA is also likely to give rise to arguments of compliance with Article 8. This essentially exempts from the IOCA regime any interception which is carried out with the consent of one of the parties to the communication. In the leading Canadian case of *R* v. *Duarte*,[24] the Supreme Court pointed out that exemptions on this ground directly contradict the principle that it is the person whose privacy is being infringed who should be afforded the safeguards. The Irish Law Commission has recently made the same point in a report on privacy.[25]

Another important area of surveillance work is intelligence-gathering through 'telephone metering'. This involves gaining information on a subscriber including the telephone numbers dialled, and the date, time and length of calls. It can involve a 'dynamic' subscriber check allowing the details to be passed on as the call is made. In addition, a mobile telephone user's whereabouts can be pinpointed through local base stations picking up both the calls and the telephone's regular signal emissions.

Despite the findings of the European Court in *Malone* that telephone metering was in breach of Article 8, it is not regulated under IOCA; instead, a statutory basis was provided by inserting a new section 45 into the Telecommunications Act 1984. This allows disclosure of communication data on the broad grounds of prevention and detection of crime or for the purposes of criminal proceedings. These are similar to the grounds for disclosure of personal data under section 28 of the Data Protection Act 1984 (soon to be replaced by section 29 of the 1998 Data Protection Act). The sufficiency of these provisions has recently been questioned in relation to e-mail data. As part of the request for access to

'metering' information under these provisions, the police have also sought and received print-outs of the contents of the communications from ISPs. However, in doing so, the police are circumventing the need for an IOCA warrant which would not be possible if the mail was sent via the public postal system, for example.[25a]

Police Act 1997

Until Part III of the Police Act 1997 came into force on 22 February 1999, the use of covert listening devices was regulated by administrative Home Office guidelines first published in 1984.[26] Surveillance carried out under these guidelines was almost certainly in breach of Article 8 because of its lack of legal basis.[27] Part III will remedy this, in part, by providing a statutory basis for some such operations, although not all.

Although Part III was largely debated in the context of regulating bugging devices, it also covers other equipment such as video cameras when the placement of the device may cause an act of trespass, criminal damage or unlawful interference with wireless telegraphy. It was the need to provide law enforcement agencies with a defence to allegations of unlawful trespass and criminal damage, rather than a desire to protect privacy rights, that primarily prompted the introduction of the legislation. However, this narrow approach means that there are significant gaps in the scope of the legislation, similar to those discussed in relation to IOCA.

First, although introduced to cover *all* listening devices, Part III covers only technical devices whose installation requires interference with property. There are several devices currently available that can be used without causing any physical interference, including long-distance sensitive microphones and equipment based on laser-beam and microwave technology.[28] The establishment of the Police Information Technology Organisation (PITO)[29] in the same piece of legislation shows the importance of new technology to modern-day policing. And although some of these 'stand-off' devices are currently too costly to employ on a regular basis, advances in technology are likely to lead to both an expanded and cheaper range of equipment and therefore to greater use in the future.

---

[22] Clive Feather *Interception of Email—Some Legal Issues*, 7 August 1998.

[23] [1997] EHRLR 540.

[24] (1990) 53 CCC (3d) 1.

[25] Law Reform Commission, *Surveillance and the Interception of Communications*, June 1998.

[25a] See Home Office proposals in recent consultation paper, n. 17a above.

[26] *Guidelines on the use of equipment in police surveillance operations*, (London: Home Office, 1984).

[27] In *R.* v. *Sultan Khan* [1997] AC 558 the House of Lords clearly considered the lack of statutory controls to be unsatisfactory although it did not expressly find a breach of Art. 8. See also the European Commission decision in *Govell* v. *UK* (1997) 4 EHRLR 438.

[28] European Parliament, *An Appraisal of Technologies of Political Control*, 1997.

[29] Part IV of the Police Act 1997.

Secondly, Part III is not to apply where the police have consent to place a device on the premises. Paragraph 2.1 of the *Intrusive Surveillance Code of Practice* that accompanies Part III says that:

'Authorisations under Part III will not be necessary where the police, the National Crime Squad, NCIS or HM Customs & Excise are acting with the consent of a person able to give permission in respect of relevant property'.

This exemption, which is based on the preservation of common law under section 93(7), was neither debated, nor referred to, during the parliamentary debates. Although its precise effect is difficult to predict, it gives rise to several issues. The first is whether police officers and others relying on it will be faced with complex questions in landlord and tenant law in trying to identify the correct person from whom to gain consent. A legal opinion obtained by JUSTICE concluded that:

'The difficulty with para.2.1 [of the Code of Practice] is that the officer concerned is potentially required to make a decision on a complex area of civil law often requiring the sight and interpretation of documents. A mistake will inevitably involve breach of privacy, acts of trespass and possibly interference with personal property and criminal damage—being the very evils, we assume, the concept of prior authorisation introduced by the [Police] Act was intended to avoid.'

The exemption also amounts to a form of 'participant monitoring'. As discussed above, creating an exemption on the basis of consent from a third party entirely fails to address the need for safeguards of the privacy rights of those who are subjected to the surveillance. In this context, it may mean that a hotel room is wired up with permission from the hotel owner, or an office is bugged on the say-so of the employer; but the persons targeted have none of the Part III safeguards. It also has the effect of excluding listening devices placed in police and prison cells from the same controls.

As the Home Office has recently made clear, the 1984 guidelines on surveillance operations will continue to regulate operations which fall outside Part III until they are replaced by new codes being drafted by the Association of Chief Police Officers (ACPO).[30] The latter will include separate codes to cover interceptions of communications that fall outside IOCA and surveillance equipment that is not regulated by Part III. Although it is intended that they will closely follow the requirements of both pieces of legislation, they will be voluntary codes of practice and, as such, raise questions

of compatibility with the legality requirement of Article 8 (see above).[30a]

The need for such codes also highlights the anomaly that, due to deficiencies in legislative drafting, there will be two regimes regulating similarly intrusive surveillance operations—one statutory under Part III with its scrutiny and monitoring safeguards and the other non-statutory governed by voluntary ACPO codes only. This anomaly is undoubtedly vulnerable to challenge when the Human Rights Act 1998 comes into force.

In addition, there are other aspects of Part III that arguably fail to comply with Article 8, such as the absence of a *general* requirement for prior independent approval of an operation. Under section 97, prior approval from a Commissioner is required only where the property involved is a dwelling, a hotel room or office or the action is likely to involve confidential information of various kinds: legally privileged, personal or journalistic. In an urgent case, even this is not to apply; the surveillance may be begun on police authorisation alone, although the Commissioner has the power later to quash or cancel it. Although it is made clear in the Code that this exception should only be relied on in exceptional circumstances, there is no parallel provision for urgency in either IOCA or the legislation covering the security services. In any event, in an age of mobile telephones and fax machines, it is questionable whether it is necessary to treat urgent applications differently. The experience in Australia is that authorising judges are able to respond quickly and there is no evidence to suggest that a requirement for prior approval even in urgent cases has had an adverse effect on police operations.

In recent years, the Security Service (MI5) has moved further into the field of combatting criminal activity. For example, since 1992 it has been the lead agency in the intelligence effort against terrorism in Northern Ireland; more recently, under the Security Service Act 1996, its role has been extended to undertake operations in support of tackling serious crime when tasked by the National Criminal Intelligence Service (NCIS). In this new law enforcement role, it may use its powers to place surveillance devices and generally search premises under the Intelligence Services Act 1994. Although these are essentially the same powers as under Part III of the Police Act, there are nevertheless some significant differences such as the lack of safeguards covering legally privileged, confidential and journalistic material.

Article 13: an effective remedy

Each of the different statutes governing surveillance— IOCA, the Police Act 1997 and the Security Service Act

---

[30] See para.10 of the Home Office Circular on implementation of Part III of the Police Act 1997, HOC 4/1999.

[30a] The ACPO Codes come into force on 1 October 1999..

1989—establishes its own separate complaint system. Under IOCA and the Security Service Act, complaint may be made to a tribunal; under the Police Act, it is to a Commissioner. Although the tribunal system has been held by the European Commission to satisfy the requirement of an 'effective remedy' under Article 13,[31] this is likely to be reopened under the Human Rights Act on one or more of the following grounds:

- Under each of the statutes, only complaints where a warrant has been issued may be investigated. This therefore provides no protection against unauthorised or unlawful interceptions; instead, these are considered to be a criminal matter for the police to investigate. However, as no reasons are given for dismissing an application and there is no duty on either the tribunal or Commissioner to refer the matter to the police, the complainant is unlikely to become aware of the distinction.
- Under IOCA and the Security Service Act, the tribunal may only apply judicial review principles. This means that it may not consider either the accuracy or the merits of the evidence put forward in support of the warrant for interception, for example. Furthermore, the tribunal's decision can neither be appealed nor judicially reviewed in the courts.
- There is no oral hearing, only limited disclosure of evidence and no reasoned decision given under any of the complaint procedures. Where the application is dismissed, the complainant is merely informed that no breach of the relevant legislation has taken place.
- In the case of Part III of the Police Act 1997, there is the potential conflict between the Commissioner's dual functions of approving warrants and investigating individual complaints. Although no doubt practices will be adopted to ensure that a Commissioner does not examine a complaint involving an application which he or she has approved, this may not satisfy the requirements of Articles 6 and 13 of the Convention that the same body should not both permit and sanction activities.[32]

The covert and sensitive nature of surveillance operations necessarily raises difficulties when it comes to applying normal principles of procedural justice to a complaint system. The recent case of *Chahal* v. *UK*[33] is an illustration of this. This concerned Mr Chahal's right to a judicial appeal against a deportation order on grounds of national security. The Court made it clear that it should be possible to employ procedures that both accommodate legitimate security concerns about the nature and sources of intelligence information and which also accord individuals a substantial measure of procedural justice.

This has led to the introduction of special procedures in the Special Immigration Appeals Commission Act 1977 that governs appeal hearings raising national security issues. It is accepted that such hearings will include material that cannot be disclosed to either the appellant or his or her representative. The Act therefore provides for the Attorney-General to appoint a special advocate to represent the interests of the applicant in those parts of the proceedings from which the appellant and his or her legal representative are excluded. Rules of evidence specify the role of the advocate, and restrict the nature and extent of any communication with the appellant. The appellant must also be given a summary of the submissions and evidence and reasons for the Commission's decision to the extent that it is possible to do so without disclosing information contrary to the public interest. In principle, this appears to be a suitable model for tribunals hearing complaints in relation to covert surveillance operations.

INFORMERS AND UNDERCOVER POLICE OFFICERS

Although the use of informers and undercover police officers is an important part of modern-day policing, their use gives rise to clear dangers. With informers, particularly those who are accomplices, there will be questions about the reliability of the information gained; with undercover policing, there are fine gradations between involvement, incitement and entrapment and therefore fine lines between what is fair and unfair.

The use of informers and undercover police officers raises two distinct issues under the Human Rights Act 1998. The first concerns fair trial rights under Article 6. Issues as to the lawfulness and fairness of the investigation may be considered in relation to admissibility of evidence, as will questions of disclosure under the Criminal Procedure and Investigations Act 1996 at the trial itself. These are largely evidential matters dealt with in other papers.[34] However, as mentioned above, Article 6 does not simply come into play during the trial; it is also relevant when key operational decisions are being made during the investigation. The recent decision of the European Court in *Teixeira de Castro* v. *Portugal*[35] involving an undercover police officers may

---

[31] *Esbester* v. *UK*, n. 13 above; *Hewitt and Harman* v. *UK* (No.2) 20317/92.

[32] See *Piersack* v. *Belgium* (1983) 5 EHHR 169.

[33] (1996) 23 EHRR 413.

[34] See also Chap. 3 of *Under Surveillance*, n. 3 above.

[35] ECtHR, judgment of 9 June 1998.

have implications for the need for operational supervision in order to comply with Article 6. The case concerned a routine 'buy and bust' exercise with undercover officers approaching the applicant to set up a heroin deal, for which he was subsequently arrested. It was held on the facts that the police conduct amounted to incitement and the evidence obtained was in breach of the fair trial provisions of Article 6.

While fully recognising the need for such operations in the fight against crime, the European Court ruled that 'the use of undercover agents must be restricted and safeguards be put in place even in cases concerning the fight against drug-trafficking'. In Portugal, this involved gaining prior authorisation from a magistrate and a preliminary investigation to establish the background of the target, both of which the undercover officers had failed to do.

The case therefore places weight on the requirements of authorisation and supervision in undercover operations if the exercise is not to breach Article 6; the same is probably true for participating informers where the risks are similar. The question therefore is whether the current, non-statutory 1969 Home Office Circular, together with unpublished internal police guidelines on undercover operations, are sufficient to ensure compliance with Article 6 in the light of this recent decision.

The second issue is the extent to which informers and undercover police officers intrude upon privacy rights under Article 8. Interestingly, the European Court appears to have taken a less straightforward approach to this kind of surveillance compared to its approach to the use of technical devices. In the case of *Ludi* v. *Switzerland*[36] the Court held that a defendant who knowingly engages in criminal activity 'must have been aware that he ran the risk of encountering an undercover police officer whose task would be to expose him' and therefore cannot rely on the protection of Article 8. This decision appears to have drawn a distinction in privacy protection between two situations: one where the surveillance takes place when it is clear that the suspect is already involved in criminal activities and where it is not. It is not a distinction, however, that the Court has drawn in the line of cases on the use of electronic surveillance. These latter apply the principle that the right to a private life exists as such, whether or not the person is engaging in criminal activity; in those circumstances where interference is justified, it should be in accordance with the rule of law to satisfy Article 8.

Even taking account of the Court's decision in *Ludi*, there are clearly circumstances when the involvement of an informer or an undercover officer may infringe a suspect's privacy rights. For example, it seems likely that an officer who insinuates himself into a suspect's home, or seeks to participate in a person's private life (as in the *Colin Stagg* case) is intruding upon a person's private rights. This could also be argued when surveillance is used in the early stages of an investigation for intelligence-gathering purposes where there is only suspicion of criminal activity. In these circumstances, it is difficult to draw a distinction between the intrusion caused by an undercover police officer and that caused by a bugging device.

Currently there is no statutory control regulating the use of informers or undercover officers by any of the law enforcement agencies or the security services. In relation to the police, there are unpublished, internal guidelines drafted by ACPO that incorporate the 1969 Home Office Circular, *Informants who take part in crime*. This is expected to be replaced by a new national code drafted by ACPO (see above) which will tighten up some of the internal procedures, including the authorisation process for using participating informers and undercover officers, and be more specific on methods of accountability, for example.

In terms of compliance with the Human Rights Act, there is again the question whether non-statutory guidelines are sufficient. While such guidelines clearly provide the basis for a coherent and systematic approach, they are nevertheless legally unenforceable. The courts may take them into account,[37] but unlike a statutory instrument, a breach of a non-statutory code cannot of itself form the basis of legal action. Additionally there is the problem of ensuring compliance with a document that does not have legal status. Research undertaken, albeit some years ago, showed that the current ACPO guidelines were more often honoured in the breach than the observance.[38] Although the new code will set national mandatory standards, the problem of cultural resistance to regulation should not be underestimated.

As the JUSTICE report acknowledges, there are clearly tensions and practical difficulties in reconciling covert practices with principles of accountability. However, as the Police and Criminal Evidence Act 1984 showed in relation to the detention rights of suspects, there are some areas of policing which are so fundamental to the integrity of the system that they need to be subject to a statutory regime of checks and balances. The use of informers and undercover police officers probably falls into such a category.

---

[36] (1993) 15 EHRR 173.

[37] See *Ameer* v. *Lucas* [1977] Crim. LR 104.
[38] See C. Norris and C. Dunnighan, *Subterranean Blues: Conflict as an Unintended Consequence of the Police use of Informers*, (Kingston-upon-Hull: University of Hull, 1996).

CONCLUSION

The 1998 Human Rights Act will clearly change the environment within which the debates on surveillance policing takes place. Clearly, some of the methods presently in use fall foul of the Article 8 requirement of having a legal base; other methods pose particular problems in terms of a fair trial under Article 6. Implementation of the Act provides both the opportunity and the necessity to re-examine and reform present laws and systems so as to ensure compliance. The alternative of allowing individual and *ad hoc* challenges before the courts risks creating a lengthy period of legal uncertainty, both for defendants and law enforcement bodies.

10

INCORPORATING THE EUROPEAN CONVENTION ON HUMAN RIGHTS; ITS IMPACT ON SENTENCING

D.A. THOMAS QC, LL.D.

The Convention is written in broad terms which reflect the concerns of the period in which it was evolved. The text is significantly older than most of the legislation which governs the English sentencing system. Its impact on the operation of the English sentencing system will depend entirely on the use which the judges choose to make of it; the text of the Convention rarely offers an obvious solution to the issues which seem likely to arise. In determining questions which arise in relation to convention rights, the English courts must 'take into account' any relevant decision of the European Court of Human Rights, the Commission or the Committee of Ministers—'the Strasbourg jurisprudence'—but on the issues which seem likely to arise in the context of sentencing, the Strasbourg jurisprudence is either sparse or non-existent, and English judges will have to make their own decisions without this assistance.

Conformity to the Convention will not demand a complete restructuring of the sentencing system, and it is unlikely that points on the Convention will be taken on a day to day basis in run of the mill cases. What seems more likely is that a small number of issues will crystallise, in which the application of the Convention will be in question, either as an aid to interpretation or as a question of incompatibility.

ABOLITION OF REQUIREMENT OF CONSENT TO COMMUNITY SERVICE ORDER

One obvious example of a possible incompatibility is the abolition of the requirement that an offender should consent to a community service order before a community service order can be made. This requirement was introduced with the community service order in 1972; it was abolished by the Crime (Sentences) Act 1997 section 38 (an Act introduced by the Conservative Government and brought into force by Labour). There are strong common sense arguments for requiring the offender to consent to such an order before it is made—it is a waste of time making an order which the offender does not intend to obey, and the requirement places an onus on the offender to disclose any circumstance which may prevent him from complying with the order.[1] Apart from this, an order by a court requiring an offender to perform unpaid work appears to be a clear contravention of Article 4(2) of the Convention—'No one shall be required to perform forced or compulsory labour.' It is difficult to see how a community service order can be brought within any of the exceptions in Article 4(3). The only relevant exception is in paragraph (a), which refers to 'any work required to be done in the ordinary course of detention imposed in accordance with the provisions of Article 5 of this Convention or during conditional release from such detention'. A community service order is a community order (Criminal Justice Act 1991 section 6); it is not a custodial sentence (see Criminal Justice Act 1991 section 31) and it is not a form of conditional release from custody. It seems inescapable that Powers of Criminal Courts Act 1973 section 14, shorn of the consent requirement in section 14(2) as a result of the implementation of Crime (Sentences) Act 1997 section 38, is incompatible with

[1] See *Hammon* [1997] 2 Cr.App.R(S) 202.

the Convention Right established by Article 4(2). The limited number of decisions of the ECHR dealing with Article 4(2) do not offer any significant help.

AUTOMATIC LIFE SENTENCE

The Crime (Sentences) Act 1997 introduced a new system of automatic life sentences. Under section 2 of the Act, an offender convicted of one of the offences included in the definition of 'serious offence' in that section, who was convicted of another serious offence before committing the later offence, must be sentenced to life imprisonment (or custody for life, if under the age of 21), unless there are ' exceptional circumstances relating to either of the offences or to the offender' which justify the court in not doing so. Some offenders who qualify for automatic life sentences under the Act would undoubtedly qualify for a discretionary life sentence in any event without reference to the Act,[2] but many who qualify for automatic life sentences under the Act would not be considered to be candidates for a discretionary life sentence. Two examples of cases decisded just before the Act came into force will make the point. The first is *Curry*.[3] The headnote reads as follows:

'The applicants pleaded guilty to robbery and possessing an imitation firearm with intent to commit an indictable offence. The applicants, both wearing balaclavas, and armed in one case with a cucumber concealed in a plastic bag and in the other with a toy gun, went into a small sub-post office and threatened the owner and a cashier. They were given £6,500. Two police officers who were in the shop arrested the applicants. Both applicants had several previous convictions. The first applicant had a previous conviction for robbery and having an imitation firearm with intent to commit an indictable offence. The second applicant had previous convictions for robbery. Sentenced to nine years' imprisonment and seven years' imprisonment respectively. Held: those who ran small sub-post offices were entitled to protection from the courts. The seriousness of the matter was compounded by the previous conviction for robbery or each applicant. The sentences were not manifestly excessive.'

As robbery while in possession of an imitation firearm is a 'serious offence' for the purposes of Crime (Sentences) Act 1997 section 2, *Curry* would have qualified for an automatic life sentence unless the court could find 'exceptional circumstances'.

A second example is *Mills*[4]:

[2] *See Attorney General's Reference No.5 of 1998 (R. v. Davies)* [1998] 2 Cr.App.R (S) 442.
[3] [1997] 1 Cr.App.R (S) 417.
[4] [1998] 2 Cr.App.R (S) 252.

'The appellant pleaded guilty to attempted rape. The appellant had a relationship with the victim over a period of about three years and they had a child. The appellant often stayed at her home, although they did not live together. The victim told the appellant that the relationship was over, but he refused to accept it. The appellant met the victim as she arrived home from a social occasion, dragged her to a grassy area and tried unsuccessfully to rape her. The appellant desisted and the victim escaped and reported the matter to the police. The victim gave evidence at committal proceedings. Sentenced to six years' with imprisonment with an order under Criminal Justice Act 1991 section 44. Held: the victim had now forgiven the appellant, and they intended to marry. As a matter of principle, the victim of a crime could not tell the court that because he or she had forgiven the offender, the court should treat the crime as if it had not happened. Attempted rape was a matter of public concern, in addition to its more immediate concern to the victim.The fact that the victim had forgiven the offender could not determine the appropriate level of sentence, but it could be taken into account as indicating the current extent of the impact of the crime on the victim. The Court had come to the conclusion that the sentence was too long; a sentence of three years would be substituted.'

The appellant in this case had a previous conviction for manslaughter, a fact to which the Court of Appeal attached no particular importance; under the Crime (Sentences) Act 1997 it would have made the appellant liable to an automatic life sentence unless the court could find 'exceptional circumstances'.

The interpretation of 'exceptional circumstances' was considered by the Court of Appeal, Criminal Division in *Kelly*.[5] The facts are taken from the headnote:

'The appellant was convicted of causing grievous bodily harm with intent. The appellant became involved in an incident between other persons at a railway station. The incident ended with the appellant sitting astride a man who had fallen to the ground, punching his face and later kicking him in the face. The victim suffered a fractured cheekbone, the loss of two teeth and a watery eye. The appellant had been convicted in March 1980 at the age of 19 of a number of robberies in the course of which firearms had been carried and on one occasion discharged. He had been sentenced to fourteen years' imprisonment; he was released from this sentence in 1988 and had no further convictions until the latest offence. Sentenced to an automatic life sentence under Crime (Sentences) Act 1997 section 2, with a period of four years specified for the purposes of Crime (Sentences) Act 1997 section 28.'

The Court of Appeal held that the cumulative effect of the youth of the offender when he committed his first 'serious offence' in 1979; the 18 year gap between the appellant's 'serious offences'; the dissimilarity between the relevant 'serious offences'; the appellant's good

[5] [1999] 2 Cr.App.R (S) 176.

record following release from his 14-year sentence in 1988; and the fact that the appellant's offence was not the most serious example of an offence under Offences against the Person Act 1861 section 18, could not amount to 'exceptional circumstances'. The Court declined to consider whether Article 2 of the Convention required a broader interpretation of the expression. Lord Bingham CJ said that recourse to the European Convention as an aid to construction of domestic legislation was permissible only in cases of ambiguity; the Court could find no ambiguity in section 2. Consideration of the conformity of section 2 with the Convention should be deferred until that issue came before the Court for authoritative decision under the Human Rights Act 1998.

When the Human Rights Act is in force, the interpretation of 'exceptional circumstances' will require reconsideration in the light of section 3(1) of the Act, which requires courts to to read and give effect to legislation 'in a way which is compatible with the Convention rights'. Article 3 of the Convention provides that 'no one shall be subjected to torture or to inhuman or degrading treatment or punishment'. There seems to be a powerful argument for saying that to impose a sentence of life imprisonment on a person when that sentence is neither deserved as proper punishment for the offence[6] nor necessary to protect the public from serious harm from the offender[7] is to subject the offender to 'inhuman . . . punishment'. In modern criminal law, there is no more severe sanction than life imprisonment; to require a court to impose that sanction arbitrarily without any rational purpose must infringe Article 3.

DETENTION AND TRAINING ORDERS

The Crime and Disorder Act sections 73 to 78 create a new system of custodial sentences for offenders under the age of 18, replacing the existing provisions which allow a court to award a sentence of detention in a young offender institution. (Detention in a young offender institution will continue in effect for those aged 18 and under 21.) A detention and training order may be for one of a number of fixed periods between four and 24 months. The change is one of name rather than substance; most offenders sentenced to detention and training orders will serve their sentences in young offender institutions alongside older offenders sentenced to detention in a young offender institution.

One feature of the new scheme is that lay magistrates sitting in the youth court will have power to award 24 months' detention and training, in place of the existing

maximum of six months for a single either way offence, or 12 months for more than one either way offence. This change, which has been made without public discussion, or even a ministerial statement that it was intended to be made, is controversial and may give rise to questions under Articles 6 and 14 of the Convention. The argument would be that the rights of an offender under the age of 18 have been substantially reduced by comparison to those of an offender over that age, and that there is accordingly inappropriate discrimination on the grounds of 'other status' in the delivery of the rights provided by Article 6.

No magistrates' court can try an offender aged 18 or over for an either way offence unless he has consented to summary trial[8]; the longest sentence which a magistrates' court can pass on an adult offender who has been tried summarily is six months, or 12 months if more than one either way offence is involved. An offender aged 18 or over cannot be sentenced to a custodial sentence of more six months for a single offence, or more than 12 months in aggregate,[9] without having had the chance to insist on trial by jury, and having his case considered by a judge of the Crown Court, whether on conviction on a trial on indictment or following a committal for sentence.[10]

An offender under 18 has no right to insist on trial by jury in any case. He can be tried summarily for any either way offence, or any offence triable only on indictment except homicide, at the discretion of the magistrates sitting in the youth court.[11] Until the enactment of the Crime and Disorder Act 1998, this lack of procedural protection for the young offender was compensated by the limitations on the sentencing powers of the youth court. If the youth court considered that the case warranted a sentence of more than six months' detention in a young offender institution in the case of one offence or an aggregate of 12 months, it was obliged to commit the offender to the Crown Court for sentence,[12] or to commit him for trial if that course was possible.[13] Even

---

[6] See *Wynne* v. *UK* (1994) 19 EHRR 333.

[7] *Weeks* v. *United Kingdom* (1988) 10 EHRR 293.

[8] See Magistrates' Courts Act 1980 s.20(3).

[9] Except where a magistrates' court activates an existing suspended sentence, or makes an order under Criminal Justice Act 1991 s. 40 in respect of an existing sentence.

[10] See Magistrates' Courts Act 1980 s. 38.

[11] See Magistrates' Courts Act 1980 s. 24.

[12] Under Magistrates' Courts Act 1980 s. 37, which is repealed by the Crime and Disorder Act, Sched.

[13] An offender under 18 may be committed for trial if he is charged with an offence in respect of which detention under Children and Young Persons Act 1933 s. 53(2) and (3) is available (all offences punishable with 14 years' imprisonment—causing death by dangerous driving and causing death by careless driving, having consumed alcohol so as to be above the prescribed limit, or indecent assault) or he is charged jointly with an adult who has been committed for trial. See Magistrates' Courts Act 1980 s. 24.

though an offender under 18 might be sentenced to two years' detention without the option or jury trial, his case would require the consideration of a judge of the Crown Court.

The effect of the Crime and Disorder Act 1998 is to remove from the offender under the age of 18 the protection of consideration of his case by a professional judge before a custodial sentence in excess of six months (or 12 months for multiple offences) is imposed. There appears to be an argument for saying that this may amount to an unjustified discrimination in relation to the right to a fair trial under Article 6 (1).

RETROSPECTIVE PUNISHMENT

Article 7(1) of the Convention concludes with the following sentence:

'Nor shall a heavier penalty be imposed than the one that was applicable at the time the criminal offence was committed.'

The principle against moving the goal posts once the game has started has immediate appeal. It is stronger when applied to the retrospective creation of new offences than to the retrospective increase in the punishment of established offences. The man who complains that actions which were lawful when he carried them out have been made criminal with retrospective effect commands more sympathy than the man who admits that he has willingly broken the law and taken the risk of the lower penalty, but would not have done so if he had known of the enhanced penalty that has subsequently been imposed for the same offence. In any event, the principle of the final sentence of Article 7(1) is open to question. A more sensible approach to the increase in penalties would be a requirement of fair notice. An offender cannot reasonably complain of an increase in the penalty for an offence if he had notice when he committed the offence that the increased penalty would (or might) apply by the time his case came before the court, even though it was not in force at that time in the sense that it could be applied to an offender appearing before the court on that day.

The principle of English law (for which it is surprisingly difficult to find much authority) is that a statute increasing the penalty for an offence is presumed not to be intended to take effect retrospectively, unless there is clear statutory language to the effect that it does.[14] If Parliament expressly so provides, a statute may take effect retrospectively. Parliament did expressly so

provide in the Drug Trafficking Offences Act 1986, which introduced the confiscation order.[15] The propriety of a confiscation order made in respect of an offence committed before the commencement of the Act was challenged in *Welch* v. *United Kingdom*.[16] The applicant was charged in February 1987 with possessing cocaine with intent to supply in November 1986, and he was further charged in May 1987 with a conspiracy to obtain cocaine with intent to supply committed between 1 January 1986 and 3 November 1986. (The confiscation provisions of the Drug Trafficking Offences Act 1986 came into force on 12 January 1987.) The applicant was sentenced to a confiscation order in the amount of £66,914, reduced on appeal to £59,914. The confiscation order was clearly lawful by reference to domestic law, given the express provisions for retrospective application in the Drug Trafficking Offences Act 1986. The European Court of Human Rights held that the order violated the second limb of Article 7.

The Government attempted to support the view that there was no violation of Article 7 with the argument that a confiscation for the purposes of the order was not a punishment or penalty, but a confiscatory or preventive measure. Given that a confiscation order can be made only by a criminal court on conviction for an offence, that it is a 'sentence' for the purposes of the Criminal Appeal Act 1968 and that it can result in the offender serving a substantial default term if the order is not satisfied, this was inevitably an uphill task.

A better line of argument might have been that the introduction of the confiscation order did not result in the possibility of a 'heavier penalty' than was applicable on the dates of the offences as stated in the indictment. Although confiscation orders have been described as 'Draconian', in reality they are no more threatening than the Wizard of Oz. The order which was made against Welch could have been made against him under different provisions which were in existence at the relevant time. A confiscation order is an order to pay an amount of money, backed up by the procedures for the enforcement of fines. Although there were special provisions in section 11 of the 1986 Act for the appointment of receivers to enforce confiscation orders, they are in substance no different from the use of civil remedies to enforce a fine through High Court proceedings, which is made possible by Magistrates' Courts Act 1980 section 87. If Welch had been convicted of the offences on the date on which they were committed, it would have been open to the Crown Court to impose on him an unlimited fine (see Criminal Law Act 1977 section 32(1)). There was at that time no statutory obligation on the Crown

[14] See *R.* v. *Penwith Justices ex parte Hay, Pender and Perkes* (1997) 1 Cr.App.R (S) 265.

[15] Drug Trafficking Offences Act 1986 s. 38(4).
[16] (1995) 20 EHRR 247.

Court to take account of the offender's means (as is now provided by Criminal Justice Act 1991 section 18).

The only differences between a fine and a confiscation order under Drug Trafficking Offences Act 1986 which might be relevant to Article 7(1) are that the decision to impose a fine is in the discretion of the court, while the making of a confiscation order was mandatory under the 1986 Act; this can be balanced against the fact that a fine can be for an unlimited amount, while the maximum amount of a confiscation order is limited to the value of the defendant's proceeds, or the amount that might be realised, whichever is the less. A court can impose a fine on the assumption that it can be paid out of expected future income, but a confiscation order is limited to the amount that might be realised at the time the order is made.[17]

There would surely have been a strong argument for saying that the enactment of the Drug Trafficking Offences Act 1986 did not expose the applicant in *Welch* to 'a heavier penalty' than the one that was applicable at the time the offence was committed. All the Drug Trafficking Offences Act 1986 actually did was to change the name of the penalty (from 'fine' to 'confiscation order'), introduce an element of mandatoriness and restrict the amount of the order.

There are two respects in which it could be said that the Drug Trafficking Offences Act 1986 exposed the offender to a 'heavier penalty'. The Act allowed the High Court to make charging orders and restraint orders. These could be made in anticipation of a confiscation order, and had to be discharged if no such order was made. The 1986 Act also permitted longer terms of imprisonment in default of payment of a confiscation order than were possible in the case of fines. In 1986, the maximum term of imprisonment in default of a fine imposed by the Crown Court was 12 months; the Drug Trafficking Offences Act 1986 included a scale of terms extending to ten years. The two scales have now been brought together as the Powers of Criminal Courts Act 1973 section 31(3A). Charging orders and restraint orders, being provisional in nature, and being made in anticipation of criminal proceedings, are probably not penalties, and the retrospective provision of such orders seems not to violate Article 7. The longer default terms probably do not violate the prohibition as on retrospective penalties as they were not truly retrospective. The default sentence would be served only in the event of a default through wilful refusal or culpable neglect occurring after the commencement date of the legislation.

Welch v. *United Kingdom* was distinguished by the Court of Appeal in *Taylor*,[18] where an order was made against an offender convicted of an offence committed after the commencement of the Act, based in part on the proceeds of drug trafficking derived from offences committed before the commencement of the Act. The Court of Appeal held that the Drug Trafficking Offences Act 1986 section 2(5) specifically permitted a court to make a confiscation order in respect of benefits derived from earlier offences which had not been covered by a confiscation order made in respect of those offences. The confiscation order did not contravene Article 7 of the Convention, as the penalty by way of confiscation order and the procedure for determining it were laid down by the 1986 Act which was in force during the whole of the period of the conspiracy of which the appellant had been convicted. The 1986 Act required the sentencer to bring into account, when assessing the proceeds of drug trafficking, those benefits which had accrued at any time, even before the commencement of the Act; but at the time of the present conspiracy, anyone embarking on drug trafficking must be taken to have known that if he were convicted, all the benefits he had obtained from unlawful conduct of that kind could be taken into account in assessing a confiscation order. The mischief which Article 7 sought to avoid was that a defendant be given a punishment greater than his offence carried at the time he committed it. The appellant had committed the present offences between 1990 and 1993, by which time the Act was fully in force and the penalties to which he rendered himself liable were well known. He must be deemed to have committed them with his eyes open to the possible consequences.

Whether or not *Welch* v. *United Kingdom* was correctly decided, it has had an important effect on legislative practice. Anything which could be treated as a retrospective increase in punishment is carefully avoided.[19] An example of the extremes to which Parliament is now willing to go to avoid an infringement of Article 7 is provided by the commencement arrangements for Criminal Procedure and Investigations Act 1996 section 58. This complex section empowers a court to prohibit the publication of derogatory assertions about third parties made by advocates mitigating in the Crown Court or magistrates' court. However, section 61 of the Act provides that section 58 applies only where

---

[17] See Drug Trafficking Offences Act 1986 s. 4(3), re-enacted as Drug Trafficking Act 1994 s. 5(3).

[18] [1996] 2 Cr.App.R (S) 96.

[19] If it is not overlooked. The commencement provisions of Criminal Justice and Public Order Act 1994 Sched. 9 para. 45 (which extended the definition of 'sexual offence' to a number of offences to which it did not originally apply) provide that the amended definition should apply to offenders convicted before the date of commencement, whose offences must have been committed before the commencement date. As the effect of this amendment was to expose the offender to the risk of a heavier penalty in the form of a longer than commensurate sentence under Criminal Justice Act 1991 s. 2(2)(b), there was a strong argument for saying that it gave rise to a potential violation of Art. 7.

the offence in respect of which the speech in mitigation was made was committed on or after the appointed day for the commencement of the section. As well as taking compliance with Article 7 to the extreme—it is difficult to see how an order restricting the publication of a derogatory assertion made in a speech in mitigation could be regarded as a 'penalty'—this provision illustrates the practical problems which Article 7 can create. It is commonplace today to see defendants sentenced for sexual offences committed many years, sometimes decades, before the trial; the sentencer must remember that section 58 does not apply to them. Cases will frequently arise where offences are committed on both sides of the appointed day. If the same speech in mitigation covers all of them (as it normally will) does the court have power to make an order or not?

In the case of the Criminal Procedure and Investigations Act 1996 section 58 this does not really matter, as the provision is unlikely to be used with any frequency, but the same question arises in the context of confiscation orders for non-drug trafficking offences in such a way as to create the possibility of major confusion. The power to make a confiscation order in such cases was introduced by the Criminal Justice Act 1988, which (like the Drug Trafficking Offences Act 1986) was made retrospective.[20] Those provisions were amended in detail by the Criminal Justice Act 1993 and more substantially by the Proceeds of Crime Act 1995. The amendments made by the Criminal Justice Act 1993 included the insertion of section 71(7A), which establishes that the standard of proof is the civil standard, were brought into force so as to apply to proceedings instituted on or after the commencement date, irrespective of the date on which the offence was committed. Was this a breach of Article 7?

The more substantial amendments made by the Proceeds of Crime Act 1995 were brought into force with much more attention to the possibility of a breach of Article 7; they apply only if every offence of which the offender is convicted in the same proceedings (whether or not a confiscation order is made in respect of those offences) was committed on or after the commencement date of the Act. This restriction does not apply where an offender asks the court to take offences into consideration. If a defendant pleads guilty to ten offences of theft or fraud, some committed before and some after the commencement date of the 1995 Act, the 1995 Act does not apply to any of the offences, even though no benefit was derived from the pre-commencement offences. If on the same facts the offender pleads

guilty to counts charging offences committed after the commencement date, and asks the court to take into consideration offences committed before the commencement date, the 1995 Act applies to all of the offences. The difficulties become worse when continuing offences committed over a period of time (such as conspiracies or offences of fraudulent trading) are involved. It is easy to see the scope for confusion.

There are plenty of other examples where a strict, or possibly over-strict, compliance with the rule against retrospective increases in penalty leads to practical inconvenience. One is the changes made by the Crime and Disorder Act 1998 in relation to revocation of parole licences. Under the parole system introduced by the Criminal Justice Act 1991, long-term prisoners are liable to be recalled to prison if their licences are revoked by the Parole Board. This procedure did not apply to short term prisoners (those serving less than four years.) A short term prisoner who failed to comply with the terms of his licence was liable to be convicted of a summary offence by a magistrates' court, which could suspend his licence for a period not exceeding six months. The Crime and Disorder Act 1998 section 103 has now abolished this procedure and applied the provisions which govern revocation of licence in the case of long term prisoners to short term prisoners as well. This change will apply only to short term prisoners sentenced for offences committed after the commencement date of section 103; an offender sentenced at some date, possibly far in the future, to a sentence of less than four years for offences committed before the commencement date, will be liable to be dealt with subject to the old procedure under the terms of a repealed statutory provision. The practical problems which this will cause are obvious. There seems to no reason why the new arrangements should not apply to all offenders sentenced after the commencement date, or even released on licence after the commencement date, so long as they have notice of their potential liability at the time of release. Oddly, the old procedure for dealing with short term prisoners will apply in future to offenders convicted of offences committed before 1 October 1992, the date on which the new parole system came into force. There was less concern in 1991 with the question of retrospectivity, and the parole system introduced by the Criminal Justice Act 1991 applied to all offenders sentenced on or after 1 October 1992, irrespective of the date of the offence.

Article 7 has now been enacted as part of English law and governs the making and interpretation of all statutes. In 1951, statutory change in sentencing law was relatively rare; the Criminal Justice Act 1948 was the first major statute dealing with sentencing since the Prevention of Crime Act 1908. We are now accustomed

---

[20] See Criminal Justice Act 1988 s. 102(4), which provides that the confiscation provisions of the Act apply to an offence committed before the commencement of the Act, provided that the relevant proceedings were instituted after the commencement of the Act.

to continuous legislation on sentencing; proposals for the next Criminal Justice Bill are canvassed before the last one has received the Royal Assent. The problem of retrospectivity is a constant one, and can produce bizarre situations.[21] It is to be hoped that the English courts will examine what is and what is not permissible in terms of the concluding words of Article 7(1), and reach conclusions which respect the underlying principle on which the Article is based, but avoid some of the difficulties which result from its overzealous application to changes which are more of form than of substance.

[21] *See Attorney General's Reference No.48 of 1994 (R.v. Jeffrey)* (1995) 16 Cr.App.R.(S) 980. The appellant was convicted on 8 November 1994 of a single count of buggery of a male person without consent, committed in October 1991. On 3 November 1994, s. 142, 143 and 144 of the Criminal Justice and Public Order Act 1994 came into force. These sections redefined rape so as to include non-consensual buggery; the maximum sentence remained life imprisonment. The change meant that the Sexual Offences Act 1956 s. 12(1) (the section under which the appellant had been convicted) applied only to consensual buggery. S. 144 of the 1994 Act revised the penalties for buggery contrary to the Sexual Offences Act 1956 s. 12. If committed with a man aged 18 or over, the maximum sentence was to be two years. If the offender had been sentenced before 3 November 1994, the maximum sentence would have been ten years. The trial judge proceeded on the basis that the maximum sentence was two years. The Court of Appeal accepted the Attorney General's submission that the intention of Parliament was not to decrease the maximum sentence for non-consensual buggery but to increase it. An offence of non-consensual buggery committed before the commencement of the 1994 Act could not be charged after that commencement as male rape, contrary to the Sexual Offences Act 1956 as amended, as this would contravene Art. 7. The maximum sentence for non-consensual buggery before the Act was ten years; after the Act it was to be life imprisonment. There was no question of the Court inflicting an increased penalty on the offender; the Court was simply declining to decrease the penalty when Parliament had evinced a clear intention to increase it for the particular form of offending of which the offender was guilty. The maximum sentence for the offence committed by the offender before the commencement of the 1994 Act was ten years' imprisonment.

11

THE HUMAN RIGHTS ACT: POST-TRIAL AND HEARING

DAVID KYLE*

THE SETTING

Ask the man in the street for a 'soundbite' comment on the news that the Human Rights Act 1998 received the Royal Assent on 9 November 1998 and he will probably say 'Great'. Ask a more informed man in the street, and he will probably say 'About time too!'. Ask a selection of players on the stage of criminal justice and not only are comments unlikely to be of soundbite length, but they may also cover the entire spectrum from delight to dismay.

At one extreme will be those who rejoice unequivocally that the fundamental rights, enshrined in the European Convention on Human Rights, are at last a part of our domestic law with all the benefits of direct interpretation by the courts of the rights, and their effect, and the compatibility of our legislation. More cynically, this might be heralded as open season to argue any aspect of evidence or procedure which looks to disadvantage a defendant as a breach of a Convention right, particularly the right to a fair trial.

At the other extreme will be those who applaud the notion of protecting Human Rights, but ask why it has to be visited on our criminal justice system. After all, we have a pretty good system, don't we? We have jury trials and the prosecution has to prove its case beyond reasonable doubt—a couple of self inflicted and devoutly cherished guarantees of a fair trial and a just outcome, neither of which are to be found in the Convention. And they will look across the Atlantic to the US Constitution and the Canadian Charter of Rights and Freedoms and wonder about experience in those countries of numerous, time-consuming arguments on Constitution and Charter points which appear to have nothing to do with justice in its widest sense and every-

* of the Criminal Cases Review Commission

thing to do with getting off on 'technicalities'. I do not claim to have researched this and I confess that my knowledge is every bit as anecdotal as the next person's. I was interested to see however that the Autumn 1998 issue of Justice reports Sedley LJ's introduction to the Justice training course on Human Rights and Employment and Discrimination Law. He referred to a case in which the Supreme Court of Canada had to decide whether the right to counsel (section 10(b) of the Charter) extended to a drunk driver arrested far inside the Arctic Circle who wanted his lawyer brought up from civilisation before he blew into the bag 'by which time he would be at best sober and at worst frozen to death'. He then went on to say this:

'If all that the legal profession does is use the Convention as the last port in a storm, much as Wednesbury irrationality is used in judicial review proceedings, then it will be rapidly devalued and sidelined. If, on the other hand, perceptive and intelligent analysis of case throws up well judged and educated arguments on Convention rights, the judiciary will both learn with the practising profession and acquire a new dimension to its own thinking and forensic instincts. This without doubt is the situation which everybody wants to see develop, but it will not happen without conscientious efforts.'

The title of this session is 'Post Trial and Hearing'. For the purpose of my contribution, I have taken this to mean the appeal stage of the criminal justice process. In one sense, of course, this could leave me open to discussing every aspect of the Human Rights Act and its impact on criminal justice, because the appellate courts will have to grapple with these matters just as enthusiastically as will the courts of trial. This mammoth task I gratefully leave to others. I intend to look at the somewhat narrower matter of the role and function of the appellate courts in the context of the Human Rights Act. I just mention in passing that, if there is one thing which stands out for me as a source of comfort, it is that so far the European Court of Human Rights has been pretty relaxed about the exercise of *discretion* by trial courts to include or exclude evidence (e.g. *Shenk* v. *Switzerland*[1]. In our case we would doubtless say that the principles by which section 78 of the Police and Criminal Evidence Act 1984 operates are very congruent with those of Article 6 of the Convention.

AN APPEAL STRUCTURE

We do have one, although this is not actually a requirement of the Convention, which can be contrasted with the 1966 UN Covenant on Civil and Political Rights, of which Article 14 specifically refers to a right of appeal in the context of fair trials. It is hard to envisage an acceptable system of criminal justice which does not have built into it some form of appeal process. For present purposes, it should be noted that, once an appeal system is instituted, it will attract the guarantees of Article 6 of the Convention.[2] This was the well known libel action against Count Tolstoy by Lord Aldington. When the Count tried to appeal, he was required to lodge almost £125,000 as security against costs. He complained to the European Court that this denied him the right of access to the courts as guaranteed by Article 6. The Court held that appellants enjoy the fundamental guarantees in Article 6 within the appellate jurisdiction. The Court also held, however, that the manner of application of Article 6 depends on the special features of the proceedings involved. The Court did not see its role as substituting itself for the competent British authorities in determining policy. Rather, its role was to review the decisions actually taken in a particular case against the yardstick of fairness. The Court went on to find that that the security for costs order pursued a legitimate aim (protection of the plaintiff should the appeal be unsuccessful) and was imposed in the interests of a fair administration of justice, since regard was had to the lack of prospects of a successful appeal.

We have two broad systems of appeal, depending on whether the case was tried by the Magistrates' Court or the Crown Court. Following summary conviction by the magistrates, any appeal by the convicted person will usually take the form of a rehearing in the Crown Court. That being the case, any Convention points can be revisited (if already rehearsed in the lower court) or taken in the Crown Court. There is nothing obvious about the exercise of the Crown Court's appellate jurisdiction which merits scrutiny in the context of the Human

Rights Act. Subject only to this: there is no restriction on how the prosecution presents its case at the appeal hearing. Some evidence might be abandoned. More significantly, additional evidence might be adduced. Could it be argued that the prosecution's ability to better its position and to have a second, bigger bite of the cherry is unfair? Logically the answer should be no, provided that, specific to the appeal hearing, the Article 6 protections are afforded to the appellant in their entirety.

It is the procedure of the Court of Appeal, where for the most part issues of fact are taken as having been settled at trial and the Court does not substitute its own view of the evidence for that of the jury, which excites a greater scrutiny against the terms of Article 6. It seems that in principle, a full oral hearing is not *necessary* for the purpose of Article 6 fairness where the only issues are matters of law. However fairness may demand such a hearing. In *Pardo* v. *France*,[3] the Commission were considering a situation where an appellant was not ready to present his case. Far from granting an adjournment, the Court proceeded to adjudicate on the merits of the case based on the written pleadings. 'The Commission recalls that the right to a fair trial holds a prominent place in a democratic society. In the case of an appeal procedure, provided for under domestic law, this right implies that counsels [sic] may take the opportunities offered by the procedure to develop their arguments fully. Thus, when it is a case of guaranteeing rights that are not theoretical or illusory but rights that are practical and effective, it is not conceivable that counsels should be prevented, as an indirect consequence of procedural devices, from arguing orally on the submissions made and from supporting them by exhibits other than those already contained in the case file.'

In our system, the process remains adversarial throughout and the full Court of Appeal is invariably prepared to hear oral argument from both sides. Indeed, in recent years the Court has reinforced the adversarial nature of the proceedings and highlighted the difficulties if this is diminished (by the Crown not opposing the appeal, particularly in fresh evidence cases: *R.* v. *McIlkenny and others*).[4] At an earlier stage, however, applications for leave to appeal are initially considered by a single judge on written application and usually without oral argument. A refusal by a single judge entitles the applicant to renew his application before the full Court of Appeal. Sometimes there will be oral argument, either because the court regards it as necessary (and grants legal aid as appropriate) or because the applicant instructs counsel privately. It follows that

---

[1] (1991) 13 EHRR 242.

[2] See *Tolstoy Miloslavsky* v. *United Kingdom* (1995) 20 EHRR 442).

[3] (1993) 17 EHRR 383.

[4] (1991) 93 CAR 287.

there are cases when the full court will refuse leave to appeal in the absence of the applicant and without hearing argument. Although, therefore, the climate in which the Court of Appeal operates appears generally conducive to the expectations of Article 6, there may be a question mark over the application for leave to appeal procedure, touching as it does on the fairness point (desirability of an oral hearing) and the right of a person 'to defend himself in person or through legal assistance of his own choosing' (Article 6(3)(c)). It may be of course that challenge to the Court of Appeal's procedures is satisfactorily answered first by the flexibility which the court itself can, and does, operate, followed by the availability of the 'long stop' remedy of application to the Criminal Cases Review Commission.

One possible area for contemplation is the Court of Appeal's approach to fresh evidence and the terms of section 23 of the Criminal Appeal Act 1968 as amended by the Criminal Appeal Act 1995.

It is self evident that on occasions the reception of evidence at the appeal stage may be necessary to the proper determination of the appeal and there must be a mechanism for the reception and consideration of that evidence if the appeal proceedings are to be fair. In *Ekbatani* v. *Sweden*,[5] the European Court held that there had been a breach of Article 6 because the Swedish court had declined to hold a rehearing and had exercised the option to dismiss the appeal without a hearing. Either option was available in accordance with Swedish law. The Court considered the wrong option had been exercised, particularly as there was the possibility of relevant new evidence. The court recognised the application of Article 6 to appeal proceedings and said that the manner of application depended on the special features of the domestic proceedings viewed as a whole (echoed in the *Tolstoy* case).

Against that—and this is the principle on which our appeal system is based—is the desirable notion that matters should not be litigated over and over again. There has to be finality. Parties to litigation ought not generally to be allowed to use the appeal process as a vehicle for shoring up their cases. Section 23 of the 1968 Act seeks to strike the balance by providing that the Court of Appeal can receive fresh evidence if it thinks it necessary or expedient in the interests of justice. In reaching this decision, the Court must consider the likely impact on the conviction, admissibility, whether the evidence is capable of belief and whether there is a reasonable explanation for not calling it at trial. On the face of it, these are perfectly acceptable factors, particularly the one about why the evidence was not adduced at trial. There are however a couple of

points to ponder. First, is it consistent with the concept of Article 6 fairness that the court should purport to determine whether the evidence is capable of belief as a preliminary to receiving the evidence? Where this evidence is to be given by a witness, the Act does not require—and indeed it may imply the opposite—the Court to hear the witness before deciding whether the proposed evidence is capable of belief. In practice, the Court does sometimes hear the witness in order to determine this preliminary question, so perhaps its own procedure imports the element of fairness which might be said to be lacking in the statute itself. Secondly, decisions made by the Court of Appeal in individual cases that the proposed evidence was *not* capable of belief, or that there was *no* reasonable explanation for the failure to call it earlier, might henceforth be more susceptible to challenge in their own right that they themselves rendered the appeal hearing 'unfair'.

As to the actual reception of the evidence, there are arguments around Article 6(3)(d) and the compatibility of procedures we have adopted (at common law and by statute, notably sections 23–26 of the Criminal Justice Act 1988) in order to allow evidence to be given other than by the mouth of a witness standing in the witness box in full view of the Court and the accused. I imagine these arguments will be as relevant to the Court of Appeal in its reception of fresh evidence as to courts of trial.

IS THE COURT OF APPEAL READY?

This is a slightly tongue in cheek question because I have no doubt that the sentiments of Sedley LJ will be roundly shared by all his judicial colleagues. But it is worth noting in passing how the Court of Appeal has expressed itself in relation to the Convention. Let me start with an extreme, and anonymous, example of the terms in which leave to appeal from a court martial conviction was refused by a single judge: 'The point about EC law has already been decided against you and in any event is bad. Mercifully, despite the intense desire of Continental bureaucrats to meddle, we still control the running of our armed forces.' More recently, we have had regard to the judgments of the Court of Appeal in *Saunders*[6] and *Staines and Morrisey*[7] when dealing with claims by convicted persons that one aspect or another of their trials were in breach of the Convention and that their convictions should be quashed.

Both cases concerned the admissibility of answers given under statutory compulsion to DTI Inspectors. In

---

[5] (1991) 13 EHRR 505.

[6] [1996] 1 Cr. App. R 463.
[7] [1997] 2 Cr. App. R 426.

Saunders, the Court said, 'English courts can have recourse to the European Convention on Human Rights and decisions thereon by the European Court of Justice [sic] *only when the law of England is ambiguous or unclear*. Saunders has taken his case to Europe on this issue and the European Commission on Human Rights has referred it to the European Court in Strasbourg. Should Saunders succeed there, our treaty obligations will require consideration to be given to the effect of the decision here. But our duty at present is to apply our domestic law which is unambiguous'. [my emphasis].

Similarly in *Staines and Morrisey* (by which time the European Court had found in Mr Saunders' favour), 'the present position is very unsatisfactory. It would appear that the appellants have or certainly may have grounds for complaining in Strasbourg and, if the penalty is enforced, and they incur costs in seeking relief, they may have claims to compensation against Her Majesty's Government. That is not, however, something which the courts can remedy. Our domestic law remains as declared by this case in Saunders. The United Kingdom is subject to a treaty obligation to give effect to the European Convention on Human Rights as interpreted by the court of Human Rights, but that again is not something which this court can enforce.'

So although in the second case, the court acknowledged the difficulty, neither judgment indicated whether the court felt that admitting evidence of enforced answers was, or was not, unfair as envisaged by Article 6. I appreciate that, in *Saunders*, the court may have been inhibited because the matter was pending in Europe and, in *Staines and Morrisey*, because Strasbourg had pronounced in Mr Saunders' favour. But I see from a 'Human Rights Update' article[8] that the authors warmly approve of a couple of cases, *R. v. Thomas*; *R. v. Flanagan*[9] and *R. v. Radak*,[10] in which the Court of Appeal did indicate their view that the decisions were in line with the Convention. Apart from suggesting that the answer to my question (is the Court ready?) should be 'Yes', these cases perhaps also reveal a degree of prescience, given that the point in issue was the admissibility of written statements under sections 23–26 of the Criminal Justice Act 1988.

THE HEART OF COURT OF APPEAL DECISIONS

Section 2(1) of the Criminal Appeal Act 1968 as amended by the Criminal Appeal Act 1995 provides that:

⁸ In (1998) 148 NLJ 1782.
⁹ *The Times*, July 24 1998.
¹⁰ *The Times*, 7 October 1998.

'Subject to the provisions of this Act, the Court of Appeal
a shall allow an appeal against conviction if they think that the conviction is unsafe; and
b shall dismiss such an appeal in any other case.'

In determining whether a conviction is safe or unsafe, in the context of the Human Rights Act, the Court of Appeal will be presented with grounds and argument about breaches of the Convention and will have to wrestle with those issues just like any other court and will have to apply sections 2 and 3 of the Act just like any other court. Anticipating and debating the nature and scope of such 'Convention points' is the mammoth task I have sidestepped.

However an interesting, and perhaps not simply an academic, question is the relationship between a breach of a Convention right and the safety of a conviction. Does an established breach necessarily mean that a conviction is unsafe, or could the Court of Appeal take the view that, notwithstanding the breach, the conviction is nonetheless safe taking into account all the other circumstances relevant to the case. And, if the court were to take this latter view, could this interpretation of 'safe and unsafe' itself be challenged as incompatible with Convention rights?

I might say that the Court of Appeal's approach to whether, at the point of appeal, a conviction is safe or unsafe is a matter of considerable domestic interest, quite apart from any Convention considerations. Before its amendment, section 2 of the 1968 Act had a menu of situations in which an appeal might be allowed, set off by a proviso to prevent unmeritorious successes. Their replacement by the single word 'unsafe' and the abolition of the proviso was a contentious amendment, although the Court of Appeal itself recognised that very often, under the old regime, no great thought was given to which menu item was being applied. With particular reference to the role of the Criminal Cases Review Commission, not only are we interested in the meaning of 'unsafe'; we are also interested in the extent to which we can and should assess the court's willingness to receive evidence favourable to the Crown (see *Gilfoyle*)[11] when deciding whether or not to refer a conviction to the Court of Appeal. Would it be a just outcome if the court finds a conviction to be unsafe in circumstances notwithstanding new evidence indicative of guilt? Linked to this of course are considerations when a retrial should be ordered under section 7 of the 1968 Act.

There are authorities in which the Court of Appeal has considered section 2 of the 1968 Act as amended.

¹¹ [1996] 1 Cr. App. R. 302.

R. v. Graham[12]

'The new provision . . . is plainly intended to concentrate attention on one question: whether, in the light of any arguments raised or evidence adduced on appeal, the Court of Appeal considers a conviction unsafe. If the court is satisfied, despite any misdirection of law or any irregularity in the conduct of the trial or any fresh evidence, that the conviction is safe, the court will dismiss the appeal. But if, for whatever reason, the court concludes that that the appellant was wrongly convicted of the offence charged, or is left in doubt whether the appellant was rightly convicted of that offence or not, then it must of necessity consider the conviction unsafe. The court is then under a binding duty to allow the appeal . . . Where the condition in section 2(1)(a) as it now stands is satisfied, the court has no discretion to exercise.'

R. v. Chalkley and another[13]

The setting for this decision was that two defendants had pleaded guilty after an adverse ruling about the admissibility of particularly damning evidence. The significance of the judgment lies in the court's view of when a plea of guilty is unsafe, although the approach to section 2(1) as amended has a general application. After reviewing a number of authorities, the court set out three propositions:

1. The single word 'unsafe', uncluttered by other similar notions serving the same end, should concentrate the mind on the real issue in every appeal from the outset;
2. A conviction would be unsafe where the effect of an incorrect ruling of law on the admitted facts would leave the accused with no legal escape from a verdict of guilty on those facts. However, a conviction would not normally be unsafe where an accused is influenced to change his plea to guilty because he recognises that, as a result of a ruling to admit strong evidence against him, his case on the facts is hopeless;
3. A mistaken or uninformed plea, or one made without an intention to admit the truth of the offence charged, is unsafe.

R. v. Pearson[14]

'The function of this court since the substitution of the new section 2(1) . . . is that we must not allow an appeal where we think the conviction is safe. No doubt where this court takes the view that an appellant did not receive a fair trial this court would not, save in the most exceptional circumstances, reach the view that the conviction was nevertheless safe. We

observe that a trial may be fair although it could be said that justice had not been seen to be done.'

R. v. Farrow[15]

The concept of the 'lurking doubt' as a basis for allowing an appeal[16] was laid to rest. The Court of Appeal thought it undesirable to place any gloss on the test formulated by Parliament which had the advantage of brevity and simplicity. In answering the simple test posed for the court by section 2(1) of the 1968 Act, the court would in different cases take account of the considerations relevant to the particular case.

As a brief overview of the position, it seems to me that the court's approach to the amended section 2(1) test can be put in a couple of propositions:

(i) If the Court of Appeal is to conclude that a conviction is unsafe, it must be able to articulate its reasons for coming to that conclusion.
(ii) Where the safety of a conviction is challenged because of a process failure, this cannot be a stand alone reason for concluding that the conviction is unsafe. The question is whether the process failure causes the court to have any doubt about the safety of the conviction taking into account all the relevant considerations as they appear to the court at the time of the appeal hearing.

'Process failure' is possibly an inelegant shorthand to cover a variety of circumstances, but it might well embrace what, under the terms of the old section 2, was described as a wrong decision on any question of law or material irregularity in the course of the trial. Breach of Convention rights is within my contemplation when using this expression, and the question is whether the Court of Appeal will be justified in balancing such a breach against the rest of the relevant circumstances in the particular case when deciding whether the conviction is safe or not. This would seem to be an outcome wholly consistent with the Court's apparent approach to the proper interpretation of section 2 as amended.

I think there are a number of reasons why the Court of Appeal can absorb the Convention dimension in this way without itself being vulnerable to criticism that its own procedure breaches Article 6. First, decisions of the European Court are confined to the interpretation of the Convention and adjudication on whether it has been violated; they do not, where the application arises out of criminal proceedings, purport to adjudicate directly on the validity or outcome of the domestic proceedings.

[12] [1997] 1 CAR 302 (HK).
[13] [1998] 2 All ER 155.
[14] 20 February 1998 (CA).
[15] *The Times*, 20 October 1998.
[16] *R. v. Cooper* [1969] 1 QB 267.

Secondly, as we have seen, although the Article 6 protections apply to appellate systems, the European Court considers that the manner of their application depends on the special feature of the domestic proceedings viewed as a whole. On this basis, it can be asserted that the function of the Court of Appeal is to review the safety of a conviction and that the fairness of the trial is properly to be considered as one, albeit important, factor in the equation. It may well be that an established breach of a Convention right will weigh very heavily with the Court of Appeal, but that is not the same as making it an absolute that, without any more, breach of a convention right necessarily makes the conviction unsafe.

There may of course be counter arguments, of which a couple occur to me. What about *Chalkley* and guilty pleas? The store we lay by guilty pleas as contributing to the efficiency, effectiveness and economy of the criminal justice system is not altogether shared elsewhere in Europe, and the idea that a guilty plea cures all may not stand up against the Convention view of a fair trial. Then again, looking at *Pearson*, could the language used by the court, which may not have had the Convention in mind at the time, rebound? Article 6 guarantees a fair trial, so it can be said that a breach of Article 6 equates to an unfair trial. Should the *Pearson* judgment be interpreted as saying that a breach of Article 6 therefore equals an unsafe conviction other than in the most exceptional (undefined) circumstances? Or is this an example of crooked thinking? The judgment of the Court of Appeal in *Mullen*[17] is interesting in this context, albeit in relation to factual circumstances outside the boundaries of the trial process itself. First, a conviction may be 'unsafe' within the meaning of section 2 of the 1968 Act as amended if the trial amounted to an abuse of process of sufficient magnitude, notwithstanding that evidence of guilt was incontrovertible and the trial itself had been scrupulously fair. Secondly, in such a situation, the Court must balance the gravity of the offence and the danger to the public represented by the offender against the nature and gravity of the abuse in question. It remains to be seen whether intervention by the Court of Appeal is to be limited, on the facts in *Mullen*, to the means by which an offender is brought within the jurisdiction, or whether a conviction founded on proceedings amounting to an abuse for whatever reason is capable of being 'unsafe'. It does however appear that the Court of Appeal continues to regard the balancing of competing factors, and not giving any one type of occurrence a 'knock out' status, as being the correct approach to the question whether a conviction is safe or not. This is also consistent with ECHR jurisprudence.

[17] [1999] Crim. L.R. 561.

ABUSE OF PROCESS

I suppose this should strictly speaking be regarded as a *pre*-trial and hearing matter, but I include it because there has been a developing jurisdiction and the Human Rights Act dimension may impact on it, with consequential involvement of the appellate courts. First, if the danger of 'last port in a storm' use of the Convention materialises, it could well do so in the guise of pre-trial abuse applications. Secondly, there may be aspects of the existing abuse of process jurisdiction which will be affected by this extra dimension, of which I have picked a couple: delay (where I see no particular problem) and entrapment/agent provocateur (where I do).

The traditional approach of English courts has always been one of reluctance to prevent a prosecution going ahead. 'It is only if the prosecution amounts to an abuse of the process of the court and is oppressive or vexatious that the judge has power to intervene. Fortunately such prosecutions are hardly ever brought but the power of the court to prevent them is of great constitutional importance and should be jealously preserved.'[18]

From more recent experience, we might think that the number of cases stayed as being an abuse of process does not altogether support the rarity suggested by Lord Salmon. It remains true that the factors which would justify a judge stopping a case before the trial starts are narrow and the decision in any given case is seen very much as one for the judge's discretion, exercised in light of the particular circumstances of the particular case, and one unlikely to be disturbed on appeal.

DELAY

This has been a particularly fruitful source of abuse applications in recent years, probably going hand in glove with the perceived inefficiencies of the Crown Prosecution Service. Although the courts have said that cases should not be stopped simply as a form of discipline against the CPS,[19] it is nonetheless true that as a general rule some form of improper act or inefficiency by the prosecution will lie behind successful abuse applications based on delay. It is also part of our present jurisprudence that old cases may be stopped simply by virtue of age, and regardless of fault, if a fair trial would be impossible. This concept of course lay at the heart of the objections to the passing of the War Crimes Act 1991. By contrast, delay occasioned by the fault or inefficiency of the defence is unlikely to result in a

[18] Lord Salmon in *Connelly* v. *DPP* [1964] AC 1254.
[19] *Ex parte Belsham* (1992) 94 CAR 382.

successful application to stop the case, subject always to the requirement that a fair trial must be possible.

Article 6(1) of the Convention entitles everyone charged with a criminal offence to a fair and public hearing within a reasonable time. For this purpose, time runs from the point where a defendant knows he is to be prosecuted. As already mentioned, in English law the time since the offence may be relevant to an abuse of process application. European cases seem to be very much in accord with English authorities on the causes and consequences of delay. For that reason we should not expect our existing approach and practice to be at odds with the Convention.

ENTRAPMENT/*AGENT PROVOCATEUR*

The position in English law is that entrapment does not of itself amount to a defence to a criminal charge.[20] I am not aware of any European authority which indicates that this in itself is inimical to Convention rights. Where however there have been defence attacks founded on entrapment, they have been fought principally on the battlefield of admissibility of evidence rather than directly on the issue of abuse of process.[21] So far so good, because, as we have seen, the European Court has taken a benevolent approach to discretionary inclusion and exclusion of evidence. There is however an overlap with abuse of process jurisdiction, as was the situation in *R.* v. *Latif and Shahzad*,[22] where the House of Lords held that the trial judge had been justified in the particular circumstances in declining to stay the proceedings as an abuse of process.

I wonder whether the Convention dimension may force the issue of entrapment matters coming more prominently into the abuse of process arena (where European cases may bite) rather than being seen as an evidential consideration.

[20] *R.* v. *Sang* [1980] AC 402.
[21] See e.g. *R.* v. *Christou and Wright* (1992) 95 CAR 264; *Williams* v. *DPP* (1994) 98 CAR 209 and *R.* v. *Smurthwaite and Gill* (1994) 98 CAR 437.
[22] [1996] 1 WLR 104.

The relevant Articles of the Convention are Article 8 (right to respect for private and family life) and Article 6. Article 8 permits 'interference' with the protected right if it is in accordance with the law and is necessary in a democratic society for a number of purposes, including the prevention of disorder or crime. Self-evidently, the best way to become 'Europe proof' over Article 8 and intrusive crime investigation techniques is to have a statutory regime against which the degree of 'interference' can be judged. We have done this for telephone taps (the Interception of Communications Act 1985) and for covert entry onto property for surveillance purposes (the Police Act 1997). No legislation sanctions or controls entrapment or the use of *agents provocateurs*. There has to be an argument that sting operations of the type mounted in the *Christou* and *Williams* cases should be controlled by legislation if they are to escape censure as being in breach of Article 8.

There are also implications for Article 6, having regard to the judgment of the European Court on 9 June 1998 in the case of *Texeira de Castro* v. *Portugal*.[23] In that case, the defendant was approached by undercover police to set up a heroin deal for which he was subsequently prosecuted. The Court found that there had been breaches of Article 6 both as to the conduct of the police (incitement) and as to the manner of obtaining the evidence against the defendant. Relevant considerations included (i) the police acting outside the statutory scheme for entrapment operations, (ii) not establishing whether the defendant was pre-disposed to commit any drugs offences and (iii) the Portuguese courts failing to address sufficiently the question whether the police had instigated the commission of the offence. Under current English law, we would probably argue that we routinely address properly the third point. As to the second, this does not appear to have been addressed by the court in *Williams*. As to the first, we may be vulnerable because we do not have a statutory regime. As I say, continuing to treat this type of activity as a matter of evidence and admissibility may not keep us safe from intervention.

[23] (1996) 22 EHRR 293.

PART III

Regulation

12

WHICH REGULATORY BODIES ARE SUJECT TO THE HUMAN RIGHTS ACT?

J. BEATSON QC*

A. 'VERTICAL' AND 'HORIZONTAL' EFFECT

Broadly speaking, Bills of Rights can either protect the rights of citizens against encroachment by the state and public bodies or can also regulate rights between fellow citizens.[1] If they only protect the rights of citizens against encroachment by the state and public bodies, their effect has been described as 'vertical'. If they also protect the rights of citizens against encroachment by private individuals and entities in some or in all circumstances, their effect has been described as 'horizontal'. Does the Human Rights Act 1998 have a 'horizontal' effect or does it only operate 'vertically', i.e. against the state?

The Human Rights Act 1998 (hereafter 'HRA') is primarily designed to give Convention rights a 'vertical' effect. Section 6 provides that individuals will be able to rely on Convention rights against public authorities and those exercising functions of a public nature. This will be so both in proceedings initiated by the individual, whether by way of judicial review or otherwise, or as a defence in proceedings initiated by a public authority or a person exercising functions of a public nature.[2] Section 6 makes it unlawful for a public authority to act or fail to act in a way which is incompatible with a Convention right. The broad effect of the provision is to create a new public law wrong. In judicial review proceedings, this will mean that infringement of a Convention right will be a question of illegality rather than one of irrationality. The Act does not create a criminal offence;[3] and a person's reliance on a Convention right does not restrict any other right or freedom conferred by or under any law having effect in any part of the United Kingdom; nor does it restrict any existing rights of action.[4]

For this reason, the question of whether, and if so the extent to which, the HRA has a 'horizontal' effect is unlikely to be significant in the context of the criminal law and criminal process. Criminal law and process are invoked and operated by public authorities so that both are thus clearly subject to the Human Rights Act.

Regulatory bodies are, however, not always characterised as public authorities and their functions cannot all be said to be functions of a public nature. While some contexts, for example companies inspections, medicine licensing and environmental regulation, are clearly examples of public law regulation, others, especially self-regulatory bodies, may not qualify. The question of 'horizontal' application is accordingly of importance in the context of regulation, especially 'self-regulation'. It is argued below that, although the position is less clear, Convention rights are also likely to have some 'horizontal' effect under the HRA's regime. The extent to which a horizontal application is possible was fiercely debated during the passage of the legislation. Concern was expressed (mainly by media interests) that the HRA would enable the courts to develop a general tort of infringement of privacy based on ECHR Article 8 and that this would weaken the freedom of the

* Rouse Ball Professor of English Law, University of Cambridge, Director of the Centre of Public Law. This account is based on a section of a forthcoming *Guide to the Human Rights Act 1998* co-authored with Stephen Grosz and the late Peter Duffy QC.

[1] See generally Clapham, *Human Rights in the Private Sphere* (1993) chs. 4, 6; Dremczewski, *European Human Rights Convention in Domestic Law* (1997) ch. 8.

[2] See HRA, s. 7(6)(a).

[3] S. 7(8).   [4] S. 11.

press.[5] This led to several explanations by government ministers as to how they anticipated the Convention rights might be relevant in an action between private parties.[6]

The effect of the HRA on individuals subject to regulation will therefore depend upon two questions. First, what persons and bodies are 'public authorities' since it is only in proceedings against public authorities that Convention rights will be directly applicable. Only the acts of public authorities and others exercising functions of a public nature are made unlawful by section 6 if they are incompatible with Convention rights. Secondly, will the HRA operate horizontally and, if so, how? In particular, what are the limits to the use of the Convention rights as a tool for the development of the common law? The broader the circumstances in which it is legitimate to so use the Convention, the less the distinction in practice (if not in theory) between direct and indirect horizontal effect.[7] These two questions are considered below.

B. WHAT PERSONS AND BODIES ARE 'PUBLIC AUTHORITY' AND SO REQUIRED TO ACT COMPATIBLY WITH THE CONVENTION RIGHTS?

(1) Overview

In order to achieve the purpose of 'bringing rights home',[8] the HRA is intended to impose the obligation to act in accordance with the Convention on any body for which the Government of the United Kingdom might find itself responsible in Strasbourg. The HRA contains no closed definition of a 'public authority'. What section 6 does is expressly to provide that the term includes a court or tribunal and any person 'certain of whose functions are functions of a public nature'.

The breadth of the Act's reach is deliberate. The Lord Chancellor made it clear that the government 'opted for a wide-ranging definition of public authority' and 'created a correspondingly wide liability' in order 'to provide as much protection as possible for the rights of

the individual against the misuse of power by the state'[9] and sought to do this by a principle rather than a list of bodies.[10] The Home Secretary stated that what was wanted was 'a realistic and modern definition of the state so as to provide correspondingly wide protection against an abuse of rights'.[11] Accordingly liability under the HRA was designed to go beyond 'the narrow category of central and local government and the police—the organisations that represent a minimalist view of the state' and to extend to those bodies in respect of whose actions the UK government is answerable in Strasbourg.[12]

The intention was to distinguish three categories: 'organisations which might be termed 'obvious' public authorities, all of whose functions are public', including courts and tribunals;[13] 'organisations with a mix of public and private functions', and organisations with no public functions', the last of which fall outside the scope of section 6.[14] 'Obvious' public authorities, such as central government and the police, would be 'caught in respect of everything they do',[15] but bodies which are public in certain respects but not in others would not be subject to section 6 if the particular act is of a private nature.[16] But, although the HRA is intended to cover two of the three categories, this is not clearly reflected in the drafting of section 6.

English law has hitherto primarily considered the distinction between the public and the private in the context of the scope of the application for judicial review and the supervisory jurisdiction of the High Court. Courts have considered when proceedings *must* be by way of judicial review and when they *cannot* be by reference to the concepts of 'public bodies' and 'public functions'. The government anticipated that the jurisprudence relating to judicial review would be drawn upon in determining what is a public authority under HRA section 6.[17]

The law on the scope of the application for judicial

---

[5] HL Debs. 24 November 1997 cols 771–779; 314 HC Debs 16 February 1998 cols 791–794; 17 June 1998 cols 399–405, 411, 413 ff. These concerns led to the introduction of what is now s. 12.

[6] See e.g. 583 HL Debs 24 November 1997 col. 783 ff, 811 306 HC Debs 16 February 1998, cols. 776–777.

[7] For this reason the approach of Hunt [1998] *PL* 423, 441–2, who rejects direct horizontal application, but argues that the effect of s. 6(3) is that norms protecting fundamental rights apply to all law so that a generous approach to the development of the common law is required, may in practice amount to the same thing.

[8] See White Paper, *'Rights Brought Home'* CM para. 2.2.

[9] HL Debs., 24 November 1997, col. 808. 583; HL Debs., col. 475 and 584 HL Debs. col. 1262. See also White Paper para. 2.2.

[10] 583 HL Debs., col. 796 (Lord Chancellor). Cf the different approach in the context of Freedom of Information, *Your Right To Know* (Cm 3818, London: HMSO, 1997).

[11] 314 HC Debs., col. 406.

[12] *Ibid.*, 406–408.

[13] S. 6(3)(a). The Act limits the proceedings which may be brought in respect of the acts of courts and tribunals and the remedies available for their unlawful acts: see s. 9.

[14] 314 HC Debs., cols. 410–411 (Home Secretary). See also 583 HL Debs., col. 796 (Lord Chancellor).

[15] HC Debs, 16 February 1998, col. 775 (Home Secretary).

[16] 584 HL Debs., col. 1232 (Lord Chancellor) and S. 6(3)(b).

[17] 314 HC Debs., col. 409 (Home Secretary); 582 HL Debs., 3 November 1997 col. 1310; Lord Williams, 583 HL Debs., col. 811 (Lord Chancellor).

review cannot, however, be determinative. First, it will be necessary for the English courts to take into account the Strasbourg jurisprudence on what constitutes the state for the purposes of the Convention, which, as we shall see, differs in material respects. Secondly, notwithstanding the Home Secretary's statement that 'the concepts are reasonably clear', the way English courts have drawn the distinction between 'public' and 'private' for the purpose of the judicial review jurisdiction has produced a complicated and not altogether consistent body of cases, using a variety of tests. Thirdly, for the purposes of judicial review, not all the acts of 'obvious' public authorities are treated as 'public'. Nevertheless, the case law on the judicial review jurisdiction is instructive.

(2) The 'public/private' distinction in the context of the application for judicial review

This is not the place for a full consideration of the way the courts have determined whether a matter is 'public' for the purposes of the application for judicial review,[18] but a brief account is instructive. Broadly, two questions are asked: first, is the proposed respondent a 'public body', and secondly, is the claim a 'public law' claim concerning a 'public' function.

(a) Is the proposed respondent a 'public body'?

This is sometimes put as asking whether its functions involve a 'public' element. The Courts have developed two tests in this context; 'source' based tests, and 'functional' tests. 'Source' based tests look to the source of a body's power. Thus, the courts ask whether a body's power is derived from statute[19] or the prerogative.[20] The classic test for the scope of the remedy of certiorari[21] asks whether the body has 'legal authority to determine questions affecting the rights of subjects'.

'Functional' tests, on the other hand, look at the nature of the power exercised by the body. The functional questions asked include the extent to which the body is institutionally or structurally controlled by government,[22] whether it exercises *de facto* non-consensual power, and whether there was a government

decision that a particular sphere should be dealt with by a self-regulatory body. If there was such a government decision, several other factors are also relevant. First, is the body supported by a periphery of statutory powers and penalties whenever non-statutory powers or penalties prove insufficient? Secondly, do EC requirements call for statutory provisions?[23] Thirdly, is the power the body exercises 'governmental in nature'? Fourthly, would a governmental body either have to exercise the function if this body did not or would government in fact exercise it.[24]

Where the source of a body's power is statute or prerogative this will generally be a decisive factor in deciding that it is 'public'.[25] Where it is not, however, it may nevertheless qualify as 'public' where the functional tests are satisfied. It is clear that central and local government and inferior courts and tribunals, the police, immigration officers, prisons, health authorities, NHS Trusts, the Legal Aid Board, the Criminal Injuries Compensation Board, executive agencies and statutory regulatory bodies are 'public' bodies and amenable to judicial review.

Apart from those 'core' cases, a number of examples can be given of bodies that have been held to be 'public' bodies for the purposes of the judicial review jurisdiction. Certain professional bodies have qualified because of the *de facto* powers they have over practitioners and those wishing to become practitioners.[26] So have the self regulating bodies recognised under the Financial Services Act 1986,[27] the Stock Exchange,[28] the Takeover Panel,[29] the Advertising Standards Authority,[30] the Association of the British Pharmaceutical Industry.[31] University visitors[32] have also qualified as has a private (or privatised) railway company in the exercise of its regulatory functions.[33] For the HRA, such bodies would

---

[18] For fuller consideration of the case law on the identification of public functions and public law see de Smith, Woolf and Jowell *Judicial Review of Administrative Action* (5th edn., 1995) 167ff; Beatson (1987) 102 *LQR* 34. See also Law Com. 226 (1994) section III.

[19] *Leech* [1988] AC 533, 561.

[20] *R. v. Criminal Injuries Compensation Bd., ex p Lain* [1967] 2 QB 864; *GCHQ* [1985] AC 374.

[21] *R. v. Electricity Commissioners, ex p London Electricity Joint Committee Co.* [1924] 1 KB 171, 205.

[22] See the cases on the incidence of privilege under the Crown Proceedings Act 1947, e.g. *Tamlin* v. *Hannaford* [1950] 1 KB 18; *BBC* v. *Johns* [1965] Ch. 32

[23] *R. v. Take-Over Panel, ex p. Datafin* [1987] QB 815.

[24] *Ibid., R. v. Advertising Standards Authority, ex p. Insurance Service plc* (1990) 2 Admin LR 77; *Aga Khan's* case [1993] 1 WLR 909; *ex p. Massingberd-Mundy* [1993] 2 All ER 207

[25] *R. v. Take-Over Panel, ex p. Datafin* [1987] QB 815, 847. But note that this will not be so where the 'claim' is not a 'public law' claim. For examples of 'obvious' public authorities, see below.

[26] *R. v. General Council of the Bar, ex p. Percival* [1991] 2 QB 212; *R. v. General Medical Council, ex p. Colman* [1990] 1 All ER 489

[27] *R. v. LAUTRO, ex p. Ross* [1993] QB 17.

[28] *R. v. ISE of the UK and Ireland, ex p. Else* [1993] QB 534.

[29] *R. v. Take-Over Panel, ex p. Datafin* [1987] QB 815.

[30] *R. v. Advertising Standards Authority, ex p. Insurance Service plc* (1990) 2 Admin LR 77.

[31] *R. v. Code of Practice Committee, ex p. Professional Counselling Aids Ltd* (1991) 3 Admin LR 697.

[32] *R. v. Hull University Prison Visitor, ex p. Page* [1993] AC 682

[33] *R. v. GW Trains, ex p. Frederick* [1998] COD 239 ;and see Lord Williams, 582 HL Debs., 3 November 1997, col. 1310). See also the example given in the debates of a commercial security company operating a privatised prison.

fall within section 6(3)(b) since only 'certain' of their functions are functions of a public nature. Accordingly, by section 6(5), in relation to a particular act, such a body is not a 'public authority' if the nature of the act is private.

But a number of bodies with similar *de facto* power have been held not to be amenable to judicial review. These include sporting bodies,[34] religious authorities (apart from the Established Church, the Church of England),[35] and certain dispute resolution bodies.[36] In these cases the courts have emphasised the non-governmental nature of the bodies rather than the *de facto* power they exercise. Although it has not been decided whether the Press Complaints Commission is amenable to judicial review,[37] it was widely assumed in the debates on the HRA that it would qualify as a body 'certain of whose functions are functions of a public nature' within section 6(3)(b).

(b) Is the claim a 'public law' claim concerning a 'public' function?

In the context of the scope of the application for judicial review a qualification has to be made to the statement that the statutory or prerogative source of a body's power will generally be decisive in deciding that it is 'public' for the purposes of the judicial review procedure. Even in such cases it also has to be asked whether the claim is a 'public law' claim. If there is a contractual relationship between the individual and the body, or if the source of its power over the individual is 'contractual', it is unlikely that it will be sufficiently 'public' to bring it within the ambit of the judicial review procedure.[38] Even if the body whose act or decision it is wished to challenge is clearly a 'public' body, the claim must be 'public'. Judicial review is considered to be an inappropriate means of challenging a public authority when that authority is acting in the capacity of a private contracting party.[39] Furthermore, an individual affected by the decision of a public body may be held not to have

a public law claim against that body where he has a contractual, tortious or restitutionary claim (a 'private' law claim) against a third party *in respect of that decision.*[40] Traditionally judicial review has also not been thought appropriate for 'commercial' or 'managerial' decisions.[41]

(3) Public authorities properly so called: the difference between the HRA and judicial review

The second question, 'is the claim a 'public law' one concerning a 'public function', shows that, for the application for judicial review, even an 'obvious' public authority is not caught in respect of everything it does. This marks a sharp distinction from what was said by the Lord Chancellor and the Home Secretary about the scope of the HRA and the effect of section 6. But, as indicated, there is an important difference between what was said in the Parliamentary debates and the wording of section 6. Section 6 does not on its face specify which bodies are 'public' in respect of all their functions and acts. To the extent that not all of the functions of a body are 'public', it must be a body 'certain of whose functions are of a public nature' within section 6(3)(b) and thus is, by section 6(5), only a public body (and therefore required to act in accordance with Convention rights) in respect of such of its acts which are 'public'.

Will the 'public law' claim limit apply in determining the meaning of 'public authority' for the purpose of HRA, section 6? Do the judicial review cases which apply it show that, even in the core category of 'obvious' public authorities, it is not possible (notwithstanding what the Home Secretary said) to conclude that all their functions are public? If so, some activities and functions of central and local government, such as those characterised as 'contractual', 'commercial' or 'managerial' may not be 'public'. It would follow that, because of the provision in section 6(3)(b) and 6(5), section 6 would only apply to those of its acts which are of a public character. Although the position is not altogether clear, this result is unlikely.

It is submitted that the domestic qualification of the concept of what is 'public' is unlikely to be appropriate in the context of HRA, section 6. First, the Strasbourg jurisprudence shows that the mere fact that a relationship is contractual is not conclusive and that protection has been afforded to employment in the public service.[42] The availability of this protection in principle

---

[34] *Law v. National Greyhound Racing Club* [1983] 1 WLR 1302; *R. v. Jockey Club, ex p. Aga Khan* [1993] 1 WLR 909; *R. v. Football Assoc., ex p. Football League* [1993] 2 All ER 833.

[35] *R. v. Chief Rabbi, ex p. Wachmann* [1992] 1 WLR 1036; *R. v. Imam of Bury Park, ex p. Sulaiman Ali* [1992] COD 132.

[36] *R. v. Insurance Ombudsman Bureau, ex p. Aegon Life Assurance Ltd, The Times,* 7 January 1994; [1994] CLC 88.

[37] *R. v. Press Complaints Commission ex p. Stewart-Brady* [1997] EMLR 185 (CA). The court left open the question whether the PCC was amenable to judicial review. However, the preponderance of opinion during the passage of the Bill was that, for HRA purposes, it would be a public authority.

[38] See n 34 above.

[39] E.g. *R. v. Derby CC, ex p. Noble* [1990] ICR 808 (dismissal of police surgeon); *McLaren v. Home Office* [1990] ICR 824 (conditions of appointment of prison officer).

[40] *R. v. Secretary of State for Employment, ex p. EOC* [1994] 1 AC 1.

[41] *R. v. National Coal Board, ex p. NUM* [1986] ICR 791, 795. Cf. *Mercury Ltd v. Electricity Corp.* [1994] 1 WLR 521.

[42] *Lombardo v. Italy* (1992) Series A No. 249–B (judge); *Scuderi*

has often been undermined in practice by the deference shown to national bodies by the Strasbourg court as part of the application of the doctrine of margin of appreciation.[43] But this does not affect the scope of the Convention concept of bodies that count as 'the state' and it is generally accepted that the doctrine of margin of appreciation should not be transposed to the domestic context.[44]

Secondly, as noted above, it is clear that the intention behind the treatment of the concept of 'public authority' in section 6 was to replicate the Strasbourg concept of the state. Indirect support for this position can also be garnered from the decisions of the ECJ and the House of Lords in *Foster* v. *British Gas*,[45] albeit in the different context of what bodies are directly bound by the equality provisions in a European Community directive. The ECJ has held that all organs of the administration, including decentralised authorities, were bound. Those engaged in commercial activities were included, as were bodies exercising a function that had previously been undertaken by a state body, but which, as a result of a governmental decision (and legislation), had been privatised.[46]

Thirdly, there are the clear *Pepper* v. *Hart* statements by the Lord Chancellor and the Home Secretary. Accordingly, the bodies within the core category such as central and local government and inferior courts and tribunals, the police, immigration officers, prisons, health authorities, NHS Trusts, the Legal Aid Board, the Criminal Injuries Compensation Board, the Parliamentary Commissioner, Local Government Ombudsmen, executive agencies and statutory regulatory bodies are obliged to act in a manner which is compatible with Convention rights in relation to *all* their activities, whether they are public or private in nature.

So, for example, section 6 will apply to employment in the public service.[47]

There may be other differences between the location of the 'public' and the 'private' divide in a domestic context not involving human rights and one in which, as a result of the HRA, the Strasbourg approach must, absent inconsistent legislation, be applied. So, for example, it has been held that only state schools are amenable to the judicial review jurisdiction; other schools 'fall fairly and squarely into the private sector' and the relationship between the pupils and the school is founded on contract.[48] But it has been held that the UK government can be liable for the violation of human rights in the disciplinary systems of independent schools since they co-exist with a system of public education and since the convention right to education is guaranteed to pupils in all schools.[49] The development of the Strasbourg jurisprudence on bodies for which there is state responsibility has been affected by the existence of positive duties on member states to secure protection of Convention rights. Where the Strasbourg institutions assume jurisdiction on the basis of a positive duty on the member state to protect individuals against violations of convention rights by other individuals, it is not necessary to decide whether the body that infringed the right in question was a 'public authority'. Thus, in the *Young, James & Webster* case[50] it was not necessary to decide whether the nationalised British Rail was a 'public authority' for which the state is responsible.

(4) Court and tribunals

The Act applies to anything done by a court or tribunal, whether the act is public or private in nature. It will apply not only to judicial acts, but also to listing and other administrative functions of the court, such as dealings with court funds, issuing of proceedings and applications and sending out notices, as well as the employment of court staff. The duty to act compatibly with Convention rights will apply in any proceedings, including those between private parties. For the purposes of discussion, the obligations arising from the judicial acts of courts and tribunals can be classified as those which are addressed directly to the courts and those which arise indirectly.

v. *Italy* (1993) Series A No. 265–A (civil servant); *Darnell* v. *UK* (1993) Series A No. 272 (health service employee); *Muti* v. *Italy* (1994) Series A No. 281–C. But claims concerning public employment have also been held to fall outside the scope of the Convention's protection: see Harris, O'Boyle & Warbrick, *Law of the ECHR* (1995) 182, 362, 381, 410.

[43] See D. Clapham, *Human Rights in the Private Sphere* (1993) 222.

[44] See Sir John Laws, [1998] PL 254, 258 and 'An Overview' above; Marshall in *Constitutional Reform in the UK: Practice and Principles* (1998) 82; Mahoney (1998) 19 HRLJ 1, 3. See also *R.* v. *Stafford JJ, ex p. Imbert*, The Times, 25 February 1999, *per* Buxton LJ, *obiter*.

[45] Case 188/89 [1990] ECR I–3313; [1991] 2 AC 306. See also Case 152/84 *Marshall* v. *Southampton & SW Hampshire* [1986] ECR 723; *Fratelli Costanzo* v. *Commune di Milano* [1989] ECR 1839; *Kampelmann* v. *Landschaftverband Westfalen-Lippe* [1998] IRLR 333.

[46] In the context of the Convention, see *Powell & Rayner* v. *UK* (1990) Series A No. 172; *Baggs* v. *UK* (1987) 44 DR 13, 52 DR 29 (Heathrow Airport)

[47] *Vogt* v. *Germany (*1995) 21 EHRR 205; *Leander* v. *Sweden* (1987) 9 EHRR 433; *Halford* v. *UK* (1997) 24 EHRR 523; *Ahmed* v. *ILEA* [1978] QB 36. Cf *Kosiek* v. *Germany* (1987) 9 EHRR 328.

[48] *R.* v. *Fernhill Manor School, ex p. Brown* (1993) 5 Admin. L.Rev. 175. See Bamforth [1999] *CLJ* 159.

[49] *Y* v. *UK* (1992) Series A No. 247–A, *Edwards* v. *UK* (1992) Series A No. 247–B; *Costello-Roberts* v. *UK* (1993) Series A No. 247–C (corporal punishment).

[50] (1981) Series A No. 44.

(a) Obligations placed directly on courts and tribunals:

certain Articles of the Convention are directed specifically at the activities of the courts. Direct obligations may be regarded as those where the order of the court, or the procedure it adopts, may amount to a violation of Convention rights. Courts and tribunals which adjudicate on 'civil rights or obligations' will be bound by the guarantees of fair trial and access to courts contained in Article 6(1) of the Convention. These guarantees apply to all proceedings relating to civil rights or obligations, whether both parties are private or one party is a public authority. a court determining criminal charges will in addition be bound to respect the minimum guarantees of criminal procedure contained in Article 6(2) and (3). Courts with powers to order detention, or bail or other forms of release from detention, or to review the lawfulness of detention, will be bound to apply the provisions of Article 5. Any court or tribunal dealing with Convention rights must also take account of the obligation under Article 13 to provide an effective remedy, even though that Article is not listed among the Convention rights in Schedule 1 to the Act.

(b) General and indirect obligations which also bind courts:

An order of a court may itself violate a Convention right, even in proceedings where no public authority is involved. For example, a judgment or fine in defamation proceedings may raise an issue of freedom of expression under Article 10 of the Convention[51]; an order that a journalist disclose the source of his information, even though made at the instance of another private litigant, may also amount to a violation of Article 10[52]; as may the grant of an injunction restraining publication[53]; or the grant of an order banning exhibition of a film.[54] The making of an *Anton Piller* order may raise property issues under Article 1 of the First Protocol[55] and orders of the court in family matters may deprive a party of his right to respect for family life under Article 8. In the examples given, the order of the court itself interferes with the enjoyment of a Convention right. The injunction restraining publication, or the damages award in the libel proceedings, prevents the exercise of the right of freedom of expression; likewise the disclosure order. However, the Convention also imposes on the state, and therefore on the courts, a positive obligation to secure respect of certain rights. In those cases, a court's failure to grant relief to an individual against interference with the right by another private party may itself amount to a violation of the Convention right in issue.[56]

The effect of HRA section 6(3)

It has been argued that the effect of section 6(3) is to subject courts and tribunals to the duty not to act in a way which is incompatible with a Convention right in all proceedings, and that this is so whether the party against whom the Convention right is being invoked is a public authority or a private person. On this view section 6(3) thus impliedly requires *direct* horizontal effect to be given to convention rights.[57] Sections 12 and 13 of the Act may appear to provide some support for this. These provisions apply where a court is considering whether to grant any relief which, if granted, might affect the Convention right of freedom of expression, and where a court's determination might affect the exercise by a religious organisation of the Convention right to freedom of thought, conscience and religion. The support for direct horizontal effect might be thought to follow from the fact that those provisions are not limited to cases to which a public authority is a party.[58]

But both the structure of the HRA and what was said during its Parliamentary passage[59] shows that section 6(3) does not have such a wide-ranging effect. It has been suggested that section 6(3) 'means only that the courts *in their own sphere* must give effect to such fundamental rights as the right to a fair trial; and to more particular rights such as a right to an interpreter'.[60] That it is proper not to give section 6(3) the widest possible meaning is shown by the structure of section 6, which is focused on the position of public authorities, and which clearly shows that it was not intended to

---

[51] *Lingens* v. *Austria* (1986) 8 EHRR 103; *Tolstoy-Miloslavsky* v. *UK* (1996) 20 EHRR 442. See also *Rantzen* v. *Mirror Group Newspapers* [1994] QB 670.

[52] *X* v. *Morgan Grampian* [1991] AC 1; *Michael O'Mara Books Ltd* v. *Express Newspapers plc and others* [1999] FSR 49; *Camelot* v. *Centaur Communications* [1999] QB 124; *Goodwin* v. *United Kingdom* (1996) 22 EHRR 123.

[53] *Sunday Times* v. *United Kingdom*, 2 EHRR 245 (1979); *Observer & Guardian* v. *United Kingdom* (1992) 14 EHRR 153.

[54] *Otto Preminger Institut* v. *Austria* (1994) 11 EHRR 34.

[55] *Chappell* v. *United Kingdom* (1989) Series A No. 152 A.

[56] See, sect. C(2) below and n. 50 above.

[57] H.W.R. Wade, in *Constitutional Reform in the UK: Practice and Principles* (Cambridge: Cambridge Centre for Public Law, 1998) 63. Hunt's suggested intermediate position ([1998] *PL* 423, 426) 'in which the norms protecting fundamental rights apply to all law, whatever its nature', is in practice likely to be very close to Wade's.

[58] 315 HC Debs., 2 July 1998, col. 536 (Home Secretary).

[59] E.g. LC HL 3rd Reading 5 February 1998, col. 840; HL 2nd Reading, 3 November 1997 cols. 1231–1232.

[60] Kentridge, in *Constitutional Reform in the UK: Practice and Principles* (Cambridge: Cambridge Centre for Public Law, 1998) 70, emphasis added. But cf his view in *Du Plessis* v. *De Klerk*, 1996 (3) SA 850, 877–8 that provisions (e.g. that in the Namibian Constitution, Art 5) that rights are to be upheld by the judiciary, which are similar to HRA s. 6(3) do support wider than purely vertical application and may equate the judgment of a court with state action, so that their absence in the South African Constitution was a strong pointer to the rights under it only having direct vertical effect.

include private individuals and entities within it. This is, for example, shown by the treatment of persons or entities only certain of whose functions are of a public nature. By section 6(5), such a person or entity will be a public authority and subject to the obligation to act compatibly with Convention rights in respect of acts whose nature is public but not in respect of acts whose nature is private. Nor do sections 12 and 13 support *direct* horizontal effect of Convention rights either in general or in the particular case of Articles 9 and 10. First, all they do is to replace the formula used in HRA, section 2 that courts 'take into account' the Strassbourg jurisprudence by a stronger but not conclusive 'have particular regard' formula. Secondly, they do not affect section 6. Accordingly, save for the case (discussed below) of situations in which member states, and thus their courts, have a positive duty to secure an individual's Convention rights against interference by other private persons or entities, it is unlikely that there will be direct horizontal effect. But, there is likely to be *indirect* horizontal effect in a number of circumstances, also discussed below, although its extent cannot be stated precisely.

(5) Other persons exercising functions of a public nature

The obligation to respect Convention rights is also imposed on any person certain of whose functions are of a public nature; but such a person is not a public authority if the nature of the particular act in issue is private.[61] It is this class of public authority which is likely to cause the most difficulty, and which occupied much time during the passage of the Bill. Critics considered that the expression was too vague to be workable, and suggested that the provision be limited, for example by publication of a list of bodies to be regarded as public authorities. As discussed above, the intention of the broad approach is to ensure that the Act covers the acts of any bodies for which it would be responsible under the Convention before the Strasbourg institutions. Only in this way can Convention rights be 'brought home', in the sense that individuals will be able to obtain remedies before national courts and tribunals rather than having to apply to Strasbourg. The Strasbourg case law on state responsibility will therefore be of considerable importance.[62]

The case law relating to amenability to judicial review, discussed above, will also play a large part in determining what are functions of a public nature for the purposes of the Act, although, for the reasons given in

the earlier discussion, the boundary will not be drawn in exactly the same way. This class of public authority will include professional bodies which exercise regulatory and disciplinary functions[63]; private commercial organisations exercising public functions; a railway company in the exercise of its regulatory functions[64]; industry-based ombudsmen; university visitors[65]; and bodies exercising (self)regulatory functions in the financial, media and other commercial sectors.[66]

A person or body in this class falls within HRA section 6(3)(b) since only 'certain' of its functions are functions of a public nature. Accordingly, by section 6(5), in relation to a particular act, such a person or body is not a 'public authority' if the nature of the act is private. It is obliged to comply with the Convention only in respect of the exercise of its public functions. When it is acting in a private capacity, for example as an employer, a commercial enterprise or a representative of a profession[67] it is not treated as a public authority.

C. EFFECT BEYOND PUBLIC AUTHORITIES: 'HORIZONTALITY'

Finally, we turn to the way the HRA may affect regulatory bodies which do not qualify as public authorities and regulatory bodies with hybrid public and private characteristics in respect of those functions which are not of a public nature.

(1) Interpretation of primary or secondary legislation:

Where the proceedings involve the interpretation of primary or secondary legislation, the HRA will affect all proceedings including those solely concerning private parties and private regulatory bodies. Section 3(1) provides that statutes are to be read and given effect in a way which is compatible with the Convention rights 'so far as it is possible to do so'. So, for example, any statutory protection of privacy or confidentiality in a particular context (for example under data protection legislation) will therefore have to be construed 'so far as it is possible to do so' to ensure compatibility with the right to freedom of expression in proceedings where all parties are private individuals or entities. Again, a statutory provision limiting the freedom of employees to belong or not to

---

[61] S. 6(5).

[62] See also n. 45 above (EC law on the 'State' for the purpose of the doctrine of direct effect of directives).

[63] *König* v. *Germany* 2 EHRR 170 (1978); *Le Compte* v. *Belgium* (1982) 4 EHRR 1; *Cascado Coca* v. *Spain* (1994) 18 EHRR 1.

[64] *R.* v. *GW Trains, ex p. Frederick* [1998] COD 239; and see Lord Williams: 582 HL Debs., 3 November 1997, col. 1310.

[65] *Page* v. *Hull University Visitor* [1993] AC 682, [1993] 1 All ER 97.

[66] See the examples given above, nn. 25–33.

[67] See nn. 34, 39–42 above.

belong to a trade union and thus limiting the freedom of association in Article 11 will have to be construed in accordance with the HRA's powerful interpretative obligation. Under this courts are, as Lord Cooke of Thorndon put it, directed to search for 'possible meanings' which are compatible with the Convention rights rather than, as under the traditional approach to statutory interpretation, the 'true' meaning.[68] The effect of section 3's direction is that where a party to private litigation founds a claim or a defence on a legislative provision, its compatibility with the Convention rights is an issue, which may properly be raised, and the court is directed to strive to interpret the provision so as to produce compatibility.

(2) Positive duties on member states to secure an individual's convention rights against interference by others

In certain circumstances the Strasbourg institutions impose positive duties on member states to secure an individual's Convention rights against interference by other persons or entities. This has occurred particularly in relation to the prohibition of torture (Article 3), the right to liberty and security (Article 5), the right to respect for private and family life (Article 8), and the right to freedom of peaceful assembly and to freedom of association (Article 11). Where it is held that there is such a positive duty, a state that is party to the Convention is obliged to ensure a practical and effective system for the protection of the right in question. In some cases, including regulatory contexts, this will include 'the adoption of measures designed to secure respect for [the right] even in the sphere of the relations of individuals between themselves'.[69]

An English court which is confronted with a fact situation in which the Strasbourg jurisprudence has imposed such positive duties will have to decide whether it is able to protect the right in question and, if so, whether it should. It is submitted that, save where prevented from so doing by incompatible UK legislation[70] or where the incompatibility of UK law can

only be remedied by the enactment of legislation, the court should in principle protect the individual's Convention rights against such interference by other persons. That would be consistent with the aim of the HRA of 'bringing rights home' and with the requirement in section 2(1) of the HRA that the Court 'take into account' the Strasbourg jurisprudence, which imposes the positive duty. Moreover, the Court is an organ of the state for which the UK is responsible under the Convention regime[71] and by section 6(3) of the HRA it is a 'public authority' and therefore under a duty not to act in a way which is incompatible with a Convention right.[72] Section 6(3) does not, for the reasons given above, create direct horizontal effect in all cases involving Convention rights. But in those cases in which the state and its organs (including the court) is under a positive duty to secure an individual's Convention rights against interference by other persons or entities it is clearly arguable that it must do so save where precluded by the HRA.

The HRA's only impediment to the enforcement of Convention rights is the doctrine of parliamentary sovereignty. A distinction must be drawn between incompatibility, which can only be remedied by legislation, and incompatibility which can be removed by the development of common law doctrine and remedies. Absent legislation which is incompatible with the Convention rights or the inability of the court to remedy the incompatibility by the development of common law doctrine, it is submitted that protection should be afforded in cases in which the state and thus the court is under a positive duty. If it is not then an appeal to Strasbourg is likely to succeed and the right in question will not have been 'brought home'.

Notwithstanding the arguments in principle favouring such protection, a number of factors suggest that in practice it will not often be granted. First, it is difficult to predict when a positive duty will be imposed by the Strasbourg institutions. The policy questions regarding violations by private individuals have been developed in the context of specific Articles[73] and the guidelines suggested for the imposition of a positive duty are very broad and open-textured. So it is suggested that there may be a positive duty where the aim of the right in question is to protect the individual's dignity, but not where is it to protect democracy, and the violation of

[68] HL Debs.,18 November 1997, col. 533. See also Lord Simon, *ibid.*, col. 536. The Home Secretary, however, stated (HC Debs., 3 June 1998, cols. 421–422) that it was not the government's intention that the courts should 'contort' the meaning of statutory words to produce 'implausible or incredible meanings'.

[69] *X and Y* v. *The Netherlands* (1985) Series A No. 91 para. 23 (Art. 8). See also *Marckx* v. *Belgium* (1979) Series A No. 31 para. 31; *Guerra* v. *Italy* (1998) 4 BHRC 63. On Art. 2, see *Mrs W* v. *UK* (1983) 32 D & R 10; *Mrs W* v. *Ireland* (1983) 32 D & R 211; *McCann* v. *UK* (1996) Series A No. 324 21 EHRR 97. On Art. 3, see *A* v. *UK* 23 September 1998, para. 22. On Art. 11, see *Young, James and Webster* v. *UK* (1981) Series A No. 44, paras. 48–49; *Plattform Ärzte für das Leben* v. *Austria* (1988) Series A No. 139 para. 32.

[70] HRA, ss. 4(2), 6(2).

[71] Eg *A* v. *UK*, n. 69 above, paras. 23–24.

[72] By s. 7(6)(b) 'legal proceedings' include an appeal against the decision of a court or tribunal, so that, if the lower court or tribunal is under a duty under s. 6(1) to give effect to positive duties under the Convention where possible and not precluded by statute, act compatibly with Convention right, that the victim may (see s. 7(1)) rely on this in any appeal.

[73] D. Clapham, *Human Rights in the Private Sphere* (1993) 240.

human rights would probably not have occurred 'but for' the absence of state action.[74] The fact that a positive duty has been imposed by the Strasbourg Court in a particular context upon another member state does not necessarily mean that such a duty would be imposed in that context upon the UK.[75] Moreover, the Strasbourg Court gives member states a margin of appreciation as to how any such duty is to be implemented.[76]

Secondly, in Strasbourg it is the state, not the individual, that is liable. Holding the individual liable would thus be to do more in a sense than 'bringing rights home': full protection of the plaintiff's rights would make an individual defendant liable in an English court where that defendant could not be liable in Strasbourg. There is, moreover, a strong reason of substance for not imposing such liability. This is that whereas where the UK is held to be under a positive duty by the Strasbourg court, any subsequent remedial legislation is not retrospective,[77] this is the normal effect of a judgment in a novel situation or where a previous decision is being overruled.[78]

Thirdly, the HRA has not eliminated the right to take proceedings before the Strasbourg court. This will still be necessary in cases of incompatible legislation where no remedial action is taken. Where a vacuum of this sort is revealed as a result of the imposition of a positive duty, the express reservation of failure to legislate from the category of unlawful acts suggests that the HRA also contemplates that the appropriate remedy for the individual is recourse to Strasbourg. The question when it is appropriate for courts to develop the common law raises fundamental questions and is considered below.[79] But the mere fact that, at the international level, a member state is under a positive duty to secure the convention rights of individuals against other individuals does not *per se* justify the development of common law doctrine to remove inconsistency.

Fourthly, with regard to the requirement in HRA, section 2, that the Strasbourg jurisprudence be taken into account, no distinction is made in section 2 between the general effect of the jurisprudence and its effect in those situations in which a positive duty has been imposed upon member states. This suggests that there is no intention that cases in which there is a positive duty should be treated differently from those where there is not (considered in the next section). In neither case are the Convention rights made conclusive. On this argument any horizontal effect in domestic law would as a matter of law be the same whether or not there is a positive duty. But where there is a positive duty, the policy of 'bringing rights home' should affect the weight to be given to the Convention right and the Strasbourg jurisprudence by a court taking it into account under section 2(1). In short, where there is a positive duty this should affect the *extent* of any horizontal effect even if it does not affect its *nature*.

(3) Convention rights as a tool for the development of the common law

The third situation in which Convention rights will have some horizontal effect is where they are used as a tool for the development of the common law to which all, including regulatory bodies, are subject. This was done by the Court of Appeal in *Derbyshire CC v. Times Newspapers Ltd.*[80] and may have been done by the House of Lords,[81] notwithstanding what their Lordships said. There are other examples.[82] Strictly speaking, this form of horizontal effect is not a consequence of incorporation since the *Derbyshire* case is only one example of its occurrence before the enactment of the HRA. But it is likely that, although there is no presumption of compatibility between common law and convention rights (as there is in the case of statutes as a result of section 2), the effect of the HRA will make courts more willing to use the Convention in this way. In the context of the South African Constitution, Kentridge JA (drawing on Canadian and German law) described this form of horizontal effect as indirect. He stated that while a fundamental right may override a rule of public law, 'it is said to "influence" rather than to override the rules of private law'.[83]

During the Parliamentary consideration of the HRA it was widely thought that Article 8 might be used by the courts to generalise the particular instances in which tort protects privacy in a piecemeal and indirect way to create a general tort, as occurred in the United States.[84]

[74] *Ibid.*, 196, 240.

[75] Compare, in relation to transsexuals *B* v. *France* (1992) Series A No. 232–C and *Cossey* v. *UK* (1990) Series A No. 184.

[76] *Markt Intern verlag* v. *Germany* (1989) Series A No. 165 (Art. 10).

[77] In the case of the creation of a criminal offence it *cannot* be retrospective (ECHR Art. 7(1)) unless the act was criminal according to the general principles of law recognised by civilised nations (Art. 7(2)).

[78] *DPP* v. *Shaw* [1962] AC 220; *Knuller* v. *DPP* [1973] AC 435; *R.* v. *R. (Rape: marital exemption)* [1992] 1 AC 599; *Kleinwort Benson* v. *Lincoln CC* [1998] 3 WLR 1095.

[79] The failure to incorporate Art. 13 is not of significance in this context because of the remedies in HRA, ss. 6–8.

[80] [1992] QB 770.

[81] [1993] AC 534.

[82] *Raymond* v. *Honey* [1983] 1 AC 1; *A-G* v. *Guardian Newspapers Ltd* [1987] 1 WLR 1248; *A-G* v. *Times Newspapers Ltd.* [1990] 1 AC 109; *R.* v. *Home Secretary, ex p. McQuillan* [1995] 4 All ER 400; *R.* v. *Khan* [1996] 3 All ER 289; *Rantzen* v. *MGN* [1993] 4 All ER 975, 994; *John* v. *MGN* [1996] 2 All ER 35 (jury awards).

[83] *Du Plessis* v. *De Klerk*, 1996 (3) SA 850, 874.

[84] See e.g. *Pavesich* v. *New England Life Insurance Co.*, 50 SE 68 (1905). See also the First Restatement of Torts, § 867.

The Lord Chancellor stated that any such development would not be the courts enforcing the Convention but developing the common law.[85] And sections 12 and 13 of the HRA, which were inserted to meet fears about the erosion of press and religious freedom, only require the courts to 'have particular regard to the importance of' the Convention rights of freedom of expression and religion.[86] While this suggests some horizontal effect, it also suggests that it is only to be what has been termed indirect effect. It has, however, been argued that the effect of section 6(3), while not creating direct horizontal effect, goes 'considerably further in the direction of horizontality' than the Canadian and South African approaches.[87] This is because it places the courts 'under an unequivocal duty to act compatibly with Convention rights' and will in some cases 'require them actively to modify or develop the common law in order to achieve such compatibility'. It is submitted that it is unlikely, at least in the early stages of the development of HRA jurisprudence, that the courts will depart from their traditional incremental approach to the judicial development of the common law.

(4) The limits to the use of the Convention rights as a tool for the development of the common law

In Canada and South Africa it has been recognised that the fact that a Bill of Rights does not directly apply to the common law in private proceedings does not mean that it is not relevant in such cases. Thus, in *Retail Wholesale & Department Store Union* v. *Dolphin Delivery*,[88] McIntyre J said that the issue of the direct applicability of the Canadian Charter of Rights was 'a distinct issue from the question whether the judiciary ought to apply and develop the principles of the common law in a manner consistent with the fundamental rights enshrined in the [Charter]'. He stated that 'the answer to this question must be in the affirmative'. A similar position has been taken by the South African Constitutional Court[89] and even before the enactment of the HRA, there were statements in the cases that the common law should be *interpreted*, so far as possible, with a predilection that it should conform to the principles of the convention. The argument that the effect of HRA section 6(3) is to impose a duty actively to consider modifying the common law to achieve compatibility with Convention rights has been noted above, as have the suggestions made during the parliamentary

passage of the HRA that one example of such development might well be a tort of invasion of privacy. But can any further guidance be given on when the courts are likely to modify the common law to make it more consistent with the fundamental values enshrined in the Convention?

A number of factors will affect the willingness of a court, normally the court of last resort, to develop the common law. First, there is the status of the particular common law rule that is under consideration. Has it been criticised in purely common law terms, as were the rules precluding the recovery of payments made in response to *ultra vires* demands for tax,[90] and payments made under a mistake of law?[91] Is it based on a public policy which no longer requires it?[92] Can it be seen as fundamental or inextricably linked to other important rules, as some but not all consider the doctrine of privity of contract to be?[93] If the rule is deeply embedded so that any modification will have a ripple effect on other rules or require consequential changes, it is likely that the view will be that any change should be by legislation rather than by modifying common law doctrine. The likelihood of judicial development will also be reduced where the common law rule has been modified by statute, as in the case of the payment of interest in respect of damages.[94] Judges are also likely to be reluctant when asked to devise a common law solution to a complex social and ethical problem.[95] Nevertheless, a number of the significant developments that have taken place recently show that important questions have remained unresolved in our common law system and that Parliament has been either unable or unwilling[96] to resolve them. Thus, until 1989 there was no English authority on the question whether medical treatment can lawfully be given to a person who is disabled by mental incapacity from consenting to it, a situation described by Lord Goff as 'startling'.[97] In such cases the judges may have no alternative but to devise a common law solution.

But beyond this it is difficult to predict the approach to a submission that a common law rule should be

---

[85] 306 HC Debs., 776–7, 314 HC Debs., 411, 414.
[86] Ss. 12(4), 13(1).
[87] Hunt [1998] *PL* 423, 441.
[88] [1986] 2 SCR 573 (Sup. Ct. of Canada).
[89] *Du Plessis* v. *De Klerk*, 1996 (3) SA 850.
[90] *Woolwich Equitable BS* v. *IRC* [1993] 1 AC 70.
[91] *Kleinwort Benson* v. *Lincoln CC* [1998] 3 WLR 1095
[92] *Thai Trading Co* v. *Taylor* [1998] 2 WLR 893 (contingency fee agreements).
[93] Cf the majority and the minority in *Trident* v. *McNeice* (1988) 62 ALJR 508. See also Lord Reid's view in *Beswick* v. *Beswick* [1968] AC 58, 72.
[94] E.g. *President of India* v. *La Pintada Cie Nav. SA (No 2)* [1985] AC 104.
[95] See e.g. Lord Browne-Wilkinson and Lord Mustill in *Airedale NHS Trust* v. *Bland* [1993] AC 789, 885, 891.
[96] *Woolwich Equitable BS* v. *IRC* [1993] AC 70, 176.
[97] *Re F. (Mental Patient: Sterilisation)* [1990] AC 1, 72 (Lord Goff of Chieveley).

modified or developed. In part the approach will depend on the view taken of the judicial role, particularly in what, in the context of the HRA, is a constitutional matter. The difficulty is illustrated in Lord Goff's speech in the *Woolwich* case. The Crown had argued that the development of the common law to provide for a restitutionary remedy to citizens who had paid tax in response to an unlawful demand by a public authority would overstep the boundary the courts traditionally set for themselves, separating the legitimate development of the law by the judges from legislation. But Lord Goff stated that he was 'never quite sure where to find' that boundary, and that 'its position seems to vary from case to case'.

There are many examples of the vitality of the common law. The view that once seemed to be gaining favour that major developments, even in areas hitherto the preserve of the common law should, in the future, be achieved by legislation,[98] is less influential among the judges. For example, in 1991 the House held that the rule that a husband cannot be criminally liable for raping his wife if he has sexual intercourse with her without her consent no longer forms part of the law of England, recognising for the first time that rape within marriage is a crime.[99] In 1993 the House had to grapple with fundamental questions concerning the scope of the principle of the sanctity of life. In the tragic *Bland* case it held, again for the first time, that doctors responsible for the treatment of a patient in a persistent vegetative state were not under a duty to provide medical treatment, including artificial feeding.[100] The creation of

relief by *Mareva* injunctions and *Anton Piller* orders is another example. Of less dramatic impact but of fundamental significance to the law of obligations, in 1991 the House of Lords recognised the principle of unjust enrichment as the unifying principle underlying liabilities to make restitution of benefits gained by the defendant at the plaintiff's expense.[101]

This vitality is particularly apparent in cases concerning the relationship of the citizen and the state, in particular the development of a system of administrative law based on the power of the court to review the legality of administrative action. It has recently been held, albeit with a European Community catalyst, that coercive orders can be made against government ministers[102] and a citizen who makes a payment in response to an unlawful demand for tax is entitled to the repayment of the money irrespective of whether the payment was mistaken or made under coercion.[103] As in the rape in marriage case, the House consciously 'reformulated' the law and 'reinterpreted' principles. Similarly, it has been held that company inspectors are not entitled to require witnesses to give undertakings of confidentiality in relation to information and documents given to them by the inspectors.[104]

These examples, particularly those in the area of public law with its constitutional dimension, suggest that the traditional incremental approach to the development of the common law need not be a significant barrier to the alignment of common law doctrine and Convention rights. The enactment of the HRA means that courts are likely to go beyond their existing predeliction that the common law should be interpreted so far as possible to conform with the principles of the Convention.

---

[98] *Myers* v. *DPP* [1965] AC 1001, 1021; *Beswick* v. *Beswick* [1968] AC 58, 72, 85; *President of India* v. *La Pintada Cie Navegacion SA* (No 2) [1985] AC 104, 111–2; *National Westminster Bank plc* v. *Morgan* [1985] AC 686, 708. But even when this was fashionable there were striking exceptions: *Rookes* v. *Barnard* [1968] AC 1129.

[99] *R.* v. *R (Rape: marital exemption)* [1992] 1 AC 599. For another example concerning criminal law and evidence, see *R.* v. *Kearley* [1992] 2 AC 228, 345 (willingness to develop the rules governing the admissibility of hearsay evidence).

[100] *Airedale NHS Trust* v. *Bland* [1993] AC 789.

[101] *Lipkin Gorman (a firm)* v. *Karpnale Ltd.* [1991] AC 548.

[102] *R.* v. *Secretary of State for Transport, ex p. Factortame Ltd.* *(No. 2)* [1991] 1 AC 603; *M* v. *Home Office* [1994] 1 AC 377.

[103] *Woolwich Equitable Building Society* v. *IRC* [1993] 1 AC 70.

[104] *Re Inquiry into Mirror Group Newspapers plc* [1999] 2 All E.R. 640, per Scott V-C.

13

IMPACT OF THE HUMAN RIGHTS ACT UPON VCOMPLIANCE: THE TAXATION VIEWPOINT

N. JORDAN*

TAX COMPLIANCE

My contribution to this session is devoted to the impact of the Human Rights Act in the field of taxation. I am conscious that the word 'taxation', quite apart from being oddly juxtaposed with 'human rights', does not actually appear in the session titles.

In fact it sneaks in under the heading of 'Compliance' Compliance is an activity (or state, or process) common to both the regulation of financial business and taxation. The common feature is that each of these involves an involuntary and submissive relationship with an agency of the state, the agent being armed with potent coercive and disciplinary powers.

The potential impact of Convention rights on the tax compliance field may prove interesting in a number of respects:

- First, all natural and corporate citizens have, at least potentially, a taxation relationship with the state. It is quite simply a much bigger field than regulatory compliance.
- Secondly, taxation is by far the most stressed and adversarial relationship which most non-criminal citizens are ever likely to have with the state. I do not mean to suggest that mature adults fail to recognise the benefits of taxation generally, only that their individual contributions are in no way hypothecated to their own benefit and there is no reciprocity. Financial regulators may provide the chance of a good living in return for obedience. Revenue and Customs do not give: they only take.
- Thirdly, the tax compliance relationship has been in existence for very much longer than any of its regulatory equivalents. Many of the administrative, proce-

dural and disciplinary aspects of the process, which have been refined and explored at length in disputes under domestic law, offer parallels to similar issues arising in the regulatory compliance process. The tax experience may therefore have something to teach.

- Fourthly, the potential application of Convention rights in tax matters has been recognised sporadically for at least two decades. UK tax issues were intermittently the subject of proceedings at Strasbourg long before the Human Rights Bill appeared over the horizon. To that extent we tax practitioners greet our regulatory brethren as newcomers.
- Fifthly, taxation involves the process whereby the state comes to enjoy a share generally between 17.5 per cent and 40 per cent of most economic activity within its jurisdiction.[1] In view of the sheer size of the resulting sums, and the infinity of circumstances to which the rules apply, it may be predicted that tax compliance will continue to be an arena in which great resources are devoted to exploring, refining and, if necessary, transforming the issues. To the extent that those issues are human rights issues, tax precedents will often be relevant to regulatory compliance; and sometimes to other much more general areas. In this respect tax law may prove to be a trailblazer for the development of the new human rights jurisdiction almost to the same extent as criminal law.

BACKGROUND

I hope I have said enough to justify the subject matter of

---

* Partner, Clifford Chance.
[1] See generally the annual OECD Revenue Statistics.

my address. Next, a little background. So long as the human rights jurisprudence was limited to the tribunals at Strasbourg, the opportunities for taking Convention points in relation to disputes with tax authorities were rather limited. The Court at Strasbourg is understandably preoccupied with the task of broadening the geographical reach of the simpler sort of human rights, primal issues of life, limb and liberty. In my experience of it, which I acknowledge is very limited compared with that of many of the other speakers, the Court shows signs of being overwhelmed even by this task and lacks the resources to develop the potential of its jurisdiction vertically as well as horizontally.

In particular, the Court lacks any real capacity for establishing matters of fact, especially complex or expert fact. In consequence it is difficult for it, when working in technical contexts, to find the balance between the private and the public good which underlies most Convention rights. How can one assess the proportionality between a purpose and the means adopted to achieve that purpose without a clear view of what the purpose is, and what those means actually comprise? How can one assess the reasonableness or objectivity of the explanations provided to justify apparent discrimination?

Working under such difficulties, the Court in Strasbourg may be tempted to escape what it sees as dilemmas of secondary importance by way of findings of fact which would raise eyebrows amongst those more familiar with the national background; or else, recognising that it is poorly placed to make the necessary factual findings, by allowing the state an unduly wide margin of appreciation, which in effect involves deferring to the factual assertions of the state authority and risks nullifying the whole human rights endeavour.[2]

It naturally follows that I give an enthusiastic welcome to the patriation of human rights. This radical step decentralises the human rights jurisdiction to a court system with the knowledge and the resources to develop it as it deserves.

CURRENT TOPICS

So how then does the human rights jurisdiction deserve to be developed in the taxation field? At first blush human rights and taxation are not obvious bedfellows. In the past I have found that mirth is the usual reaction to the idea that a great corporation might bring a human

rights case to protest its tax demand. That perception seems to be changing quite fast. Already the notion of claiming human rights seems less exotic, less grandiloquent, than it used to do. Once one accepts the idea that human rights amount to a code to regulate the balance of rights between individuals and the state, it is perfectly natural that Convention points should arise across the whole range of private relationships with public authority and not be confined to the sort of elemental moral confrontation which the phrase 'human rights' still evokes when taken in isolation.

What then are the Convention rights which bear upon UK tax compliance? And what current tax issues may be affected? Before starting on this journey I would like to adopt the note of caution sounded by other speakers who have talked about the impact upon the criminal process. When one really comes down to it, the contents of the Convention have a slightly fortuitous quality. It was, after all, a negotiated document. Whether or not any burning fiscal issue happens to have a human rights dimension is a little accidental. No doubt the great majority of issues between taxpayers and the tax authorities will proceed on their way much as they did before and this will particularly be true of substantive tax issues as opposed to procedural or disciplinary issues.

Here are a few of the exceptions. I will proceed through the Convention rights in the order in which they appear in Schedule 1 to that Act, flagging up certain current controversies which I think may be affected and looking at some of those controversies in more detail to consider what the possible human rights outcomes may be.

Taking the Convention rights in order, therefore, we come first to

Article 4: 'Prohibition of slavery and forced labour'

Paragraph 3 of the Article, which defines certain exemptions to the prohibition, provides at (d) that forced and compulsory labour should not include 'any work or service which forms part of normal civic obligations'. There will therefore be a dusty answer for anyone who maintains that the obligation to fill in a tax return is a breach of his Convention rights. However the compliance labour imposed upon some classes of citizen goes far, far beyond this. It has always been a distinguishing feature of the UK fiscal system that the taxation authorities seek to tap cashflows as far upstream as possible. Thus, employers account for the income tax on wages; banks account for interest on deposits; and similar arrangements exist of course in many other fields and in relation to value added tax and national insurance contributions. In effect, all these paymasters are compelled to act as unpaid tax collectors. This involves a huge burden of work for many such surrogate

---

[2] Consider e.g. the very weak passages on the Inland Revenue's argument about double taxation in *National and Provincial Building Society and others* v. *UK* (Case 117/1996/736/933-935) [1997] STC 1466, paras. 60 and 61 (at 1482).

taxpayers in respect of liabilities which are not their own. This burden is commonly enforced by severe penalties for failure. There has never previously been any form of proceeding through which persons in this position could seek redress for any perceived unfairness in the obligations placed upon them. Perhaps Article 4 now provides it.[3]

I think it would be helpful to give an example to show why this might be a serious and not a frivolous issue. Take the example of interest payments made gross by banks and other deposit-takers. Every year many billions of pounds are paid to depositors by banks and building societies. The basic rule is that interest is paid under deduction of lower rate tax,[4] but as many small depositors are not liable to tax (housewives for example) there is provision for banks to run gross accounts. Certain formalities are naturally required before a depositor may receive his interest gross. Appropriate certificates have to be given.[5]

Unfortunately, the draftsman of the legislation provided that the necessary certificate was invalid in the event of any omission or inaccuracy in any of the information required to be provided. He included no threshold of materiality. Since the information required includes, for example, the depositor's full postcode,[6] it follows that if a depositor opens a gross account with the wrong postcode then the bank, which is hardly likely to be aware of the error, is in breach of the law by paying interest gross on that account. This state of affairs is of course unlikely to be discovered until the Revenue carries out one of its occasional compliance audits. A sizeable bank might have a million or more such accounts, so it is inevitable that a proportion of them will be found to contain trivial defects of one sort or another. Subject to very limited extra-statutory tolerance by the Inland Revenue, these defects put the bank in default of its obligation to deduct and remit lower rate tax.[7]

Since the bank is in default, it is liable to pay not merely the missing tax but also interest on late payments and, in principle at least, penalties as well. All this, remember, on income which is not its own income but the income of its depositors, and in respect of which it is acting merely as an unpaid tax collector.

So far, so onerous, but there is nothing shockingly unfair about this. After all, the bank can in principle at least recoup the money from its own depositors[8]; and those depositors, if genuinely not liable to tax (which is of course likely, since there is no obvious correlation between forgetting your postcode and tax fraud) the depositors can then recover the tax as an overpayment to the Inland Revenue.

The fly in the ointment is that the Inland Revenue's auditors do not look at a million accounts. What they do, very naturally, is look at a tiny proportion of the total population of accounts and extrapolate statistically to estimate the total number of defective accounts. Estimated assessments are then raised upon that basis, against which the bank must pay. Since this amount is not reconciled to identified depositors the bank has no way of recouping the tax (and interest and penalties). Worst of all, unless you assume that every single person who makes a clerical error in his or her certificate is also a tax avoider, then the vast majority of this 'tax' which the bank is forced vicariously to pay is actually not due at all, from anyone. It is a complete and utter windfall to the tax authority, the cost of which falls on the unpaid tax collector.

Against that sort of fact-set it is perhaps easier to imagine that a successful Convention point might be brought under Article 4.

Article 6: 'right to a fair trial'

Paragraph 1 of the Article provides 'In the determination of his civil rights and obligations . . . everyone is entitled to a fair . . . hearing . . . by an independent and impartial tribunal established by law.' This is a key provision from a tax point of view. Assuming for the moment that tax liabilities fall within the expression 'civil obligations', then it might be taken for granted that tax laws are in full compliance. Of course almost every issue which arises between a citizen and a tax authority as to what the citizen's rights and obligations are (as distinct from the question of what they should be) comes provided with a right of appeal to the Special Commissioners, the VAT tribunal, some similar body, or to the Courts themselves.

However Article 6 is believed by some to be of key importance in relation to the issue of retrospective tax legislation.[9] Such legislation is commonly, though not invariably, introduced in response to a defeat or an impending defeat of the tax authorities before the domestic courts. The question posed is whether, by procuring a retrospective amendment of the law in its own favour, in proceedings to which it is itself a party,

[3] In *Four Companies* v. *Austria* (App. No. 7427/76) the Commission ruled that what we in the UK know as PAYE obligations could come within Art. 4 but that on the facts they fell within Art. 4 (3)(d).

[4] TA 1988 s. 480A and s. 4(1A).

[5] TA 1988 s. 480B.

[6] See Income Tax (Deposit Takers) (Interest Payments) Regs. 1990/2232, reg. 5 (e)(1) and Sched.

[7] TMA 1970 s. 17 and Income Tax Building Societies Regs. SI 1986/482, regs. 10 and 12.

[8] TA 1988 s. 480A.

[9] See *A,B,C and D* v. *UK* (App. No. 8531./79), 23 DR 203 and *Building Societies* case, above n. 2.

the tax authority is in effect denying the taxpayer the right to a fair hearing by an impartial tribunal. This question is closely bound up with certain wider issues arising out of retrospective legislation, which I will tackle below in the discussion under Article 1 of the First Protocol.

Paragraph 3 of Article 6 provides for certain minimum rights for anyone charged with a criminal offence. Most relevantly, sub-paragraph (c) entitles such a person 'if he has not sufficient means to pay for legal assistance, to be given it free when the interests of justice so require'. (This provision will be familiar from the *Community Charge* case.)

As other speakers have pointed out, the question of what amounts to a criminal offence is broadly an 'autonomous' one: that is to say, signatory states cannot simply side-step these requirements by labelling as 'civil' procedures which objectively have the character of criminal proceedings. This is an area of potentially huge significance in relation to tax compliance because, as in relation to regulatory compliance, UK tax statutes bristle with offences and penalties of one kind or another, the vast majority of which have traditionally been classified as non-criminal (with a view to avoiding the need to comply with the full rigours of the criminal law) but which are yet plainly and confessedly punitive in their general intent or effect. The impact of bringing such matters within the ambit of legal aid would, one imagines, be quite considerable.[10]

At all events let us give honour to a certain Mr Sweeney, a pioneer of this form of claim, but who suffered the fate of most pioneers. As long ago as 1984 Mr Sweeney, who had a long history of failing to make tax returns, appealed to the High Court against certain penalties awarded against him by the General Commissioners of Tax in Maidstone.[11] The day before the hearing he telexed the court, apparently from Denmark, asking for an adjournment on grounds of lack of funds to prepare his case and praying in aid the provisions of the European Convention. An uncomprehending court ruled that the Convention was not justiciable in England and that in any event the relevant provisions related only to criminal proceedings which (in the absence of argument) tax penalties were presumed not to be.

The Inland Revenue may find it less easy to dispose of the next such claim.

Article 8: 'right to respect for private and family life'

As with so many of these dippings into the Convention, someone coming to the matter for the first time might have difficulty in seeing anything of the faintest relevance to taxation in paragraph 1 of the Article, 'Everyone has the right to respect for his private and family life, his home and his correspondence'.

The key provision is however the last, 'his correspondence'. Others more versed in Convention law than I may be able to clarify whether 'everyone' in this context includes corporations. Even if limited to individuals this provision has potential application to very large numbers of taxpayers, in as much as the power of the tax authorities to demand access to private papers is ever-increasing and their practice in exercising that power appears to become more aggressive.[12]

My own particular interest here lies in whether this right reinforces the doctrine of legal privilege in relation to tax matters. Put shortly, does the qualifier in paragraph 2 of the Article, that 'there should be no [such] interference by a public authority . . . except such as in accordance with the law and is necessary in a democratic society in the interests of . . . the economic well-being of the country' preserve any right of access which the Inland Revenue may have to material which in conventional terms is protected by legal privilege?

Once again, some background is necessary to explain the point. The Inland Revenue's flagship information power is contained in sections 20 to 20(D) of the Taxes Management Act 1970. This provides extensive powers to call for, or indeed to seize, documents and other information. The power is not limited to obtaining documents from the taxpayer himself. It also enables documents believed to be relevant to the taxpayer's affairs to be demanded from others, including the taxpayer's barristers and solicitors. As you might expect, the right to call for a taxpayer's documents from his lawyers is qualified (section 20(B)(8)) to the effect that lawyers cannot be obliged 'to deliver or make available, without their client's consent, any document to which a claim to professional privilege could be maintained'.

---

[10] See e.g., *Benedoun* v. *France* (App. No. 12547/86), 24 February 1994, Series A, No 284, 18 EHRR 54 (tax geared penalty for *mauvaise foi* subject to this Art.), *AP MP and TP* v. *Switzerland*, Case 71/1996/690/882) 29 August 1997, 26 EHRR 541 (heirs not liable for penalty for testator's tax fraud) and *JJ* v. *The Netherlands*, Case 9/1997/793/994 (tax penalty equal to 100% of tax charged a criminal charge—damages awarded for breach of Art.).

[11] *Sweeney* v. *General Commissioners for Maidstone* [1984] STC 334.

[12] The French tax authorities are no less aggressive: see *Funke* v. *France* etc. App. No. 10828/84, 25 February 1993, 16 EHRR 297, 332 and 357 (raid on home by tax authorities without warrant—there being no need for such a warrant in French law at that time) For another example of limit of tax powers see Commission case of *X (Hardy-Spirlet)* v. *Belgium* (App. No. 9804/82), 7 December 1982, 31 DR 231 (tax authorities asked for details of expenditure: X did not wish to reveal intimate details of personal life; tax authorities successfully invoked Art. 8(2)).

This provision may spare legal advisers from embarrassment but does not necessarily protect their client, the taxpayer. This is because the power to address information demands to the taxpayer himself contains no equivalent protection for privileged material. Furthermore, it is not limited to the documents in his possession but also embraces documents in his power. Thus, if privileged documents are in the taxpayer's possession it is unclear (at best) that he is entitled to withhold them. Even if the privileged documents are held by the taxpayer's solicitor or barrister it is not clear that the Inland Revenue may not require the taxpayer to call for such documents, which would of course normally be within the taxpayer's 'power', at least if he had paid his bills. (The lawyer in such a case might of course argue that an involuntary request for documents, from a coerced client, was one which it was neither necessary nor proper for him to meet.)

This is clearly a difficult as well as a sensitive question. Most commentators take the view that a modern court would be unlikely to imply into the section any protection for legally privileged documents which the draftsman has not in fact expressly included. For myself I feel that the draftsman working in 1970 may well have regarded the sanctity of privileged documents as being something so obvious as not to need stating at every point where it was relevant. Had the matter come before a court in, say, 1971, I conjecture that that is what would have been decided. Conversely, if the matter came up for decision in present times, I think it would likely go the other way. It may well be that the Human Rights Act's requirement that statutes be construed in a manner consistent so far as possible with Convention rights would now restore the balance to the original position.

Article 14: 'prohibition of discrimination'

It is very easy to postulate a tax which amounted in object or effect to a fiscal persecution of some unpopular minority. The windfall tax apart, such things do not normally occur in the UK. Nevertheless the prohibition of discrimination may still have relevance in a number of contexts.[13]

The first, which I shall come back to in more detail, relates once again to retrospective legislation designed to fix the outcome of current proceedings to which a tax authority is party.

The second, rather more vague, is the question of the extent to which it is constitutionally permissible to enact tax laws which have the linguistic form of measures of general application but which are in fact tailor-made to address the circumstances (for better or for worse) of a single identified taxpayer. For example, section 134 of the Finance Act 1982, an obscure provision concerning the valuation for tax purposes of ethane feedstock of North Sea origin, was, it seems, enacted for the sole purpose of subsidising the trading position of a single chemical plant in an area of Scotland where unemployment locally was very high, at the expense of its Southern competitor, and all with nil or negative effect on the tax revenues overall. That at any rate is the picture that seems to emerge from subsequent review proceedings.[14]

Everyone is familiar with the notion that taxes are sometimes designed to engineer social or economic results which are seen as desirable in themselves, as well as simply to raise revenue for the state's spending purposes. It could hardly be otherwise. However the idea of a tax which, in effect, reflects the outcome of a negotiation with a single person seems to lack the quality of universal application which one associates with the very notion of law. This is an extremely difficult area which I will touch upon again under the general heading of what would constitute a bad or impermissible tax from a Convention standpoint.

A third area of discrimination which I would expect to see giving rise to a significant number of human rights cases is that of tax residence. Like most developed tax systems the UK seeks to impose tax upon non-residents in respect of profits, gains or other taxable events which have some connection, often a very slight connection, with the UK. Since it is obviously not possible to extend UK taxing measures to non-residents generally, special provision has to be made for non-residents. Hundreds of such special rules, many intensely complex, are scattered throughout the tax statutes. Many of them were drafted with anti-avoidance in mind and hence are couched in excessive terms. Because of this, and because of the sheer complexity of the special arrangements for non-residents, their differential treatment can produce strange results, some intended, some probably not. One of the simplest examples has already been corrected. The long-standing rule that repayments of overpaid tax to residents carried interest whereas non-residents were repaid without interest is now gone—thanks to the European Court of Justice's interpretation of the non-discrimination Articles in the EC Treaty.[15] I expect that as we go along other examples, more complex but no easier to justify, will be discovered.

---

[13] Thus the Commission decision in *McGregor* v. *UK* (App. No. 30548/96) that TA 1988 ss. 259(1)(c) and 261A(3) discriminated against him being male led to changes in FA 1998 s. 26(3).

[14] *R.* v. *AG, ex p. ICI* (1984) 60 TC 1.

[15] Case C-330/91 *R. v IRC ex p. Commerzbank AG* [1993] STC 605; the offending provision was TA 1988 s. 825(1); the reform proposal was announced in Inland Revenue Press Release of 23 July 1993.

Article 1, first protocol: 'protection of proprty'

Last but not least—in fact last and most—I come to Article 1 of the First Protocol. This Article consists of three inter-related rules:

First—'Every natural or legal person i.e. explicitly including a company is entitled to the peaceful enjoyment of his possessions'.
Secondly—'No-one should be deprived of his possessions except in the public interest'.
Thirdly—'The preceding provisions shall not, however, in any way impair the right of a State to enforce such laws as it deems necessary . . . to secure the payment of taxes or other contributions or penalties'.

Convention case law, including in particular the *Gasus Dosier* decision in 1995,[16] emphasises that the margin of appreciation in determining what is in the general interest by way of taxation is very wide, but not limitless. A state cannot circumvent the first rule, which upholds the right to peaceful enjoyment of possessions, by labelling any act of confiscation 'a tax'.

Hitherto the European Court's attention has been directed to this matter (at least so far as UK taxation is concerned) only with regard to a single category of tax legislation, namely retrospective tax legislation.[17] This is of course a category which has always been seen as controversial, particularly in the case of retrospection designed to turn defeat into victory with regard to matters already before the courts. However there is no reason why Convention scrutiny should be confined to the special case of retrospective tax legislation. In principle any measure which is sufficiently unfair and unreasonable in its effects might be held to be non-compliant as being disproportionate or (which may be another way of saying the same thing) as being a tax in name only.

This is an area which I have always found to be one of acute difficulty. It is easy to say that an outrageously discriminatory tax would be unreasonable—and unlawful too, if any means of redress could be found. I think it was Jeremy Bentham who posed the example of a tax upon persons with blue eyes. Where discrimination is in issue, it is a free-standing ground of non-compliance. That is to say, a complaint may succeed under Article 14 alone even if the matter is not also considered to be an unjustified deprivation of possessions under Article 1 of the First Protocol.

However, as soon as one moves away from the obvious example of gross discrimination it becomes extraordinarily hard to formulate any helpful criteria by reference to which a substantive tax provision can be assessed as being so unfair, unreasonable, excessive or disproportionate as to fall outside even the wide margin of appreciation permitted under Article 1 of the First Protocol. There is of course some domestic history of attempts, occasionally successful attempts, to strike down UK legislation where the offending provision appeared in secondary rather than primary legislation—usually a matter of pure chance. If the objectionable rule was in secondary legislation then one could bring review proceedings upon the useful, if slender, fiction that Parliament would never authorise the Inland Revenue to act unreasonably. A lucky plaintiff might find that Parliament itself had provided the criteria by reference to which the unreasonableness of the provision could be established. It might for example have enacted the enabling section in terms inconsistent with the secondary legislation subsequently made under it. Or the minister might in Parliament have expressed the Government's intentions with sufficient clarity that the subsequent provision could be seen to collide with the intention.

Otherwise, it is really not easy to say what makes a tax unfair because, at the risk of seeming flippant, it is in the nature of tax to be unfair. Tax is a confiscation. You pay your money and you get nothing back. (A pattern of behaviour which in any other context can be guaranteed to excite the suspicion of auditors, insolvency practitioners, and indeed tax inspectors!) Nearly all taxpayers enjoy benefits purchased by tax-funded expenditure but there is no traceable connection between the two things (with the heavily qualified exception of National Insurance contributions). Given that taxation is inevitable in all advanced societies, except Monte Carlo, what—if anything—would put a tax beyond the pale?

Certainly I think it would be very difficult to attack a taxing measure as non-compliant simply because it had no reasonable prospect of fulfilling its advertised intentions. In the 1960s there was briefly a tax in the UK called Selective Employment Tax. This sought to put the British economy on a more secure footing by distinguishing between non-productive workers (bad) and productive workers (good). By taxing the provision of non-productive jobs it was thought that millions of shirkers in the service industries could be driven back into the 'real' economy, transforming the nation's finances at a stroke and ensuring full employment for evermore. It is difficult to think of any fiscal measure in any country at any time which was less likely to achieve its aims,[18] but if such a measure were reintroduced

---

[16] *Gasus Dosier* v. *Netherlands* (App. No. 15375/88), 23 February 1995, 20 EHRR 403.
[17] Above n. 9.

[18] See Dennis Healey, *The Time of my Life* 369, observing that it worked so well that overmanning became a crippling burden on manufacturing companies for years to come.

today I feel sure that any court would hold that the margin of appreciation in a democratic society includes the right to embark upon crackpot schemes.

One possible candidate for non-compliance would be a fiscal measure which levied tax on any given source at a rate in excess of 100 per cent, as for example, the old Betterment Levy (which preceded Development Land Tax) was capable of doing. The description of taxes as 'penal' is a very overworked epithet, but a tax at over 100 per cent is properly so described. By taking more than the totality of the proceeds of any given transaction it must be regarded as punishing the taxpayer for having undertaken that transaction in the first place. Whatever else may be a tax, a genuinely punitive measure would in my view not be.

RETROSPECTION

By far the largest potential area of Convention application, so far as substantive taxing measures are concerned, remains the special case of retrospection. Retrospection is not of course peculiar to the tax field and the most famous example—the War Damage Act of 1965—did not in fact involve tax at all. In practice, controversial instances of retrospection almost invariably arise in the tax field where such measures have in recent years become entirely routine.

The theoretical objections to retrospective legislation are well known. In essence, a retrospective measure (tax or any other) enacts a fiction as to what the law was. Thus, it promulgates two rival versions of what the law is supposed to have been at one and the same time. This is in principle destructive of the rule of law. If retrospection were to be adopted promiscuously, why should anyone have any more respect for the existing law than they do for any of the infinite range of non-existing laws by which the existing law may at any moment be supplanted, for the past and present as well as for the future?

This objection cannot however be regarded as absolute. For one thing, the same problem occurs to some degree with judge-made law, due to the doctrine that decisions of the courts, including decisions on appeal which reverse a ruling below, relate back to an earlier time. Thus legitimate expectations may be defeated by judges as well as by the legislature. (At least yours and mine may be. The Inland Revenue, as so often, is in a special position: claims for repayment of excess tax are, pursuant to section 33 of the Taxes Management Act, 1970, disregarded if the original excessive computation 'was in fact made . . . in accordance with the practice generally prevailing at the time').

The ECHR has itself twice now in UK cases[19] confirmed that retrospection may be Convention compliant, whilst keeping the door firmly open to the possibility that in appropriate circumstances it would not be.

The particular sub-set of the problem of retrospection which interests me most, and which may I think be regarded as an aggravated example of the practice, is retrospection introduced by the fiscal authorities in order to reverse an actual or anticipated defeat in the courts. This unattractive habit is extraordinarily prevalent in the UK.

Section 62 of the 1987 (No. 2) Finance Act sets the modern style, sometimes known as the 'fruits of victory' formula. Subsection (2) provided:

'(2) Nothing . . . above affects—

(a) . . . the judgment of any Court . . . given before 17th March 1987 [i.e. some four months before the 1987 Act received Royal Assent], or

(b) the law to be applied in proceedings on appeal to the Court of Appeal . . . where the judgment of the High Court . . . which is in issue was given before that date,

but, subject to that, the amendment made . . . above shall be deemed always to have been made.'

The practical result of this measure therefore was that the taxpayer (a Mr Padmore) was allowed to keep the benefit of the judgment he had obtained on 16 March 1987 subject to the Inland Revenue's rights of appeal (which the Inland Revenue subsequently took and lost).[20] Everyone else similarly placed (at least unless they had some special arrangement with the Inland Revenue) had their rights confiscated.

The *Building Societies* case which went to Strasbourg was a further such case.[21] Three societies launched proceedings based on the success of domestic proceedings brought by the Woolwich, which had obtained a declaration that certain secondary legislation was *ultra vires*.[22] The Inland Revenue admitted that it had no defence whatever to the claims brought by the three societies. Nevertheless it introduced retrospective legislation to destroy these claims. (In fact it did so no fewer than three times in three separate Finance Acts, as the claims showed remarkable vitality and proved extremely difficult to kill off). Only after that did the societies proceed (unsuccessfully) to Strasbourg.

[19] Above n. 9
[20] See *Padmore* v. *IRC*, 62 TC 352.
[21] *National and Provincial Building Society and others* v. *UK* (Case 117/1996/736/933-935) [1997] STC 1466.
[22] *R.* v. *IRC ex p. Woolwich Equitable Building Society* (1990) 63 TC 589.

The governmental response to all such criticisms is robust. It says that to the extent that decisions of the courts reveal that previous policy choices were incorrectly rendered into statute (or perhaps just poor choices) then it is not merely permissible but praiseworthy to intervene so as to restore matters to what was (or should have been) intended.

The Inland Revenue's moral position is arguably reinforced wherever the retrospective measure contains a 'fruits of victory' formula for the original litigant whose successful proceedings brought the matter to notice. An alternative view is that, far from reinforcing the Revenue's position, such carve-outs render the retrospective legislation vulnerable, because the discrimination involved is blatant. (Which is not of course to say that it is incapable of being reasonably justified: many might feel that the fruits of victory formula represents a reasonable compromise between the subject's right to justice and Government's right to govern).

I assume, given that the formula was adopted at least as long as 12 years ago, that the reason the draftsman adopted an anonomysing formula, whereby Mr Padmore was identified by reference only to the date of his judgment, was not because of any anxiety in connection with Article 14 of the Convention but rather in order to avoid falling foul of Parliament's own procedures with respect to hybrid bills.[23] Be that as it may, this form of discrimination was ruled acceptable by the ECHR in the *Building Societies* case (where the Woolwich had enjoyed a similar saving from retrospection). However, that decision was firmly rooted in findings of fact peculiar to the proceedings. It by no means follows that this favourite drafting formula will always be regarded as compliant.

Apart from the discrimination (Article 14) involved in a carve-out in favour of the taxpayer first past the post, fiscal retrospection is potentially open to challenge under Article 1 of the First Protocol. Retrospection designed to validate an earlier invalid purported charge necessarily must itself be regarded as a charge to tax (it imposes the charge which the earlier provision failed to impose); and a charge to tax must always be a deprivation of possessions. Always remembering that there is a particularly wide margin of appreciation in regard to taxation or purported taxation, it remains the case that the measure is susceptible to a finding of non-compliance if the Court concludes that it was disproportionate. The Court's review of proportionality in such a case may well be influenced by the general truism that retrospection makes for legal uncertainty and by its nature destroys legitimate expectations. In striking the required

balance between subject and state, there are therefore some heavy weights already in the debit scale.

The other obvious ground of challenge to the type of retrospection I have described is the one I mentioned earlier, under Article 6 of the Convention itself—denial of the right to a fair hearing. There is here a preliminary point on whether purported tax demands are or are not within the phrase 'civil rights or obligations'. In this respect the building societies were successful at Strasbourg but on the particular facts of the case their rights were actually claims to restitution of monies unlawfully exacted. There is some authority for the view that a tax demand is not a 'civil obligation', but the European Court has taken the view that consequential civil rights arising out of tax demands can be; whether this will in time lead to a view that a tax demand is a civil obligation is a matter for speculation.[24] It may be that the answer to this question would be influenced by whether or not the demand is actually a valid one, as opposed to whether a fair hearing has been denied in respect of it.

The Inland Revenue has a ready, if rather unattractive, answer to the charge of denial of a fair hearing. The answer is that retrospective legislation in the usual form does not deny anyone the right to take their grievance to a fair hearing by an impartial and independent tribunal. Any taxpayer who wishes remains welcome to do so. It is merely that the law has been altered so that he is bound to lose. Legal proceedings are not sporting contests: a tribunal does not cease to be fair simply because one side has no chance of winning: if the law is firmly against the taxpayer then it is quite right and fair that he should have no chance of success.

When I first heard this line of argument I must say that it struck me as sophistry of the most repulsive kind. If one party to litigation has the practical power (the House of Commons being a totally ineffective safeguard where technical tax provisions are concerned) to rewrite the law in its own favour then any subsequent hearing is, to speak plainly, a show trial—just as much as it would be if the law had been left alone but the tribunal had been suborned.

I have come to accept that the matter is more difficult. If one says that the law must never be retrospectively changed, in any circumstances, pending a hearing, then one is really saying that the litigant enjoys a right to veto over the enactment of any retrospective legislation. This veto may be limited, in that it does not arise until (say) the taxpayer gives notice of his desire for the fair

---

[23] For another example see FA 1984 s. 58(2) and Sched. 12 Part II; this is explained in N. Lawson, *The View from No 11*, 354–5.

[24] The original view may be found in *Darby* v. *Sweden* (App. No. 11581/85), 23 October 1990, Series A, no 187 (1991) 13 EHRR 774. For the view that obligations arising out of tax can be within Art. 6 see *Editions Perispocope* v. *France*, 26 March 1992, Series A no 234 (1992) 14 EHRR 597.

hearing to which he is entitled. It may be further limited by confining it to the litigant's own affairs. However both these limitations cause as many problems as they solve. The first would attach a wholly inappropriate significance to the formal issue of proceedings or to some other (and what other?) moment at which the particular taxpayer's right to veto legal change might be said to accrue. The second restriction raises all the problems of discrimination already discussed. Why should a widespread grievance be redressed by a race with only one possible winner?

It may be argued that the taxpayer's real grievance in this situation is that the law has been changed against him; and one can make a fair case for saying that this is not a compelling grievance if he has already failed in, or has not taken, the Article 1 argument, i.e. he has failed to show that the retrospective measure which has (in practice) stifled his fair hearing is one which should never have been made.

In my own view, the grievance of the taxpayer in this situation is twofold. The taxpayer is really saying: (1) I would have won under the law as it was; and (2) the retrospective change in the law was unjustified. This is a terribly frustrating position for the taxpayer to find himself in. Experience shows that Government spokesmen will be quite ruthless in denigrating the legal claim they are proposing to destroy. It will be suggested that the taxpayer's original complaint was doomed to failure and is only being stifled in order to spare the public purse the costs of a successful defence; or that the taxpayer's grievance could only have succeeded by exploiting a technical 'loophole'; that the resulting profit would have been an unmeritorious 'windfall' achieved at the expense of his fellow taxpayers; that the taxpayer has gone back upon a long-established understanding of what the law was which everyone else was content to accept; that the retrospection is not really retrospection at all but simply helpful 'clarification'; etc etc. (This process of softening-up the target has a long tradition. In the debate on the Indemnity Act following the First World War, a Government spokesman explained that the retrospection was only necessary to deal with certain 'smart alecks' who 'had taken legal advice', the taking of (correct) advice being apparently conclusive proof of bad character.)

The taxpayer's frustration arises because many of these accusations would have been put to the test were the original proceedings allowed to go forward to a fair hearing on the original law. But if the retrospective measure is passed (as it always is) the justifications advanced for it will never be tested. In effect, a legal inquiry is supplanted by a political one, in which the taxpayer is not heard.

Ugly though this process undoubtedly is, I cannot myself see much hope for attacks upon retrospection which rely upon Article 6 alone and not also upon Article 1 or Article 14.

LEGITIMATE EXPECTATIONS

Before I close I would like to mention two other areas. The first of these concerns the legitimate expectations of taxpayers who have been encouraged or permitted by tax officials to suppose that their affairs would be dealt with in a particular way (whether or not that treatment was strictly in accordance with statute) and who are then disappointed by a subsequent change of position on the part of the tax authority.

This is a very familiar situation which gives rise to a fair amount of review litigation under domestic law. Once upon a time it was thought that such claims were not competent, on the ground that however clear the representation might have been, a mere official could not alter the tax laws as laid down by Parliament. In more recent times the courts have accepted that a taxpayer may be entitled to rely upon sufficiently clear representations by the tax authority, provided of course that the taxpayer himself has been open and candid in his own disclosure leading to the ruling in question.

It is a common complaint amongst tax practitioners that, although the principle is clear, it is almost impossible to win such cases, largely because the standard of disclosure required is both uncertain and unrealistically high, so that fault of some kind is almost always found. (The other, pragmatic, view is that most such claims fail because the Revenue concedes the strong ones.)

A particularly interesting example occurred some five years ago in *R. v. CIR, ex parte Matrix Securities Limited*.[25] That involved a tax scheme where clearance for a particular (and astonishingly favourable) tax treatment had been unconditionally given by the Inspector of Taxes in response to a letter drafted by the taxpayer's legal advisers. The Inland Revenue subsequently withdrew its clearance. The taxpayer unsuccessfully sought review and appealed all the way to the House of Lords, losing at every stage. The case has always intrigued me because, although all but one of the nine judges who heard the matter agreed that the Inland Revenue was not bound, because of the inadequacy in the taxpayer's disclosure, the judges found it impossible to agree amongst themselves just what the defect had been. The House of Lords found unanimously against the taxpayer on a wide variety of grounds, but only one

---

[25] [1994] STC 272 (HL) affirming [1993] STC 774 (CA); for a much fuller explanation of the factual background see the judgment of Park J in *Matrix Securities Ltd* v. *Theodore Godard* [1998] STC 1.

of those enjoyed the support of more than two of the five judges. That ground, with which all five agreed, was that the disclosure was deficient because it had been addressed to the Inspector of Taxes rather than to the Head Office of the Inland Revenue. Quite a picky requirement one might say, in the absence of any explicit obligation to communicate with the Revenue at one level rather than another,[26] and made no more impressive by the fact that all three judges in the Court of Appeal rejected precisely the same argument.

I have not researched the point but I merely mention, as a lively possibility, that taxpayers will find some support in the Strasbourg jurisprudence for a more generous attitude to be taken towards legitimate expectations engendered by the tax authorities, whether in transaction-specific correspondence or in more general statements of practice.

Finally, I end this brief review by mentioning the *Marks & Spencer* case in which the High Court has recently ruled against Marks & Spencer but, I understand, leave to appeal to the Court of Appeal has been granted.[27] This is a VAT case and usefully reminds us that Human Rights Convention points may and should, wherever possible, be run in conjunction with European Community law points. To some extent, VAT is ahead of the game in that ECHR principles can be run before domestic courts in VAT cases even without the Human Rights Act.

[26] Especially when the Revenue had issued statements in 1986 and 1990 that taxpayers should address their questions in the first instance to their local inspector and not usually to Head Office—*Matrix Securities Ltd* v. *Theodore Godard* [1998] STC 1 at 31–3.

[27] *Marks and Spencer plc* v. *Customs and Excise Commissioners* [1999] STC 205.

The background to the case is that prior to July 1996 HM Customs suffered a series of heavy reverses before the courts, giving rise to potential VAT repayment claims estimated at billions of pounds. The Government responded by announcing its intention retrospectively to curtail repayment rights from six years (from the date of payment or longer where VAT is paid by mistake) to three. Following much hostile comment to the effect that this measure was likely to be in breach of both Community law and ECHR principles of legitimate expectation and peaceful enjoyment of possessions (since ECHR principles are implied into Community law irrespective of the enactment of the Human Rights Act), the Government amended its legislation so as to extend the three year time limitation period to claims *by* Customs as well as claims *from* Customs.

Although this response removed one potential line of attack against the legislation, there are still many others. Unfortunately, the VAT Tribunal and Moses J in the High Court have failed to rise to the challenge and have effectively narrowed the applicability of Community law/ECHR rights in the VAT arena to virtual non-existence. It is hoped that these judgments will be reversed on appeal. There is also other litigation in this area expected to come before the courts later this year which again will be relying on Community law/ECHR principles, and I await this with interest.

If nothing else I think the existence of this litigation confirms the point that I made at the outset, that so far as taxation is concerned the human rights jurisdiction is already running. It is certainly too early to say how significant its effects will be, but to my mind the proper test of the Act's success should be this, that by the next election the Government bitterly regret having enacted it!

14

HUMAN RIGHTS AND CORPORATE WRONGS: THE IMPACT OF THE HUMAN RIGHTS ACT ON SECTION 236 OF THE INSOLVENCY ACT 1986

R.C. NOLAN*

I INTRODUCTION

Lawyers are increasingly aware of the major impact the Human Rights Act 1998 ('the 1998 Act') will have on what they commonly regard as 'commercial law', far removed from the traditional realm of 'human rights law'.[1] They have thought about how the 1998 Act will affect various public (or at least quasi-public) regulatory processes, such as those established under the Financial Services Act 1986 (soon to be replaced by a new Financial Services and Markets Act), and how it will influence the conduct of investigations by state-nominated inspectors, such as those appointed to examine a company's affairs under Part XIV of the Companies Act 1985. Relatively little attention has been paid to the subject matter of this paper, the 1998 Act's impact on inquiries into a company's dealings and affairs under section 236 of the Insolvency Act 1986.[2]

In order to assess the impact of the 1998 Act on section 236, it is useful first to outline the very wide powers conferred by the section, and then the manner in which courts have hitherto controlled the exercise of those powers, to protect those affected by them from oppression, before turning to the possible consequences of the 1998 Act for section 236. In short, it is likely that the courts' current approach to section 236 will have to change.

II THE POWERS CONFERRED BY SECTION 236 OF THE INSOLVENCY ACT 1986

The liquidator, receiver or administrator of a company is generally a private individual, rather than a state functionary, but nevertheless section 236 of the Insolvency Act 1986 confers 'an extraordinary power to assist him in obtaining information about the company's affairs',[3] a power also described as 'drastic and far-reaching'.[4] The section enables the court, on application of 'the office-holder' (a term which includes liquidators, administrators, administrative receivers and the official receiver),[5] to summon before it for examination any officers of the company, or any person known or suspected to be indebted to the company, or to possess property belonging to the company or information about it. The court may also order any officer of the company, or anyone in possession of information about it, to swear an affidavit containing an account of his dealings with the company, or to produce relevant books, papers and records. These powers are backed by substantial coercive sanctions: the court may issue a warrant for the arrest of a person in breach of an order made under

* Fellow of St Johns College Cambridge, University Lecturer in Law.
[1] See e.g., Lidbetter, *Company Investigations and Public Law* (Oxford: Hart Publishing, 1999); Davies, 'Self-incrimination, Fair Trials and the Pursuit of Corporate and Financial Wrongdoing' in B.S. Markesinis (ed.), *The Impact of the Human Rights Bill on English Law* (Oxford: Oxford University Press, 1998).
[2] Such examinations are addressed by Davies, *Ibid*.

[3] *In re Castle New Homes Ltd.* [1979] 1 WLR 1075, 1080G, *per* Slade J, referring to s. 268 of the Companies Act 1948, one of the statutory predecessors to s. 236 of the Insolvency Act 1986. See also *In re British & Commonwealth Holdings plc (No. 2); Joint Administrators of British & Commonwealth Holdings plc* v. *Spicer & Oppenheim* [1993] AC 426, 439D, *per* Lord Slynn.
[4] *In re Rolls Razor Ltd. (No. 2)* [1970] Ch. 576, 583D, *per* Megarry J, also addressing s. 268 of the Companies Act 1948.
[5] Insolvency Act 1986 ss. 234(1), 236(1).

section 236, or a warrant for the seizure of books, records or such like in the possession of that person.

Case law which considers section 236 shows just how extraordinary the provision is. Section 236 confers an unfettered discretion on the court.[6] It empowers the court to order the examination of a person relevant at any time, whether or not there are pending criminal or civil proceedings against him to which the examination might be material.[7] An order under section 236 may be made even though it exposes the subject of the order to the risk of personal liability.[8] Further information obtained from a person through use of the section can be disclosed to prosecuting authorities that have the necessary powers to compel production, and such information is *prima facie* admissible against the informant at his subsequent criminal trial, though the trial judge would have jurisdiction to exclude it.[9] The section impliedly abrogates the examinee's privilege against self-incrimination.[10] Information obtained from a person under section 236 is *prima facie* admissible in civil proceedings involving that person.[11] Naturally, lawyers who acted for a company cannot claim legal professional privilege in respect of their communications with the company if and when they are required to reveal such communications pursuant to section 236: the privilege belongs to the company, not to them.[12] Indeed, in exceptional cases, section 236 might be capable of

overriding the privilege from disclosure which attaches to legal advice in the possession of someone subject to an order under the section, even though the advice was not given to the company in question.[13] However, an order under section 236 should not override the privilege attaching to advice or opinions generated in the context of actual or anticipated litigation.[14]

The need for the inquisitorial powers conferred by section 236 is plain.

'The process under section 268 [of the Companies Act 1948, a predecessor of section 236 of the Insolvency Act 1986] is needed because of the difficulty in which the liquidator of an insolvent company is necessarily placed. He usually comes as a stranger to the affairs of a company which has sunk to its financial doom. . . . In any case, there are almost certain to be many transactions which are difficult to discover or to understand merely from the books and papers of the company. Accordingly, the legislature has provided this extraordinary process so as to enable the requisite information to be obtained.'[15]

'A liquidator or administrator comes into the company with no previous knowledge and frequently finds that the company's records are missing or defective'[16].

Nevertheless, the courts are well aware of the potential for oppression within the powers conferred by section 236 or its predecessors,[17] which extend back to section 115 of the Companies Act 1862. In order to guard against these potential injustices, the courts have laid down guidelines for the exercise of discretion under section 236. These safeguards largely address the question whether a liquidator, or other office-holder, should be allowed to take advantage of the section and, if so, by what means. They also seek to put some limits on what may be done with information gathered under the section.

The remainder of this paper will address those safeguards, and then consider whether they are sufficient in the light of the 1998 Act. It is very doubtful that they are. Finally, the paper will consider some wider implications of the 1998 Act for section 236.

---

[6] *In re Rolls Razor Ltd. (No. 2)* [1970] Ch. 576, 593, *per* Megarry J; *In re John T. Rhodes Ltd.* [1987] BCLC 77, 79–80, *per* Hoffmann J.

[7] *North Australian Territory Company* v. *Goldsborough* [1893] 2 Ch. 381, 384, *per* Lord Esher MR; *In re Bletchley Boat Co. Ltd.* [1974] 1 WLR 630, 637, *per* Brightman J; *In re Castle New Homes Ltd.* [1979] 1 WLR 1075, 1088-9, *per* Slade J.

[8] See *Cloverbay Ltd.* v. *BCCI* [1991] Ch. 90, 103A, *per* Browne-Wilkinson V-C, in the context of an order against an officer of the company concerned.

[9] See *Hamilton* v. *Naviede; In re Arrows Ltd. (No. 4)* [1995] 2 AC 75 in relation to all these issues, and Insolvency Act 1986 s. 433. As regards disclosure of information obtained by means of s. 236 see also *Soden* v. *Burns* [1996] 3 All ER 967.

[10] *Bishopsgate Investment Management Ltd.* v. *Maxwell* [1993] Ch. 1; *Hamilton* v. *Naviede; In re Arrows Ltd. (No. 4)* [1995] 2 AC 75, 93, *per* Lord Browne-Wilkinson.

[11] See Insolvency Act 1986 s. 433 and the Civil Evidence Act 1995. Note also the Insolvency Rules 1986 (SI 1986/1925) rule 9.5(2)–(4) and *Re Esal (Commodities) Ltd (No. 2)* [1990] BCC 708, 718B–C and 723H, *per* Millett J, as regards leave to use information obtained under s. 236 in subsequent litigation. The grounds on which Millett J thought leave should be granted are too narrow: *Hamilton* v. *Naviede; In re Arrows Ltd. (No. 4)* [1995] 2 AC 75, 102E–G, *per* Lord Browne-Wilkinson. Further, information obtained by means of s. 236 should, *a fortiori*, be *prima facie* admissible in civil proceedings against a person, given that it would be so admissible against him in a criminal trial according to *Hamilton* v. *Naviede; In re Arrows Ltd. (No. 4)* [1995] 2 AC 75.

[12] *In re Brook Martin & Co (Nominees) Ltd.* [1993] BCLC 328, 336g–h, *per* Vinelott J.

[13] *Ibid.*, at 336–7, *per* Vinelott J. The position in Australia is different: see *Re Compass Airlines Pty. Ltd.* (1992) 10 ACLC 1380, addressing s. 597 of the Australian Corporations Law, which broadly corresponds to s. 236 of the Insolvency Act 1986.

[14] *Re Highgrade Traders Ltd.* [1984] BCLC 151, addressing s. 268 of the Companies Act 1948, one of the statutory predecessors of s. 236 of the Insolvency Act 1986.

[15] *In re Rolls Razor Ltd. (No. 2)* [1970] Ch. 576, 591–2, *per* Megarry J.

[16] *Cloverbay Ltd.* v. *BCCI* [1991] Ch. 90, 102, *per* Browne-Wilkinson V-C.

[17] *In re North Australia Territory Co.* (1890) 45 ChD 87, 93, *per* Bowen LJ; *In re Castle New Homes Ltd.* [1979] 1 WLR 1075, 1089G, *per* Slade J.

III THE COURTS' APPROACH TO THE POWERS CONFERRED ON THEM BY SECTION 236 OF THE INSOLVENCY ACT 1986

The first, obvious, protection for the subject of an application under section 236 is that the liquidator, or other office-holder, must show why the examination should be ordered, or why an affidavit should be sworn, or why documents should be produced.[18] However, protection from irrelevant or immaterial applications, though necessary, is clearly far from sufficient: a liquidator might well want information from a proposed examinee which, though highly relevant, could nevertheless prejudice the examinee significantly. The courts have therefore imposed further controls over the discretion conferred by section 236, controls which reflect the purpose they have attributed to that section.

In *British & Commonwealth Holdings plc* v. *Spicer and Oppenheim*,[19] the House of Lords held that the purpose of section 236 was very broad: to enable the office-holder to carry out his task, which, in the case of a liquidation, includes the beneficial winding-up of the company concerned, as well as the provision of information to public authorities where the liquidator is authorised or required to make such disclosure.[20] The purpose of the section is no longer restricted to enabling a liquidator (or other office-holder) to 'reconstruct the company's knowledge' of events and dealings before his appointment.[21] However, the section 'is not to be used for giving a litigant (just because he is an office-holder) special advantages in ordinary litigation'.[22] The court's discretion under section 236 must therefore be exercised after a careful balancing of all the factors involved:[23] in particular, the court will have regard both to the reasonable requirements of the officer-holder to carry out his task and the need to avoid making an order which is unnecessary, unreasonable or oppressive to its subject,

such as an order which would give the office-holder an unfair advantage in litigation.

The practical result of these generalities was formerly the so-called 'Rubicon Test'[24]: 'a rule of thumb under which relief under s. 236 would be withheld if office-holders had already commenced proceedings against, or definitely decided (mentally crossed the Rubicon) to proceed against the proposed witness [i.e. examinee]'.[25] This test was rejected in *Cloverbay Ltd* v. *BCCI*,[26] because its application often depended on ascertainment of the office-holder's state of mind, something which led to many undesirable disputes of fact: the 'Rubicon Test' was an impractical test. In the *Cloverbay* case, the Court of Appeal recommended a return to a more 'case-by-case', empirical approach to making orders under section 236.[27] Nevertheless, recent cases have indicated that the 'Rubicon Test' had at least a 'germ of truth' in it.[28] The courts still do not want to make a order under section 236 if the liquidator, or other office holder, of a company would thereby gain an unfair advantage in litigation. Consequently, when litigation by, or involving, the office-holder is on foot, or imminent, the courts are very unwilling to make any order under section 236 against another party to that litigation, or against witnesses in the action, which might give the office-holder such an unfair advantage.[29]

A court may also choose the particular type of order it makes under section 236 with a view to protecting the subject of its order from oppression. The courts regard an order for oral examination as potentially the most oppressive order they can make under section 236; less likely to be oppressive is an order to swear an affidavit deposing to the affairs of the company in question, and least likely to be oppressive is an order for the production of documents relating to the dealings or affairs of the company.[30] Consequently, a court may be more

---

[18] *In re John T. Rhodes Ltd.* [1987] BCLC 77, 79h, *per* Hoffmann J; Insolvency Rules 1986 (SI 1986/1925) rule 9.2(1).

[19] [1993] AC 426, 439D, *per* Lord Slynn.

[20] *Hamilton* v. *Naviede; In re Arrows Ltd. (No. 4)* [1995] 2 AC 75, 102–3, *per* Lord Browne-Wilkinson.

[21] *British & Commonwealth Holdings plc* v. *Spicer and Oppenheim* [1993] AC 426, 439C, *per* Lord Slynn, disapproving contrary *dicta* in *Cloverbay Ltd.* v. *BCCI* [1991] Ch. 90.

[22] *Re Atlantic Computers plc* [1998] BCC 200, 208F–209A, *per* Robert Walker J, citing *In re North Australian Territory Co.* (1890) 45 Ch. D 87; *In re Bletchley Boat Co. Ltd.* [1974] 1 WLR 630; *In re Castle New Homes Ltd.* [1979] 1 WLR 1075 and *Re Esal (Commodities) Ltd.* [1990] BCC 708. See also *Cloverbay Ltd.* v. *BCCI* [1991] Ch. 90, 102E, *per* Browne-Wilkinson V-C.

[23] *British & Commonwealth Holdings plc* v. *Spicer and Oppenheim* [1993] AC 426, 437A–440A, *per* Lord Slynn. See also Lord Woolf's judgment in the Court of Appeal in the same case, [1992] Ch. 342, 392–3.

[24] *In re Castle New Homes Ltd.* [1979] 1 WLR 1075.

[25] *Re Atlantic Computers plc* [1998] BCC 200, 208E, *per* Robert Walker J.

[26] [1991] Ch. 90.

[27] *Ibid.,* at 102, *per* Browne-Wilkinson V-C, and at 106F, *per* Nourse LJ.

[28] *Re Bishopsgate Investment Management Ltd. (No. 2)* [1994] BCC 732, 739E, *per* Hoffmann J; *Re Atlantic Computers plc* [1998] BCC 200, 208F, *per* Robert Walker J.

[29] Consider *Re J.N. Taylor Finance Pty. Ltd.* [1998] BPIR 347, 369F–370C, *per* Evans-Lombe J. This was a case on s. 426 of the Insolvency Act 1986 (assistance to foreign insolvency courts) which looked at the authorities on s. 236 for the purpose of deciding whether to make an order under s. 426 in aid of the Supreme Court of South Australia, which, under Part 5.9 of the Australian Corporations Law, had directed the oral examination of various people concerned in the collapse of the company and a related entity. See to like effect *Re Southern Equities Corporation Ltd.* (High Court, unreported, 1 March 1999).

[30] See *Cloverbay Ltd.* v. *BCCI* [1991] Ch. 90, 103C, *per* Browne-Wilkinson V-C.

willing to make an order for the production of documents than an order for oral examination.[31]

The courts can also control access to information generated by means of section 236. Under rule 9.5(2) of the Insolvency Rules 1986[32] leave of the court is required in order to gain access to the written records and answers generated in an oral examination under the section, or to affidavits sworn in compliance with an order under the section, unless the person seeking access is an office-holder who could have sought an order under section 236 itself. Another way in which the courts have controlled the use of information procured under section 236 is by subjecting those who obtain such information to an implied, qualified duty of confidentiality in respect of it.[33] However, the duty does not prevent an office holder from using information obtained by means of section 236 in the performance of his tasks. So, for example, a liquidator may use such information (with leave if needs be) in civil litigation undertaken for the benefit of the company,[34] and he can disclose it to state bodies when required or authorised to do so.[35]

Control exercised by a court or tribunal over the evidence which may be used before it can provide further protection from the oppressive use of section 236: if a court or tribunal limits the use which may be made of information procured under the section, it can thereby limit the prejudice which might be caused by such use. So, for example, when faced with the possibility that information obtained under section 236 might be tendered at the trial of the person who provided it, in order to prove he committed an offence, the House of Lords held that the use of such self-incriminating information could be controlled by the trial court and, indeed, should be controlled (if at all) by the trial court, rather than by the court which originally made the order under section 236.[36]

In summary, the courts' protection for those who are the subject of an application under section 236 focuses primarily on the timing of the application in relation to other surrounding circumstances, particularly pending, or immanently anticipated, litigation by, or involving, the office-holder who seeks the order under the

section. Protection can also be given in other ways, by the type of order made under the section, or by the subsequent control of the information obtained under the section.

When the Human Rights Act 1998 comes fully into force,[37] and introduces rights into English law (the 'Convention Rights') which are derived from the European Convention on Human Rights,[38] the courts will doubtless have to consider whether the techniques evolved so far to prevent oppression under section 236 will provide sufficient, or appropriate, protection for the Convention Rights of anyone who might be prejudiced by action under the section. It is unlikely that they do. In order to see this, it is necessary to examine the relevant Convention Rights, and the way they are incorporated into English law.

IV THE RELEVANCE OF HUMAN RIGHTS

The most relevant Convention Rights are established by Article 6 of the European Convention on Human Rights. Article 6 guarantees the right to a fair trial. The first, general, sentence of Article 6(1) concerns both civil and criminal trials and provides that:

'In the determination of his civil rights and obligations or of any criminal charge against him, everyone is entitled to a fair and public hearing within a reasonable time by an independent and impartial tribunal established by law.'

Article 6(2) and (3) provides more specific rights for the defendant in a criminal case.

It is unlikely, according to the jurisprudence of the European Court of Human Rights, that an oral examination undertaken by a court pursuant to section 236, or any other action taken pursuant to the section, would itself attract the application of Article 6. That is because the European Court of Human Rights has drawn a distinction between the adjudication of rights, to which Article 6 applies, and the investigation of facts, to which it does not apply, and an oral examination under section 236 is part of an investigation, rather than an adjudication, as is swearing an affidavit or producing documents in compliance with an order under the section. This distinction is demonstrated by *Fayed* v. *UK*[39] and *Saunders* v. *UK*.[40] Both cases concerned a challenge to the activities of Department of Trade and Industry inspectors who had been appointed under Part XIV of

---

[31] See *Re J.N. Taylor Finance Pty. Ltd.* [1998] BPIR 347.

[32] SI 1986/1925.

[33] See *Hamilton* v. *Naviede; In re Arrows Ltd. (No. 4)* [1995] 2 AC 75, 102–3, *per* Lord Browne-Wilkinson. See also *Soden* v. *Burns* [1996] 3 All ER 967.

[34] See n. 11 above.

[35] *Hamilton* v. *Naviede; In re Arrows Ltd. (No. 4)* [1995] 2 AC 75, 102–3, *per* Lord Browne-Wilkinson.

[36] See *Hamilton* v. *Naviede; In re Arrows Ltd. (No. 4)* [1995] 2 AC 75 and s. 78 of the Police and Criminal Evidence Act 1984. Particular reference was made in the *Arrows* case to *Rank Film Distributors Ltd* v. *Video Information Centre* [1982] AC 380.

[37] See in particular Human Rights Act 1998 ss. 3 and 6.

[38] UKTS 38 (1965); Cmnd. 2643.

[39] Judgment of 21 September 1994, Series A No. 294–B, (1994) 18 EHRR 93.

[40] Judgment of 17 December 1996, App. No. 19187/91, (1996) 23 EHRR 313, [1997] BCC 872.

the Companies Act 1985 to examine the affairs of various companies, and in their reports had made adverse findings against respectively Mr Fayed and Mr Saunders. The activities of the inspectors were held not to fall within the scope of Article 6, being investigations rather than adjudications: although the inspectors' reports were unflattering, to say the least, about Mr Fayed and Mr Saunders, the reports themselves did not determine any legal right or obligation so as to fall within Article 6. Convention Rights become relevant, however, when it is proposed to make use of information obtained under section 236 in criminal or civil proceedings.

In a criminal case, the problem will be that someone other than an office-holder, a prosecutor, wishes to use information obtained by the office-holder under section 236 against the very person who provided the information under compulsion of the section. Such information is admissible as evidence as a matter of English law, though the trial judge would have jurisdiction to exclude it.[41] However, it is now clear from *Saunders* v. *UK*,[42] that Article 6(1) generally prohibits the use in criminal proceedings of evidence which tends to incriminate a person if that evidence was obtained from him under compulsion, or the threat of compulsion—for example, by means of an order under section 236. Consequently, the protection for a defendant inherent in a criminal court's discretion to exclude evidence against him is not by itself sufficient to vindicate the defendant's Convention Rights: such a discretion does not eliminate the possibility that self-incriminating evidence obtained under compulsion, or threat of coercion, will be used in a criminal trial, contrary to Article 6(1).

The other controls evolved by the courts to guard against the oppressive use of section 236 are of little help here. The courts' general unwillingness to grant an office-holder's application under section 236 if he has commenced, or is likely to commence, an action involving the respondent to his application actually provides the respondent with little protection from the risk that self-incriminating evidence will be used against him in criminal proceedings. Litigation by the office-holder involving a particular person who is the subject of an application under section 236, or even the possibility of such litigation, bears no particular relationship to the likelihood or conduct of a prosecution against that person. While any refusal to make an order under section 236 makes it less likely that self-incriminating evidence will be produced in the first place, the courts'

unwillingness to grant an application under the section makes it no less likely that self-incriminating evidence will be generated in those cases where an order is in fact made, nor does it prevent the use of self-incriminating evidence which is obtained under the section. Furthermore, the controls which the courts have imposed over the use of information gathered under section 236 do not ensure the exclusion of self-incriminating evidence given by a person in compliance with an order under section 236: there are may ways in which prosecuting authorities may lawfully come into possession of such evidence, which is clearly admissible in court.[43]

The issues raised by section 236 in the context of a civil trials are another matter.[44] Here, the main problems are, first, that the office-holder himself may wish to procure information by means of section 236 for use in litigation by him and, secondly, that the office-holder may seek to use information already obtained by him under the section in litigation to which he is party. The liquidator may also wish to release information to someone else involved in litigation who would find the information useful for the purposes of his action.

Article 6(1), which refers to the right to a 'fair hearing' in very open-ended language, has been interpreted as the basis of various specific rights in the context of a civil trial. Most importantly for present purposes, the right to a fair hearing requires compliance with the principle of 'equality of arms':[45] 'as regards litigation involving opposing private interests,[46] 'equality of arms' implies that each party must be afforded a reasonable opportunity to present his case—including his evidence—under conditions which do not place him at a substantial disadvantage *vis-à-vis* his opponent'.[47]

While the European Court of Human Rights has also held that Article 6(1) does not require national courts to follow any particular rules of evidence, whether in a civil

---

[41] See n. 36 above.

[42] Judgment of 17 December 1996, App. No. 19187/91, (1996) 23 EHRR 313, [1997] BCC 872. See also *Funke* v. *France*, Judgment of 25 February 1993, Series A No. 256–A, (1994) 16 EHRR 297.

[43] *Hamilton* v. *Naviede; In re Arrows Ltd. (No. 4)* [1995] 2 AC 75, 102H–103G, *per* Lord Browne-Wilkinson.

[44] The extent to which the privilege against self-incrimination is, or should be, available outside a criminal trial is discussed in Davies, n. 1 above. It is not intended to address the point further in this paper.

[45] *Neumeister* v. *Austria*, Judgment of 27 June 1968, Series A No. 8, (1968)1 EHRR 91; *X* v. *Federal Republic of Germany* 6 YB 520, 574 (1963).

[46] This is how the English courts clearly understand litigation by a liquidator for the benefit of the company and those 'interested' in its assets: see *Cloverbay Ltd.* v. *BCCI* [1991] Ch. 90, 108D, *per* Nourse LJ.

[47] *Dombo Beheer* v. *Netherlands*, Judgment of 27 October 1993, Series A No. 274-A at para. 33, (1993) 18 EHRR 213, 229–30. See also *Feldbrugge* v. *Netherlands*, Judgment of 29 May 1986, Series A No. 99 at para. 44, (1986) 8 EHRR 425, 436–7; and *Van de Hurk* v. *Netherlands*, Judgment of 19 April 1994, Series A No. 288, (1994) 18 EHRR 481.

or a criminal trial,[48] the question whether information obtained under section 236 can be used in civil litigation is more than just a question of the admissibility of such information as evidence: it could constitute a matter of substantive unfairness, in breach of Article 6(1), if its use would place one litigant at an unfair advantage *vis-à-vis* another. The liquidator, or other office-holder, has a means of access to information, section 236, which is not available to litigants generally; consequently use of information obtained under the section could put the person using it at an unfair advantage in a civil action, and therefore infringe the principle of 'equality of arms'. Indeed, the English courts themselves appear to take this view, for they often speak of, or allude to, the oppression inherent in placing a liquidator or other office-holder at an unfair advantage in civil litigation through the use of section 236.[49] Such advantage could take the form of allowing the liquidator in effect to take pre-trial depositions, contrary to current English practice in civil litigation; to have earlier discovery of documents than is allowed under the Civil Procedure Rules,[50] and, indeed, to obtain documents which would not be available under those rules.

So the ability of one party in a civil action to use information obtained by means of section 236 might well be characterised as unfair for the purposes of Article 6, because it infringes the principle of 'equality of arms'. If it is, then the courts will have to ensure that such unfairness does not occur once the 1998 Act comes fully into force and obliges them to uphold Convention Rights in general, and rights under Article 6 in particular. It is questionable whether the means they have developed so far to control the potentially oppressive effects of section 236 will be sufficient for the task. Three main forms of control have been identified: first, the courts' unwillingness to order an examination under section 236 when litigation involving the office-holder concerned is pending, or imminently anticipated, and the examination could give the office-holder an advantage in that litigation; secondly, the courts' choice of what sort of order to make under the section, and thirdly, the ability of courts and tribunals to regulate the use of information obtained by means of the section.

The courts' disinclination to make an order under section 236 which might give an office-holder some

advantage in anticipated or pending litigation does reduce the likelihood that another party to the litigation will have his right to a fair trial infringed: the courts' disinclination makes it so much less likely that section 236 will create 'inequality of arms' between parties to the litigation, in breach of Article 6(1). Indeed, the courts' desire to maintain a 'level playing field' in litigation forms the justification for their current approach to section 236 in the context of a pending or anticipated action.[51] However, it is quite possible that information might be obtained by a liquidator in an oral examination undertaken before any litigation was on foot. Use of such information in any subsequent action might breach the principle of 'equality of arms'. So the courts' unwillingness, once litigation is anticipated, to make an order under section 236 which could give the office-holder an unfair advantage in the litigation may indeed help to ensure that trials are fair, within the meaning of Article 6; but it provides no guarantee of such fairness.

The type of order made under section 236 would appear to provide little protection for the Convention Rights of a person against whom proceedings may be brought by a liquidator, or other office-holder, who has taken advantage of the section. The means by which information is obtained (oral examination, the swearing of an affidavit or the production of documents) bears no necessary connection to the nature of the information provided, nor the use to which it can be put. So, for example, a liquidator could obtain an unfair advantage in civil litigation by means of an order under section 236 that a defendant, intended defendant or witness should swear an affidavit which, in effect, amounted to a pre-trial deposition not otherwise obtainable. And again, by use of section 236, a liquidator could obtain discovery of documents from his opponents earlier and more widely than is allowed under the Civil Procedure Rules.[52] This too might be stigmatised as an unfair advantage for the liquidator in the litigation, a breach of the principle of 'equality of arms'.

The ability of a civil court to regulate the use of information obtained by means of section 236 could provide strong protection for the Convention Rights of someone who had been subjected to an order under section 236. However it has not done so to date. First, relevant information obtained by means of section 236 is *prima facie* admissible as evidence in a civil case,[53]

---

[48] It is for each state to lay down its own rules of evidence: *Schenk v. Switzerland*, Judgment of 12 July 1988, Series A No. 140 at para. 46, (1991) 13 EHRR 242, 265–6. This approach by the Court is hardly surprising given the very different legal systems of the states which are party to the Convention.

[49] See e.g. *Re J.N. Taylor Finance Pty. Ltd.* [1998] BPIR 347, 369G–370B, *per* Evans-Lombe J. See also the cases cited at n. 22 above.

[50] See now Part 31 of the Civil Procedure Rules.

[51] See n. 22 above and the text thereto.

[52] In *Cloverbay Ltd.* v. *BCCI* [1991] Ch. 90, 103C, Browne-Wilkinson V-C adverted to the possibility of a liquidator obtaining early discovery and inspection of documents by use of s. 236, but he did not mention the possibility that a liquidator might be able to obtain more documents by use of the section than under the relevant rules of court for discovery and inspection.

[53] See n. 11 above.

but it was hitherto thought that evidence could not simply be excluded in civil proceedings because of the manner in which it was obtained.[54] Secondly, while the defendant in an action can object to the claimant using information against him which he provided under compulsion of section 236,[55] and while someone wishing to use information gathered under section 236 may need to obtain leave of the court in order to inspect documents created pursuant to the section,[56] this does not constitute anything like full control over all the material which might be obtained or generated pursuant to section 236. Indeed, the Companies Court will very likely allow an office-holder to use any information he obtained by means of section 236 in a subsequent civil action brought by him.[57] Finally, as has been noted, there is a duty of confidentiality attaching to information obtained by means of section 236, but the duty does not prevent an office holder from using such information in the performance of his tasks.[58] Consequently, this duty of confidentiality is of relatively little use as a protection for a litigant's rights under Article 6.

V RESPONSES TO THE HUMAN RIGHTS ACT 1998

It is clear that Article 6, and the 1998 Act, will require that information obtained under section 236 should not be used to incriminate the person from whom it was obtained. Once the 1998 Act comes fully into force, admission of such self-incriminating evidence cannot remain a matter of discretion for the court before which a criminal trial is taking place: that court will simply have to exclude self-incriminating evidence obtained under compulsion, unless the defendant himself introduces the evidence, or the charge against the defendant concerns his failure or refusal to answer questions he is

obliged to answer, or his failure to answer them truthfully and as fully as required by law.[59]

Furthermore, section 3 of the 1998 Act, which will require courts to interpret and give effect to legislation (such as section 236) in a manner compatible with Convention Rights, may be construed as allowing, or indeed obliging, a court to control the use of information gathered pursuant its order under section 236, and in particular to direct that self-incriminating information should not be used against the person who provided it.[60] Though the court making an order under section 236 might well be less well informed than a subsequent trial court about the use to which information obtained under the section might be put, it could give the subject of its order the security of knowing that any information he gives in compliance with the order will not be used in breach of his Convention Rights.

In the context of civil litigation the 1998 Act may well have other consequences for the exercise of the courts' discretion under section 236, and for the use of information obtained by means of the section. Currently, control of section 236 is largely directed to ensuring that the section is not used to give a litigant, just because he is an office-holder, special advantages in ordinary civil litigation.[61] This is a specific application in English law of the principle of 'equality of arms', premised on the view that the office-holder is an ordinary litigant, on a par with his opponent.[62] Nevertheless, when the 1998 Act comes fully into force, the courts may have to place firmer controls than they do at present on the use of information obtained by means of section 236, to ensure that 'equality of arms' in civil litigation is maintained: current control of the section might be insufficient to protect litigants' Convention Rights, for the reasons set

[54] It was thought that a civil court hearing an action had no general discretion to exclude relevant evidence: see *Phipson on Evidence* (Sweet & Maxwell, London, 14th edn., 1990) §§28-29-28-23; *Cross and Tapper on Evidence* (Butterworths, London, 8th edn., 1994) 215–8, and *Keane on Evidence* (Butterworths, London, 4th edn., 1996) 40–1. It is now clear that rule 32.1 of the Civil Procedures Rules confers such jurisdiction, which can be used to exclude evidence whose prejudicial effect outweighs its probative value: *Grobbelaar* v. *Sun Newspapers Ltd.* (Court of Appeal, *The Times*, 12th August 1999).

[56] Insolvency Rules 1986 (SI 1986/1925) rule 9.5. As indicated in the text to n. 36 above, the discretion to grant leave under rule 9.5 should not be exercised to deny access to information obtained under s. 236 which is required for the purposes of a *criminal* trial: *Hamilton* v. *Naviede; In re Arrows Ltd. (No. 4)* [1995] 2 AC 75, 105C–107F, *per* Lord Browne-Wilkinson.

[57] *Re Esal (Commodities) Ltd. (No. 2)* [1990] BCC 708, 723H, *per* Millett J.

[58] See the text to nn. 33–35 above.

[59] In February 1998, as a direct result of *Saunders* v. *UK*, Judgment of 17 December 1996, App. No. 19187/91, (1996) 23 EHRR 313, [1997] BCC 872, the Attorney General issued guidelines to prosecutors, indicating that they should not use self-incriminating evidence obtained under compulsory processes such as Part XIV of the Companies Act 1985, unless the defendant himself introduces the evidence, or else the charge against the defendant relates to his failure to supply information required of him by law. Interestingly, the guidance did not mention s. 236, probably because information obtained under that section is most commonly obtained and used by an office-holder as a private individual, not by the state, or by someone acting on its behalf or at its behest. However, the exceptions to the prohibition on the use of self-incriminating evidence appear to be equally applicable to evidence obtained under s. 236.

[60] See Sealy & Milman, *Annotated Guide to the Insolvency Legislation* (5th edn., London: CCH 1998), 274, suggesting that *Hamilton* v. *Naviede; In re Arrows Ltd (No. 4)* [1995] 2 AC 75 may have to be reconsidered in so far as it holds that a court making an order under s. 236 should not impose restrictions on the use in a criminal trial of information gathered pursuant to its order.

[61] See n. 22 above and the text thereto.

[62] See e.g. *Cloverbay Ltd.* v. *BCCI* [1991] Ch. 90, 108E, *per* Nourse LJ.

out in Part IV above. It is, however, difficult to predict what form such controls might take.

Once again, it is quite possible that section 3 of the 1998 Act, by requiring a court to interpret and give effect to section 236 in a manner compatible with Convention Rights, will allow or oblige the court making an order under section 236 to control the use of information gathered pursuant its order.[63] Equally, when a court has to consider exercising its discretion under rule 9.5 of the Insolvency Rules 1986 to allow access to information obtained by means of section 236, section 3 of the 1998 Act arguably obliges the court to ensure that an applicant for access cannot use such information to gain an advantage in civil litigation which would infringe a defendant's Convention Rights. Finally, section 6 of the 1998 Act, which prohibits a court from acting in a fashion inconsistent with any Convention Right, may be taken to oblige a civil court to use its discretion under rule 32.1 of the Civil Procedure Rules to exclude any evidence obtained under section 236,[64] if its use would give the office holder an unfair advantage, in breach of his opponent's rights to equality of arms under Article 6.

It is hard to anticipate any wider effects of such increased control over the use of information obtained under section 236. Increased control might encourage wider use of section 236, because the courts would feel that such control provided adequate protection against abuse of the section, obviating the need to refuse a section 236 application when litigation by the applicant is pending or contemplated. However, increased awareness of the need to safeguard Convention Rights may simply encourage the courts to impose new controls on the use of information obtained by means of section 236, while leaving existing controls on the section unaltered. In either case, the 1998 Act may well make section 236 less useful to liquidators and other office-holders, who often wish to use the section precisely with a view to civil litigation. Just how much less useful section 236 might become would depend on the strictness of the courts' practice in excluding evidence which resulted from an order under section 236, and which might produce an 'inequality of arms' in the action before it—that is, whether the court would exclude only information directly obtained by an office-holder under the section, or whether it would also exclude evidence derived from the information obtained under the section.[65]

Yet any reconsideration of section 236 in the light of the 1998 Act does not necessarily compel these conclusions. The use by a liquidator, or other office-holder, of information obtained by compulsion under section 236

can only infringe a principle of 'equality of arms' in litigation if it is assumed that the office-holder and his opponent start off as equals, and that the use of section 236 can therefore give the office-holder an unfair advantage. In reality, this assumption very rarely holds good. As noted earlier, the office-holder normally takes up his office ignorant of the affairs of the company.[66] In litigation on behalf of the company, he is usually at a distinct disadvantage, for the company has often 'lost its memory'. There are many reasons for this. Perhaps proper records were never kept, or were destroyed; maybe those who know the relevant facts, and were the 'mind of the company' at the time they occurred, cannot now be contacted, or are unwilling to give evidence, possibly because the office-holder is now making a claim against them. The reality is that a liquidator or other office-holder rarely begins or undertakes litigation 'equal in arms' with his opponent. Consequently, it is more realistic to see an office-holder's use of section 236 not as putting him at an unfair advantage over his opponents, but rather as bringing him back to equality with them. If that is the case, then use of information obtained by means of section 236 need not necessarily breach the principle of 'equality of arms', nor need it infringe any Convention Rights, so long as the privilege against self-incrimination is respected. This is not to say that a liquidator or other office-holder should have *carte blanche* to use section 236 as he will: the potential for oppression still remains within the section, and the courts will still have to limit that potential. For example, it would still be necessary to prohibit the disclosure of information by a office-holder unless he is specifically authorised or required to divulge it. Also, it might be appropriate to distinguish between applications made under section 236 by different types of office-holder, so as to allow greater use of the section by a liquidator or an administrator, as opposed to an administrative receiver: a liquidator or an administrator acts for the benefit of a wide class of creditors of a company, whereas an administrative receiver acts principally for the benefit of the debenture holder who appointed him. What such a new approach does, however, is to recognise that an application under section 236 should not necessarily be stigmatised because the applicant office-holder seeks an order which may improve his position in litigation.

It is possible, and highly desirable, that the higher courts will reconsider section 236 in this way. There are indications of dissatisfaction with the current approach to the section in the judgment of Hoffmann J (as he then was) in *Re John T. Rhodes Ltd*,[67] and in the dissenting judgment of McCowan LJ in *Cloverbay Ltd.*

---

[63] See n. 60 above and the text thereto.
[64] See n. 54 above.
[65] Such questions are discussed in Davies, n. 1 above.

[66] Again, see the text to nn. 15 and 16 above.
[67] [1987] BCLC 77.

v. *BCCI*.[68] Both judges seem to favour the sort of approach shown by the Australian courts to the equivalent discretions conferred by Part 5.9 of the Australian Corporations Law. That approach involves open acknowledgement of the fact that the legislature has given liquidators, and other office-holders, statutory means of obtaining information they might not otherwise be able to collect precisely because of the difficulties they face in performing their tasks.[69] Consequently, the timing of an oral examination under Part 5.9 is not so restricted as that of its English equivalent under section 236, and information gained by a liquidator under Part 5.9 can be used by him in litigation, even against the person who provided it.

That is not to say the subject of an order under Part 5.9 has no protection from oppression by the order: far from it. The potentially most oppressive order under Part 5.9, an order for oral examination, is tightly controlled for the protection of the examinee. So, for example, the court ordering the examination has power both statutory (under section 596F of the Corporations Law), and inherent,[70] to give directions about the conduct of the examination. The court conducting the examination will not permit a dress rehearsal of cross-examination in relation to current proceedings,[71] nor will it permit an examination to be conducted for the purpose of destroying the credit of a witness in pending litigation.[72] Legal professional privilege is respected and protected.[73] The examinee has the right under section 597(16) to be represented by Counsel, who may take objections to particular questions, or to the examination itself, if the questions, or the examination as a whole, are oppressive. Under section 597(4), the court,

on the application of either the examinee or the liquidator, may order that the examination be held in private. An examinee is entitled to claim the privilege against self incrimination pursuant to section 597(12A) by prefacing his answers with the word 'privilege'. Section 597(12A) does not entitle the examinee to refuse to answer a question, but it does mean that his answer may not be used in criminal proceedings against him, or in proceedings against him for a penalty. Last in this summary, but not least, the Australian courts, like their English counterparts, have control over what evidence can be used before them, a power which can be used to eliminate the possibility of oppression under Part 5.9 of the Corporations Law.[74]

VI CONCLUSION

The enactment of the Human Rights Act 1998 necessitates a re-examination of section 236 of the Insolvency Act 1986. The use of section 236 in defiance of the privilege against self-incrimination must become a thing of the past. The other effects of the 1998 Act on section 236 are less easy to predict. The principle of 'equality of arms' in litigation, which is part of the right to a fair trial under Article 6 of the European Convention on Human Rights, may mean that further restrictions are placed on use of the information gathered under the section. This may make section 236 far less useful, and could make the important commercial and social tasks of a liquidator, or other office-holder, even more difficult than they are at present. Yet any such undesirable effects on section 236 are not inevitable if the courts recognise that use of section 236 more often than not merely puts an office-holder on a par with those against whom he may take action.

---

[68] [1991] Ch. 90, 108 ff.

[69] See e.g. *Hamilton* v. *Oades* (1989) 166 CLR 486; *Grosvenor Hill (Queensland) Pty. Ltd.* v. *Barber* (1994) 120 ALR 262. See generally *CCH Australian Corporations & Securities Law Reporter* (North Ryde, NSW: CCH, 1990—present) §§ 5.7B.0005–5.7B.0100, and Robson (ed.), *Robson's Annotated Corporations Law* (4th edn., Sydney: 1999) 668–82.

[70] See e.g. *Hong Kong Bank of Australia* v. *Murphy* (1992) 28 NSWLR 512, 523, *per* Gleeson CJ, on the conduct of an oral examination under s. 597 which probed into admissions made in the course of 'without prejudice' negotiations.

[71] *Hong Kong Bank of Australia* v. *Murphy* (1992) 28 NSWLR 512, 518–9, *per* Gleeson CJ.

[72] *Re Hugh J. Roberts Pty. Ltd. (in liq.)* [1970] 2 NSWR 582, 585, *per* Street J.

[73] *Re Compass Airlines Pty. Ltd.* (1992) 10 ACLC 1380.

[74] See e.g., *Hong Kong Bank of Australia* v. *Murphy* (1992) 28 NSWLR 512, 523, *per* Gleeson CJ, on the admissibility of admissions made in the course of "without prejudice" negotiations which came to light in the course of an examination under s. 597 of the Corporations Law. Note also that while Australian civil courts formerly seemed to be like their English counterparts in having no discretion to exclude relevant evidence (see n. 54 above and Byrne and Heydon, *Cross on Evidence* (4th Australian edn., Sydney 1991: §11130), those jurisdictions which have adopted the Uniform Evidence Act (e.g. New South Wales, in 1995) may now possess such a discretion by reason of s. 135 of that Act (see Ligertwood, *Australian Evidence* (3rd edn., 1998), § 2.16).

15

FINANCIAL SERVICES AND THE HUMAN RIGHTS ACT

GEORGE STAPLE QC*

I suspect financial services is one of those areas where, at any rate for a while, the Human Rights Act would have gone largely unremarked, at least until a major case came forward. But it has been given much greater immediacy as a result of the Government's consultation on the new regulatory regime and the publication of a draft Financial Services and Markets Bill.

When we talk of financial services we think principally of the City of London. At the risk of stating the obvious, the City can fairly claim to be one of the world's pre-eminent financial centres. In spite of the decline of sterling as a reserve currency London is a leading centre of global currency and capital markets. There were, at the last count, some 555 foreign banks in London, more than any other city in the world. The Foreign Exchange Market has a daily turnover of $640 billion representing 30 per cent of global business and more than the turnover of the next three largest centres, New York, Tokyo and Singapore put together.

London rivals New York and Tokyo as the leading fund management centre, and more foreign companies are listed on the London Stock Exchange than any other (525 in June 1998). This compares with 454 foreign listings on NASDAQ and 193 on the French *Bourse*, with 220 on the German exchanges.

In 1996 the London Metal Exchange traded 1 billion tonnes of metal valued at $2 trillion, while 60 per cent of Eurobonds are traded in London and 75 per cent of secondary bond trading takes place here.

I could go on, but statistics are boring. It is sufficient to say that the financial services industry in this country is huge. It accounts for a fifth of the UK's gross domestic product. As the Treasury has recently put it in the course of the consultation on the Bill:

* Partner, Clifford Chance, former Director of the Serious Fraud Office.

'Financial markets are central to the efficient allocation of resources within the economy, for maintaining financial stability and for supporting enterprise. If abuse and financial crime become commonplace, then the efficiency and liquidity of those markets will be damaged. People will either choose to do their business on better regulated markets or enter fewer transactions. The result will be an increase in costs for both direct and indirect users of the market and, ultimately, economic under-performance.'

In other words the City needs effective regulation.

HISTORY OF REGULATION IN THE UK

Regulation can come in many different forms. As in the past, it can be a word from the Bank of England privately informing a banker of the limits of prudent commercial conduct. At the other end of the spectrum, it can involve large teams of regulators operating within financial institutions as day by day they go about their business. What may be appropriate for one kind of business in one particular market may not be appropriate for another kind of business in a different market.

Until a decade ago the UK lacked comprehensive regulation of the financial services sector. It relied on a combination of piecemeal statutory intervention and so-called self regulation. It lacked a securities commission, or other similar agency, with overall control of the investment sector.

So the approach to regulation, in so far as there has been an approach at all, has until very recently been based on a relatively small group of bankers and market men in the City knowing how to behave. In so far as they did not behave, the criminal law would take care of them, and they would be prosecuted before the courts.

The Stock Exchange had a set of rules, fairly informally enforced by a disciplinary committee and the commodity traders would enforce the rules of their own markets. As for banks, that was down to the Governor occasionally, and almost imperceptibly, raising an eyebrow. Mergers and acquisitions were policed, as indeed they still are, by the Takeover Panel, a non statutory body staffed mainly by the investment banks sending people on secondment.

It seemed to be enough to keep things in order, and at the same time not to discourage the taking of risk—but only the right amount of risk. Indeed it enabled London to develop very nicely as a financial centre. Occasionally there was a scandal, which the City of London Police, and possibly the Department of Trade, would investigate, and in rare cases charges would be brought under the Prevention of Fraud (Investments) Act. And that was about it.

CHANGE

This lightness of touch was not, however, going to be good enough in the new era of global markets ushered in by the abolition of exchange control in 1979 and Big Bang in the mid 1980's, which essentially meant dual capacity for those licensed to do business on the Stock Exchange and the introduction of outside capital for members. As the Conservative Government brought in its huge programme of privatisation millions of ordinary people were encouraged to invest their savings in the equity markets and make personal provision for their pensions.

A new system of regulation was clearly going to be necessary. And so with the coming into force in 1988 of the Financial Services Act, there began the reform of investor protection in the UK.

But over the last ten years there have been a number of cases where the new system has been perceived to have failed. There have been spectacular collapses like BCCI and Barings and others which, though less traumatic, have nevertheless been very serious.

We may, of course, have done better than we think. One of the problems with deterrence, which is after all a principal purpose of regulation, is that you can never measure it. You cannot measure how much fraud and other mischief has been prevented, or at least sent elsewhere, by the mere existence of a regulatory and prosecuting system, and, indeed most importantly, the culture of compliance that has developed within firms. But it cannot be denied that there have been too many scandals, and, fairly or unfairly, much of the blame has been laid at the doors of the regulators for allowing them to happen.

THE NEW REGIME

So there has been considerable impetus ten years on to look again at the system. Indeed the demand for change has been pretty loud. Much concern has been expressed about the system's self-regulatory nature. The Government has not shrunk from the challenge. It has placed further reform of financial regulation high on its list of priorities. As you know the Government was no more than three weeks in office when the Chancellor announced a total restructuring of the regulatory regime. When complete, it will bring to an end the system of self-regulation which has existed up until now, and replace it with a fully statutory scheme. The new legislation has found a place in this year's Queen's Speech.

The prospect, therefore, is for a Financial Services Authority drawing on the experience of practitioners, but not allowing them to regulate themselves, with four statutory objectives namely:

(a) maintaining confidence in the financial system;
(b) promoting public understanding of the system;
(c) protection of consumers; and
(d) reducing financial crime by regulated persons.

It is hard to quarrel with any of that, and the Financial Services Authority will, we are told, aim to ensure that the costs of regulation are proportionate to its benefits. The new organisation will be able to adopt a risk-based approach to supervision. In other words supervision is likely to be heaviest where risk is greatest. It will look to senior management of regulated firms to be responsible for their financial soundness and proper conduct of their business – an attempt to learn the lessons of Barings and a number of other cases where management systems appear totally to have failed.

There is much work to do, but as a first step the banking supervision functions of the Bank of England have been transferred to the new regulatory body together with all its staff. By the year 2000 almost everything that happens in the City will be within the remit of the new Financial Services Authority. It will bring together no less than nine bodies at present responsible for banking supervision, investment business, insurance companies, building societies and the regulation of Lloyd's. It will have a massive task, for which those regulated, rather than the taxpayer, will be expected to pay.

The FSA's mandate includes both the retail and wholesale sectors. Past experience suggests that more regulation is needed in the retail sector. Whereas increased oversight is not wanted on the wholesale side, where players are judged better able to make their own risk assessment.

One reason why the UK's old method of product by product regulation has proved increasingly ineffective is the structural change that has taken place in the financial services industry. As the dividing lines between banks, insurance companies and securities firms have become blurred and financial conglomerates have begun to engage in multiple activities, regulators in segregated organisations have found that focussing on products yielded only an incomplete picture of what was going on.

Because firms allocate capital and calculate risk on a group wide basis, it makes sense to redesign the regulatory system by shifting the emphasis from product based supervision towards a group based approach.

The focus it seems will be on a firm's approach to risk, and on the quality of senior management, rather than on junior managers responsible for individual products. So in future, senior management will no longer be able to plead ignorance of their subordinates' misdemeanours and escape censure, as has so often happened in the past.

But it has to be recognised that the success of the new Financial Services Authority will ultimately be judged, not so much on its record of keeping City firms day by day on the straight and narrow, but rather, when disaster strikes and investors lose money, on whether the FSA's enforcement and disciplinary process is seen to be effective. That will in turn depend upon the system's integrity, and whether it meets the rigorous test of justice and fairness set by the new legal framework in which it must operate, underpinned by the incorporation of the European Convention on Human Rights as part of English law.

THE NEW DISCIPLINARY APPROACH

The end of self regulation means that regulators can no longer rely on the club ethos and expect participants to take their medicine without protest, for the good of the club. Those who are the subject of enforcement proceedings by the regulator are increasingly likely to ask whether they have been treated fairly and in accordance with their human rights. Both the manner in which the FSA sets up its enforcement procedures, and the way in which the tribunal, to which its decisions, when contested, will be referred, performs will need to have regard to this.

FSA'S POWERS AS REGULATOR

For the last five months the Treasury has been consulting on the form of the proposed legislation to set up the new authority. We have had before us the draft Financial Services and Markets Bill, a formidable measure by any standard, containing some 233 clauses and 10 schedules. We have been able to see the shape of things to come.

The authority will be responsible for authorisation, without which it will be a crime to carry on any regulated activity in virtually the entire financial services industry. It will also have a rule making, advisory and policy making function. The proposed legislation will give the FSA an extremely wide range of powers to investigate, discipline, fine, intervene in the business of, sue and prosecute regulated firms.

In its role as investigator the FSA will be able to

1. compel answers from witnesses on oath,
2. compel authorised persons to hand over information and documents,
3. hire a competent person to conduct an investigation,
4. enter premises of an authorised firm *without* a warrant,
5. investigate individuals suspected of not being fit and proper or in breach of the FSA's principles of conduct,
6. enter domestic premises with a warrant,
7. compel delivery of other documents held by third parties, and
8. compel lawyers to divulge the names and addresses of their clients.

This is a formidable armoury, not, I think, available to any UK regulator under the current system. Unusually the individuals who will exercise these powers will not be Crown servants or police officers. They will be employees of the FSA, which is a private company limited by guarantee. The functions of the FSA will be given to it directly by statute. The FSA will, however, be accountable to Treasury ministers and through them to Parliament. Members of the FSA board will be appointed by, and may be removed by, the Treasury. The FSA will, therefore, be a public authority subject to judicial review.

It will be able to take disciplinary action against firms and their employees, and will itself have the power to fine, publish a statement of misconduct and to order restitution or disgorgement of profits.

There will be a 'civil' fines regime to punish those guilty of market abuse, and the authority will have wide powers of intervention in businesses to control their activities and their assets. It will also be able to seek injunctions in the civil courts restraining contravention of the new legislation or dealing with assets.

Finally the authority will have powers to prosecute for misleading statements (i.e. offences similar to those under Section 47 of the present Financial Services Act) and also for money laundering and insider dealing.

From that brief statement of the powers of the new authority, it will be very obvious that with a staff of some 2000 and a yearly spend of over £150 million, it will be an immensely powerful regulator. It behoves us all clearly to understand the nature of the animal that is about to be given legal life.

I do not personally need convincing that for effective regulation in a complex area strong powers are needed, and I am sure the intention is that they will be used with the utmost care and discretion, or, as the FSA has put it in relation to the proposed compulsory investigation powers, 'in a manner that is proportionate to the concern that has given rise to the investigation or enquiry and fair to those whose conduct is the subject of enquiries and those required to provide assistance in those enquiries'. However regulators are no more immune to human failing than anyone else, and, if they are to have these powers, basic safeguards are needed against the possibility of abuse.

The Government is rightly proceeding with caution. The announcement that the new legislation will be scrutinised by a joint committee of both Houses before it begins its parliamentary progress is evidence of this. It is important because considerable anxiety has been expressed about whether the safeguards to be built into the proposed regime are, in fact, adequate, and whether they will pay proper regard to ordinary principles of natural justice and, in particular, to the provisions of the European Convention on Human Rights.

THE DRAFT BILL

Much of the comment on the draft Bill has centred on the process by which the FSA will reach its enforcement decisions. There is also concern about the vagueness of the definition of the market abuse offences.

There is a wide feeling that, if the integrity and effectiveness of City regulation is to be maintained, it is critical that basic principles of fairness are not sacrificed in the cause of administrative efficiency.

The disciplinary and enforcement process, as presently drafted, gives those accused of wrongdoing few protections, until after the authority has decided to censure or fine them. Although the Act will put in place an independent tribunal administered within the court system to which appeals from FSA decisions can be taken, as the Financial Times recently put it, 'legal protection should begin much further upstream'.

THE PROCESS

As presently drafted the Bill provides that, having conducted an investigation, the FSA may issue a notice warning of disciplinary or enforcement action. The notice will describe the proposed fine or statement for publication. Reasons must be given, but evidence on which the decision is based need not be set out.

The alleged offender will have 28 days to make representations. And within a reasonable time after that, the FSA has to decide what to do. If it decides to impose penalties, it has to issue what is called a decision notice setting out,

1 The date on which the decision takes effect
2. The reasons for the decision
3. Notification of the right of appeal to the Tribunal

It had appeared that, in contrast to the present regime operated by the self regulating organisations (SROs) under the 1986 Financial Services Act, the FSA would not only investigate, but *itself* decide whether an offence had occurred. At present such decisions are taken by independent tribunals run by the SROs. There is, nothing as yet in the draft Bill to provide for anything similar under the new regime. Nor is there anything to say whether disciplinary action can be settled or compromised.

If the FSA decides to impose a penalty, it will be able to publish whatever information it thinks appropriate about the proceedings. If dissatisfied with the FSA's decision, it is for the firm or the individual concerned to take the initiative and mount an appeal to the independent appeal tribunal to be known as The Financial Services and Markets Tribunal.

The existence of this appeal procedure is probably sufficient to ensure that the new regime complies with Article 6 of the European Convention on Human Rights. Article 6 entitles everyone 'to a fair and public hearing within a reasonable time by an independent and impartial tribunal established by law'. However much of the concern that has been expressed has been about the lack of fairness inherent in the process within the FSA itself, before the appeal stage is reached. The FSA was apparently not only to be the investigator, with the massive powers to which I have referred, but also prosecutor and judge. And finally at the end of the process it would pocket the fine!

That this had, at least, the perception of unfairness, or as the cases on bias put it 'the lack of a clear eye', seems now to have been acknowledged by the Authority, and indeed the Treasury. The FSA has just published a statement entitled 'Enforcing the New Regime', and just before Christmas the Chief Secretary to the Treasury announced measures to ensure that enforcement procedures of the new regulator are fair and transparent and that it will not act as judge and jury in its own cause.

THE FSA'S ENFORCEMENT COMMITTEE

In addition to the protections provided by the appeal tribunal, the FSA has recognised that it must put in place its own arrangements and procedures to ensure that those subject to administrative enforcement action are able effectively to exercise their right to make representations before a decision is taken.

The FSA has announced that an Enforcement Committee, a sort of court of first instance, will be established to decide whether disciplinary sanctions, restitution orders or civil fines should be imposed. The FSA board will appoint a full time chairman of the Enforcement Committee, who is likely to be an experienced lawyer. The committee will be drawn from a panel of practitioners and public interest representatives. If the case is substantially contested there will be the opportunity to make representations, and to see the factual evidence on which the FSA relies. With leave it will be possible to have an oral hearing. By this means the FSA intends that the judicial function of deciding on breaches and penalties will be separated from its prosecution function. Such a committee would have some of the features of the tribunals currently provided by the self regulating organisations under the existing legislation.

We must now await the Bill itself, but the Chief Secretary has said, in an apparent reference to the functions of the Enforcement Committee, that it will contain a statutory duty on the part of the Financial Services Authority to establish and publish procedures and a duty to act in accordance with those procedures. The Bill will also contain an express right to see the evidence on which a case rests and there will be a duty on the FSA to disclose such evidence. Further, the FSA will be prevented from publishing any details of enforcement action until the appeal process has been completed. He added that there will no longer be any power to make rules to decide what evidence should be inadmissible before the appeal tribunal.

All this is very welcome news, and gives much greater confidence in the fairness of the regime that is being set up. It would be good to see the independence of the Enforcement Committee enshrined in the Bill, but it must now be said that the Government and the FSA have demonstrated their intention to ensure a disciplinary process that provides consistent, fair and transparent results in which the industry and the public can have confidence.

ECHR CONCERNS

However in spite of this very considerable progress, there remain two other areas where human rights issues are of concern. They are whether the disciplinary framework and the civil fines regime is indeed 'civil' or whether they are 'criminal', and the vagueness of the definition of the market abuse offences.

The disciplinary offences are found in a number of different parts of the draft Bill. They apply to 'approved persons' employed in regulated activities, and to 'authorised persons', who will usually be firms. An 'approved person' is guilty of misconduct if he fails to comply with a statement of principle (Clause 48), or by being concerned in a firm's breach of a statutory requirement (Clauses 50 to 54). They are punished by fines or public censure.

An 'authorised person' may also be fined or censured (Clauses 135 and 136) if the Authority considers he has been in breach of a statutory requirement under the Act. Separately the Bill confers powers on the FSA to impose 'civil fines', where a person has engaged, or has induced another person to engage, in 'market abuse' (Clauses 56 to 58).

THE MARKET ABUSE OFFENCES - 'CIVIL' OR 'CRIMINAL'?

What constitutes 'market abuse' is found in general terms in the statutory precepts which are to be supplemented by a code (Clauses 56 and 57). The fine may be unlimited and recoverable as a civil debt (Clause 62).

Broadly the draft code, so far published, identifies two types of activities which constitute market abuse (a) market manipulation, which would include artificial transactions, price manipulation and disseminating misleading information and (b) misuse of privileged information. These offences are not classified as criminal, indeed they are specifically labelled as 'civil'. But under the Strasbourg jurisprudence whether the conduct is 'civil' or 'criminal' for the purpose of the Convention will depend on objective tests. What any particular conduct is labelled is only a starting point. (*Engel* v. *Netherlands* (1976) 1 EHRR 647, series A No 22). In order to decide whether the far more stringent protections available in criminal proceedings under Article 6 should apply, the courts will also look at (a) the nature of the offences and (b) the severity of the penalties to which those charged with them are exposed.

There is little doubt that the penalties of censure and fine are intended to have a deterrent and punitive purpose, and 'civil fines' for market abuse can apply to anyone breaking the rules, not just those authorised and approved and within the regulatory regime. The market abuse offences of information misuse and market manipulation are civil equivalents of the existing criminal offences of insider trading under the Criminal Justice Act 1993 and market manipulation under section 47 of the Financial Services Act 1986. It would be surprising if the courts were to classify the proposed market abuse offences differently for Convention purposes.

As to the severity of the penalties, the fines which may be levied are unlimited, although they will be proportionate to the gravity of the offence. The level of fines under the existing system has already reached £2 million mark (Morgan Grenfell re European Unit Trusts).

DISQUALIFICATION

There is, however, some authority from Strasbourg to suggest that certain offences under the disciplinary framework, as opposed to the market abuse offences, could be considered civil rather than criminal, for instance conduct which currently results in a 'disqualification direction' under Section 59 of the Financial Services Act 1986. In other words where someone has shown himself not to be 'fit and proper', it is possible that, applying the objective tests to which I have referred, it may not be regarded as criminal conduct for the purpose of the Convention.

In a number of cases concerned with regulatory proceedings, which related only to those engaged in a particular market or profession, it has been held that the proceedings are not criminal. In *APB* v. *IMRO* (Application 30552/96, 15 January 1998) the proceedings involved an intervention order and the fitness and properness of a member. In *X* v. *United Kingdom* (Application 28530/95, 18 January 1998) which related to the Secretary of State's objection to an applicant's appointment as the chief executive of an insurance company on the ground that he was not fit and proper was assumed to be civil in nature. In *Wickramsinghe* v. *United Kingdom* (Application 31503/98, 8 December 1997)the GMC and Privy Council's decisions as to the applicant's fitness to practice medicine were held not to be criminal for the purposes of the Convention.

These cases all involved regulatory proceedings where it could be said that the orders were more for the protection of the public than punitive. But disqualification can also be a severe penalty, a substantial element of which is purely punitative. It goes directly to a person's livelihood, reputation and property. Deterrence is also a principal purpose.

THE CONVENTION SAFEGUARDS

So it does seem pretty clear that, with the possible

exception of disqualification cases, the disciplinary framework and market abuse provisions of the draft legislation will be regarded as criminal in nature. As a result the Convention will confer a number of important protections on people facing disciplinary or market abuse proceedings.

1. Most significantly, the right to the presumption of innocence means that evidence obtained by use of the FSA's compulsory powers against a defendant would not be admissible as part of the case against him. This would be in line with the decision in *Saunders* v. *United Kingdom* (1996) 23 EHRR 313, where the admission in evidence at the applicants' trial of transcripts of evidence of interviews with DTI Inspectors was held to violate Article 6(1), because at the time of the interrogation he was under a duty to answer the questions - a duty which was enforceable by criminal proceedings for contempt.

2. The right would again be infringed if the internal tribunal or the appeal tribunal were to adopt a standard of proof on the balance of probabilities (the civil standard) rather than the criminal standard of beyond a reasonable doubt.

3. The right to equality of arms would require that people without adequate means should be provided with financial help, at least in complex cases, to enable them to secure representation before the tribunals.

VAGUENESS OF THE OFFENCES

The second remaining area of concern relates to the actual definition of 'market abuse' for the purpose of the so called civil fines regime. The key element of the definition in Clause 56 of the draft Bill is that the behaviour in question 'is likely to damage the confidence of informed participants that the market is true and fair'.

It is, of course, a well established principle of law that an offence must be clearly defined, so that an individual can foresee the legal consequences of his actions. The particular form of culpability required for the commission of an offence must be reasonably foreseeable, and must not be altered retrospectively.

It is, strongly arguable that the very general terms of Clause 56 offend against Article 7 of the Convention, which is designed to ensure that offences are clearly defined. Because the provisions are so general, it will be impossible to tell whether particular conduct falls within the offences. Although the draft code under Clause 17 of the Bill is much more specific than Clause 56, it does not have the force of law. It merely provides evidential weight of the breach.

Lord Lester and Javan Herberg's joint opinion on the

draft Bill for a number of City institutions (reproduced in the Appendix) expresses the view that it would be a breach of Article 7 for a person to be convicted of a market abuse offence where his conduct was not prohibited by the Code – let alone where the conduct was actually permitted by the Code.

They have suggested that the point could be met by amending Clause 56 so that, whilst evidence of a breach of the Code would continue to be evidence to support an allegation of market abuse, evidence that the behaviour in question did not fall within the Code would be a defence to a market abuse charge.

CONCLUSION

These are important issues. It is very much in the interests of the Government, consumers and the financial services industry itself that the new legislation is seen to work, and to work fairly. If at the first challenge, it is found wanting in this respect by the Courts, the new regime's credibility will be severely damaged. It is vital that the Government gets it right. They were wise to consult. There has been a huge response, and it appears that changes will now be made to accommodate many of the concerns that have been expressed. No doubt that process will continue when the Bill comes under the scrutiny of the joint parliamentary committee. Above all a balance must be struck whereby effective and efficient regulation is established, ensuring fairness to those charged with offences and at the same time avoiding the delay, complexity and increased costs, which have so bedevilled the criminal and civil justice systems when dealing with financial matters.

POSTSCRIPT

Following these remarks, which were made on 9 January 1999 a joint committee of the House of Lords and the House of Commons was appointed to consider the draft Financial Services & Markets Bill. The joint committee delivered two reports dated respectively 27 April 1999 and 27 May 1999.[1] HM Treasury responded on 17 June 1999 and the Financial Services & Markets Bill was introduced in the House of Commons on the same day. The Government has sought to respond to some of the criticisms contained in the reports of the joint committee and some improvements to the Bill have been made.

The major objection to the draft Bill was that the proposed market abuse regime created offences which were "criminal" within the meaning of the European Convention on Human Rights, but failed to provide the additional safeguards required by Article 6 of the Convention. The arguments are set out in full in the joint Opinions of Lord Lester of Herne Hill QC, Javan Herberg and Monica Carrs-Frisk, which form annexes C and D to the first report of the joint committee and which are reproduced below. The Government has partially recognised this concern by giving some further protection to defendants to market abuse proceedings.

In Clause 144 of the Bill, it is now provided that a statement made by a person in compliance with a requirement imposed by an investigator is generally admissible in any proceedings. But it may not be adduced against that person, or questions relating to it asked, by the prosecution in criminal proceedings, other than for charges in relation to the provision of false information, or by the Financial Services Authority in proceedings before the tribunal to determine whether a penalty for market abuse should be imposed. It may, however, be adduced, or a question relating to it may be asked, by the person himself, or by those acting on his behalf. It can be used by the prosecution or the FSA in cases against another person, or in cases against that person where the charge relates to the provision of false information.

Furthermore, it is now proposed that financial support should be provided to defend market abuse proceedings in appropriate cases, and the Government intends to restrict the scope of the market abuse regime to market participants.

Similar human rights concerns were raised in relation to the FSA's enforcement and disciplinary powers. The Government has not accepted these concerns.[2]

In relation to the decision-making process within the FSA, Clause 340 of the Bill provides that the procedure must be designed to secure among other things that the decision which gives rise to the obligation to give a warning notice or decision notice is taken by a person not directly involved in establishing the evidence on which that decision is based.

The FSA must rebate fine income to the regulatory community and it cannot include its costs in any fine.

The power to enter premises without a warrant has been removed, and by Clause 146 a warrant will now be required for entry to any premises. A Justice of the Peace, or Sheriff in Scotland, before issuing the warrant

---

[1] HL Paper 50–1 HC Paper 328–1, 1998–99 (First Report), and HL Paper 66 HC Paper 465, 1998–99 (Second Report).

[2] HL Paper 66 HC Paper 465, 1998–99 Evidence p. 3 paras 10 and 11.

must be satisfied that there are reasonable grounds for believing that one of three sets of conditions is satisfied namely:

(i)   a request for information has not been wholly complied with and that the documents or information may be found on the premises concerned; or

(ii) the premises are the business premises of an authorised person or appointed representative, that information or documents on those premises could be required by the Authority or the investigator, but that a request for that information or those documents would not be complied with, or would result in the information or documents being removed, tampered with or destroyed; or

(iii) a serious offence has been, or is in the process of being, committed, and that there is information or there are documents on those premises which are relevant to that offence, which could be required by the Authority or the investigator, but which would not be produced, or which might be removed, tampered with or destroyed.

16

HUMAN RIGHTS AND
MARKET ABUSE

MICHAEL BLAIR QC*

It is not easy to follow a contribution as impressive and compressed as the one we have just heard from Laws LJ,[1] and what follows will inevitably be on a much more restricted and specialist canvas.

I would, however, like to make four points, partly in response to the contribution from George Staple Chapter 15 above, and I will conclude with one personal observation.

ENFORCEMENT OF STANDARDS

I imagine that it will be common ground here today that, if regulation of financial services or of any other central area of the United Kingdom's life is to be put in place, it must be put in place for real. This means that regulation must be enforced, and that enforcement must be fair, effective and accountable. The accountability, in terms of policy, in the area of regulatory enforcement lies to Parliament through ministers, while the accountability, in terms of the quality of casework, rests squarely with the specialist tribunal and the courts.

In the financial services area, the regulators aim to be robust and proactive, but sensible and fair-minded. There is no question of our seeking to indulge in any excess, or undue enthusiasm. If we wish to gain and retain the respect of the community, we have to be able to behave sensibly and maturely.

NARROWING OF DIFFERENCES

Over the last six months or so there has, in the market abuse area, and, indeed, in relation to financial regula-

* General Counsel, Financial Services Authority.
[1] See Overview, 11 above.

tory enforcement more generally, been a debate about methods and arrangements. Initially, the difference between some commentators and what the Government and the Financial Services Authority was proposing was relatively deep. But the consensus is now much closer than it was before.

It is important not to overstate the problem. Ministers mean to live within the confines of the Human Rights Act 1998, and the European Convention itself. Furthermore, with the coming into force of section 19 of the Act of 1998, Ministers will have to express a public opinion that the Bill is in conformity with the Convention requirements at the outset of the parliamentary proceedings, probably later this spring. There is, however, still some difference between some of the commentators and ourselves on the actual meaning of the Convention requirements themselves. This centres on two particular areas:

(a) Is the market abuse proposal criminal in nature? and
(b) Is it clear enough?

As to the first of these, it seems important to look at the issue in its context. The subject matter concerns the need for high quality market facilities in the UK investment markets, ensuring that they are clear of abuse, well informed and efficient in operation. Most, if not all, of those that will be subject to the new requirements will be practitioners working in those markets. For them, therefore, the issues look somewhat like those that apply to the learned professions, such as the Bar or solicitors or accountants. Equivalent arrangements for securing high standards of conduct to mutual benefit exist in those areas, and are normally characterised as civil. It is, therefore, not hard to conclude that, for the regulated community at least, the proposals can be characterised as civil, or, if there is any lingering doubt, could be refashioned so that such a characterisation can properly be made. In his contribution to this conference, for instance, George Staple has concluded that 'fit and proper' requirements across the whole breadth of the regulated community (which could be as many as 30,000 firms) can properly be characterised as civil in nature. And I respectfully agree with that assessment.

There are, I agree, some remaining issues about the inclusion within the proposed regime of 'outsiders', that is, typically, the end users, or unregulated customers. The question here may depend in part on whether it is proper to characterise these persons, albeit not market practitioners themselves, as inside the market mechanism in the sense that they may be dependent on mutual, synallagmatic obligations to behave honourably and sensibly.

The second question is whether the proposed legislation is clear enough not to fall foul of the Convention obligations about ascertainability of requirements imposed on the individual.

There is of course a need to ensure that the high level requirements, currently in clause 56 of the draft Financial Services and Markets Bill, fit together with the code which the Financial Services Authority would publish under clause 57 'for the purpose of helping to determine whether or not behaviour amounts to market abuse'. As the market abuse proposals developed in 1996–7, the draft code was published before the Bill itself was drafted, and the conceptual framework for each of them does not yet fully dovetail with the other. Once that has been done, however, it should be possible to conclude that the eventual section, supported with the explanatory and more detailed code, gives sufficient certainty for these important and sensitive markets. I hope, however, that we will all resist the temptation, as English lawyers, to look at the material in the traditional style frequently accorded to English criminal statutes. Other jurisdictions, including that of Scotland, seem to be more comfortable with higher level principles, even in the criminal context, than the English and United States lawyers traditionally are. The *Handyside* case maybe instructive here.

OPTICAL DIFFERENCE

My third point relates to a difference of approach that I have detected in this conference and beforehand. Most commentators on the market abuse proposals seem to regard the subject as a *bilateral* topic, that is a form of arm-wrestling between the regulator and the person under investigation or discipline. This approach is reinforced in the context of the Human Rights Convention, which is often seen as focussing on the

relationship between the individual and the state. In the regulatory community, however, we tend to see this subject as a *trilateral* one, with the third limb being the victims of the antisocial conduct concerned.

The police have this optical problem as well, since they are often seen by their critics as the forces of the state massed against the individuals, whereas, in their own approach, they are keeping the peace as between malefactors and the public at large. In our case, the trilateral nature of our job is more emphatic than that of the police, since we have powers to require redress, repair of injury, and rectification. In addition, we operate a compensation scheme which provides for financial recompense if a firm with liabilities is unable to pay: and we 'tax' the remainder of the industry in order to deliver that redress.

I suppose that both these approaches are, in a sense, valid, but, in saying that, I do hope that those who see the issue as bilateral are equally willing to accept that the trilateral construction has validity as well. There are, for instance, outstanding legal issues, deriving from the European Convention on Human Rights, in the Ombudsman area: and, indeed, I spent a good deal of last week dealing with the human rights of a number of locals on the LIFFE exchange whose capital had been damaged by a most imprudent gamble by a 'rogue trader', resulting in the paying away not only of his assets but of other clients whose assets were in the same pool as his.

INTERNATIONAL NATURE OF THE PROTECTIONS

My last point touches on some of the issues of construction that will confront our courts when the new legislation is commenced. As this conference has shown, we need, or some of us need, to relearn a lesson that we learned in 1971–4, when the United Kingdom joined the European Communities. Once the Human Rights Act is in force, this is not only domestic law in the United Kingdom, but European law operating in the context not simply of one legal system but of a large and expanding number. So the amount of clarity required is on a European scale. And not every element of English criminal procedure is protected, but only those that are embedded in the broad and high level language of the Convention itself. The English tradition of detailed criminal formulation is not a guaranteed Convention right, and, indeed, it is foreseeable that the need for legal certainty in convention terms may on occasion create issues about a very detailed and convoluted approach. If the law is not comprehensible even to skilled lawyers, how can the man in the street be expected to know about it? A good example here is the standard of proof: it is largely an Anglo-Saxon concept, and, in so far as there is a difference between George Staple QC and Buxton LJ on the question whether it is protected by the convention, I tend to side with the Lord Justice.[2]

PERSONAL REFLECTION

Finally, a personal remark. My legal career began in or about 1965, when I was, I believe, the first United Kingdom Stagiaire in the European Commission of Human Rights in Strasbourg. This was before the United Kingdom accorded the right of individual petition, so we were dealing with German, Norwegian and Danish cases among others. We were working in wooden shanties thrown up to house the initial staff required to establish the Council of Europe.

And it rather looks as though my legal career will come to its end on retirement at about the time when the legislation on human rights in the United Kingdom finally comes into effect.

---

[2] See Ch 6 above.

APPENDIX

COUNSELS' OPINIONS ON THE IMPACT OF THE ECHR ON THE DRAFT FINANCIAL AND MARKETS BILL

The two Joint Opinions of Lord Lester of Herne Hill QC and Javan Herberg, and Lord Lester of Herne Hill QC and Monica Carrs-Frisk are reproduced here by kind permission of the British Bankers Association, the International Swaps and Derivatives Association, the Institutional Fund Managers Association, Clifford Chance, Freshfields and Linklaters & Paines.

(1) IN THE MATTER OF THE DRAFT FINANCIAL SERVICES AND MARKETS BILL

JOINT OPINION

1. We are asked to advise whether the proposed disciplinary framework contained in the draft Financial Services and Markets Bill ("the Bill") is likely to infringe any of the Articles of the European Convention on Human Rights (and in particular, Article 6) in the form in which the Convention will be incorporated into United Kingdom law under the Human Rights Act 1998. We base our advice upon the draft Bill as published in July 1998, and upon the draft Guidances and Codes published under the Bill.

2. In our view, for the reasons set out below:

(a) Even before the incorporation of the Convention by the Human Rights Act, Convention rights will be relevant in construing the Bill, in that the courts will have regard to the Convention and to Convention law in interpreting ambiguous provisions, or in themselves exercising discretionary powers.

(b) Once the Human Rights Act comes into force, the courts will have to construe the Bill so as to be compatible with Convention rights if at all possible, even if this involves a strained rather than a natural interpretation of its provisions. Furthermore, in our view, the FSA, as a public administrative body, will in principle be liable in damages if it acts in breach of a Convention right, notwithstanding the statutory immunity from damages claims (except in cases of bad faith) conferred by paragraph 17 of Schedule 1 of the Bill.

(c) Turning to the disciplinary provisions of the Bill,

Article 6 of the Convention provides far more stringent protections if those provisions are considered to be "criminal offences" for the purpose of the Article. In our view, it is strongly arguable that all of the disciplinary offences, and in particular the Market Abuse offences, are indeed "criminal" in that sense. This is because the nature of the offences, and the nature and severity of the penalties to which the person concerned is exposed, are such that, having regard to the Convention case law, it is unlikely that the courts will accept that the characterisation in the Bill of the offences as "civil" is determinative of their true nature. Accordingly, the safeguards for the determination of criminal charges are likely to apply to disciplinary proceedings under the Bill.

(d) Applying the protections conferred by Article 6 to the disciplinary provisions of the Bill:

    (i) the right to an independent and impartial court, and the right to a fair trial, is satisfied by the right of appeal to the Tribunal, but only to the extent that (a) the appeal is (as it appears to be), *de novo*, full, and with the burden of proof remaining on the FSA; and (b) the individual or commercial entity affected is not prejudiced by the" first instance" determination against him or it by the FSA;

    (ii) the principle of equality of arms and the right to legal assistance under Article 6(3)(c) may require, in complex cases, that an individual without means is provided with financial assistance to secure representation before the Tribunal;

    (iii) the presumption of innocence may be infringed if the standard of proof before the Tribunal is interpreted to be proof on the balance of probabilities (as the FSA appear to contemplate, at least in relation to Market Abuse offences), rather than proof to a criminal standard or to a "high" civil standard;

(iv) the presumption of innocence and the privilege against self-incrimination will be violated in breach of Article 6 if, as is presently proposed, information obtained by the FSA by compulsion is admitted in evidence in proceedings before the Tribunal relating to disciplinary or market abuse offences;

(v) the Market Abuse offences as defined in the Bill are framed at such a high level of generality that they do not satisfy Article 7(1) of the Convention, which requires, in accordance with the principle of legal certainty, that an offence must be clearly defined in law so that a person may foresee the legal consequences of his or its own actions. This violation is not wholly cured by the more detailed Code to be issued under the Bill, because it is currently proposed that the Code will have no more the evidential effect, so that conduct not prohibited by the Code might still be found to be in breach of the statutory offence;

(vi) once the United Kingdom has ratified Article 4 of Protocol No. 7 of the Convention, as the Government proposes to do in the near future, the Bill will be in violation of that Article to the extent that it allows "dual prosecution" of a person for breach of the criminal law (for insider dealing or breach of s. 47 of the FSA 1986) and for breach of the Market Abuse rules.

The Structure and Proposed Disciplinary Framework of the Bill

3. We will not set out in any detail the proposed structure of financial regulation contained in the Bill, nor the proposed disciplinary framework (within which we include the market abuse provisions of Part VI of the Bill), which is summarised in our Instructions. In essence, the Government proposes to replace the existing system of financial regulation with a single regulator called the Financial Services Authority ("FSA"). Although a private company limited by guarantee and funded by a levy on those it regulates, the FSA will be a public authority exercising statutory and delegated powers and subject to to judicial review. The FSA will have disciplinary powers over authorised entities and approved persons (who, typically, will be employees or officers of authorised entities), as well as, in some instances, any person committing certain prescribed offences. The proposed disciplinary offences with which we are

here concerned will all be created by the Bill at a fairly high level of generality, and will be supplemented by Codes and Guidance made under the legislation.

4. The disciplinary framework under consideration is contained in a number of different parts of the Bill.

a) Part V of the Bill ("Employment in regulated activities") contains, at clauses 50–54, disciplinary powers in respect of approved persons. An approved person who, as it appears to the FSA, is guilty of a failure to comply with a Statement of Principle under Clause 48 or is knowingly concerned in a contravention by a connected authorised person of a statutory requirement may be disciplined by the imposition of a "fine" (clause 50(3)(a) or public censure (clause 50(3)(b). Clause 52(4) provides for the recovery by the FSA of the amount of the unpaid fine as a civil debt due to it.

b) Part XII of the Bill ("Disciplinary measures") creates (at clauses 135–141) a similar disciplinary framework in respect of authorised persons. Where the FSA considers that an authorised person has contravened a requirement of or under the Bill, it may impose a "financial penalty" (clause 136) or a public censure (clause 135). The financial penalty is again recoverable by the FSA as a civil debt (clause 139(4)).

c) Quite separately, Part VI of the Bill confers powers upon the FSA to impose what are described as "civil fines" for "Market Abuse". By virtue of Clause 58, if the FSA is satisfied that a person has engaged, or has induced another person to engage, in Market Abuse (as defined in general terms in clause 56 ("the Statutory Precepts") and to be supplemented by a Code published under clause 57), it may impose upon that person a fine of such amount as it considers appropriate. Clause 62(4) again provides for recovery of an unpaid fine by the FSA as a civil debt.

We are not asked to advise upon those provisions of the Bill dealing with fitness and propriety, and the withdrawal of authorisation or approved status.

The Impact of the Human Rights Act 1998

5. It is important to summarise the relevance of Convention rights both now and after the coming into force of the Human Rights Act 1998. Once that measure is in force, the courts will have much more power and responsibility for tackling the range of problems raised by our Instructions, to the extent that those problems have not been adequately

addressed by Government and Parliament in shaping the Bill.

6. The Convention is not yet part of English law. However, this does not mean that Convention rights are at present irrelevant when construing statutes or declaring the common law. When interpreting legislation that has an impact upon the rights guaranteed by the Convention, the courts apply a presumption that, in the absence of clear words, Parliament does not intend to exercise its legislative powers in breach of the Convention. Accordingly, the courts have regard to the Convention and its case law when interpreting ambiguous legislation: *R. v. Secretary for the Home Department, ex parte Brind* [1991] 1 AC 696 (HL). They also have regard to the Convention law when the common law is uncertain or incomplete: *Derbyshire County Council v. Times Newspapers Ltd* [1992] AC 534 (HL). Where the courts themselves exercise discretionary powers (for example, when granting injunctive relief or exercising appellate functions in relation to excessive awards of damages for libel), they seek to ensure that those powers are exercised in accordance with the Convention: see e.g., *Attorney-General v. Guardian Newspapers Ltd (No. 2)* [1990] AC 109 (HL); *Rantzen v. Mirror Newspapers (1986) Ltd* [1994] QB 670 (CA). What the courts cannot do at present is to require the FSA (as distinct, for example, from the Appeal Tribunal in exercising its *judicial* powers) to exercise its *administrative* powers in accordance with Convention rights: *ex parte Brind*, above. However, in the absence of a statutory or executive indication to the contrary, the courts will treat ratification of the Convention as giving rise to a legitimate expectation that the decision-maker will act in conformity with Convention rights at least when exercising prerogative powers: *R. v. Secretary of State for the Home Department, ex parte Ahmed and Patel*, judgment of the Court of Appeal of 30 July 1998, as yet unreported, per Lord Woolf MR.

7. We should add that, quite apart from the Convention, it is well established under general principles of English public law that, to ensure fairness, the courts will imply words into a statute where the words are ambiguous or incomplete: see e.g., *Wiseman v. Borneman* [1971] AC 297 (HL). It is a principle of legal policy that the law should be just. When construing the Bill, the courts will therefore presume that Parliament intended to observe this principle, and therefore strive to avoid a construction that leads to injustice: see e.g., Bennion *Statutory Interpretation* (3rd ed., 1997) pp.

614–16. Where necessary the courts will have regard to Article 6 of the Convention and its case law for this purpose: see *Raymond v. Honey* [1983] 1 AC 1 (HL) and its progeny.

8. However, when the Human Rights Bill is enacted and brought into force, the courts will have to go much further. Where possible they will have to construe legislation so as to be compatible with Convention rights, for example, by reading into the Act sufficient procedural safeguards to comply with Article 6. This may involve a strained rather than a literal or natural construction of the statutory language. The courts will not be empowered to strike down or set aside primary legislation which cannot be construed compatibly with Convention rights. However, it is the Government's repeatedly declared intention that the courts should strive where possible to avoid having to declare a statutory provision to be incompatible with Convention rights. It is to be expected that the courts will devise new principles of interpretation to make statutes compatible with the Convention. They are unlikely to adopt the doctrine of implied repeal in respect of primary legislation enacted after the coming into force of the Human Rights Act, but will probably require nothing less than an express intention to repeal or amend a provision of that Act or a Convention right.

9. Another important consequence of the Human Rights Act will be that it will make it unlawful for a public authority, such as the FSA or the Appeal Tribunal, to act in a way which is incompatible with a Convention right. Every public power (for example, of the FSA or the Appeal Tribunal) that interferes with Convention rights (such as the right to a good reputation, or to property, or to personal privacy, or to a fair hearing by an independent court or tribunal) will have to be invoked only where necessary and applied in accordance with the principles of proportionality and legal certainty.

10. In the case of an administrative body, such as the FSA, if it acts in breach of a Convention right, it will in principle be liable in damages under the Human Rights Act where an award of damages is necessary to afford just satisfaction to the victim of the breach. However, paragraph 17(1) of Schedule 1 to the Bill provides that neither the FSA nor any person acting on its behalf shall be "liable in damages for anything done or omitted in the discharge, or purported discharge, of the [FSA's] functions." Paragraph 17(3) disapplies paragraph 17(1) if "the act or omission is shown to have been in bad faith".

11. The effect of this provision, which is effectively the equivalent of the existing section 187 of the FSA 1986, is somewhat obscure. We doubt whether it would be construed by the courts as immunising the FSA against a claim brought under the Human Rights Act for breach by the FSA of a Convention right, since this would prevent victims of such breaches from enjoying effective domestic remedies for such breaches and effective access to justice: cf., the European Court's judgment of 10 July 1998 in *Tinnelly and McElduff* v. *United Kingdom*. We consider it to be more likely that the courts will treat the immunity conferred by paragraph 17(1) of Schedule 1 as confined to liability for anything done or omitted to be done under the Bill read in isolation from the Human Rights Act. However, we suggest that this is a matter which needs to be clarified with the Government.

12. The Human Rights Bill is likely to receive the Royal Assent by the end of 1998, but it is unlikely to be brought fully into force until the year 2000. During the hiatus, the courts will be unable to give direct effect to Convention rights.

13. Although the Human Rights Act will empower and require the courts where possible to make the Bill compatible with Convention rights, and to provide effective remedies where, for example, the FSA discharges its functions in a manner which breaches Convention rights, it is the responsibility of Government and Parliament to enact the Bill in a form that does not authorise or require breaches of Convention rights. We therefore hope that the Government will be persuaded by the process of consultation on the Bill to modify its terms so as to minimise the risks of breaches of Convention rights. It is plainly in the public interest for the executive and legislative branches of government to do their best to create a user-friendly statutory scheme that reduces the need for legal proceedings under the Human Rights Act.

Article 6 of the Convention and its relevance

14. Article 6 of the Convention provides as follows:
"(1) In the determination of his civil rights or obligations or of any criminal charge against him, everyone is entitled to a fair and public hearing within a reasonable time by an independent and impartial tribunal established by law . . .
(2) Everyone charged with an offence shall be presumed innocent until proved guilty according to law.
(3) Everyone charged with a criminal offence has the following minimum rights:
(a) to be informed promptly . . . and in detail of the nature and cause of the accusation against him;
(b) to have adequate time and facilities for the preparation of his defence;
(c) to defend himself in person or through the legal assistance of his own choosing or, if he has not sufficient means to pay for legal assistance, to be given it free when the interests of justice so require;
(d) to examine or have examined witnesses against him and to obtain the attendance and examination of witnesses on his behalf on the same conditions as witnesses against him . . .".

15. There are thus special procedural safeguards for proceedings involving the determination of criminal charges, in Article 6(2) and (3), notably as regards the presumption of innocence, including protection against self-incrimination. That is why it is important to know whether the disciplinary proceedings under the Bill are to be regarded as criminal or civil in nature for the purposes of Article 6. However, even if the proceedings are to be regarded as civil rather than criminal, we emphasise that the requirements of Article 6(1) apply for example, as regards a fair hearing by an independent and impartial tribunal, and the principle of equality of arms.

16. The procedural rights protected by Article 6, like other Convention rights, apply equally where a commercial entity is the "victim" of the conduct complained of, as where an individual is involved; see e.g. *Air Canada* v. *United Kingdom* (1995) 20 EHRR 150 (complaint of breach of (inter alia) Article 6(1) by company). Thus our analysis applies whether disciplinary proceedings are brought against an individual (whether as an approved person or otherwise) or against a legal person such as an authorised entity.

17. We agree with our Instructing Solicitors that, in spite of the statutory description of the fines as "civil", it is strongly arguable that, for the purposes of the procedural guarantees contained in Article 6 of the European Convention on Human Rights, they are to be treated as criminal in nature. The case law of the European Court of Human Rights in this area is complex and sometimes inconsistent and unclear. We shall endeavour to summarise the relevant principles thus far developed by the Court for the purpose of deciding whether there is a "criminal charge" in terms of Article 6. However, we should observe that, although our courts will have to have regard to the case law of the European Commission and Court of Human Rights, they will not be bound

by the Strasbourg decisions. These are likely to be cases where the European Commission or Court has allowed the public authorities of the Contracting States a wide margin of appreciation or discretion, and where our courts will feel able to adopt a more robust interpretation of Convention rights, as domestic rather than international courts. This is especially the case where traditional common law concepts of due process, natural justice and fairness are woven together with Article 6 of the Convention in cases where a person's livelihood, reputation, or property is at stake.

Ascertaining whether there is a "criminal offence" within the meaning of Article 6 of the Convention

18. In general, the European Court of Human Rights has repeatedly emphasised that a restrictive interpretation of Article 6 of the Convention would frustrate the aim and purpose of that provision, bearing in mind the prominent place which the right to a fair trial holds in a democratic society: see e.g., paragraph 30 of the Court's judgment of 26th October 1984 in *De Cubber* v. *Belgium*, Series A no. 86, (1985) 7 EHRR 236.

19. The concept of "charge" in Article 6 consists of "the official notification given to an individual by the competent authority of an allegation that he has committed a criminal offence": *Deweer* v. *Belgium*, Series A no. 35, (1980) 2 EHRR 439; *Eckle* v. *Germany*, Series A no. 51, (1982) 5 EHRR 1. However, the existence of a criminal charge is not always dependent on there being an official act. It may in some instances take the form of other measures which carry the implication of such an allegation and which substantially affect the situation of the suspect: *Foti* v. *Italy*, Series A no. 56, 5 EHRR 313, judgment of 10th December 1982; *Brozicek* v. *Italy*, Series A no. 167, 12 EHRR 371.

20. To determine whether an offence qualifies as "criminal", as distinct from disciplinary or administrative, for the purposes of the safeguards contained in Article 6 of the Convention, a realistic and substantive approach is required. The *first* matter to be ascertained is whether or not the text defining the offence belongs, in the domestic legal system, to the criminal law; *secondly*, the nature of the offence, and *thirdly*, the nature and degree of severity of the penalty that the person concerned risked incurring must be examined, having regard to the object and purpose of Article 6, to the ordinary meaning of the terms of that Article, and to the laws of the Contracting States: paragraph 32 of the judgment of the European Court of Human Rights of 24th

September 1997 in *Garyfallou AFBE* v. *Greece, Reports* 1997–V; affirmed in paragraph 56 of the European Court's judgment of 2nd September 1998, in *Lauko* v. *Slovakia* (as yet unreported).

21. In answering the question whether the classification under domestic law belongs to criminal law or to disciplinary or administrative law, the descriptions given by the relevant domestic law have only a relative value: paragraph 52 of the European Court's judgment of 21st February 1984, in *Özturk* v. *Germany*, Series A no. 73. If the applicable domestic law classifies the offence as criminal, this will be decisive. But, because of the dangers of evasion of the guarantees of Article 6, where the domestic law classifies the proceedings as "civil" or "disciplinary", the domestic classification is no more than a starting point: paragraph 82 of the Court's judgment of 8th June 1976 in *Engel* v. *Netherlands* (1976) 1 EHRR 647, Series A no. 22. The assessment must therefore be made on the basis of objective principles. That is why the Court has developed the second and third criteria. For example in *Campbell and Fell* v. *United Kingdom*, Series A no. 80, (1985) 7 EHRR 165, the fact that the prison offences with which the applicants were charged belonged to disciplinary law and were not a "criminal cause or matter" under domestic law was not decisive.

22. For Article 6 to apply it suffices that the offence in question is "criminal" in nature in terms of the Convention, or that it has made the person concerned liable to a sanction which, in its nature and degree of severity belongs in general to the "criminal" sphere: paragraph 55 of the Court's judgment of 25th August 1987, in *Lutz* v. *Germany*, Series A no. 123, (1988) 10 EHRR 182. The second and third criteria are alternative and not cumulative criteria: paragraph 57 of the European Court's judgment in *Lauko*, above. However, a cumulative approach may be adopted where the separate analysis of each of the three criteria does not make it possible to reach a clear conclusion as to the existence of a "criminal charge": *Lauko*, above, citing paragraph 33 of the *Garyfallou AEBE* judgment; and paragraph 47 of the Court's judgment of 24th February 1994 in *Bendenoun* v. *France*, Series A no. 284, (1994) 18 EHRR 54 (where proceedings for tax evasion leading to large financial penalties were held to be criminal proceedings for the purpose of Article 6, even though they were described as "tax penalties" rather than "criminal penalties", and the surcharges were imposed by the Revenue under the supervision of

the administrative courts and not by a criminal court, and they were calculated in direct proportion to the tax originally evaded, and they were not an alternative to a custodial penalty).

23. Under the second criterion, it is necessary first to consider whether the norm in question is addressed exclusively to a specific group in one or more specific capacities or whether it is of a generally binding character. A provision of disciplinary law, for example, may be addressed only to those who belong to the disciplinary system (such as members of the armed forces, or members of a profession (see e.g. *Wickramsinghe* v. *United Kingdom* (Appln 31503/96, admissibility decision). However, even where this is the case, the disciplinary offence may still be criminal in nature for the purposes of Article 6: see e.g., *Campbell and Fell* above. The case law on whether or not a norm is a generally binding character is somewhat uncertain: see e.g., the Court's judgment of 23rd March in *Ravnsbörg* v. *Sweden*, Series A 283–B, paragraphs 31–33.

24. In a number of recent admissibility decisions, the Commission has held or assumed that regulatory proceedings which relate only to those engaged in the particular market or profession are civil for the purposes of Article 6(1): see *APB* v. *IMRO* (Appln 30552/96, 15 January 1998) (IMRO proceedings relating to intervention order an fitness and properness of member were assumed to be civil in nature); *X* v. *United Kingdom* (Appln 28530/95, 18 January 1998) (regulatory proceedings relating to the Secretary of State's objection to the Applicant's appointment as Chief Executive of an insurance company on the basis that the Applicant was not fit and proper as required by Insurance Companies Act 1982 assumed to be civil); *Wickramsinghe* v. *United Kingdom* (Appln 31503/96, 8 December 1997) (GMC and Privy Council's decision as to the Applicant's fitness to practice medicine was expressly held not to be a criminal matter but civil for the purposes of Article 6). However, in each case it is clear that the Commission's view turned not on the fact that the norm was not of general application to the public at large, but rather on the fact that the power at issue was open to exercise not for punitive reasons but for protection of the public, by the exclusion of an unfit person from the industry or profession, whether temporarily or permanently.

25. If the norm is sufficiently general, it then becomes relevant to ascertain the purpose of the penalty. Where a fine has a deterrent and punitive purpose,

this is sufficient to show that the offence is criminal in nature in terms of Article 6 of the Convention: *Lauko*, above. The fact that the commission of the offence is not punishable by imprisonment and does not give rise to a criminal record are not decisive of the classification of the offence for the purpose of the applicability of Article 6: *Lauko*, citing paragraph 53 of the *Özturk* judgment. Furthermore, the relative lack of seriousness of the penalty at stake cannot deprive an offence of its inherently criminal character: *Lauko*, citing paragraph 54 of the *Özturk* judgment.

26. In *Lauko*, the applicant was found guilty of what was described under domestic law as a minor offence (namely, without justification accusing a family of causing a nuisance). He was fined and ordered to pay costs. The Constitutional Court dismissed his constitutional complaint that there had been no fair and public hearing in his case and that the administrative authorities dealing with it had not been impartial. The complaint was dismissed on the ground that it involved only a minor offence and therefore not subject to examination by a court. However, the European Court held that, even though the offence was not defined as criminal by domestic law, it was criminal in nature for the purposes of Article 6 because of the general character of the legal rule infringed by the applicant and the punitive purpose of the fine imposed upon him.

27. The third, and in many cases decisive, criterion is that of the nature (as distinct from the purpose) and the severity of the penalty with which the violator of the norm is threatened. Even if the purpose of the sanction does not make the second criterion applicable, because the scope of the violated norm is not of a general character, the nature and severity of the penalty may still make Article 6 applicable: see e.g., the Court's judgment of 27th April 1991 in *Demicoli* v. *Malta*, Series A no. 210, (1992) 14 EHRR 47.

28. Outside the sphere of disciplinary proceedings, where "fiscal penalties" are imposed, if they are of a punitive nature, such as fines and disqualification, they give the proceedings a criminal character for the purposes of Article 6: see e.g., *Lutz* v. *Germany*, Series A no. 123, (1988) 10 EHRR 182 ("regulatory" petty road traffic offences punishable by fines and disqualification from holding a driving licence for a period of one to three months and that had been decriminalised were treated as criminal in nature, because they were deterrent and punitive).

Application of the Convention principles to the "civil fines" under the draft Bill

29. The fact that the Bill describes the fines as "civil" is, for the reasons we have explained above, no more than a starting point in the analysis. In our view, a consideration of each of the second and third criteria referred to above point strongly to the conclusion that at least some if not all of the disciplinary offences under the Bill are criminal in character.

30. Considering first *the nature of the offences*, it is clear that both the civil fines for disciplinary offences and for market abuse are of a generally binding character; indeed they are in this respect markedly different from the disciplinary rulebooks of the SROs, which generally took effect only by virtue of the contractual relationship between the members and the SRO. This is therefore the first clear point of distinction as regards the Commission's admissibility decision in *APB Limited v. IMRO* (above), where express reference was made to the self-regulating nature of IMRO's system of maintaining internal discipline (at p. 13 of the transcript). The disciplinary framework of the Bill is imposed by or under statute, and it is imposed (in the case of Market Abuse offences) upon any person or body contravening their terms, whether authorised or not. In this respect, there is a slightly stronger case for believing that the Market Abuse offences are "criminal" than the more general disciplinary offences upholding the Principles and other standards set out in or under the Bill (Parts V and XII), which only apply to authorised or approved persons.

31. The criminal nature of the offences created by the Bill appears most clearly from the nature of the Market Abuse offences. The "Statutory Precepts" set out in clause 56 of the Bill create "offences" of "information misuse" and "market manipulation". "Information misuse" (Clause 56(1)(b)(i) of the Bill) is, in effect, a civil equivalent of the insider trading regime. The draft Code of Conduct published in June 1998 provides that a person may not deal (etc) where he possess "privileged knowledge" (i.e. information which other market users could not legitimately get, for example because confidential) of "disclosable information" (i.e. information which will at some time be disseminated on the relevant market) which is "relevant information" (i.e. information which a market user would reasonably regard as significant in deciding whether to deal).

32. In our view, it would be very surprising if the Article 6 protections which plainly apply to the criminal offence of insider trading were not to apply to the very similar offence of misuse of privileged information. Indeed, the Bill will for the first time confer upon the FSA the power to prosecute for the existing criminal offences of insider dealing and misleading statements and practices under section 47 of the Financial Services Act 1986, so that the FSA will be in the position of having to chose, when faced with "insider dealing-type" conduct, whether to exercise its criminal powers under the Criminal Justice Act 1993 or whether to exercise its Market Abuse powers (or both). In our view, the courts (including the Appeal Tribunal) are likely to treat both as criminal in nature for Convention purposes.

33. Similar considerations apply to the Market Abuse offence of market manipulation (clauses 56(1)(b)(ii) to (iii)). This offence is further subdivided into "dissemination of misleading information", "artificial transactions" and "price manipulations", at least some of which would fall under section 47 of the Financial Services Act 1986—in respect of which the FSA is also for the first time given a prosecutorial role.

34. It is, in our view, not a sufficient distinction that the existing criminal offences under the CJA 1993 and FSA 1986 are backed by the sanction of imprisonment, whilst the Market Abuse sanctions are purely financial (or denunciatory). As we have already noted, the sanction of imprisonment is clearly not a necessary condition for the offence to be regarded as criminal. Furthermore, it is significant that the purpose for which fines are to be levied under clause 58 of the Bill has been described by the FSA (which under clause 59 of the Bill is obliged to prepare and publish a statement of its policy as to the imposition and amount of fines) in its Consultation Paper No, 10 (Market Abuse, Part 1, June 1998) as including not merely restitution to any identifiable victims, and the disgorgement of any profits made, but also "a fine aimed at deterring [the] misconduct" (para. 6, page 4; see also paras 132–136, p. 31). In our view, a sanction which has as its aim a deterrent effect upon society generally (since Market Abuse offences apply to all; not merely to authorised persons) is a hallmark of a criminal offence.

35. The nature and severity of the penalty (the third criterion referred to above) also points to the criminal nature of the Market Abuse offences. The fines which may be levied are unlimited, except for the need for the FSA to seek to ensure that they are

proportionate to the gravity of the offence. In serious cases, the fines are likely to be very substantial; as our instructing solicitors note, SRO fines have recently increased very substantially, with IMRO fining the Morgan Grenfell companies £2 million (by consent) in connection with the Peter Young Unit Trusts affair, and SFA fining SBC Warburg (as it then was) in the region of £4–500,000 (by consent) in the Regional Electricity derivatives case (which case, incidently, concerned conduct which appears to be a central preoccupation of the "information misuse" provisions of the Bill). There is every likelihood that the FSA will seek to continue, it not to increase, the recent level of fines.

36. It is true that the sanction for non-payment is enforcement as a civil debt rather then committal to prison, but on balance, in our view, the importance of this is outweighed by the other factors, and the courts are likely to decide that these fines have a criminal connotation.

37. The position is less clear-cut in relation to the disciplinary regimes under Parts V and XII of the Bill. Since these regimes will only apply to approved and authorised persons respectively, it might be argued that such offences are closer to a scheme of internal regulation rather than punitive sanction, and thus, by extension from the Commissions's admissibility decision in *APB* v. *IMRO* (above) may be considered as civil in nature. However, in our view the nature of the disciplinary schemes is inconsistent with this analysis. Not only are they imposed by statute, and can lead to unlimited fines or "financial penalties", but it is notable that they operate quite separately from the powers relating to fitness and propriety, under which authorisation or approval can be withdrawn or not granted (the subject matter of *APB* v. *IMRO*). In our view, it is more probable that these powers too will be found to be criminal in nature.

Application of Article 6 safeguards to the Disciplinary Framework

38. It follows that the safeguards, for the trial and determination of criminal charges contained in Article 6 should in our view, apply to the determination of guilt and the imposition of fines under the draft Bill. The main Article 6 safeguards are the right to a fair trial by an independent and impartial court or tribunal, the principle of equality of arms, and the presumption of innocence, including the privilege against self-incrimination. We shall consider each of these concepts and its relevance. In considering the extent to which the Bill's disciplinary framework meets these standards, it is necessary to consider the framework as a whole, including the available rights of appeal: see e.g., *Bryan* v. *United Kingdom*, Series A no. 335–A, (1996) 21 EHRR 342. But where a person faces serious criminal charges, he is entitled to a first instance tribunal which fully meets the requirements of Article 6(1): *Finlay* v. *United Kingdom* (1997) 24 EHRR 221 at paragraph 79.

Right to a Court

39. The FSA as an administrative authority with enforcement powers is not an independent and impartial court or tribunal within the meaning of Article 6, whatever internal procedures are devised to ensure natural justice before it reaches its decisions. Not only does it have conferred upon it the roles of investigator and prosecutor of disciplinary offences, but it will also apparently retain for its own use the proceeds of fines, as well as costs made in its favour. Accordingly, even if the FSA constructs relatively elaborate internal procedures to be followed before it arrives at decisions to impose disciplinary penalties (for example, by affording those affected a full internal hearing), these are not likely to fulfil the requirements of Article 6(1).

40. If, as we consider to be the true position, enforcement proceedings under the Bill are properly to be regarded as involving serious charges to be classified as criminal in nature, then, as we have indicated, the person affected is entitled to a first instance tribunal which fully meets the requirements of Article 6(10: see e.g., *Finlay* v. *United Kingdom* (1997) 24 EHRR 221. In our view, the Bill satisfies this requirement. It provides for a right of "appeal" by way of a *de novo* hearing before the Financial Services and Markets Appeal Tribunal ("the Tribunal"), and thereafter an appeal on point of law to the High Court. The Tribunal will satisfy the Article 6 requirement that it be "independent and impartial"; its members are to be taken from a panel of lawyers and a lay panel selected by the Lord Chancellor. It will form part of the Court service. Since the Tribunal will have the power (and the obligation) to consider appeals from decisions of the FSA *de novo* and on the merits, in practice the Article 6 requirements will be satisfied if the *Tribunal* meets those requirements, irrespective of the procedure adopted internally by the *FSA* (unless the FSA's decision itself causes such prejudice as to preclude a fair trial; see paragraph [46] below).

41. It should be emphasised, however, that the above conclusion rests on the assumption that although the Tribunal is described as an "Appeal Tribunal", in practice it can and will provide a full and unfettered hearing of the case. Limitations upon the Tribunal's ability to do so will automatically risk a violation of Article 6. Thus, we note that clause 68(3)(c) provides that the Tribunal may hear any arguments by the appellant not raised at the time that the FSA made its decision "save in specified circumstances". If circumstances are specified which prevent an appellant from raising arguments which he reasonably did not make to the FSA (because, for example, he was not aware of the case against him, or was not given a full and adequate opportunity to make representations), then we believe that there would be a violation of Article 6 (see similarly, the assumption as to the Tribunal's power to receive fresh evidence at paragraph 54 below).

Equality of Arms

42. The principle of equality of arms applies to civil as well as to criminal proceedings as an essential ingredient in a fair trial: see e.g., *Dombo Beheer* v. *Netherlands* (1993) 18 EHRR 213; and *Ruis-Mateos* v. *Spain* (1993) 16 EHRR 505. The principle requires that everyone who is a party to proceedings must have a reasonable opportunity of presenting his case to the court under conditions which do not place him at a substantial disadvantage vis-à-viz his opponent. There must be a fair balance between the parties: see e.g. *De Haes and Gijsels* v. *Belgium* (1997) 25 EHRR 1.

43. The principle of equality of arms requires that the parties to civil proceedings should be entitles to cross-examine witnesses: see e.g., Application no. 5362/72, *X* v. *Austria* 42 CD 145 (1972) (European Commission of Human Rights). A principle underlying Article 6 as a whole is that judicial proceedings should be adversarial: see e.g., *McMichael* v. *United Kingdom* (1995) 20 EHRR 205; *Mantovanelli* v. *France* (1997) 24 EHRR 370. Furthermore, Article 6(3)(d) expressly confers a right upon a defendant in criminal proceedings to cross-examine adverse witness.

44. It appears likely that the procedures which the Tribunal will adopt will, in general, meet these requirements. One possible area of difficulty, however, concerns the right to legal assistance, which may arise both under the principle of equality of arms (in circumstances in which the FSA will no doubt be represented by lawyers) and independently under Article 6(3)(c), which requires legal assistance to be provided "when the interests of justice so require". Under the existing regime, concerns have recently been expressed about the ability of individuals facing substantial SRO disciplinary proceedings to defend themselves (in circumstances where they may have been dismissed by their employers); for example, in the Barings and Morgan Grenfell cases. There will be situations where the interests of justice may require financial assistance for legal representation and for the retention of expert witness in complex disciplinary cases. In our view, there is a real risk of a breach of Article 6(3)(c) unless provision is made (whether in the Bill or elsewhere) for financial assistance in such cases. Indeed, it is at least arguable that even if the proceedings were merely to be classed as civil in nature, financial assistance might be required under Article 6(1) in a sufficiently serious and complex case; see e.g. *Airey* v. *Ireland* (1979) 2 EHRR 305.

45. We have considered whether the principle of equality of arms (or indeed, any aspect of Article 6) may be infringed by the fact that the Bill confers upon the FSA powers not only to take action for suspected Market Abuse, but also to prosecute for criminal offences (as traditionally understood) such as insider dealing and offences under section 47 of the FSA 1986. As our instructing solicitors point out, there may well be circumstances in which the simultaneous availability of both powers is oppressive to the person under investigation, in that there may be enormous pressure to accept a market abuse fine in circumstances where there remains a risk of prosecution. Indeed, the FSA's Consultation Document on Market Abuse (Consultation Paper No. 10, Pt 1) reveals that although the FSA intends ordinarily to consider first whether to prosecute and only then (para 141, p. 33) whether to exercise market abuse powers, it leaves open the possibility that "evidence may come to light in civil or regulatory proceedings [for market abuse] which require reconsideration of whether criminal prosecution is warranted" (para 143, p. 34).

46. In our view, however, the potential availability of the two sets of powers is unlikely of itself to constitute a breach of Article 6 (save in relation to double jeopardy, as to which see paragraphs 68 and 69 below). Provided that each procedure it itself fair and complies with the principle of equality of arms, there is no authority to suggest that the fact that the person under investigation may be placed in a difficult position itself constitutes a breach of Article 6. We would point out, however, that were the FSA in

practice to act in an oppressive manner, this might well give rise to a *domestic* judicial review challenge for abuse of discretion: if, for example, the FSA either (i) went against its guidance in refusing to consider whether to prosecute (in accordance with the Code for Crown Prosecutors) *before* considering Market Abuse remedies; or (ii) decided to reconsider criminal proceedings in the light of a failure to force an admission or settlement of a Market Abuse charge, where there was no genuinely material new evidence warranting such reconsideration.

47. We have also considered the point raised by our instructing solicitors as to the potentially oppressive effect of the extra-territorial reach of the market abuse provisions. Clause 56(4)(b) has the effect that the market abuse provisions catch conduct which takes place outside the United Kingdom, but which occurs "in relation to" qualifying investments traded on a relevant market in the United Kingdom. Although we agree that the provision is sweepingly drafted, we do not consider that it violates Article 6, or indeed any Convention right. Nothing in the Convention prevents conduct committed abroad with an impact within a contracting state from being made unlawful.

Fair Trial

48. Even where the principle of equality of arms is satisfied, there may still be a breach of the requirements of a fair trial. A good recent example arose in *Niderhost-Huber* v. *Switzerland*, Judgment of 18th February 1987, where the applicant brought civil proceedings against a company from which he had been dismissed as chairman and managing director, seeking arrears of salary and a severance payment. In the course of the Swiss proceedings, the Cantonal Court transmitted the appeal to the Federal Court together with the case file and one page of observations which were not communicated to the applicant. The Court found that, since the observations had not been communicated to either party, no infringement of equality of arms had been established. However, the Court observed that the concept of a fair trial also implies in principle the right of the parties to a trial to have knowledge and comment on the evidence adduced or observations filed (citing, inter alia, the Courts judgment of 20th February 1996 in *Lobo Machado* v. *Portugal* (1996) 23 EHRR 79 for the principle that the requirements derived from the right to adversarial proceedings are the same in both civil and criminal cases). The Court described the right to adversarial proceedings

as a "fundamental principle" and held that the right to a fair trial had been violated even though the observations did not present any fact or argument which, in the opinion of the Swiss courts, had not already appeared in the impugned decision. The Court stated (paragraph 27) that "What is particularly at stake here is litigants' confidence in the workings of justice, which is based on, *inter alia*, the knowledge that they have had the opportunity to express their view on every document in the file."

49. As we understand the position, although there may be no right to disclosure of all information gathered or considered by the FSA in making a disciplinary order, the appellant will have sight of all material which the FSA discloses to the Tribunal. Further, the Tribunal will itself have the power to make disclosure orders against the FSA. This would appear to meet the requirements of Article 6. Although the Appellant may not have an unfettered right to adduce new evidence before the Tribunal (if the Lord Chancellor's rules circumscribe that right by requiring, for example, that the fresh evidence could not reasonably have been produced to the FSA at the earlier stage), we anticipate that the Tribunal's power to allow fresh evidence would nonetheless be sufficient to comply with Article 6; the Tribunal will, in appropriate cases, no doubt allow fresh evidence where it can be shown that the individual could not earlier have anticipated its relevance (because, for example, of limited disclosure by the FSA).

50. More generally, the Appeal Tribunal would not be required by virtue of the requirements of Article 6 to adopt the same evidential standards as would be applied by a domestic criminal court—with regard, for example, to the admissibility of hearsay evidence. The European jurisprudence generally accords states a wide margin of appreciation as to what procedures may be adopted, provided that the presumption of innocence is respected (as to which, see below), and provided that the procedures overall respect the right to a fair trial. We do not consider, on the material before us, that the Tribunal procedures contemplated generally fail that test, save in the specific respects referred to below.

The Presumption of Innocence

51. If the proceedings are criminal in nature, so as to give rise to the presumption of innocence guaranteed by Article 6(2), then the overall burden of establishing guilt must remain with the prosecution: see e.g., *Lingens and Leitgens* v. *Austria* (1981) 4 EHRR 373. Any rule which shifts the burden of

proof in a criminal case, or which applies a presumption operating against the accused, must be confined within reasonable limits: *Salabiaku* v. *France* (1988) 13 EHRR 379. Even if the proceedings are civil in nature, they are, of course, subject to the requirements of fairness and a fair balance between the parties, inherent in Article 6 as a whole.

52. In *Allenet de Ribemont* v. *France* (1955) 20 EHRR 557, the French Minister of the Interior and a number of senior police officers held a press conference shortly after the applicant's arrest in which they named him as one of the instigators of a murder. The European Court of Human Rights held that the presumption of innocence could be violated not only by a judge or a court but also by other public officials. Although Article 6(2) could not prevent the authorities from informing the public about investigations in progress, it required that they did so with all discretion and circumspection necessary if the presumption of innocence was to be respected. The statements at the press conference contained a clear implication that the applicant was guilty and therefore violated Article 6(2).

53. The position under the Bill appears to be as we understand it, that no public censure (or other penalty) imposed by the FSA will be implemented before the hearing of any appeal by the Tribunal (because clause 68(5) provides that a decision appealed against does not have effect until the appeal, and any further appeal to the High Court, has been finally disposed of). We note, as our Instructing Solicitors point out, that clause 211, dealing with Decision Notices, provides that decisions must "specify the date upon which the decision takes affect" (clause 211(1)(b)) and that the FSA may "publish such information about the matter to which a decision notice relates, in such way as it considers appropriate" (clause 211(5)). In our view, those provisions must be taken to be subject to the effective stay on implementation of any decision contained in clause 68. On that basis, it appears that the presumption of innocence will not be infringed by action of the FSA before an appeal is heard.

54. If we were wrong in our interpretation of the above provisions, and it is intended that action may be taken by the FSA before an appeal to the Tribunal is heard and determined, then the position would be very different. In that scenario, a person might, for example, be found guilty of a disciplinary offence by the FSA and effectively punished by publication of a public censure before any appeal to the

Tribunal could be heard. Not only would it then be strongly arguable that the presumption of innocence would be infringed, but more fundamentally the incompatibility of the FSA's internal procedures with Article 6 would come into play: there would have been an effective determination and punishment without recourse to an impartial tribunal. However, as we have explained, we do not consider that this vice is in fact inherent in the statutory scheme.

55. As to the burden and standard of proof before the Tribunal, we note that the FSA's Consultation Paper 10 on Market Abuse suggests (at paragraph 7) that the burden will be on the FSA, but only "on the balance of probabilities". If this is intended to suggest that the standard will effectively be 51 per cent (at least in relation to the Market Abuse offences), rather that the usual civil standard which may be more onerous in serious cases (on the *Hornal* v. *Neuberger* principle: [1957] 1 QB 247 (CA)), then the proposal is likely to infringe the presumption of innocence. The case for an infringement would be reinforced by the argument that there was a breach of Article 14 (non-discrimination) read with Article 6, because of the unjustified distinction between the standard in criminal cases in the strict sense (for example, for insider dealing) and the standard in Market Abuse or other disciplinary cases.

56. It is arguable that the burden of proof ought to be even more stringent than the sliding civil standard; that, assuming that the proceedings are found to be criminal in nature, the criminal standard ought to apply; see, in the domestic context, *Re A Solicitor* [1993] Q.B. 69 (where allegations is disciplinary proceedings are essentially criminal, then the criminal standard applies) and *R* v. *Police Complaints Board ex p. Madden* [1983] 2 All ER 353. However, even in the domestic context, the position is anything but settled; compare *Re A Solicitor* with *R* v. *Hampshire CC ex p. Ellerton* [1985] 1 All ER 599 (fire officers' disciplinary proceedings to be decided on flexible civil standard even where grave allegations of corrupt practice made) and *R* v. *Maidstone Crown Court ex p. Olson* (QBD, Unreported, 18 May 1992) (standard for determining whether taxi driver "fit and proper" is civil, even though the allegation constituted a criminal offence). In the closest existing parallel to the Tribunal, the present Financial Service Tribunal (which hears appeals from certain authorisation and expilsion decisions of the ex-Securities and Investments Board) has adopted a sliding civil test

in its decisions, notwithstanding the serious nature of allegations made; see *In the Matter of Peter James West and Paul Bingham* (published decision of the FST of 18 November 1994).

57. In any event we have some doubts as to whether the application of the sliding civil standard would violate the presumption of innocence within Article 6. In the first place, there is no overriding Convention requirement that where an offence is criminal in nature, proof must be "beyond reasonable doubt". Ans in any event, recent decisions by SRO Tribunals have demonstrated that they are capable of adapting the civil standards, in cases, where very serious allegations are made, so as to be to all intents and purposes indistinguishable from the criminal standard: see e.g. *SFA* v. *Capel Myers* (unpublished decision of the SFA Disciplinary Tribunal, October 1995).

58. The FSA's Consultation Paper 10 on Market Abuse proposes that a breach of the FSA's Code on Market Abuse will itself provide "evidential weight" that the Statutory Precepts have been infringed (at paragraph 5; p. 3). Whether or not this will constitute a partial shifting of burden of proof away from the FSA (and clause 57(6) of the Bill suggests that it will not), we consider that this is not likely to infringe the presumption of innocence, given the Convention case law on the point (see *Salabiaku* v. *France*, above).

Privilege against Self-Incrimination

59. The right to a fair trial in a criminal case includes the right of anyone charged with a criminal offence to remain silent and not to contribute to incriminating herself: *Funke* v. *France* (1993) 16 EHRR 297. In *Murray* v. *United Kingdom* (1996) 22 EHRR 29, the European Courts of Human Rights held that, although not specifically mentioned in Article 6, the right to remain silent under police questioning and the privilege against self-incrimination are generally recognised international standards which lie at the heart of Article 6. In *Saunders* v. *United Kingdom* (1996) 23 EHRR 313, the European Court held that the right not to incriminate oneself cannot be reasonably confined to statements of admission of wrongdoing or to remarks which are directly incriminating. Information obtained under compulsion whcih appears on the face to be of a non-incriminating nature, such as mere information on questions of fact, may later be deployed in criminal proceedings in support of the evidence given by the person during the trial or otherwise undermine his credibility. Therefore, the

right or privilege against self-incrimination protects a person not only from being forced to supply answers of a directly incriminating nature, but also answers which would provide the factual basis from which liability could subsequently be established. Accordingly, the admission in evidence at the applicant's trial of transcripts of evidence of interviews with DTI inspectors violated Article 6(1) since at the time of the interrogation he was under a duty to answer the questions which were enforceable by criminal proceedings for contempt.

60. As our Instructing Solicitors note, the investigatory powers given to the FSA by the Bill include the power to compel attendance of any person to answer questions on oath (clause 99) and to produce documents, or to seize documents without a warrant (clause 101). The use of such material in subsequent disciplinary proceedings (including Market Abuse proceedings) is expressly authorised by the Bill. By virtue of clause 104(4), a statement made by a person in compliance with a requirement imposed under clauses 97 to 99 is admissible in any proceedings. Clause 104(5) creates an exception for evidence in "criminal proceedings", no doubt in an attempt to meet the requirements of Article 6. However, the exception in clause 104(5) is not intended to cover Market Abuse or disciplinary offences.

61. In our view, provided that the criminal provisions of Article 6 are found to be applicable to such offences, the use of such material is a clear contravention of Article 6, in the light of the decisions in *Murray* and *Saunders*. This is an area of the most serious potential mismatch between the statutory scheme and Article 6 of the Convention, and it is essential that the mismatch should be removed in the legislation itself, rather than leaving it to the courts to attempt to imply appropriate Article 6 safeguards into the legislation.

Vagueness

62. Article 7(1) of the Convention, which prohibits the retrospective imposition of criminal offences and penalties, includes the principle that the criminal law must not be extensively construed to the detriment of an accused; an offence must be clearly defined in law so that an individual may foresee the legal consequences of his actions: *Kokkinakis* v. *Greece* A 260-A (1993), 17 EHRR 397 (EctHR para 52). The principle has clear limits; the European Court has permitted (and it is likely that domestic courts will similarly permit) the clarification and development of existing statutory and

common law offences, providing that such development is "reasonably foreseeable" by the accused (for example, the extension of the offence of rape to cover spousal rape: *SW* v. *United Kingdom*, Judgment of 22 November 1995, A-335-B, p. 42; *X and Y* v. *United Kingdom*, Appln 8710/79, D&R 28 (1982), p. 77. Nevertheless, the particular form of culpability required for the commission of the offence must be reasonably foreseeable and must not be altered retrospectively.

63. In our view, it is strongly arguable that the very high level of generality of the Market Abuse offences, as contained in the Statutory Precepts in Clause 56 of the Bill, offend against Article 7(1). Clause 56 purports to cover behaviour described as "market abuse" which takes place "in relation to" qualifying investments traded on a relevant market which satisfy one or more of the conditions laid down in clauses 56(1)(b), and which is "likely to . . . damage the confidence of . . . informed participants that the market, so far as it relates to investments of that kind, is a true and fair market" (see further paragraphs 31 and 33 above). Not only are the offences far less clearly defined than their "criminal" counterparts contained in the Criminal Justice Act and Financial Services Act, but, most strikingly, the FSA's own Consultation Document on the proposed Code on Market Abuse illustrates the range of open questions as to whether particular conduct not only *will be* but *should be* treated as falling within the Market Abuse offences (see, to take one example, the FSA's discussion of the offence of misuse of privileged information, at paragraphs 71 to 125 of Consultation Paper 10). The point is not merely that the Statutory Precepts are capable of more than one interpretation; it is rather that they are framed at such a high level of generality that they leave entirely undetermined whether particular conduct falls within the offence.

64. The Bill, and the FSA, seek to meet the obvious uncertainty created by the Statutory Precepts by means of the Code, to be issued by FSA under Clause 57 of the Bill "for the purpose of helping to determine whether or not behaviour amounts to market abuse". The Draft Code and accompanying consultation document are obviously framed at a much greater level of specificity; although the Code inevitably still leaves considerable grey areas, we accept that were the Code to have the force of law, it is likely that any objection based upon Article 7(1) would fail. However, the Code does *not* have the force of law, or anything like it. Its status, under Clause 57, is merely (by subclause (6)) that it "may

be relied on so far as it tends to establish whether or not . . . behaviour amounts to market abuse". As noted at paragraph 58 above, the Consultation Paper interprets that provision as meaning that the Code will provide "evidential weight" of the infringement of or compliance with the Statutory Precepts.

65. In our view, there is a real risk that the Code will not meet the objections to the uncertainty of the Statutory Precepts. It would, in our view, be a breach of Article 7 for a person to be convicted of a market abuse offence where this conduct did not fall within conduct indicated by the Code to constitute an offence—let alone where the conduct was actually permitted by the Code.

66. In these circumstances, we suggest that the point could be met by amending clause 57(6) so that, whilst evidence of a *breach* of the Code could continue to be evidence to support an allegation of market abuse, evidence that the behaviour in question did not fall within the terms of the Code would be a defence to a market abuse charge.

67. We have also considered whether the charge of vagueness might also apply to the disciplinary offences under Parts V and XII of the Bill. It is right that these offences also incorporate by reference codes or standards drawn up under the Bill (for example, by clause 50(1)(c), a person may be guilty of misconduct by failing to comply with a statement of principle issued under clause 48, or otherwise by knowingly being concerned in a contravention of a requirement imposed "under" the Act). However, unlike the market abuse offences, the standards referred to in Parts V and XII are not merely "evidential"; they constitute the offence. The same charge of imprecision, therefore, does not apply, and we would expect that these parts of the Bill would meet the Article 7 requirement, provided that the statements of principle and other "requirements under the Act" are not themselves hopelessly vague.

Double Jeopardy

68. Article 4 of Protocol No. 7 of the Convention provides that "No one shall be liable to be tried or punished again in criminal proceedings under the jurisdiction of the same State for an offence for which he has already been finally acquitted or convicted in accordance with the law and penal procedure of that State." Provided that our conclusion that the Market Abuse offences are, in substance, criminal in nature is correct, there would appear to be a clear breach of Article 4 of Protocol

7 in permitting dual proceedings to arise.

69. At present, the United Kingdom has not ratified Protocol No. 7 of the Convention, and it therefore offers no protection in respect of alleged violations. However, the Government announced before the recess its intention to ratify Protocol No. 7 in the near future, when Parliament enacts further legislation to bring domestic law into full harmony with Protocol No. 7. When this takes place, it will in our view have the effect of creating a violation of the Convention to the extent that dual proceedings are in fact permitted.

Lord Lester of Herne Hill QC   Javan Herberg

Blackstone Chambers
Blackstone House
Temple
London EC4Y 9BW

27th October 1998

(2) IN THE MATTER OF THE DRAFT FINANCIAL SERVICES AND MARKETS BILL

JOINT NOTE OF ADVICE

1. Further to the joint Opinion with Javan Herberg of 27 October 1998, we are asked to advise on two issues:

   (a) whether the institution of disciplinary proceedings by the Financial Services Authority ("FSA") purely on the basis of a breach of one of its proposed statements of principle could potentially infringe Article 7 of the European Convention on Human Rights ("ECHR");

   (b) whether, in the light of the policy statements in Chapter 5 of the FSA's Consultation Paper 17, the nature of the disciplinary proceedings which the FSA will be empowered to bring under the Financial Services and Markets Bill("the Bill") is criminal or civil.

2. For the reasons given below, we consider that (1) the conviction of a firm of a disciplinary offence purely on the basis of a breach of one of the statements of principle, where the conduct in question does not fall within any detailed rule, evidential provision, code or guidance, would be contrary to Article 7 of the ECHR; and (2) disciplinary proceedings under the Bill would be treated as criminal in substance for the purposes of attracting the procedural safeguards guaranteed by Article 6 of the ECHR.

Article 7 of the ECHR

3. As the earlier joint Opinion advised, Article 7 of the ECHR, which prohibits the retrospective imposition of criminal offences and penalties, includes a requirement in accordance with the principle of legal certainty than an offence must be clearly defined in law, so that an individual may reasonably foresee the consequences of his actions. See *Kokkinakis* v. *Greece* (1993) 17 EHRR 397: an offence is sufficiently clearly defined to satisfy Article 7 where any individual can to a reasonable degree foresee from the wording of the relevant provision and, if need be, with the assistance of the courts' interpretation of it and with the benefit of legal advice, what acts and omissions will make him liable. Respect for the principle of legal certainty requires the act which entails the individual's criminality to be clearly set out in law. The requirement is satisfied where it is possible to determine from the relevant statutory provision what act or omission entails criminal liability. The principle of legal certainty is a general principle of European Community and Convention law, and is in part of the constitutional and legal systems of many common law and civil law countries. We would expect German firms, for example, who have automatic authorisation, to be astonished by the lack of adherence to the principle of legal certainty enshrined in their constitutional and legal system.

4. Insofar as disciplinary offences under the Bill are to be regarded as criminal for the purposes of the ECHR (as to which see below), the definition of those offences must comply with the principle of legal certainty guaranteed by Article 7 of the EHCR. We are asked to advise in relation to the institution by the FSA of disciplinary proceedings for a breach of a statement of principle issued by the FSA. We will assume for these purposes that the disciplinary offences provided for in Parts V and XII of the Bill are criminal rather than civil, with the result that the requirement of certainty in Article 7 of the ECHR applies.

5. Consultation Paper 13, published in September 1998, sets out the FSA's proposed Principles for Business ("the Principles"). (We are instructed that the consultation paper on principles for approved persons has not yet been published.) The Principles are extremely widely and vaguely drawn. For example, Principle 1 provides that "A firm must conduct its business with integrity"[1], and Principle 5 states that "A firm must observe proper standards of market conduct". They are "high-level precepts" and binding "obligations" (paragraph 1 of Consultation Paper 13).

6. It is intended by the FSA that the implications of the

Principles will be elaborated in binding rules, evidential provisions and guidance (see paragraph 9 of Consultation Paper 13). However, it is important to note that the FSA has indicated that there may be instances when disciplinary action will be taken in respect of conduct which is not identified in any such rule, evidential provision or guidance. We have in mind, in particular, the following statements by the FSA:

(a) ". . . the Principles may be relevant in situations for which no rule or guidance yet exists. In such situations firms and supervisors alike need to be prepared to make judgments based on the values embodied in the Principles." (Consultation Paper 13, paragraph 10);

(b) ". . . since the Principles as a general statement of regulatory requirements are designed to be applicable in new or unforeseen situations, and in situations in which there is no need for guidance, the FSA's evidential provisions and guidance should not be viewed as exhausting the implications of the Principles themselves." (Consultation Paper 13, Annex A, paragraph 6);

(c) ". . . disciplinary action for breach of a Principle may often be appropriate where there has been a breach of related detailed Rules, evidential provisions/Codes of Conduct and/or guidance. However, there may also be circumstances in which it will be legitimate for the FSA to take disciplinary action based exclusively on a breach of one or more of the Principles." (Consultation Paper 17, paragraph 94).

7. In our view, the Principles are so widely and vaguely drafted, that the conviction of a person of a disciplinary offence on the basis of an alleged breach of a Principle, where the conduct in question does not fall within a rule, evidential provision or guidance, would amount to a breach of the requirement of legal certainty in Article 7 of the ECHR. We do not consider that the Principle alone will enable the members of a firm to foresee to a reasonable degree what acts and omissions will make it liable (see *Kokkinakis* (above)). We find further support for our view in the recent judgment of Brooke LJ in *Westminster City Council* v. *Blenheim Leisure Limited & Ors* (judgment of the Divisional Court of 12 February 1999; unreported; New Law Online Case 499020801). Brooke LJ observed, in relation to the possibility of conviction of a criminal offence on

the basis of a breach of a Rule operated by Westminster Council that "The Licensee shall maintain good order in the premises" that:

"The Council would do well, in my judgment, to tighten up the language of Rule 9 if it wishes to be able to use it to prohibit activities like these on licensed premises after the Human Rights Act 1998 comes into force. The extension of the very vague concept of the maintenance of good order to the control of the activities of prostitutes may have passed muster in the days when English common law offences did not receive critical scrutiny from national judicial guardians of a rights-based jurisprudence, but those days will soon be over. English judges will then be applying a Human Rights Convention which has the effect of prescribing that a criminal offence must be clearly defined in law. I do not accept Mr Carter-Manning's submission that it is impossible to define the kind of conduct his clients desire to prohibit with greater precision, or that it is satisfactory to leave it to individual magistrates to decide, assisted only by some fairly arcane case-law, whether or not activities of the type of which the Council complains in this case amount to a breach of good order so as to render the licensees liable to criminal penalties."

8. The FSA has stated that it will not invoke the Principles as a basis for disciplinary action in an arbitrary and unpredictable fashion, but that it should be able to take enforcement action where "it is clear that the conduct in question violates the Principles, regardless of whether any detailed Rule, Code or evidential provision has strictly been breached; or the behaviour in question is closely analogous to behaviour which would constitute a breach of a detailed Rule, Code or evidential provision . . ." (paragraph 95 of Consultation Paper 17).

9. These statements by the FSA do not, in our opinion, meet the concern as to legal uncertainty to which we have referred. We consider that it should be possible for the FSA to prescribe with a reasonable degree of certainty the conduct which will amount to a breach of a Principle in the detailed rules, evidential provisions, codes of conduct and guidance that are to be published in relation to the Principles, and that it would not be reasonable to expect a firm to foresee that acts and omissions falling outside such detailed rules, evidential provisions, etc, might render it liable to disciplinary action for breach of a Principle.

Article 6 of the ECHR

10. We are also asked to consider the nature of disciplinary offences under the Bill, in the light of Chapter 5 of Consultation Paper 17. Chapter 5 deals with

---

[1] A breach of Principle 1, which the FSA notes is a "moral concept", is stated by the FSA to be likely to amount to one of the gravest breaches of the Principles (see Consultation Paper 13, paragraph 26).

disciplinary offences other than market abuse (which is dealt with in Chapter 6), and we assume, therefore that Instructing Solicitors are mainly concerned with these offences. We will, however, also briefly revisit the offence of market abuse.

11. So far as concerns the disciplinary offences provided for in Parts V and XII of the Bill (i.e. offences other than market abuse), we have found nothing in Chapter 5 of Consultation Paper 17 (or indeed in the speech by Mr Howard Davies of 3 March 1999) to cause us to differ from the view expressed in the joint Opinion of 27 October 1998, that such offences are likely to be treated as criminal in substance for the purposes of attracting the procedural safeguards of Article 6.

12. It is well-established in the jurisprudence of the European Court of Human Rights that even where the offence is classified as being civil in nature as a matter of domestic law, it may be criminal for the purposes of Article 6 of the ECHR where the nature of the offence (including the purpose of any sanction) *or* the nature and degree of severity of any penalty so indicates (see e.g. *Lauko* v. *Slovakia*; judgment of the European Court of Human Rights of 2 September 1998, as yet unreported).

13. Chapter 5 of Consultation Paper 17 makes it very clear that it is a major purpose of the exercise of the FSA's powers to impose a financial penalty and/or to make a public statement to deter Authorised Firms or Approved Persons from future breaches and to deter others from misconduct (see paragraph 82, as well as paragraphs 104 and 107). Where a penalty has a deterrent and punitive purpose, this is sufficient to show that the offence is criminal in terms of Article 6 (see *Lauko*, above). The statements as to the purposes of disciplinary action contained in Chapter 5 of Consultation Paper 17 lend support, therefore, to the conclusion that disciplinary offences under the Bill are criminal.

14. Mr Howard Davies, in his recent Chancery Bar Association and Combar Spring Lecture (delivered on 3 March 1999) stated that good arguments could be made to the effect that the proposed civil fines regime for market abuse is civil in nature (see page 11 of the written lecture). He referred to the facts that there was no penalty of imprisonment, that the purpose of the fining power was primarily to protect and compensate organised investment markets, that the market abuse regime (although it would apply beyond the authorised community) would be linked in its scope to those persons who chose to take advantage of the facilities of organised investment

markets, and that the criminal courts would not be involved. Mr Davies fairly accepted that the issue is "by no means clear cut" (page 11).

15. The arguments deployed by Mr Davies are not, in our view, persuasive in relation to the offence of market abuse:

(a) The fact that an offence is not punishable by imprisonment and does not give rise to a criminal record is not decisive of the classification of the offence for the purposes of Article 6 (see *Lauko*, above, and *Ozturk* v. *Germany* (1984) 6 EHRR, ECtHR);

(b) As for the purpose of the market abuse regime, Mr Davies has stated that the purpose is primarily one of protection and compensation, but it is clear from Consultation Paper 17 that this involves deterrence as an important objective (see e.g. paragraphs 138 and 144). In paragraph 144 of the Paper, it is provided that any civil fine for market abuse will reflect two main considerations, the first of which is stated to be "the need to provide an adequate disincentive to future abuse . . .". The fact that deterrence is a major purpose of the market abuse regime provides strong support for the argument that this offence is criminal for the purposes of the ECHR. It may be as a matter of domestic law that an allegation of market abuse is different from an allegation that the criminal law has been breached (paragraph 126 of Consultation Paper 17) but that is not in any way determinative of the position under Convention law;

(c) As for the argument that the market abuse regime is linked to those persons who take advantage of the facilities of organised investment markets, we do not think that this provides any indication that the offence is civil rather than criminal. Even if (which is not accepted)[2] the market abuse regime were linked to those

---

[2] It is arguable, for example, that a French bank trading in France in the shares of a French company might be guilty of market abuse, on the basis that its behaviour satisfied the conditions in clause 56(1)(a) and (b), and on the basis that clause 56(1)(c) would be satisfied because such conduct would be likely to affect the confidence of participants in the London Stock Exchange or LIFFE markets, where those shares were listed on the London Stock Exchange, or were a constituent element of the Eurotop 100 on which LIFFE has listed a futures contract. Similarly, the actions of a person trading in, say, the commodity Brent Oil in Singapore might fall within clause 56(1), on the basis that they would be likely adversely to affect the market in Brent Oil futures which are traded on IPE in London. By clause 56(4)(b) market abuse may include behaviour in relation to qualifying investments traded on a market to which Part VI applies which is situated in the United Kingdom even if such behaviour takes place outside the United Kingdom.

persons who take advantage of the facilities of organised investment markets, the offence is still of general application, just as a road traffic offence is of general application, albeit that it will in practice only apply to those who chose to drive a car. In any event, as was pointed out in the Joint Opinion of 27 October 1998, whether or not an offence is of general application is not a conclusive factor (see e.g. *Campbell and Fell* v. *UK* (1985) 7 EHRR 647, where prison discipline offences were held to be criminal for the purposes of Article 6). The decisive test is what is at stake for the individual or firm, the gravity of the offence, and the severity of the potential sanction.

16. We consider, therefore, that the offence of market abuse is likely to be characterised as criminal in relation to the ECHR. We also consider that it is strongly arguable that the other disciplinary offences established by the Bill are to be regarded as criminal, for these main reasons: (1) whilst these offences apply only to authorised or approved persons, they are created by statute and are, unlike the disciplinary rules of the old SRO's, not dependent on any contractual relationship; (2) deterrence is a major purpose of disciplinary action, and (3) the fines and penalties that may be levied may be very substantial (being on the face of the Bill unlimited).

17. We should add, that the argument that disciplinary proceedings are of a criminal nature is particularly compelling in the light of the fact that the disciplinary proceedings operate separately from the powers relating to fitness and propriety, under which authorisation or approval can be withdrawn or not granted.

18. The decisions of the French courts in the *Oury* case, to which Instructing Solicitors have drawn attention, provide further powerful support for our view that where heavy financial sanctions are imposed by a disciplinary tribunal as a punishment, the offence is properly to be regarded as criminal for the purposes of Article 6, so as to give rise to the full protection of the procedural safeguards in Article 6.

19. The Court of Appeal's judgment in Dame Shirley Porter's pending appeal may cast further light on the approach of English courts to this important matter.

Lord Lester of Herne Hill QC
Monica Carss-Frisk

7 April 1999

Blackstone Chambers
Blackstone House
Temple
London EC4Y 9BW